Nationalism, Liberalism, and Progress

Volume 1

A volume in the series

Cornell Studies in Political Economy

EDITED BY PETER J. KATZENSTEIN

A full list of titles in the series appears at the end of the book.

Nationalism, Liberalism, and Progress

Volume 1

THE RISE AND DECLINE OF NATIONALISM

ERNST B. HAAS

CORNELL UNIVERSITY PRESS

Ithaca and London

First published 1997 by Cornell University Press

Printed in the United States of America

Library of Congress Cataloging-in-Publication Data
Haas, Ernst B.
    Nationalism, liberalism, and progress / Ernst B. Haas.
        p.   cm.—(Cornell studies in political economy)
    Includes index.
    Contents: v. 1. The rise and decline of nationalism
    ISBN 0-8014-3108-5 (cloth : alk. paper : v. 1)
    1. World politics—1989–   2. Nationalism—History—20th century.
3. Liberalism—History—20th. century.   I. Title.   II. Series.
D860.H33   1997
320.54—dc21   96-48439

Cloth printing   10   9   8   7   6   5   4   3   2   1

Contents

Preface

The 1960s were dominated by notions about the cold war. During the 1970s the world was preoccupied with oil shocks and inflation. In the 1980s we welcomed the end of the cold war and the flowering of global free marketeering. But the 1990s are the decade of nationalism.

The media tell us that nationalism is evil. Nationalism implies aggression, the ethnocentrism of extreme self-assertion, ethnic cleansing, and even genocide. We wonder why the brave new world order of the late 1980s has been sullied by this throwback to earlier history. This book is dedicated to the demonstration that the dark view of nationalism is historically simplistic and morally misleading.

Nationalism can have all the negative attributes mentioned, but it need not, and it has not always displayed them. Nationalism is one of the core organizing principles and key experiences of modern human life. It is a feeling of collective identity that is experienced as mutual understanding among people who will never meet but who are sure that they belong to a community of others just like them, and different from "outsiders." "Insiders" possessed of this feeling wish to have their own state.

The sentiment of collective identity is associated *exclusively* with modernity, with life involving exposure to mass media and relatively easy communication, with the hope for increasingly better living standards that are achievable through human effort alone, owing little to faith or supernatural forces. Nationalism is the defining collective identity of modernizing humankind living in separate states. Whether it will always remain that is one of the key issues explored in this book.

Nationalism comes in many varieties: liberal, totalitarian, and religious. Religious nationalists seek to come to terms with secular modernity by defining the insider self without tearing it from tradition. Put differently, even though nationalism is an aspect of modernization, its followers do not necessarily wish to endorse a purely secular form of modern life. Another purpose of this book is to explore whether it is possible to combine traditional religious values and institutions with the modernizing thrust of nationalism.

Liberalism and secularism are twins. Most of the cases studied in this volume illustrate this relationship. But not all of them. Some display a link between totalitarian values and the desire for a collective identity; others explore efforts to moderate modernity with religious institutions and values. Liberalism and nationalism need not go together. Secularism and nationalism may be antagonists as well. Still another purpose of this book is to ascertain under what conditions liberal-secular nationalism triumphs over its rivals.

Why should that matter? This question brings us to the normative subtext of this work. I entertain the hypothesis that there has been enormous progress in human life if we think in material terms. I also suspect that this progress is due to some of the lessons taught us by the Western Enlightenment. I hold that human collectivities are able to learn, to change their institutions and practices to make things better for themselves. And I hold that this learning occurs by humankind's thinking analytically and searching for causal patterns, modes of thinking associated with the Enlightenment.

Nationalism was a human invention designed, in a sense, to make life better for collectivities suffering the pangs of modernization. Nationalism should be studied so that we can ascertain how collectivities learn most effectively. This book inquires whether liberal nationalists learn more readily than others, whether liberal nationalism is to be welcomed outside its origin in the West because it is more likely to lead to human progress than any other kind of collective identity.

All of this is explored in the form of fifteen country case studies, selected from all continents and major world cultures. Five appear in this volume; the remainder will be treated in a second volume. The five treated here are "old nationalisms," societies that achieved the status of nation-states by 1880. Several became exemplars on which later nationalists and nation-builders modeled themselves. In four of the five, the intellectual elite professed something like a nationalist consciousness by 1750. The second volume deals mostly with societies whose national identity is largely a result of the modernizing thrust the imperialism of the "old" nation-states imposed on them.

The enormous intellectual debts I owe to many people who helped with the case studies and theoretical formulations are recorded in the appropriate chapters. The same is true of funding agencies that supported parts of the work. My interest in nationalism was aroused by having lived in Germany in the 1930s. Because of the particularly brutal Nazi sense of collective identity, I wanted to experience a more benign sense of "insiderness." I found it in the liberal nationalism of the America to which my family emigrated. My work falls into the still evolving ontological and epistemological tradition called constructivism. Its outline is not yet clear; nor is it based on a firm consensus of its followers. My understanding of constructivism was enhanced greatly by many discussions with Peter Haas. Such analytic rigor as is achieved in this book is also due to my friendship with Rupert Emerson and my encounters with Karl W. Deutsch. Rupert Emerson's famous course at Harvard, "Nationalism and Imperialism," was the seed for a similar course I offered for many years. This book is largely the result of the teaching effort, to which my students contributed at least as much as I. Karl Deutsch's *Nationalism and Social Communication* persuaded me at the very beginning of my academic life that history can be formally analyzed, not merely told as stories.

None of my work would have been possible but for the fact that Hil has allowed me to shape my life so as to combine scholarship with things which, I suspect, will turn out to be much more important.

ERNST B. HAAS

Berkeley, California
June 1996

Nationalism, Liberalism, and Progress

Volume 1

CHAPTER ONE

Reason and Change in International Life

Charles Darwin wanted to establish two hypotheses as plausible. One held that man and mammals had descended from more primitive species, an inference from the more basic claim that all species had "evolved" from more primitive ancestors. In addition, he urged that evolution had occurred *because* of natural selection. Even though the two hypotheses could be considered independently of each other, Darwin wanted to link them. My objective is less grandiose, but similar in some ways. I want to explore the hypothesis that progress has occurred in international politics, but I also want to argue that progress has occurred *because* our conceptions of what constitute political problems, and of solutions to these problems, have been increasingly informed by the form of reasoning we label "scientific." Perhaps the hypothesis suggests a corollary: the diffusion of this mode of thought from its home in eighteenth-century Europe to the far corners of the planet is creating a universal problem-solving technique. Cosmopolitanism may thereby be associated with human progress and thus transform international politics.

"If my theory of relativity is proved successful," remarked Albert Einstein, "Germany will claim me as a German and France will declare that I am a citizen of the world. Should my theory prove untrue, France will

I am grateful to Emanuel Adler, Robert Keohane, David Laitin, Rick Doner, and John Ruggie for rigorous criticism. A part of this text was published under the same title in Robert L. Rothstein, ed., *The Evolution of Theory in International Relations* (Columbia: University of South Carolina Press, 1991).

1

say that I am German and Germany will declare that I am a Jew."[1] However accurate this observation may have been in 1930, I seek to show why it need not be true in general, and certainly not in the future. I advance the immodest claim that theories of international politics ought to recognize the role of the changing knowledge of nature and society that actors carry in their heads. These theories must come to realize that collective learning occurs.

My emphasis on knowledge and learning might tempt readers to classify me as an idealist, an advocate of the force of ideas as the main engine of history. The charge must be laid to rest immediately. I take my stand squarely with Max Weber: "interest (material and ideal) not ideas directly determine man's actions. But the world views, which were created by ideas, have very often acted as the switches and channeled the dynamics of the interests."[2] Material interests, according to Weber, are the things people want for their well-being, for their wealth, health, and peace. Ideal interests cover the things people want for their emotional and spiritual happiness. Both are interests in the sense political scientists use that term: they lead to specific demands for action (or inaction) made of the state by its citizens, derived from what people consider their most basic needs. Both kinds of interests are formed by ideologies, by systematized bodies of ideas people carry in their heads. Neither kind becomes politically relevant largely or exclusively *because of* the ideas that legitimate the demands. Thus I eschew any intimation of inevitability, irreversibility, or historical necessity.

This is a book about nationalism-as-rationalizer of social collectivities. It is based on the hunch that we are not reentering the world of 1914 and that the *Volksgeist* is not staging a comeback. It is derived from the conviction—from my social construction of reality—that nations result from the appropriate combination of rewards and punishments handed out by rulers, and that people, when given the chance, respond instrumentally to these inducements. National identities are chosen, not genetically implanted, and they are subject to change. Yet none of this denies that nationalist convictions are sometimes held tenaciously, that they provide the socially constructed realities of human actors that the socially constructed reality of the analyst must sort and interpret.

My inquiry is thus part of the instrumentalist tradition of scholarship in which individuals are considered able to choose an identity for themselves without being fated by history to occupy ordained slots. Instru-

---

[1] Remarks made at the Sorbonne, as reported by Robert K. Merton, *The Sociology of Science* (Chicago: University of Chicago Press, 1973), p. 120.

[2] Quoted in Wolfgang Schluchter, *The Rise of Western Rationalism: Max Weber's Developmental History* (Berkeley: University of California Press, 1981), p. 25. The commentary on the quotation is Schluchter's.

mentalist students of nationalism excel at studying how state builders anywhere in the world go about providing incentives for the diverse populations they wish to integrate into their realm, while providing disincentives for those who would rather give their loyalty to the state builder across the river. Instrumentalist theories depend heavily on the concept of social mobilization, pioneered by Karl Deutsch, connoting "an overall process of change, which happens to substantial parts of the populations in countries which are moving from traditional to modern ways of life" and "in which major clusters of old social, economic and psychological commitments are eroded and broken and people become available for new patterns of socialization and behavior."[3]

My emphasis is on the role of the ideas in the heads of the actors. Nevertheless, ideas cannot cause events to happen unless they fall on fertile soil first. The potential leaders who propagate them must find an attentive audience, and social conditions must be fluid enough to allow the aroused public to make gains at the expense of their rulers. The old structure must already be weakened to enable new ideas to challenge it successfully.

Ideas are experienced by actors. The interplay of the ideas with facilitating or inhibiting structural conditions is analyzed and interpreted by the observer, by the observer's construction of reality. Ideas are the switches that make a set of actors travel on one historical track rather than another, achieve one form of coherent collective life or another, or no form at all if the track leads nowhere. Ideas, in the form of ideologies about the origin, function, place, and mission of the nation, furnish the visions of various futures available to actors. The actors themselves throw the switches of their own further evolution. But the observer specifies the antecedent patterns and foresees the range of possible outcomes. The analyst's socially constructed reality delineates the tracks along which the actors can travel; there is no "natural reality" out there to be discovered. The observer asks where the tracks lead, whether there are new switches down the line, and, above all, whether the actors have enough free will to throw these switches once more when they decide they do not enjoy the scenery along the route or made a mistake about the destination. Neither interests nor ideas just "cause" humans to engage in a particular mode of behavior. To be sure, actors derive their interest from ideas in their heads. But the historical significance of these realities is determined by the analyst's biases and concerns. The outcomes of historical sequences for which we seek explanation (the

---

[3] The core work is Karl Deutsch's *Nationalism and Social Communication* (Cambridge: MIT Press, 1953). Quotations from "Social Mobilization and Political Development," *American Political Science Review* 55, no. 3 (1961): 493–94.

dependent variables of the inquiry) are imagined by observers as they project the utopias imagined by the actors onto the stage of history.

I explore the hypothesis that progress occurs because social collectivities, including nations, are able to make use of knowledge acquired as a result of systematic inquiry, scientific knowledge. I argue that progress occurs most readily if knowledge is "consensual," if the relevant community of actors agrees, however temporarily, on constructs of cause and effect and the choice of appropriate means to attain stipulated ends. Consensual knowledge *can* emerge; it is not *destined* to emerge. I grant that such a consensus must originate in the personal ideological commitments of the actors on the political scene. But I also insist that the origin of ideas does not determine their eventual shape or influence on policy. If competing scientific research programs can overcome their origins by blending into more comprehensive programs later, so can policy prescriptions with their roots in economics and sociology. Consensual knowledge is best thought of as the confluence of streams of thought that began as ideological knowledge and eventually transcend any personal or class-based characteristics of their founders. Does such a construct also contain *my* ideology of how things ought to work out? It certainly does insofar as my own intellectual commitment is to the notion of a rationality that can be universally practiced, but I hope to demonstrate that this notion is not merely my personal preference, that it enjoys general validity.

If we consider as progress the retreat of the great ancient scourges of famine—death from epidemics and unceasing toil unaided by technology—there is no doubt that the tide turned during the eighteenth century. As Fernand Braudel pointed out, "What has changed entirely is the rhythm of the increase in life. At present it registers a continuous rise, more or less rapid according to society and economy but always continuous. Previously it rose and then fell like a series of tides."[4] Population rose steadily in Europe and Asia, while remaining more or less stable elsewhere. Hunger receded because people's diets were enriched by the diversification of crops, a change made possible by the improvement in communications. Plague, cholera, and typhus ceased to take the toll in lives they had claimed previously. Cities grew to unprecedented size. Improvements in metallurgy, water, and steam power made possible a way of life to which we are heirs. The eighteenth century is the watershed of mankind's material progress. Perhaps more important, it also invented the *idea* of progress and attributed it to man's ability to reason scientifically.

[4] Fernand Braudel, *Capitalism and Material Life, 1400–1800* (New York: Harper Torchbooks, 1975), p. 1 and chap. 1.

I hypothesize that progress is global because scientific rationality is being globalized by way of secular cosmopolitanism. I have to show that such a diffusion is taking place and that it penetrates into all corners of the globe, not merely the bastions of Western culture. I am advancing the risky thesis that we, as a whole, are better off because we know more and that we know more because we use a particular mode of defining and solving problems. Knowledge is a key engine of progress. But it is not the only engine, and scientific problem-solving techniques could not find a fertile soil unless material interests and conditions provide appropriate incentives.

A Two-Step Model of Recognizing Complexity: Disappointment as the Trigger of Learning

My hypothesis is evolutionary. It holds that human collectivities choose more complexly and discriminatingly as they come to know and understand more. It holds that things get better for us as our routines for choosing become capable of searching for solutions that get more sophisticated in recognizing complexity. Modern history seems to me to have unfolded in a direction consistent with this thought. Consequently, a much larger proportion of the global population than before the eighteenth century now lives at a more tolerable standard of life despite two terrible world wars and almost incessant local warfare since 1945.

Suffering and disappointment are the stimuli that cause collectivities to examine past experiences and reinterpret them. Dissatisfactions with unpleasant events and outcomes, repeated many times, stimulate the search for answers that contain different and more abstract explanatory schemes. The kind of suffering I have in mind always involves experiences for which a social or political explanation is required. If the reason for one's unhappiness lies in the individual psyche, in the will of God, or in personal shortcomings, there is no trigger for collective learning. Actors must locate the cause of the unhappiness in society, the economy, the government, or the global situation.

My evolutionary hypothesis is a two-step affair. Secular rationality develops first at the level of the state; increases in secular rationality eventually trigger a transformation of the state into a nation-state. The successful formation of nation-states goes hand in hand with a deterioration of some aspects of international relations. As trade and communications increase, so do war and imperialism. The successful formation of more rationalized national communities entails a greater amount of discord among such communities. Local happiness is achieved at the cost of international strife. A transnational second step is not taken until some elites come to the conclusion that problems cannot be resolved at

5

the level of the nation-state, that collective action among several (or all) states alone can provide solutions. When this conceptual threshold is crossed, the same secular rationality that harnessed knowledge to local political choice will also be applied to relations among nations. However, insights reconceptualizing phenomena in more complex ways may differ among issues; what works in economics and ecology may not work in military-strategic matters.

But what kind of evolutionary position is this? It is not Darwinian because, aping Lamarck, I emphasize volition and self-reflection on the part of the evolving entity. It avoids the stock-in-trade of evolutionary theorists in sociology and anthropology because I see no regular stages to be attained; I avoid the notions of "adaptive fitness" and "potential to adapt," and I despair of finding evidence of culturegenic coevolution. The functionalist logic of inherent needs perpetuates a myth. I see no warrant for judging some forms of organization as "higher" and "lower," and I eschew the criteria used by most evolutionary thinkers for attributing superiority to specific traits.

The entire conception is evolutionary only in the sense that older institutions and beliefs are thought to change (not to adapt in the Darwinian sense) in such a way that people learn how to solve their collective problems to their increasing satisfaction. It is evolutionary also because a mechanism akin to natural selection guides the descent of beliefs and institutions. Older institutions and beliefs "evolve" into successors preferred by members of a society. Thus, modernization theory can explore patterns of change without also holding that the changes must be *innately* progressive, superior, higher, more adaptive, more flexible, and fitter to ensure the future survival of the society.[5]

The historical sequence I imagine is shown on Figure 1-1.[6] If this scheme turns out to describe accurately what has gone on at the national level in most countries and places, and if I can show that the growth of international rule-governed life has developed as a result of disappointment with the performance of the nation-state, then I will have shown

---

[5] The evolutionary theories of Marvin Harris and Gerhard Lenski come close to covering the historical episodes of concern to me. Both seek to account for "modernity"—industrial society—in terms of regular stages from earlier forms of social organization. Both seek causal explanations for evolution by studying the interaction between technological, social-organizational, and ideological forms. They differ in their respective emphases on material causes (Harris) and quasi-functional ones (Lenski). They agree in considering social complexity, the ability to process energy and information, as the hallmarks of high evolutionary attainment, and in that sense both offer progressivist theories. None of the biological theories of evolution that seek to subsume social evolution come close to meeting my concerns. See the discussion in Stephen K. Sanderson, *Social Evolutionism* (Cambridge, Mass.: Blackwell, 1990), chaps. 7 and 8.

[6] The variables in the right-hand column are defined closely and operationalized in my *When Knowledge Is Power* (Berkeley: University of California Press, 1990), chap. 4.

Figure 1-1. Evolution of rationalization

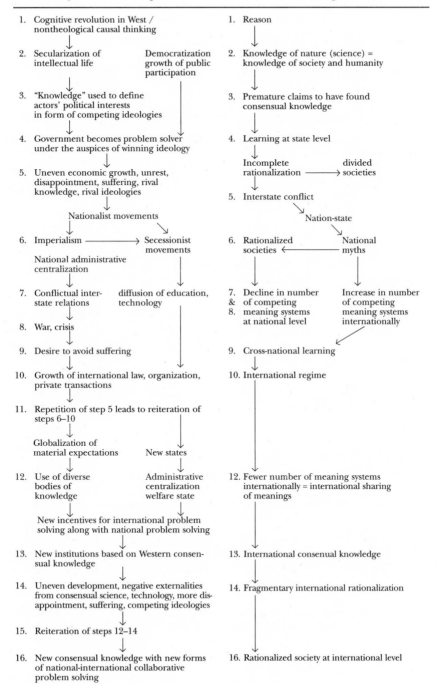

Key events expressed as stylized historical process

1. Cognitive revolution in West / nontheological causal thinking

2. Secularization of intellectual life   Democratization growth of public participation

3. "Knowledge" used to define actors' political interests in form of competing ideologies

4. Government becomes problem solver under the auspices of winning ideology

5. Uneven economic growth, unrest, disappointment, suffering, rival knowledge, rival ideologies

    Nationalist movements

6. Imperialism ⟶ Secessionist movements

    National administrative centralization

7. Conflictual interstate relations   diffusion of education, technology

8. War, crisis

9. Desire to avoid suffering

10. Growth of international law, organization, private transactions

11. Repetition of step 5 leads to reiteration of steps 6–10

    Globalization of material expectations   New states

12. Use of diverse bodies of knowledge   Administrative centralization welfare state

    New incentives for international problem solving along with national problem solving

13. New institutions based on Western consensual knowledge

14. Uneven development, negative externalities from consensual science, technology, more disappointment, suffering, competing ideologies

15. Reiteration of steps 12–14

16. New consensual knowledge with new forms of national-international collaborative problem solving

Historical process expressed as interacting variables

1. Reason

2. Knowledge of nature (science) = knowledge of society and humanity

3. Premature claims to have found consensual knowledge

4. Learning at state level

    Incomplete rationalization ⟶ divided societies

5. Interstate conflict

    Nation-state

6. Rationalized societies ⟵ National myths

7. Decline in number   Increase in number
& of competing   of competing
8. meaning systems   meaning systems
    at national level   internationally

9. Cross-national learning

10. International regime

12. Fewer number of meaning systems internationally = international sharing of meanings

13. International consenual knowledge

14. Fragmentary international rationalization

16. Rationalized society at international level

that things have progressed—that things have gotten better—because of the role of reason in human affairs.

Interdependence, Reciprocity, Rationality, Learning

The persuasiveness of this thesis, of course, depends crucially on a series of assumptions. An increase in interdependence among sections and groups within nation-states and a sharp increase in international interdependence are postulated as true. More than mutual dependence on scarce natural resources and an asymmetrical dependence on trade and money are involved. I also postulate increasing interdependence in the sense of sequential production or sequential decision processes not under the control of a single actor. There is interdependence in the sense of asymmetrical dependence on knowledge in someone else's possession. In sum, interdependence becomes a multifaceted constraint on simple "rational choice" or straightforward strategic choice.

I assume actors to be rational, but not in the sense of optimizing their choice of means as they seek to attain some set of universally valued ends. A rational actor fashions choice in conformity with practices (norms) accepted by his reference group; a rational choice is designed to maximize gain and minimize loss as defined by these culturally and contextually specific norms. Following Arthur Stinchcombe, I believe that this form of rational choice implies the existence of knowledge specialists who develop knowledge capable of becoming consensual. Such knowledge can then be used to justify collective decisions, shape conceptions of self-interest, and provide a continuing stream of information relevant to the long-term integration of the group.[7]

Rather than expecting actors to consider asset specificity or transaction costs my relaxed form of rational choice among self-interested actors in such a situation entails the behavior pattern exchange theorists label *reciprocity*. Each encounter among actors is dominated by the assumption that there will be need for future encounters and bargains. This, generally speaking, creates incentives to behave that set up a pattern of sequential exchange in which the benefits will eventually be seen as equivalent (though not necessarily at the time of the exchange) and the actions of each party are contingent on the prior actions of the other in such a way that eventually good is returned for good, and bad for bad.

Learning then, includes the ability of a collectivity to recognize patterns of interdependence and to devise decisional techniques that in-

---

[7] See Arthur L. Stinchcombe, "Reason and Rationality," in Karen S. Cook and Margaret Levi, eds., *The Limits of Rationality* (Chicago: University of Chicago Press, 1990).

8

creasingly succeed in attaining normatively desired ends (values) by way of practicing reciprocity.

Next, I explore further the notion of progress and its dependence on reason and science. Despite the fact that our realities are "socially constructed," there are some beliefs—derived from the very science made possible by the Enlightenment's belief in reason—that withstand the argument about total cultural and contextual relativity. There is a selectionist test for establishing "truth," however temporarily. The sociologists of science who suggest that a social science derived from a relativistic argument about truth can never be more than just another ideology must be confronted. If they are right, why accept an argument about the relationship between improvements in international life and scientific rationality as more than just another liberal dogma?

TYPES OF PROGRESS

When the Enlightenment thinkers invented the modern idea of progress, they thought that increased human knowledge about the world would lead to increases in human power to control the world. Moreover, increases in human virtue, also springing from the growth in knowledge about the world, would improve the manner in which the power is exercised. Increases in happiness for all would be the result of this fortunate juxtaposition. Progress in science is thus linked to the improvement of politics and political choice. Scientific progress leads to moral progress. Few seemed to worry about the content of the morality, about the specific items that constitute human happiness. Nor was there much concern about whether all, some, or only a few humans subscribe to the particular morality. It is not this version of progress I wish to investigate. Still, I share with the Enlightenment prophets the concern with showing that progress hinges on collective choices to alter the state of the world. I define progress as *directional change for the better*. There is no need to assume that directional improvement is uniform; not all potential beneficiaries of the improvement need benefit at the same time and the trend need not be uninterrupted. Nor does this definition imply irreversibility. We are talking about *net* progress.

Substantive Progress

How can we know what constitutes an improvement without referring to some standard of valuation, some value? It is impossible to avoid using some evaluative scheme, but we can still preserve generality by not using purely personal moral standards, even though the valuation is subjective.

9

Change for the better must mean change in terms of something that is valued by all, or almost all, not merely by the observer. All of humankind wants to be wealthy, healthy and to live in peace; all of us want to be free of the fear of being killed wantonly. Desires for a healthy, wealthy, and relatively peaceful life can be considered universal substantive values. Even though the hope for peace has almost always been belied by the prevalence of war and violent death, our times differ from earlier ones in that all governments at least profess the necessity for peace and increasingly act in conformity with their rhetoric. I deliberately exclude the desire for democratic institutions and for basic human rights because these do not appear to me to be universal aspirations, but temporally and culturally specific ones.[8]

Progress: Ends or Means?

Substantive progress is a result, a condition that comes about because of specific antecedents we wish to pinpoint as we talk about reason, knowledge, science, dissatisfaction, democratization, centralization, and nation building. I stress that progress is not the dependent variable of this enterprise; it is a label summing up the hypothetical direction of the historical process under investigation. The investigation may even disclose that progress is not occurring, or that it can be found only in a few places.

Moreover, there is need to clarify additional connotations of the term *progress* that relate to the conceptionalization of change. Progress, defined subjectively, also means that people entertain expectations of improvement, that they have reason to hope for a better and more secure life. These expectations acquire a normative form: people come to expect that they have a *right* to specific improvements. What accounts for such beliefs? Why do people demonstrably hold them now, but did not before the eighteenth century, even though they surely have hoped for a better life since paleolithic times? A constructivist observer answers that with the Enlightenment a method for deliberately creating improvements came into being; a procedural (or cognitive) notion of progress emerged. A constructivist holds that cognitive progress is the means that makes possible the subjectively defined end of substantive progress.

Who or what creates the improvements? Who makes use of the procedure? The answer varies with culture, geography, and political system.

---

[8] The issue of what is the moral content of the idea of progress in international affairs is explored in *Ethics & International Affairs* 9 (1995). My own view of ethics in international affairs is thoroughly consequentialist. I therefore identify with Russell Hardin's "International Deontology," pp. 133–46, and reject Brad R. Roth's argument in "Evaluating Democratic Progress: A Normative Theoretical Perspective," pp. 55–78.

Certainly progress can be brought about by private individuals and private organizations. Nevertheless, in our times the progressive use of procedures designed to bring about improvements in people's lives is associated with *public* action, with collective action by government, and, in the case of international regimes, by several governments. What concerns me here is the attempt to plan and control change by collective action. This implies the regulation or restraint of private actors. The reliance on public collective action in bringing about change is one lesson learned by many polities from the dissatisfactions engendered by the Enlightenment's view of progress.

Cognitive Progress and Its Critics

Apparently, our species is the only one that possesses the power of self-reflection along with an ability for enormously complex symbolic communication. The ability to improve our lot by self-analysis is an aspect of cognitive progress. So is the reliance on abstract concepts, information technology, and self-conscious planning. Social pressure that results in the planning of services that give us more health, wealth, and peace are part and parcel of cognitive progress, and so is the capacity of the state to control, to plan, to meld social pressures and technology into programs for human betterment. It is only since the Enlightenment that it is considered legitimate to see humans as the sole agents of their own progress, not as subjects of divine or impersonal forces. The world I seek to understand is one of secular rationality in which we make our own future, though not, as Karl Marx reminded us, always just as we wish.

But, subjectively, people often reject the progressive aspects of secularism. Let us recall that the increase in interdependence, global and local, is linked historically to the increase in secularism because secular thinking facilitated the full flowering of technology and industrialism. We also know that neither technology nor industrialism is considered unqualifiedly progressive: since the 1960s we have been inundated with evidence of the negative externalities associated with science, technology, and industry irrespective of their benefits in terms of health and wealth. Moreover, reason and knowledge lose their objective consensual base once we recall that both philosophers of science and scientists are divided on two core issues: they disagree over the validity of the fact-value distinction, and they dispute whether the determinants of scientific progress are "internal" to science or due to "external" forces such as government funding, prevalent ideologies, and coincidence with non-scientific interests. Many scientists, but by no means all, believe that, although the logic of inquiry and the methods used in research are uniform, orderly, systematic, and self-correcting, the order of nature discov-

11

ered by these means need not be equally tidy. Turgot's announcement of the onset of the reign of reason 250 years ago turns out to have been somewhat premature.

Truth? Between Relativism and Positivism

How can I rescue the plausibility of my hypothesis about substantive and cognitive progress in view of this uncertainty concerning the status of scientific truth? I attempt a thumbnail sketch of my epistemology of relativism.[9]

The sketch is inspired by a double conviction that, imperfect or not, scientific thinking must be part of the argument. I need not emphasize that political change since Turgot cannot be understood unless changes in science, technology, and industry are made part of the explanation. Less obviously, it is equally true that we all think differently about public affairs since the Enlightenment because we order our cogitations in terms of material problems and separable, manipulable solutions. We think of political action as meliorative in much the same fashion.

That admitted, it also remains true that practitioners of science entertain widely different views on what, at any one moment, constitutes knowledge; social scientists diverge even more in their beliefs. Our way out of this conundrum must be the recognition that consensus about what is true cannot ever be had at the beginning of a research project; a final closure on what is true may also elude us. Knowledge, even what passes for a consensus, is always an approximation, always subject to amendment and even refutation.

Postivists insist on the possibility, even the desirability, of separating facts from values; radical relativists among philosophers of science deny that this is possible. Moreover, they claim that the mere assertion of separation is a camouflaged attempt at ideological manipulation. I hold

---

[9] My chief debt concerning these matters is to Larry Laudan's work, whose "pragmatic" epistemology in the philosophy of science is my own. See his *Science and Relativism* (Chicago: University of Chicago Press, 1990) and *Progress and Its Problems* (Berkeley: University of California Press, 1977). I also rely on Donald T. Campbell's "descriptive epistemology." See his "Unjustified Variation and Section Retention in Scientific Discovery," in F. J. Ayala and Theodosius Dobzhansky, eds., *Studies in the Philosophy of Biology* (New York: Macmillan, 1974). My selectionist argument comes from Stephen Toulmin, *Human Understanding* (Princeton: Princeton University Press, 1972). Truth and truth tests in the social sciences I find congenial come from Burkhart Holzner and John H. Marx, *Knowledge Application* (Boston: Allyn & Bacon, 1979); Holzner, *Reality Construction in Society* (Cambridge, Mass.: Schenkman, 1968); Peter L. Berger and Thomas Luckman, *The Social Construction of Reality* (Garden City, N.Y.: Doubleday/Anchor, 1967). For a full statement of my epistemological position, see my "Reason and Change in International Life: Justifying a Hypothesis," in Robert L. Rothstein, ed., *The Evolution of Theory in International Relations* (Columbia: University of South Carolina Press, 1991).

that facts can be distinguished from values, but only in retrospect. Only after truth claims associated with a given research tradition have passed an appropriate reality test can they be considered established irrespective of whatever ideological baggage or institutional bias may have been associated with the initial research.

What are these reality tests? I rely on Stephen Toulmin's "population selectionist" argument: "what is 'sound' in science is what has proved sound, what is 'justifiable' is what is found justifiable, what is 'internally relevant' is what turns out to be internally relevant. Since any strategic redirection of a science may lead to a redrawing of its boundaries, none of these discoveries can ever be absolute or final."[10] Science is merely a process of selection among the viable and less viable variant of thought, all of which originate in the ways of thought, the meanings, shared by members of the society in which these events occur. A transcultural sharing of truths that have survived the selectionist test is possible when the respective practitioners agree on what is to be achieved, what problem is to be solved. If that condition is not met, then what is "science" in one culture may legitimately be called "error" or "superstition" in another.

No clear selectionist test is available to tell the difference between social scientific knowledge and ideological assertion. What eventually becomes consensual may well originate as someone's ideology. What is available are self-correcting procedures for making systematic observations within a framework of agreed meanings. Even then, what may come to be taken as true reflection of reality results from institutionalized challenges to the claims and assertions of one's fellow professionals. The protagonists many never achieve agreement on a single perspective or theory, but their students and successors will, because subsequent generations will retain what is useful for solving their new problems and abandon assumptions and theoretical baggage that no longer serve their needs.[11]

And so, even after making allowance for the excessive optimism of the

---

[10] Toulmin, *Human Understanding*, pp. 259–60.

[11] This can happen only under conditions of academic freedom. The official enshrinement of a single perspective that precludes challenge, whether under the auspices of state, party, or professional association, will remove the chief reality test and condemn all claims to the status of ideology. That was the fate of Chinese astronomy and of Soviet genetics. Nonideological consensus implies that most members of a profession agree that a problem exists, that the reasons for that problem can be isolated by using agreed sets of criteria and methods, and that the same criteria and methods can be employed in devising solutions to the problem. Consensus is not so much about substance as about the idea that human solutions to human problems are possible, that human ingenuity and systematic analysis are all that is needed to understand the problem, and that planning and design are effective, practical activities. For an indictment of this "scientistic" view, see Charles E. Lindblom, *Inquiry and Change* (New Haven: Yale University Press, 1990).

Enlightenment, and after expressing respect for the concerns of relativists, a case remains for linking science and reason to the achievement of human progress. I must now show how collective learning relies on reason and knowledge, whether it is aided or impeded by nationalism and liberalism.[12]

Sharing Meanings

Shared meanings are systematic understandings of cause-and-effect relationships about specific phenomena shared by people irrespective of whether they are liberals, Marxists, fascists, Buddhists, Muslims, Christians, or atheists. These transideological bridges must be buttressed by cognitive structures that command general respect. In modern times, these structures are those associated with scientific reasoning. The strengthening and extension of theses structures are other ways of describing cognitive progress, which is itself the result of groups of professionals doing their normal work. Decades and centuries of such work can then result in shared meanings. The sharing of meanings eventually brings about the melding of beliefs concerning phenomena that affect human welfare. Lessons learned by widely distributed participants in the sharing of meanings in many parts of large countries or even the entire world eventually bring about changes in local beliefs that had long remained immune from these global trends.

Nested Problem Sets and Decisional Ambiguity

"If we accept values as given and consistent," says Herbert Simon, "if we postulate an objective description of the world as it really is, and if we assume that the decision maker's computational powers are unlim-

---

[12] Given my position on relativism, my self-imposed verbal conventions on key terms are as follows. Reason cannot be distinguished from science. Reason is the human ability to study systematically the order of nature and of culture. Reason and science refer to our minds, not necessarily to what our minds discover. Still, like our intellectual ancestors in the eighteenth century, I hold that reason is the antonym of passion, faith, intuition, and bias. Knowledge is nothing absolute. I see no warrant for identifying the knowledges of nature with the knowledge of morals and of policy. Knowledge is no more than the temporary consensus of a group of practitioners that a "problem" should be defined in a certain manner, the causes and effects be arranged in an agreed pattern, that the ends and means relating to a "solution" to the problem be identified. Collective rational choice is the process of policymaking that conforms to and respects such a temporary consensus, including whatever perceived structural constraints may enter into it.

ited, then two important consequences follow. First, we do not need to distinguish between the real world and the decision maker's perception of it; he or she perceives the world as it really is. Second, we can predict the choices that will be made by a rational decision maker entirely from our knowledge of the real world and without a knowledge of the decision maker's perceptions or modes of calculation. (We do, of course, have to know his or her utility function.)"[13]

Political decision makers choose "under ambiguity," not in the way just sketched. Decision making "under ambiguity" differs fundamentally from what is normally considered to be rational behavior by individuals seeking to optimize or maximize. Problems of ambiguity include the following. There is often no determined or even probable outcome to be associated with a decision-making routine. Choice is often constrained by a condition of strategic interdependence in which the opposing choosers find themselves, a condition of which they are fully aware. Preferences are often not clear, or not clearly ordered, because the decision is not being made by a single individual but by a bureaucratic entity. There may also be a mismatch between the assumed casual links constituting the problem the organization is called on to resolve and the causal theory underlying the internal arrangements of units, plans, and programs designed to solve the problem. Decision-making models that are supposed to draw on the lessons of history, that are predicated on the actors' deliberately learning from prior mistakes, are badly flawed because the lessons of history are rarely unambiguous: different observers certainly offer varying and equally plausible interpretations of past events that often mar decision making in the present. Learning, under such circumstances, consists of recognizing the desirability of a different process of decision making, a process that copes a little better with ambiguity. Simon explicitly avoids specifying what, substantively speaking, ought to be learned. Under procedural rationality, learning means designing and mastering an alternative process.[14] Decisions made under ambiguity remain rational because the choosers do the best they can under the circumstances. They do not act randomly. They attempt to think about trade-offs, even though they are unable to rank-order their preferences. In short, they "satisfice."

Despite the tendency to satisfice, how does it happen that public policies designed to improve our material life, our health, and our ability

---

[13] Herbert A. Simon, "Rationality in Psychology and Economics," in Robin M. Hogarth and Melvin W. Reder, eds., *Rational Choice* (Chicago: University of Chicago Press, 1986), pp. 26–27.

[14] James G. March, *Decisions and Organizations* (London: Blackwell, 1988), pp. 12–14.

to live in peace politically owe a serious debt to the work of physicists, chemists, biologists, economists, and sociologists? How does it happen that this debt can take the form of new ways of thinking, of defining problems, of anticipating new problems and possibilities? In short, how is it that science can be linked to charting and planning the future of societies? The answer requires the idea of nested problem sets. Nested problem sets are bundles of public policies arranged so as to define and solve human problems in such a way as to be consistent with the knowledge claimed by prior intellectual aggregation, associated with scientific investigation. If there is consensus on the intellectual aggregation, the nested problem set also is likely to become consensual; if there is continuing disagreement among rival ways of aggregating, the rivalry will be reflected in competing nests.

The rearrangement of nests of concepts relating to public policy occurs in political organization, not in scientific endeavors: bureaucracies, legislatures, parties, pressure groups, courts. It is there that ideas of how things could be different are argued out, compared, voted on, fought about, and funded. We can think of the components of these nests as hierarchies of information undergoing rearrangement into ever more complex flowcharts. Items are moved about, subsumed under different headings designed to serve more complex purposes. We change arrows of causation between boxes as our understandings of causes and effects undergo change and as the purpose to which the information is to be put becomes more comprehensive. Nesting involves the combination, elimination, substitution, and subsuming of concepts intended to lead to more comprehensive political action, thus giving us the political counterpart of intellectual aggregation.

At each higher level of aggregation, alleged and experienced interdependencies become more complexly linked. At each higher level, earlier ideological cleavages become less salient. And at each higher level, the terms of political conflict are more easily redefined in such a way as to make unilateral insistence, the desire for absolute victory by one side, less attractive. The more complexly we nest our problem sets, the more we enmesh ourselves in the fate of others.

Redefining Nested Problem Sets: Adaptation and Learning under Bounded Rationality

I argue that problems are redefined through one of two complicated processes that I call *adaptation* and *learning*. Learning differs from adaptation in its dependence on new knowledge that may be introduced into decision making:

16

Adaptation	Learning
Behavior changes as actors add new activities (or drop old ones) without examining the implicit theories underlying their programs. Underlying values are not questioned.	*Behavior changes as actors question original implicit theories underlying programs and examine their original values.*
Ultimate purposes of the action are not questioned. Emphasis is on altering means of action, not ends. Technical rationality triumphs.	*Ultimate purpose is redefined, as means as well as ends are questioned. Substantive rationality triumphs.*
New ends (purposes) are added without worrying about their coherence with existing ends. Change is incremental without any attempt at nesting purposes logically.	*New nested problem sets are constructed because new ends are devised on the basis of consensual knowledge that has become available, as provided by epistemic communities.*

Adaptive behavior is common, whereas true learning is very rare. The very nature of bureaucratic institutions is such that the dice are loaded in favor of the less demanding behavior associated with adaption. This is true even if we restrict the type of rationality required for learning to the bounded variety.[15]

Cognitive Progress and Shared Meanings

Substantive progress can certainly occur at the local and the national level. It does not require cognitive progress on a global scale. Cognitive progress is more easily achieved among collectivities and individuals who already share a common culture, a culturally mediated set of beliefs about daily life. Ideological convergences occur more readily when the believers are members of the same cultural group. The mutual overlapping of divergent ideologies can occur first at local levels, in response to locally experienced interdependencies following technological or economic innovations, without awaiting the results of the centralized nation

---

[15] The case for the difficulty of learning under conditions of bounded rationality is starkly made by John Steinbruner, who reminds us that the recurrence and imperfect mastery of misperceptions by the actors must be taken for granted. That leaves us with the boundedly rational patterns of choice Steinbruner calls *cybernetic* and *cognitive*. See his *Cybernetic Theory of Decision* (Princeton: Princeton University Press, 1974). For an excellent summary of this theory, see Robert Cutler, "The Cybernetic Theory Reconsidered," *Michigan Journal of Political Science* 1, 2 (Fall 1981). Janice Stein and Raymond Tanter, in *Rational Decision-Making* (Columbus: Ohio State University Press, 1980), apply and illustrate the theory very convincingly.

building in the nineteenth and twentieth centuries or of more recent transnational trends.

Historically, shared meanings among literate elites emerged first in large geographic spaces unified by shared high cultures: in the Greco-Roman world, in China, in the Islamic realm, in the cultural-geographic space once occupied by Hindu culture, and in the Christian world of medieval Europe. Here shared meanings cut across and often ignored political boundaries. This world came to an end with the emergence of the territorial nation-state, which fragmented elites who had been united by common beliefs, but it unified underlying masses who had previously lived in the isolation of villages and towns. The nation-state became the agent for ushering in improvement of humankind's condition. The nation-state "rationalized" collective life. Nationalism provided several formulas for making local life better for most people. But, quite possibly (and quite certainly if Rousseau was right), it did so at the price of making international life more miserable. One of our tasks, therefore, is to determine what kind of nationalism is compatible with both international and national happiness.

The territorial state became a national state, an entity whose population made the transition from impassive and inert subject to participant; nationalism implied accountability of some kind to the populace. Rulers mattered less and people mattered more. The legitimacy of the state was believed to rest on the approval of its inhabitants. The nation-state was seen as a more effective guarantor of human happiness, a better problem solver because it combined decision making that uses consensual knowledge with a populist collective identity. A world made up of nation-states was seen as the harbinger of peace and welfare among nations. The expansion of some nation-states into major empires after 1870 was interpreted as further confirmation of the paean to substantive and cognitive progress.

Since the end of World War II two new trends have shown us the unreliability of this imputed directionality of political evolution. For the most part the empires broke up, giving rise to a large number of new states, a few of which are even nation-states. Territorial jurisdictions multiplied after 1960. At the same time, the meaning of exclusive territorial jurisdiction was beginning to be questioned and with it the significance attached to territorial sovereignty. A number of new sources of suffering surfaced for which most territorial states seemed to have no answer: endemic poverty defying purely local solution, military weakness beyond the remedy of any national military effort, and pollution of the seas and the atmosphere that transcends political frontiers. Solutions for each of these called into service more complex schemes of intellectual analysis and interpretation than had been en-

18

listed before. More sharing of meanings across borders and within countries surely took place as well. The upshot, however, was the recognition that territoriality itself is a source of the problem, because solutions put in place in one country cannot work unless all others also afflicted apply the same solution.

Many consider global consensus on these points as evidence of transnational progress:

- The rich have an obligation to give economic aid and improve the welfare of the poor.
- There are distinct limits on the unilateral manipulation of national trade and monetary policies.
- Creditors have responsibilities for considering the welfare of debtors.
- Everyone has an obligation to consider the impact of industrialization (and associated trade and investment issues) on the quality of the natural environment.
- Everyone is committed to the practice of sustainable development.

The prevalence of such a consensus undermines the territorial exclusiveness of nation-states, old and new. But for many other purposes, that exclusive shell remains the aspiration of rulers and followers alike. Nationalism as the principle for organizing human collectivities is enhanced and undermined at the same time.

Liberal nationalists accept the undermining; nationalists who seek to construct their identities along integral or syncretist lines do not. Chapter 2 is devoted to the close analysis of nationalist ideologies and their implications for the design of institutions and policies. The final component in the case for the plausibility of my hypothesis that science/ reason are causally linked to progress in international life deals with the affinity between nationalism, liberalism, and consensual knowledge.

Liberalism and the Sharing of Meanings

The maturing of consensual knowledge as a component of political decision making went hand in hand with the victory of the nation-state as the predominant form of territorial governance; it also is undermining that predominance. How can nationalism simultaneously be the handmaiden of boundedly territorial and of global governance? I hypothesize that only the kind of nationalism we call "liberal" is consistent with the progressive transnational sharing of meanings. The remainder of this study shows how well founded this provocative assertion may turn out to be.

I associate liberalism with a certain procedure for the making of collective decisions, not with a distinct moral substance. My hypothesis

19

about reason and change in international life is substantively amoral. If we think of morality as the acceptance of a specific doctrine, a specific set of values superimposed on a set of concrete decisions, we cannot associate moral content with my hypothesis about change for the better. The very notion of shared meanings must eschew attachment to a given doctrine, a prespecified scale of values that is known to be less than universal in its appeal. The evolution of contested values into shared values cannot begin with the unilateral assertion of the superiority of a single one. If Western rational thought is held out as superior, it must be proven so on the basis of its voluntary acceptance by other cultures.[16] We cannot dictate a moral code beyond stipulating the universal preference for secure life, health, wealth, and peace.

Minimally, liberalism, at all times and everywhere, is a form of government that employs decision-making procedures that provide for the representation of all major social and economic interests and ideologies and allow almost unrestricted discussion. It uses voting procedures that prevent the tyranny of majorities and minorities without committing itself to a single substantive formula of justice, rights, or expectations.

This is a minimal definition that enables me to accommodate political experiences that differ in their commitments to various notions of justice and world order. Many will insist on a notion of liberalism that is substantively Rawlsian: utilitarianism with social justice; others will stress social justice and denigrate utilitarian values. Some will argue that liberalism implies a commitment to a peaceful world order; others stress a missionary liberalism that accepts the use of force in international politics.[17]

---

[16] For a postmodernist effort to show that Western liberal writing on nationalism and state building is hopelessly distorted by secular-rational biases, see Partah Chatterjee, *The Nation and Its Fragments* (Princeton: Princeton University Press, 1993).

[17] See Yael Tamir, *Liberal Nationalism* (Princeton: Princeton University Press, 1993), for a conceptualization very different from mine. She thinks of liberal nationalism as a beneficial tolerance for the "Other" in multicultural polities. To define liberal nationalism exclusively in such terms, however, limits the sweep of the concept. Tamir is careful to distinguish this notion of liberal nationalism from the cosmopolitanism many Liberals profess. Also consider the burgeoning literature on the proposition that "democracies do not fight each other" (Michael W. Doyle, "Liberalism and World Politics," *American Political Science Review* [December 1986]: 1151–63). Bruce Russett suggests that democracies do not fight each other for ideological and normative reasons, in *Grasping the Democratic Peace* (Princeton: Princeton University Press, 1993). For a much more qualified discussion of the same proposition, see Zeev Maoz and Nasrin Abdolali, "Regime Types and International Conflict," *Journal of Conflict Resolution* (March 1989): 3–36. My treatment is explicitly designed to avoid the assumption that nationalism usually implies aggressiveness because it is rooted in some deep-seated folk culture that is immune to the Kantian civilizing influence of liberalism. Allegedly, such folk culture–based nationalisms always demonize the "other" and thus behave as Bosnians did after 1991. This view of nationalist rationalization singles out the cases of Germany and Russia as warnings of what will happen if this model catches on outside Europe, rather than the more benign French and British experiences. For an

Liberalism-as-process allows exactly the intellectual and institutional space required by a pragmatic formula of openness.[18] It permits more than one way of organizing a polity or conferring a collective identity and the unfolding of consensual knowledge. Open debate, continuous political participation, and decision by voting facilitate the mingling of ideas and the spinning of webs of common meaning to a greater extent than do hierarchical-authoritarian institutions whose rule rests on faith, fear, and force. In short, liberal institutions favor learning because they admit the rational-analytic mode of acting more than any other set of institutions. Liberal nationalism, more than any other, favors reason and progress.

---

extended argument along these lines, see Liah Greenfeld, *Nationalism* (Cambridge: Harvard University Press, 1992).

[18] I take courage from Richard Rorty's argument that philosophical pragmatism is the same thing as liberalism-as-process and that liberalism should not be defined substantively as a particular conception of justice. His notion of liberalism, like mine, has a special elective affinity with human progress. Like me, he argues that liberalism is relativistic and encompasses a special scientific-cultural dialogue for which other value systems do not have a natural elective affinity. See his *Objectivity, Relativism, and Truth* (Cambridge: Cambridge University Press, 1991), pt. 1.

CHAPTER TWO

Nationalism: An Instrumental Social Construction

The shape of international links, expectations, and patterns cannot be understood, I believe, unless we demonstrate why the most important units, nation-states, evolved as they did. Hence I will show how and why the analytical concepts necessary for the understanding of nationalism—culture, modernization, social mobilization, assimilation—differ and overlap and why the overlaps themselves must be conceptualized before we can show which form of nationalism has triumphed and whether it will continue to triumph or give way to some other political form.

Discussion is hindered by the tragic fact that *all* the terms we use suffer from sharply contested meanings in scholarly discourse. If nationalism is a set of meanings constructed by nationalists themselves, then the vocabulary for generalizing about them is socially constructed by each observer. This chapter presents my construction.

KEY TERMS DEFINED

Nation, Nationalism, Rationalization

The definitions I offer are consistent with the socially constructed universe of variables, paths, and elective affinities presented later. Nation

I gratefully acknowledge the critiques of earlier versions provided by David Collier, Russell Faeges, Ernest Gellner, David Laitin, Yosef Lapid, and John Odell. Many of my former and nationalism imply a situation in which popular awareness of, and some degree of popular participation in, politics prevail. I emphasize that many of the about one hundred eighty states currently in existence are not nation-states.

A *nation* is a socially mobilized body of individuals who believe themselves united by some set of characteristics that differentiate them (in their own minds) from outsiders and who strive to create or maintain their own state. These individuals have a collective consciousness because of their sentiment of difference, or even uniqueness, which is fostered by the group's sharing of core symbols. A nation ceases to exist when, among other things, these symbols are recognized as not truly differentiating the group from outsiders. A nation is an "imagined community" because these symbols are shared vicariously with fellow nationals over long distances, thus producing expectations of complementary and predictable behavior from fellow nationals. A government is not considered legitimate unless it is thought to represent such a group. A nation is a group of people who wish to practice self-determination. *Nationalism* is a belief held by a group of people that they ought to constitute a nation or that they are already one. It is a doctrine of social solidarity based on the characteristics and symbols of nationhood. A *nation-state* is a political entity whose inhabitants consider themselves a single nation and wish to remain one.[1]

People's ideas about themselves mark physical and cognitive boundaries between "us" and "them." As one caveman said to his son as he hurled rocks at another caveman across the valley, "It's Ok . . . as long as we have *them*, it justifies *us*."[2] These bodies of ideas contain notions of governance "for us," proposals for specific institutions, such as political constitutions, legal systems, rules of property. Shared values do not automatically produce agreements on institutions; yet values and institutions ought not to contradict one another if they are to eventuate in

research assistants made important suggestions, notably Michael Gorges, Peter Kingstone, Joseph Brandt, Richard Snyder, Felicia Wong, and Wesley Young. I also thank the University of California's Institute on Global Conflict and Cooperation and its Center for German and European Studies for financial support. A somewhat different version was previously published in *Millennium* (Winter 1993): 505–46.

[1] I am determined to transcend and avoid these commonly encountered semantic associations of the term *nationalism* because they are tainted by specific ideologies or represent socially constructed realities other than mine: resistance to imperialism, modernization under nondependent conditions, authoritarian right-wing sentiments or governance, liberal democratic sentiments or governance, xenophobia, ethnocentrism, the source of authentic self-esteem, the benign values of the West, the evil values of the Third World, or the perverted values of eastern Europeans.

[2] As depicted on a cartoon by "Wiley." *Washington Post*, Writers' Group, 1993.

orderly life in a single political space. Values and institutions must become coherent if actors prefer orderly life. The process of making them coherent is called *rationalization.* In the formulation developed by Max Weber, it is the acceptance by the group of a particular form of rationality.

Rationality and Global Rationalization

I treat nationalism as a form of rationality, an effort to impose coherence on societies undergoing change. I tailor the study of nationalism to exploring a core hypothesis: there is a particular form of nationalism—liberal nationalism—that is likely to be the most successful in integrating societies that are undergoing change. In addition, it is the only form of rationalization that is likely to bring coherence to most polities in their interactions. As the recent history of Western Europe suggests, many people come to think that even liberal nation-states are less and less able to satisfy their citizens without closer transnational collaboration. They also suspect that liberalism is more likely to give coherence to global society than any other form of rationalization. However, the plausibility of this hypothesis in no way suggests that rival forms of nationalism do not have considerable staying power; they will continue to inform the choices of modernizing societies for a long time before having run their course.

We are concerned only with two of the four types of rationality distinguished by Weber, substantive and formal rationality.[3] Collectivities made coherent by a substantive rationality choose appropriate ends–means patterns by subjecting choice to a superordinate value system, a religion or a secular dogma. The establishment of coherence involves the subordination of concrete ends (and of means appropriate to their realization) to the more basic values of redemption, realization of an earthly utopia, general welfare, or the minimization of sin. Ways of organizing the economy of family life, of governance, and of relating to outsiders (other nations) are derived from a given substantive rationality. Any highly articulated ideology that systematically seeks to integrate its components into a logical whole is a form of substantive rationality. So are specific nationalist programs and bodies of demands. They provide blueprints

---

[3] Because Max Weber often changed his mind and never discussed rationalization in a final manner there is no consensual interpretive opus on this topic. I have drawn on the following sources even though they disagree somewhat with one another. Wolfgang Schluchter, *The Rise of Western Rationalism: Max Weber's Developmental History* (Berkeley: University of California Press, 1981); Stephen Kalberg, "Max Weber's Types of Rationality," *American Journal of Sociology* 85 (1980): 1145–79.

for a more coherent form of political organization, a nation-state with a specific constitution and mission.

Weber also spoke of formal rationality, an effort to subject various substantive rationalities to a single overarching consensual logical structure; that structure seeks to make coherent various partially competing substantive rationalities. There is always a tension between substantive and formal rationality that, Weber believed, would be resolved by the triumph of formal rationality, which he also considered a uniquely Western invention. No other civilization had ever sought to subordinate the major components of collective life coexisting in a single polity under a single rational scheme of things, not even the Chinese. The possible triumph of formal rationality implied the modernization of the world on Western terms as the universally preferred mode of collective political organization. The triumph of formal rationality would be manifest in the victory of a single *modern* set of values, by its acceptance by most of the population of a polity as the institutional mode for resolving internal conflicts. Logically, formal rationalization need not entail a polity organized as a nation-state; in practice, however, the centralization of government and economy in modernizing states has joined the two.

In Weber's view, the great religions served as substantive rationalizers. They also are important in shaping nationalist doctrines and in defining institutions advocated by nationalists. Conflicts among religions, and between religious and secular principles of giving coherence to a polity, constitute instances of unresolved tensions among substantive rationalities. Each religion led to the evolution of an elite culture representing a specific ethical system, thereby transforming the beliefs and practices of its believers away from magic, though not in equal measure. The larger systems of meanings generated differed according to whether the cultural matrix was Western-Christian, Byzantine-Christian, Islamic, Buddhist, or Hindu, even though only Western christendom held beliefs favoring that aspect of modernity we call capitalism. Historical experiences associated with all of them have led to the formation of self-conscious nations. It was Weber's belief that such convergences among cultural streams as are clearly occurring now will be based on the dominant technical rationality of Western culture, which will eventually result in a universal formally rational world.

How can we relate this abstract projection into terms that respect the actual choices made by real-life nationalists? I hold that actors construct their own realities and fashion their behavior in terms of what they infer from that reality. They do not act randomly; nor do they reenact without reflection some primordial instinct of self-assertion. Their behavioral repertoire certainly and prominently includes their substantive rationalities. But nationalists remain constrained, like every actor in a collective

25

setting, by the rules of satisficing, by the need to calculate the opportunity costs of making alliances or stressing this or that theme, by the imperative of recognizing relations of strategic interdependence with other actors.[4] Even the formulation of a nationalist ideology involves deliberate choice.

In *my* social construction of nationalism, behavior is thought to rest on a calculation of benefits attending one's actions, *material as well as ideational and moral benefits.* One's calculations are governed by an epistemology self-conscious about truth tests, as well as by an ontology heavily influenced, if not dominated, by material causes. When collective behavior is so "rationalized," actors have banished magical and prescientific views of the nature of things; actors seek causal connections among phenomena and no longer think on the basis of unexamined assumptions; and the end–means chains adopted are subjected to verification by standardized methods. A consistently rational polity implies that like cases will receive like treatment, that routines determine action, not ad hoc choices. It also implies a certain amoral quality with respect to the choice of means, as anything that works is likely to be picked as the appropriate way to reach an end. In such a society all spheres of knowledge are subject to a single analytical mode of reasoning that refuses to divide nature, society, and the transcendental into separate spheres of consciousness. In short, a fully rationalized society, under modern conditions, approaches Weber's formal rationality.[5]

Table 2-1 summarizes the indicators for judging degrees of rationalization.

MODERNIZATION, SOCIAL MOBILIZATION, ASSIMILATION

Three of the core concepts for discussing nationalism-as-rationalizer are analyzed in detail in this section. The fourth, culture, is taken up in a later section when we focus on ethnonationalism.

---

[4] The conceptual challenge facing theorists of nationalism includes the "macro-micro" problem, the question of how the ideology-based demands of nationalist elites and followers can be made to fit their calculations of advantage derived from structural data, usually dealing with economic performance. For a solution that stresses the instrumental over the primordial line of causality, see H. Meadwell, "The Politics of Nationalism in Quebec," *World Politics* 45 no.2 (1993): 203–41.

[5] For an appreciation of how my social construction of the socially constructed identities invented by nationalists differs from the social constructions pioneered by other theorists (and to what extent mine is indebted to theirs), see the survey of theoretical approaches provided by Anthony Smith, "The Nation: Invented, Imagined, Reconstructed?," *Millennium* 20, no. 3 (1991): 353–68.

Table 2-1. Indicators of rationalization and derationalization

Indicator	Successful nation-state	Disintegrating nation-state
Political succession	There is a formula for determining that peaceful succession exists and is followed consistently	No formula exists, or one exists, but it is not consistently followed; coups, cabals, assassinations take place
National myth in education	There is a general agreement that the content of school curriculum contains core values	Dispute over the content of public school curriculum exists; some claim wrong values are represented, demanding more cosmopolitan or particularistic values
Religious institutions	There is a consensus on having either (1) an official state church or (2) a complete separation of church and state	Groups demand that existing arrangement be either weakened or strengthened
Civil religion	There is a consensus that core religious values (possibly straddling several religions) form part of the national myth, or an agreement that they are purely private in a secular state	Groups demand that either the religious or secular elements be changed
Cultural uniformity	There is a consensus on assimilating cultural minorities into the majority culture, or an agreement to protect and keep minority cultures	Minorities challenge the prevailing norm of assimilation, or majority questions preservation of separate minority cultures
Language	A single official language alone is acceptable in public and business life, or several such languages enjoy equal status	The continuation of official or favored languages is challenged
Income distribution	There is a general commitment to downward income redistribution via welfare state policies and social entitlements	There is no commitment to downward income redistribution via public policy
Workers' organizations	Workers' organizations are allowed a role in national economic decision making	Workers' organizations are denied any autonomous role in macroeconomic matters
Farmers' organizations	Farmers' organizations are allowed a role in national decision making	Farmers' organizations are denied any autonomous role in macroeconomic matters

27

Table 2-1 (continued)

Indicator	Successful nation-state	Disintegrating nation-state
Payment of taxes	Taxes are accepted as legitimate and are consistently paid by citizens	Taxes are systematically evaded, and/or certain taxes are considered illegitimate
Conscription (where used)	Conscription is accepted as legitimate, and evasion is minimal	The legitimacy of conscription is widely challenged, and draft evasion is common
Fighting wars (where applicable)	Military personnel are willing to fight	Military personnel evade fighting
Administrative coherence	There are clear definitions of mandates and respected jurisdictional boundaries in and among administrative agencies; civil service rules, and norms prevail	There is widespread redundancy and overlapping among administrative agencies, making it hard to determine who has a mandate to do what; inconsistent observation of civil service rules and norms; widespread corruption
Foreign policy	Public is willing to accept government's definition of country's external role and interests; public opinion accepts changes in policy	Foreign policy is highly controversial; existing policies and changes in policy are routinely challenged by important political groups
Peaceful change	Public agrees that only constitutionally sanctioned legal procedures can be used to alter policies	Some major actors proclaim the right to use extraconstitutional (or even violent) means to effect change and act accordingly
Legitimacy	Institutions representing the public (whether democratic or not) are accepted as adequate and right	There are challenges to the adequacy of existing representative institutions

Rationalization and Modernization

Rationalization means integrating diverse ways of perceiving into a single social vision and to make that vision coherent with a set of institutions. This integration can be brought about by many elite cultures, not merely the West's. Rationalizing a polity is the core challenge facing elites presiding over societies undergoing modernization.

Modernization is defined by the anthropologist Manning Nash as "the growth in capacity to apply tested knowledge to all branches of production; modernity is the social, cultural, and psychological framework that facilitates the application to science to the processes of production."[6] Modernization is often thought of as being synonymous with industrialization. Instead, I emphasize the drift away from such feudal attributes of society as local isolation, subsistence agriculture, illiteracy, rigid social hierarchies, lack of central authority, and inherited status. The core aspect of modernization of concern to me is the advent of mass education and of exposure to ideas independent of face-to-face contact. Students of comparative modernization processes summed up the shift from tradition to modernity by noting that the change involves finding the solutions to five "crises" besetting all societies since the Industrial Revolution first struck:

1. *Identity.* Extending of an active sense of membership in the national community to the entire populace; in essence, this is the issue of making state equivalent to nation.
2. *Legitimacy.* Securing a generalized acceptance of the rightness of the exercise and structure of authority by the state, so that its routine regulations and acts obtain voluntary and willing compliance.
3. *Participation.* Enlarging of the numbers of persons actively involved in the political arena, through such devices as voting, party or other group activity, extending eventually and ideally to the entire polity.
4. *Distribution.* Ensuring that valued resources in society, such as material well-being and status, are available on equal terms to all persons and that redistributive policies inhibit heavy concentrations of wealth in a few hands.
5. *Penetration.* Extending the effective operation of the state to the farthest periphery of the system.[7]

Nation and nation building refer especially to the first of these crises. Crawford Young illustrates identity formation by evoking the case of the hypothetical Indian peasant. That person is *simultaneously* a cultivator by occupation and a tenant by social status, a member of an extended kin network and head of a household. He is also a member of a particular ritual group (subcaste) and of a larger grouping of subcastes organized for

---

[6] Manning Nash, *Unfinished Agenda* (Boulder, Colo.: Westview Press, 1984), p. 6. Nash rescues modernization theory for comparative studies by removing the teleological features used earlier. For an Indian endorsement of these views, see B. N. Varma, *The Sociology and Politics of Development* (London: Routledge and Kegan Paul, 1980).

[7] Crawford Young, *The Politics of Cultural Pluralism* (Madison: University of Wisconsin Press, 1976), p. 75. Young is paraphrasing the discussion in Leonard Binder et al., *Crises and Sequences in Political Development* (Princeton: Princeton University Press, 1971).

political action. In addition, he is a member of a linguistic group, a Hindu, a citizen of a state in the Indian federation, and a client of a locally important person (perhaps the landowner whose tenant he is, who may also be the local chief of a political party or of a caste organization). The acquisition of a *national identity* then means that our Indian peasant *also* sees himself as a citizen of the Indian federation and that this identity evokes *more* loyalty than all the others. Building the national identity is the crucial activity in rationalization because it allows the rulers to become legitimate, share power, raise standards of living, and administer the entire country effectively by giving people a set of symbols that make them subordinate their parochial and partial identities to the larger one.

Processes of change often are slow, uneven, discontinuous, and confined to enclaves in the state. As was true in most of Latin America during its so-called national period, something we should label "frozen" or "partial" rationalization occurs. Most of the conditions enumerated do not yet obtain, but because the elite segment of the country *is* cognitively and institutionally integrated (though not necessarily along modern lines), the polity functions even though the large rural mass is not part of the elite culture. I sketch the relationship of rationalization to modernization in Figure 2-1. Societies located in cell 1 lack mass-based nationalism altogether, although some elite strata may entertain nationalist ideologies without being able yet to influence government; such states are still stable. Those located in cell 3 illustrate the phenomenon of frozen rationalization because modernization is absent or confined to a small elite, a temporary condition certain to be upset as innovative ways penetrate the society. Nationalist ideologies are important only insofar as they contain the elite's formula for governing; they do not yet

Figure 2-1. Rationalization and modernization

	Modernization is	
	Incomplete	Complete
Incomplete	1. France 1750, Mexico 1900	2. France 1900, Mexico 1990
Rationalization is		
Complete	3. Mexico 1950	4. France 1950

relate to identity at the mass level. Frozen rationalization cum modernization highlights a setting of potential value conflict between untouched folk cultures and elite cultures infected with aspects of formal rationality. Societies located in cell 2 have completed the transition to urbanindustrial-bureaucratic dominance, but there is too much dissensus on the features covered on Table 2-1 to consider them rationalized, whereas those in cell 4 have achieved almost full coherence.

Following Gellner I now present a stylized summary of a process of change that is constructed around the notions of agrarian and industrial society and uses the core concepts of elite and folk cultures. Agrarian society is nonnational because its social structure is characterized by discontinuous communication patterns and heterogeneous symbolic content. A few specialized, usually hereditary, status groups, organized horizontally, profess a common high-literate culture and rule over a vertically organized, illiterate, and isolated peasantry attached to various folk cultures. An exogenous force (foreign conquest, a new religion, a sudden increase in the availability of capital, a technological change) triggers massive change. Peasants are "mobilized" by moving into armies, factories, cities; they acquire a taste for middle-class amenities. They aspire to some of the perquisites of the elite culture but fail to achieve anything like political and economic equality during the early stage of industrialization. They become available to play the social roles that fit their new statuses, to leave behind the role of peasant-cultivator. The newly mobilized but "unassimilated" may eventually succeed in acquiring the linguistic and numerical skills needed to pass into the elite culture, thereby losing whatever cultural factors distinguished them earlier from the ruling groups. To do so, however, they usually have to fight for educational and political equality. Once the assimilation is completed, the polity is rerationalized along more egalitarian lines than before.[8]

The Mobilization-Assimilation Balance

That, however, is only one possible outcome. Those undergoing mobilization need not choose to shed their traditional ways. They may wish to remain "traditionals" who cherish their folk culture by not learning the elite language, not converting to the right religion, and refusing to shed the traits that impede assimilation. In other settings, the dominant elite may block the desire for assimilation of the mobilized by active discriminatory measures. In either case, the mobilized but unassimilated

[8] See Ernest Gellner, *Nations and Nationalism* (Ithaca: Cornell University Press, 1983), chaps. 2 and 3. The concepts of social mobilization, assimilation, and mobilization/assimilation were developed by Karl W. Deutsch, *Nationalism and Social Communication* (New York: Wiley, 1953).

will deliberately form political movements to force their way onto a different track that is expected to lead to wealth, status, power, or recognition as the despised elite's equal. The mobilized-unassimilated forge identities in opposition to those who prevented their peaceful entry into the elite's culture. In multicultural situations, for example in the disintegrating Habsburg, Ottoman, Qing, and British empires, things are complicated in this fashion because the mobilized have often good reason to resist assimilation into the empire's elite culture because to assimilate may mean giving up self-respect, status, wealth, or power.[9] Hence the mobilized-unassimilated may begin to act out their frustration. They will exclude themselves from not only the benefits of industrialism but also the upward mobility that might otherwise have been theirs. These circumstances propel them to the definition of an alternative identity that retains much of the folk culture and may end as a type of nationalism quite different from those who choose to merge with the old elite. The alternative mobilization-assimilation balances and imbalances are shown on Figure 2-2.

Figure 2-2. The mobilization-assimilation balance and rationalization

Modernization is

	Incomplete	Complete
Assimilation is — Incomplete	1. Not a nation-state	2. National identity contested
Assimilation is — Complete	3. Proto-rationalized state	4. Rationalized nation-state

In cell 3 we find a few polities that seem rationalized now because a small elite rules unchallenged by the traditional folk still undergoing mobilization; things will change—and nationalist creeds will multiply— once the degree of mobilization is such as to pose severe challenges for

[9] I call attention to the existence of a compelling literature that, on grounds of rational choice, explains and predicts the failure of assimilation in multicultural settings and therefore questions the possibility of rationalizing such societies via institutions under the control of one dominant group. See Alvin Rabushka and Kenneth A. Schepsle, *Politics in Plural Societies* (Columbus, Ohio: Merrill, 1972). David Laitin, *Language Repertoires and State Construction in Africa* (Cambridge: Cambridge University Press, 1992).

the elite to assimilate the newcomers rapidly. Countries in cell 1 are not yet nation-states, though many are on the way. In cell 2 we find the most volatile mixture: a fully mobilized population not yet successfully assimilated but conscious of rival ideologies claiming to establish collective identities. Successfully rationalized nation-states inhabit cell 4, although they may not remain there; only here do we find the cognitive and institutional integration that is able to cope with all five of the "crises" of modernization. Yet the outcome need not be "modern," or formally rational. In our days, the countries in cell 4 constitute a minority of existing states.

How can we tell when countries have passed from cells 1 and 3 into 2 or 4? Only a stratum of the population not part of the elite can experience social mobilization, such as the peasantry, the urban skilled and unskilled groups, and the urban bourgeoisie (if kept out of the governing elite). Typically, an unmobilized population is illiterate, not part of a market economy extending beyond the immediate locality, rarely travels outside that area, and depends on the extended family for all social and support services (unless such services are supplied by religious bodies). Sons inherit the occupations of their fathers. The state is perceived as a remote oppressor, to be evaded by guile or flight. Countries undergoing rapid social mobilization would look as pictured in Table 2-2.

Table 2-2. Rapid social mobilization

Description	Average annual total population or income added (%)		Ten-year growth rates (%)	
	Range	Median	Range	Mean
Shift into any substantial exposure to modernity, including rumors, demonstrations of modernity of mechanisms	2.0 to 4.0	3.0	—	—
Shift into mass media audience (radio, movies, posters, press)	1.5 to 4.0	2.75	—	—
Increase in voting participation	0.2 to 4.0	2.1	2–40	21
Increase in literacy	1.0 to 1.4	1.2	10–14	12
Change of locality of residence	1.0 to 1.5	1.25	—	—
Population growth	(1.9 to 3.3)	(2.6)	—	—
Occupational shift out of agriculture	0.4 to 1.0	0.7	4–10	7
Change from rural to urban residence	0.1 to 1.2	0.5	1–12	5
Linguistic, cultural, or political assimilation	0.5 to 1.0	0.25	—	—
Income growth	(2.0 to 8.0)	(5.0)	—	—
Income growth per capita	—	(2.3)	—	—

SOURCE: Wolfgang Zapf and Peter Flora, "Differences in Paths of Development: An Analysis for Ten Countries," in S. N. Eisentstadt and Stein Rokkan, eds., *Building States and Nations* (Beverly Hills, Calif.: Sage, 1973), vol. 1, p. 177. Reprinted with permission.

We can also say that in a polity undergoing mobilization most of the following conditions hold:

- The literacy rate remains about 50 percent.
- Peasants are able to move freely from countryside to city.
- Children no longer are compelled to follow their father's occupation, although most do.
- Everyone is exposed to television and radio messages.
- The subsistence agricultural sector is shrinking but remains important.
- Industrialization is confined to enclaves.
- The extended family and religious organizations remain the chief suppliers of social services.
- There are few intermediate organizations (such as modern interest groups), and the ones that exist rarely function translocally.
- Those who earn their living in the modern sector typically feel hostile toward it.
- Attitudes toward the state are ambivalent; sometimes the state remains a distant oppressor to be evaded, but more often it is seen as a potential benefactor.

Elites who try to provide direction and help to the mobilized-unassimilated struck by the forces of modernization are engaged in rationalization *if* they provide a coherent set of values and institutions. And now, at last, the conceptually focused reconstruction of the historical paths to nation-statehood can be undertaken.

Historical Paths to the Nation-State

A very respectable and respected scholarly tradition argues that, while nationalism is distinctly a phenomenon of the modern world and ought to be considered a core principle in the study of rationalization and derationalization of modern polities, nationalism is also causally and contextually linked to liberal democracy and not "authentically" to any other mode of governance.[10] Put into historical terms, the argument holds that the only "authentic" nationalisms occur in countries in which

[10] This argument was made by Arnold Toynbee and Hans Kohn and is the subject of the work of Elie Kedourie. See his *Nationalism* (London: Hutchinson, 1969) and *Nationalism in Asia and Africa* (New York: Meridian Books, 1970). For an exhaustive and erudite discussion of many different meanings of nation and nationalism and an intelligent sorting of what they imply for political action, see Frederick Hertz, *Nationality in History and Politics* (London: Routledge and Kegan Paul, 1944). Hertz himself prefers the "subjective" con-

the state "built the nation," in which the nationalist bourgeois counter-elite that displaced the state-building nobility was culturally identical to its antagonist, and in which the major part of the population has not yet been socially mobilized. Multicultural settings are inhospitable to the establishment of successful nation-states. So are situations in which the old elite and the counterelite do not subscribe to the same cultural norms. Nation-states that do not originate as the heirs of a previously established single state are expected to have great trouble achieving legitimate authority, especially if the claim to nation-statehood occurs after the completion of social mobilization.

I now present a typology of historical paths that fits most nation-states. That typology impugns the argument that liberal democracy and nationalism have a unique affinity. Most comparative accounts of nationalism shy away from positing modal historical sequences, repetitive phases in the evolution of nation-states. Some accounts attempt this for Eastern Europe, others for Western Europe, but none seeks to include Asian or Latin American experience as well.[11] Liberalism is clearly not the only ideology that served as the basis for rationalizing polities. The evidence that continues to unroll anew every time we turn on the TV news suggests that nonliberal ideologies enjoy tremendous popularity. There are dozens of countries that go through modal patterns of development different from the French and British experience of the eighteenth and early

---

ceptualization to which I also subscribe, and he gives ample reason for rejecting the arguments associated with nationalism I impugn here.

[11] I am not the first to try my hand at creating a historical sequence typology. Charles Tilly and Stein Rokkan attempted similar feats with respect to the creation of centralized states in Western Europe. Their efforts complement mine without covering the same ground because they deal with the period before the nineteenth century, the period of state, not nation-building. See C. Tilly, ed., *The Formation of National States in Western Europe* (Princeton: Princeton University Press, 1975), and S. Rokkan, "Territories, Nations, Parties," in Richard L. Merritt and Bruce M. Russet, eds., *From National Development to Global Community* (London: George Allen & Unwin, 1981), pp. 70–95. The most complete and comprehensible account of Rokkan's approach is Peter Flora's, "Stein Rokkan's Makro-Modell der Politischen Entwicklung Europas: Ein Rekonstruktionsversuch," *Kölner Zeitschrift für Soziologie und Sozialpsychologie* 33, no. 3 (1981): 397–436. Miroslav Hroch, in *Social Preconditions of National Revival in Europe* (Cambridge: Cambridge University Press, 1985), also attempts something similar. Hroch's reasoning is functionalist, seeing "needs" in historical development conforming to the "necessary" development of capitalist societies. Anthony Giddens offers a treatment of the path-determined history of nationalism that in some respects parallels mine. However, Giddens thinks of nationalism as resulting *from* the form of rationalizations that involves the routinization of most socioeconomic interaction patterns in modern states, a form of psychological adaptation toward which people gravitate as their life becomes routinized. I stress the opposite: rationalization by way of routinization *follows* the acceptance of nationalist beliefs. Moreover, Giddens is really only interested in types A and C on my list, as is Rokkan in "Territories, Nations, Parties." For Giddens, see his *The Nation-State and Violence* (Berkeley: University of California Press, 1985).

nineteenth centuries. We ought to analyze these patterns before we declare any single case to be uniquely authentic.

I repeat that my own social construction of reality is responsible for this choice of questions-serving-as-variables. I assume the dominance of instrumental motives among actors: they choose to act as nationalists for instrumental reasons. I chose the variables because they correspond to my inductive reading of case histories; they represent my way of imputing patterned instrumental behavior to actors following the limited number of paths blazed by modern history. I assume a weak causality in the actual association of variables, a causality no stronger than that of elective affinities. And I remain agnostic on the core question: Do origins strongly bias the evolution of later patterns and behaviors?

Five questions should be asked of each case, each historical experience of which we have some knowledge; the answers can be yes or no.

1. *State in place.* Are the institutions of the state essentially in place at the time of the nationalist self-assertion?
2. *Social Mobilization.* Is social mobilization substantially complete at the time the effort is made to create or assert the existence of a nation? More specifically, has most of the population become available for new social roles? Do the advocates of nationhood, the mobilized-unassimilated, contain only individuals who are fully mobilized, or do we find individuals among them who have not quite shed all the traits of tradition?
3. *Acceptance of the elite culture.* Do the mobilized-unassimilated accept the elite's culture as their own?
4. *Multiculturalism.* Are the mobilized-unassimilated all of the same culture? If not, are the claims of the mobilized-unassimilated concerned essentially with the elimination of inferiority based on cultural criteria? Do the mobilized-*partly* assimilated base their claims for nationhood on the alleged denial of cultural recognition by the elite?
5. *Equality.* Are the claims of the mobilized-unassimilated concerned essentially with equality of status and wealth?

All judgments by the analyst-observer are made at the time when demands for separate nation-statehood are first brought forth with great force. Sorting the answers to these questions into patterns yields five common types:[12]

[12] Ernest Gellner makes the same point somewhat differently. In the oldest nation-states there was no conflict between the state and the culture of those who took it over. In central Europe, those who captured or fashioned the states professed the same culture as their non-national predecessors, but they needed to imbue the masses with that culture. In East-

I. Type A
  1. State institutions are in place.
  2. Counterelite accepts culture of old elite.
  3. Social mobilization is advancing, but incomplete.
  4. Mobilized-unassimilated are articulate, but not numerous.
  Example: France in 1789

II. Type B
  1. State institutions are in place.
  2. Counterelite is internally divided about which elite culture (among several possible ones) ought to be adopted. It also is divided on which aspects of folk culture should be featured.
  3. Social mobilization is not far advanced, but accelerating.
  4. Mobilized-unassimilated are numerous and articulate.
  Example: India in 1940

III. Type C
  1. No state exists. Counterelite has to build one by seceding or by unifying several states.
  2. Counterelite is internally divided, just as in Type B.
  3. Social mobilization is underway, but its impact is uneven.
  4. Mobilized-unassimilated are numerous and articulate.
  Example: Germany in 1850

IV. Type D
  1. State is extremely weak, and localism prevails.
  2. Counterelite is culturally ambivalent, rejecting foreign elite culture and unsure about local folk culture(s).
  3. Social mobilization is frozen at a low level.
  4. Mobilized-unassimilated are few in number, but articulate.
  Example: Brazil in 1930

V. Type E
  1. There is no state because secession is just occurring.
  2. Counterelite is a portion of the former ruling elite, thrust against its will into a new role; its attitude toward local folk culture and rival elite cultures is ambivalent.
  3. Social mobilization is complete or very far advanced.
  4. Mobilized-unassimilated are the victims of former oppression or discrimination.
  Example: Ukraine in 1990

---

ern Europe, state and culture had to be fashioned simultaneously because the nationalists rejected the culture of their "oppressors." In the former Soviet realm, the same was true, "but the 'natural' development was distorted by 70 or 40 years of communism" (*Encounters with Nationalism* [Cambridge, Mass.: Blackwell, 1994], p. 192).

Building Blocks of Identities and Solidarities

As J. Nagata pointed out, "Ethnic identity is a unique blend of affective, expressive and basic ties, sentiments and loyalties with (sometimes blatantly) instrumental, calculated, political interests, and the latter are explained and given meaning by the former."[13] This statement illustrates the mystification so often engendered by the celebration of ethnicity in conjunction with the denunciation of nationalism. Admirers of ethnic identity offer a circular definition that makes impossible the isolation of antecedent and consequent conditions; they also suggest that instrumental motives are significant only within the matrix of meaning given by the ethnic womb. My definition of building blocks of identity is intended to banish mystification and anthropological bias.

Why are the mobilized-unassimilated so often dissatisfied? Status, religion, race, and language are the most common building blocks of national identities. My instrumentalist commitment makes me seek out actors' resentments as privileged causes.

Status as Shaper of Identity

The term *equality* is shorthand for talking about perceptions of status deprivation. One of the chief motivations for political action is the rectification of such perceived deprivation, the improvement of one's condition relative to that coveted and already attained by someone else. The striving to improve the income of one's group, the opportunities for upward mobility by means of access to educational facilities, the recognition of one's natural language as a means for achieving these benefits, or the opportunity for learning a more useful language—all these are standard instruments to improve one's status. Because it implies the elimination of barriers between classes or other status groups, the improvement of one's status is the same thing as striving for equality. In politics this search includes the demands to participate in decision making and for equality under the law.

When does status (or income) deprivation become a definer of identity? What does it have to do with nationalism? Striving for equality may serve as a boundary marker for group solidarity in its own right or in combination with cultural boundary markers. In the second case the phenomenon known as a cultural division of labor obtains: the status and occupational hierarchy of society covaries with cultural attributes. This is illustrated when most coalminers in Britain are Welsh, most street-

---

[13] J. A. Nagata, "In Defense of Ethnic Boundaries," in C. Keyes, ed., *Ethnic Change* (Seattle: University of Washington Press, 1981), p. 112.

sweepers in India are members of the scheduled castes, and most domestic servants in Brazil are blacks. However, the bourgeois nationalists
in Western Europe, whose demands created the modern nation-states,
defined their solidarity in terms of class and in the search for equality
alone.

The search for equality is the most pervasive and the most basic definer of group solidarity. It becomes a definer of identity as well when it
is reinforced by cultural differentials and by active discrimination on the
part of the ruling elite. Our prototypical Indian peasant becomes a caste-
defined, language-denominated nationalist when he acts out his resentment at not being assimilated by the ruling elites, when he blames his
poverty on discrimination—real or imagined—made possible by the linguistic and ritual group markers. He translates his frustration into nationalism when he joins a group that advocates secession from India as
a means of escaping the alleged discrimination. But he confirms his
allegiance to the Indian nation when he joins a group that seeks upward
mobility by relying on New Delhi's legislation.

Culture as Shaper of Identity

What is "culture"? It is nothing more mysterious than a "system of ideas
and signs and associations and ways of behaving and communicating."[14]
Normally, the sharing of meanings implied by these activities must be
accomplished through the medium of a commonly understood natural
language that motivates people to action even though these individuals
are not part of face-to-face groups or closely related kin. The concept of
culture loses significance if it can be made to refer to face-to-face groups
as well as to impersonal collectivities.

An elite culture is a system of meanings that encompasses geograph-
ically scattered collectivities and individuals who may never encounter
one another in person. It uses a language sophisticated enough to articulate and communicate abstract ideas about law, cosmology, origins, futures, and science; it maintains itself through the medium of specialized
skill-and-status groups, such as clerics, administrators, and nobles, as well
as academics or mandarins. In premodern times, important elite cultures
were the Latin-based Christian system of meanings in Western Europe,
Greek-based Christianity in Eastern Europe, Arabic-based Islam in North
Africa and West Asia, and Mandarin-based Confucian culture in East
Asia. A folk culture lacks specialized skill groups, prevails in small, com-

---

[14] Gellner, *Nations and Nationalism*, p. 7. Young, *Politics of Cultural Pluralism*, pp. 12–13,
says that he uses the term *communal* as a synonym for *cultural* and that *ethnic* means essentially the same thing as *cultural, linguistic,* or *racial* as an identifier of solidarity and identity.
I agree with him.

pact but relatively isolated localities, and lacks a language capable of expressing abstract and potentially universal ideas, though it may be very rich in conveying powerful meanings in small groups.

But what is the relationship between culture and the "objective" attributes of nationhood on which so many theorists and ideologists insist? The most common building blocks of national identity are language, religion, and race. These are the characteristics most often singled out by advocates of nationalism as the attributes that mark off one nation from another; supposedly they furnish the source of "legitimate" nation-statehood. I use culture as a collective term, the sum and aggregate of these building blocks. One speaks of the existence of a culture *after* these separate characteristics of a people have had a chance to blend and enrich on another.[15]

India and Switzerland contain more than one linguistically defined group of citizens; Brazil and Indonesia count several races; many countries contain several very self-conscious religious communities. Are all of these groups actual or potential "nations" with a marked identity within their present states? Are they potential secessionists who challenge the right of the present state to call itself a nation-state? Sikhs, Gujaratis, Tamils, and Bengalis are indeed potential nations *if* enough people identified with each religiously, racially, and linguistically defined group opt for the more restricted identity, opt for secession. However, if they instead continue to subordinate their separate identities to a common Indian identity that they recognize as encompassing and superseding the local attachments, they remain Indian nationalists and supporters of the Indian nation-state, multicultural though it is. Multiculturalism may, but need not, be inconsistent with nation-statehood. One hundred and fifty years of civil peace in multicultural Switzerland make my point; all four Swiss cultural groups define themselves as Swiss above all else. All depends on the character of the rationalization formula adopted as each country moves away from its origins.

---

[15] Stein Rokkan, in my judgment, erred in overidentifying the evolution of territorially based identities in Western Europe with ethnic-linguistic building blocks. See his argument in Tilly, *Formation of National States.* For an impressive demonstration of just how plastic these building blocks were in the prenational settings of the Holy Roman, Byzantine, and Islamic empires—which were the geographical-political settings in which my five ideal types operated—and why no unique causal role ought to be assigned to any specific combination of attributes, see John A. Armstrong, *Nations before Nationalism* (Chapel Hill: University of North Carolina Press, 1982), pp. 164–67 and pp. 197–200. I make absolutely no claim that these building blocks must all be present in any given case or that they must occur in some special combination. Moreover, I have omitted the notion of custom as an attribute of culture because I am unable to determine what it means apart from religiously sanctioned practices or modes of behavior associated with class, caste, or status group.

*but their definition
are not
necessarily the same*

Ethnonationalism: Is It a Useful Concept?

Why did the Soviet Union and Yugoslavia, both multicultural entities, break up in 1991, whereas Britain, Spain, and France, also multicultural, did not? Note that in all these cases, the dissatisfied were fully mobilized decades if not centuries ago. Moreover, they were fully assimilated into the elite culture to the extent that they wished to be assimilated; they were not the victims of systematic discrimination for being Slovene, Lithuanian, Welsh, Catalan, or Breton. It was not the mobilized but unassimilated in Central Asia and Ukraine who seceded, but members of the Uzbek, Turkmen, and Ukrainian communist elites, who, formally speaking, were as assimilated into Soviet elite culture as one could be according to Marxist-Leninist orthodoxy.

The concept of ethnonationalism has been finding favor to cover the anomaly of culturally based expressions of strong dissatisfaction with what had been supposed to be highly successful nation-states that had put the travail of social mobilization behind them long ago. Ethnonationalism is the currently popular manifestation of what is more generally known as *primordialism*, the belief that nations are "real" (not imagined) entities. Nations so defined differ from other territorially defined units of governance (such as city-states, empires, and states, which are not nation-states) because their inhabitants define their identities in cultural terms exclusively. Nationalists who already possess, or strive to create, ethnically defined nations tend to glorify peasant culture and incorporate traditional peasant themes into contemporary ideological assertions in an effort to restore some features felt to have been lost.[16]

Recognizing the validity of ethnonationalism as an explanatory concept violates the historical sensitivities of both liberals and most Marxists: "The Jacobin conception clearly labeled ethnicity in politics as reactionary. Most works in social science in the period after the Second

---

[16] Gellner argues for the existence of "ethnographic nationalism," by which something very similar to ethnonationalism seems to be meant (*Encounters with Nationalism*, p. 29). He does not claim that primordial qualities underlie this ideology. Anthony D. Smith, however, argues that the extent to which nations are "imagined" by nationalists is limited by certain prior cultural features of a primordial kind; therefore, the instrumental nation-building efforts of communist elites were bound to fail ("Ethnic Identity and Territorial Nationalism in Comparative Perspective," in Alexander J. Motyl, ed., *Thinking Theoretically about Soviet Nationalities* [New York: Columbia University Press, 1992], pp. 47–48). David Laitin explores in detail the modal circumstances under which incomplete assimilation into the elite culture occurs even though opportunities for complete assimilation exist in many cases, and when and why such incomplete assimilation develops into an ethnonationalism that can become political. He brilliantly shows that no primordial mysteries are needed to explain such processes in "The National Uprisings in the Soviet Union," *World Politics* 44, no. 1 (1991): 139–77.

World War assumed that interaction and cooperation in modern society are based on secular, rational norms and on an exchange of services rather than on ethnic bonds and cultural loyalties. Marxism, or at least most interpretations of Marxism in the 1950s and early 1960s, quite clearly entertained the idea that, in capitalist societies, class solidarities will in due time supersede solidarities rooted in culture, language, race, and religion."[17]

Even though liberals and Marxists disapproved of ethnonationalism (before the 1970s) because of its antisecular derationalizing implications, the existence of the phenomenon and its increasing prominence in some modernized societies cannot be denied. I argue that ethnonationalism is just as instrumental and reasoned a response to perceived discrimination as the demands of the unassimilated in the later stages of social mobilization; it stresses cultural attributes as political markers without making them an essential building block. I believe that ethnonationalists, being modern and sophisticated people, are easily bought off. Believers in primordialism—a form of essentialism—cannot accept this formulation. How does the *ethnie* differ from any other kind of culturally self-defined unit? Hence, I make no use of the distinction between "ethnic" and "civic" conception of national identity. The contrast is ahistorical because it makes a fluid situation appear to be fixed.

NATIONALIST IDEOLOGIES AND NATIONAL MYTHS

If the allegedly unique rationalizing prowess of liberal nationalism is to be dethroned, it becomes necessary to spell out how the paths to nation-statehood other than Type A can work. Perhaps it would be more in keeping with my leading hypothesis about the potential formal rationality of liberal nationalism to wonder whether paths B, C, D, and E *can* work. In any event, the task is to spell out the range of historically held beliefs about the nature and mission of nations—nationalist ideologies—and to inquire into what happens if one of these "wins" the competition by becoming the dominant myth of a specific nation. Before doing either, it is necessary to distinguish national sentiments from nationalist ideologies and myths.

National sentiment is a belief among intellectuals and other literate groups that they constitute a nation and ought to practice self-determination at some time in the future, even though the condition of

---

[17] Erik Allardt, "Changes in the Nature of Ethnicity: From the Primordial to the Organizational," in M. O. Attir, B. Holzner, and Z. Suda, eds., *Directions of Change* (Boulder, Colo.: Westview Press, 1981), pp. 87–88 and pp. 100–115.

42

even partial social mobilization has not yet been attained. The concept is necessary because we have to recognize sentiments of solidarity—perhaps potential solidarity would be more accurate—in situations of literary self-consciousness, as in Elizabethan England, the early risorgimento, in Russia under Alexander II, or in Brazil in the 1820s.[18]

Such an elite sentiment must be sharply distinguished from nationalist ideologies. A nationalist ideology is a body of arguments and ideas about a nation advocated by a group of writers and accepted by a specific political movement. Nationalist ideologies embody political programs. They arise only after social mobilization has gone on long enough to have resulted in the availability of mass publics attentive to the message. They refer to the specifically "nationalist" content of whatever ideologies are in political competition. Hence they provide an additional dimension for talking about the content of liberalism, conservatism, socialism, and fascism, not a contrasting one. There were no nationalist ideologies prior to the late eighteenth century.

Continuing strife among rival ideologies claiming different bases of identity and contrasting missions and different institutions for their nation is proof of unsuccessful rationalization. Such strife provides evidence that the socially mobilized are split and that they cannot agree on the characteristics that make them different from other nations. They cannot reach agreement on the unique institutions that ought to govern their state. The society does not seem able to come to terms with the strains of modernization. A certain ideology may succeed in capturing the state for a limited period and then enact its program. But if a rival ideology takes over soon thereafter and scraps the policies of its predecessors, we are entitled to wonder whether a more pervasive nationalism ever really characterized the entire population, whether an accepted core body of values ever existed.

I reserve the term *national myth* for the situation in which the clamor among ideologies has been transcended to the extent of resulting in a core of ideas and claims about selfhood commonly accepted by all the socially mobilized. Put differently, the national myth represents those ideas, value, and symbols that most citizens accept despite their being divided into competing ideological groups. The myth represents the overlap among ideologies. It is possible, of course, that the bearers of a

---

[18] The best treatment of nationalist sentiments is by Armstrong, *Nations before Nationalism.* He establishes a set of "mythomoteurs," clusters of beliefs about group identity in traditional empires that influence later nationalist ideologies because they are differentially embedded in social structures. Anthony Smith ("Ethnic Identity," pp. 50–51, m. 16) uses these to create three modal types of prenationalism that are thought to shape the later path of nation-state formation, thereby combining primordially defined notions of identity with various social structures found in traditional societies.

specific ideology capture the state and eventually succeed in imposing their beliefs on everybody. Their ideology then becomes the myth. It is also possible that no single ideology ever wins finally and that the myth is made up of items on which rival ideologies have compromised. In either event, evidence that a national myth prevails is also evidence of successful rationalization.

Nationalist Ideologies Compared: A Typology Raisonnée

The difference between agrarian and industrial societies, explained Ernest Gellner, is both cybernetic and semantic. Agrarian societies are prerational because they feature "the coexistence within them of multiple, not properly united, but hierarchically related subworlds, and the existence of special privileged facts, sacralized and exempt from ordinary treatment." In industrial societies, "all facts are located within a single contiguous logical space . . . statements reporting them can be conjoined and generally related to each other . . . one single language describes the world and is internally unitary . . . there are no special, privileged, insulated facts or realms, protected from contamination or contradiction by others, and living in insulated independent local spaces of their own."[19] The difference between the two also also is expressed in the contrast between beliefs that not only claim to be "true" but also provide the sole criteria for judging all "truth" (e.g., dogmatic universalist religion), and beliefs that admit the contingent nature of truth claims, the possibility that truth is not revealed for all time but unfolds gradually in conformity with relativistic cognitive criteria (i.e., the post-Enlightenment scientific tradition). Gellner's formulation suggests that nationalist ideas are part of the transition to the rational (i.e., modern) mode of social being because they express the societal thrust toward homogeneous perception and homogeneous social organization and behavior.

Typically, nationalist ideologies make assertions about key contentious aspects of the solidarity being urged. Because they challenge, advocate, or seek to come to terms with the impact of modernity, all nationalist ideologies must be concerned with the validity of the core values of the traditional culture. *Revolutionary* ideologies seek to get rid of traditional values; *syncretist* ideologies seek to amend or retain them, differing on

---

[19] Gellner, *Nations and Nationalism*, p. 21. This formulation suggests that I am committed to a functionalist mode of reasoning that asserts that state builders deliberately adopt a certain ideology of nationalism to maneuver in the treacherous waters of transition to something other than an agrarian society—that there is something in the structural logic of transitions that implies some determinate outcome in the human logic of myth makers and ideologists. I am by no means committed to this position. Functionalism is incompatible with an epistemology of elective affinities.

the extent of intercultural borrowing that ought to be fostered. Ideologies make assertions about the nation's claim to historical uniqueness, to the territory that the nation-state ought to occupy, and to the kinds of relations that should prevail between one's nation and others. Nationalist ideologies also contain constitutional and institutional programs on how the nation ought to be governed. Finally, these ideologies advance ideas on the historical mission of the nation ranging from quiet self-perfection to conquest or the restoration of some golden age.

Seven nationalist ideologies recur in comparative history, four revolutionary and three syncretist in emphasis. Despite their differences, all seven have certain characteristics in common that distinguish them from premodern ideologies. All are populistic; they all derive their appeal from the claim that "the people" of a certain territory (not a class or status group) have an innate right to self-determination. All are progressive because they reject all or some of the historical past; they believe in the efficacy of human intervention to change history for the better. And all are rational because they diagnose a challenge and prescribe a response; they embody distinct notions of cause and effect, ends and means; matching means to ends is not usually random, emotional, passionate, willful, or romantic.

But the differences between the two main types also must be stressed. Revolutionary ideologies insist on drastic institutional change. Certain types of social groups are to be removed. Relations among remaining and new groups must become totally different. The old elite must go, and a new elite compatible with populism and progress must take its place. Syncretist ideologies are unwilling to be this drastic. They do not represent a sharp break with the past, only some compromise with it. They often reject the values of modernity, though they seek to incorporate its techniques and some of its institutions.

If Gellner is right, then the status of liberal nationalism is again being privileged. The modern qualities being acclaimed are more often associated with countries rationalized under liberal ideological auspices than with other ideologies. To the extend that the entire world yearns to become "industrial," then the victory of liberal nationalism over its rivals implies the victory of a global formal rationality over squabbling substantive ones. It would eventually imply the rationalization of the world under liberal auspices, the global end of nonliberal ideologies.

But what if the competing substantive rationalities are successful enough to satisfy people for lengthy periods of time? What if the traditional and the modern manage to coexist, however uncomfortably, in the same polity? Is it possible that such "modern" features as industrial and bureaucratic organization, at the state as well as the interstate levels, are somehow compatible with such "nonmodern" ones as religious fun-

45

damentalism and racial exclusiveness? In that case, formal (modern, industrial) rationality is not sweeping the world and the content of international relations continues to be infused with many ideologies and myths, not just one.

The purpose of our sociological study of national identity is to find out which claim is the better one. The winning pattern, conjoined with the particular historical path on which it progresses, allows us to offer modest predictions about the choices various types of nationalists are likely to make. Tables 2-3 and 2-4 summarize the seven types.

Revolutionary Ideologies

Revolutionary ideologies tend to be more internally coherent than syncretist ones. They embody a sharper sense of technical rationality. They are willing to trade off values quite ruthlessly, whereas their syncretist rivals are often hesitant and inconsistent in their choices. All nationalist ideologies stress the short run over the long term because none appreciates that over the long haul any set of major institutional changes triggers unforeseen and possibly unwanted consequences, inconsistent with the values being urged. But syncretist ideologies are much more likely to suffer from the uncertainties of the long run. Revolutionary ideologies are consistent in urging inclusive popular participation, whether voluntaristic or manipulated. Syncretists tend to fudge the issue of participation, alternating between voluntary modes and manipulation, between elections and repression, between individual rights and the obligation to submerge oneself in the collectivity.

Revolutionary ideologies of nationalism include "liberal" and "integral" variants. Each, in turn, must be subdivided. Liberals break down into "Jacobins" and "Whigs," integralists into "Leninists" and "racists." Jacobin liberals reject traditional values and institutions completely and wish to replace them. Whigs also reject them but look for replacements more cautiously. Both believe that liberal societies have many international affinities and ought to borrow from one another. Jacobins derive the nation's claim to historical distinctiveness from alleged cultural homogeneity; thus they profit from whatever processes of homogenization and centralization may have been brought about by predecessor regimes. Whigs prefer the legitimacy of historical continuity to cultural homogeneity, as did John Stuart Mill and Nehru. Both types agree that the area occupied by whatever group defines itself as "the nation" is the proper territory of its state. Both also agree that relations among liberal nations ought to be peaceful. However, Jacobins and Whigs are willing to use force against nonliberal antagonists to make them progress toward liberalism, to aid in their liberation, and to colonize them for their own

Table 2-3. Attributes of revolutionary nationalist ideologies

Dimension	Liberalism		Integralism	
	Jacobin	Whig	Leninist	Racist
What should be done about the core values of the traditional culture?	Reject outright	Reform gradually	Reject outright	Reject substance but retain symbols
What ought to be borrowed from other cultures?	Borrowing is good; liberals ought to borrow from each other	Borrowing is good; liberals ought to borrow from each other	Borrow from other Leninists	Borrow selectively from other racists
What is the nation's claim to historical differences?	Cultural superiority and homogeneity	Historical continuity	Class defined as resistance to imperialism within specific territory	Racial superiority or historical continuity
What territory is properly the nation's?		Whatever area is occupied by the group defined above		
How should the nation relate to other nations?	Spread liberalism by example and by war if appropriate	Make peaceful contribution to the expansion of liberalism	Permanent struggle; diffuse values and institutions by force and/or example	Permanent struggle; need for survival, endemic hostility toward others
What is the proper institutional structure for the nation?	Representative democracy; natural rights for individual citizens	Representative democracy; natural rights for individual citizens	Totalitarian rule via a vanguard group incarnating the nation; rights inherent in nation, not individual	Totalitarian rule via a vanguard group incarnating the nation; rights inherent in nation, not individual
What is the historical mission of the nation?		Continuous self-perfection and the global diffusion of creed	Bring about classless society	Ensure survival of the race
Examples	Danton, Jefferson, Wilson, Cavour, Heine	Mill, Nehru	Stalin, Tito, Ho, Mao	Mussolini, Hitler, Kita Ikki, Codreanu

Table 2-4. Attributes of syncretist nationalist ideologies

Dimension	Reformist	Traditional	Restorative
What should be done about the core values of the traditional culture?	Many modern values are good and usable; mix with good traditional values	Distrust modern values, very cautiously borrow	Reject existing traditional values in favor of restoring values of a past golden age
What ought to be borrowed from other cultures?	Values as well as techniques and institutions	Only techniques and institutions needed, not values	Only techniques, not institutions or values
What is the nation's claim to historical distinctiveness?	Historical longevity	Cultural superiority as evidenced by historical longevity; race	Religious revelation, scriptural authority
What territory is properly the nation's?	Usually, but not always, the existing state	Area of existing state	Area occupied by people to whom the revelation was made
How should the nation relate to other nations?	Cooperatively and peacefully, after survival is ensured	Ambivalently because of continuing fear for survival	Hostilely and distrustfully; need for struggle/vigilance
What is the proper institutional structure for the nation?	Variable	Various corporate devices to limit popular participation and legitimate leadership of traditional groups	Theocracy
What is the historical mission of the nation?	Ensure its own survival and self-perfection	Ensure its own survival	Restore the golden age
Examples	Gandhi, Senghor, K'ang Yu-wei, Mazzini, Afghani, German Romantics	Stein, Maurras, Meiji reformers, many Confucianists, Indian Muslim reformers	Tilak, Khomeini, Al-Banna, Slavophiles

good. Jacobins are somewhat more aggressive in their proselytizing zeal. All liberal nationalist advocate representative democracy, natural rights, and the free participation of all citizens in government. Jacobins believe that the historical mission of the nation is not merely continuous self-perfection but also the global diffusion of the creed. Whigs prefer to confine matters to continuous self-perfection.

There has been an elective affinity, to say the least, between liberal nationalism and late-nineteenth-century imperialism.[20] The missionary power of the creed was obvious in the allied occupation of Germany and Japan after 1945. Liberal nationalism believes in the possibility of a peaceful world order but does not consistently work for it. Not all varieties of liberal nationalism favor an egalitarian domestic social order; only in the twentieth century have the successors of the original Jacobin Liberals embraced the tenets of the welfare state. Whig Liberalism embraced capitalist principles and private property as a sacrosanct principle of social life, as necessary aspects of democratic governance, until the 1940s; now Whigs tolerate aspects of social democracy.

When we examine the integralist family of ideologies, such ambiguity vanishes fast. Racists and Leninists also reject the old order and its values, although racists sometimes pretend to retain some of its symbols, as in Hitler's playing with pre-Christian themes, Mussolini's appeals to Roman grandeur, and Kita Ikki's to Shinto ideas. Borrowing from other integralist societies is praiseworthy. What group of people is to be selected as "the nation"? Leninists came to opt for the particular class, or coalition of classes, that resists imperialism in a specified territory in preference to ethnic groups that resisted imperialism. Racists use a racial criterion or arguments about historical continuity or both. Both ideologies advocate a totalitarian mode of government by a vanguard of the elect that incarnates the nation as a collectivity. Both assume that the nation must struggle for survival because it is constantly threatened by attack from hostile external forces. Racists glorify war and self-assertion as part of the national's mission. Leninists accept war as inevitable as long as imperialism continues to live, but they glorify only wars of national liberation. For the racist, the mission of the nation is to ensure its own survival; for the Leninist it is the ushering in of a classless society. The idea of a harmonious international order is alien to racists and

---

[20] Liberal nationalism legitimated the building of the British, French, and American colonial empires after 1870. The very origin of the word *empire* in modern political discourse is associated with populism and the national mission to diffuse it. Liberal nationalism inspired much of colonial administration and explains the responses of the first generation of anticolonial nationalists in Africa and Asia. See, for instance, Richard Koebner and H. Schmidt, *Imperialism* (Cambridge: Cambridge University Press, 1965); Rupert Emerson, *From Empire to Nation* (Cambridge: Harvard University Press, 1960).

Leninists. As long as the contrast between liberal and integral nationalism remains as stark as the historic ideologies suggest, the idea of a
rationalized world seems far-fetched. But then, the successors of Stalin,
Mao, Hitler, and Tojo sensed that clinging to ideological purity is not
always wise.

How can integral nationalists shed their views, abandon the myth, as
they have done since the 1980s? Arthur Koestler's disillusioned communist hero gave the answer:

> This is a diseased century. We diagnosed the disease and its causes with
> microscopic exactness, but wherever we applied the healing knife a new sore
> appeared. Our will was hard and pure, we should have been loved by the
> people. But they hate us. Why are we so odious and detested?
>
> We brought you truth, and in our mouth it sounded a lie. We brought
> you freedom, and it looks in our hands like a whip. We brought you the
> living life, and where our voice is heard the trees wither and there is a
> rustling of dry leaves. We brought you the promise of the future, but our
> tongue stammered and barked.[21]

It is one of the ironies of integral-totalitarian nationalism that a national community first imagined only by the rulers for purposes of control becomes vivid enough for the individuals so earmarked as to acquire
a social reality for them even though it was imposed by an alien elite.
Such ethnic "nationalities" are found in China and in the former Soviet
Union. The overriding purpose of the Beijing and Moscow regimes was
the assimilation of non-Han and non-Slavic populations into the majority
culture; but in furthering this objective the communist, for tactical reasons, thought it wise to encourage local cultural identities even when
these had been hardly visible originally. Hence they assigned formal and
official "nationality" labels to everyone and gave certain concrete privileges to minority groups, apparently hoping to accelerate assimilation
by these affirmative action–like steps. But official designations that were
at first externally imposed social constructions soon became "real" for
their beneficiaries who learned to claim the special privileges as their
birthright and to take very seriously the identities artificially created for
them.[22]

---

[21] Arthur Koestler, *Darkness at Noon* (New York: Macmillan, 1941), p. 58.
[22] Such people in China have disporportionately agitated for reforms of communism
instead of claiming separate statehood for their nationality, unlike the experience in the
Central Asia and Caucasian republics where ex-communist leaders embrace the local culture as the definer of a new national identity. The case is documented by D. C. Gladney,
Muslim Chinese (Cambridge: Harvard University Press, 1991).

Syncretist Ideologies

All syncretist doctrines hinge on the relationship between religion and governance, between the diverse substantive rationalities of religious legitimation and religious solidarities and the formal rationality of uniformity of worldview.[23] The three kinds of syncretist disagree on how much of the revolutionary ideologies ought to be accepted in their countries.

Reformist syncretists, such as Mohandas Gandhi, Léopold Senghor, Kang Yuwei, Mazzini, or the German romantics, consider many modern values as desirable, provided they can be mixed appropriately with traditional values to be retained. However, such ideologists feel that not all traditional values are worthy of retention, particularly those closely associated with a diffuse agrarian order. Reformists want to borrow values, along with institutions and techniques, from the modernizers. Their claim to nationhood for their own countries rests on historical longevity. They demand only the existing state for the nation's home. They seek peaceful and cooperative relations with others, *after* the survival of their nation seems assured. Democracy may or may not be the featured form of government; various forms of authoritarian rule by the elite that understand the proper mixture of values is more common. The historical mission of the nation is to bring about its own survival and protection, which implies heavy borrowing from nonindigenous cultural sources in order to succeed. Among the successful reformist syncretists we could list some of the Meiji reformers, South Korean leaders, and perhaps the postindependence regimes in the Ivory Coast and Senegal.

Traditional syncretists distrust nonindigenous values and have no intention of introducing them. They remain deeply attached to religious systems that shape the local culture: Confucianism, Islam, Hinduism, Catholicism. However, such people are quite willing to take over such nonindigenous practices as industrial technology, scientific education, mass literacy, and sophisticated military forces. More important, they are willing to adapt indigenous institutions to the extent necessary to incorporate these practices, for example through the introduction of conscription, compulsory public education, and even aspects of industrial organization. Traditional syncretists persuade themselves that they can borrow techniques and institutions without also accepting the values that

---

[23] *Syncretism* is a term that originated in the writings of historians of religious movements who sought to show how one sect selectively borrows from another. The extension of the same idea to studies of anticolonial revolts is nicely illustrated in the case of the Boxers in Shandong Province during the 1890s. See S. Harrell and E. Perry, "Syncretic Sects in Chinese Society," *Modern China* 8, no. 3 (1982): 296–300, for material showing how a mixture of Buddhist and Taoist ideas was used to challenge Confucian political orthodoxy in an effort to reform the Qing government.

go with them. Their claim to national distinctiveness rests on an argument for historical cultural superiority over their rivals that often takes a racial form, as in the work of Charles Maurras, some of the late Qing Confucianists, and Rabindranath Tagore. They claim as the nation's realm the territory of the existing state, but they are ambivalent about the nation's relations with other countries because of their strong fear that they may not survive. Ensuring survival is the nation's main mission, which calls for an indigenous cultural renaissance along with the introduction of nonindigenous institutions and practices. The mode of governance preferred by traditional syncretists is corporatism designed to contain and channel popular participation while legitimating the leadership of traditional groups, as clearly expressed by one of the earliest latecomers, Prussia's Baron vom Stein.

Restorative syncretists reject foreign values and institutions completely. They merely want the foreigner's most powerful techniques: his armies and factories. In fact, they take the position that the values actually professed by their own governments are already dangerously corrupt and must be replaced by pure and authentic indigenous values. They are restorers because they wish to get rid of foreign moral and institutional accretions and bring back the purity of an earlier golden age. They rely on religious revelation and scriptural authority: the Vedic texts for Tilak, the Koran for Khomeini and Hassan al-Banna, the Christian Bible for the Slavophiles. Who is the nation? The people to whom the revelation was made, irrespective of where they might live.

In the setting of anticolonial revolts, revolutionary and various syncretist ideologies typically compete, giving us a range of possible national myths as the eventual winners. The typical sequence of events was roughly as follows. As a result of the introduction of Western laws, economic patterns, and especially the immigration of Western settlers, a certain segment of the colonized population is torn away from traditional pursuits by being absorbed into the modern sectors of the economy and eventually into the Western educational system. Moreover, such mobilized indigenous persons usually acquire a marked taste for Western products, ways, and values only to be rebuffed and humiliated by the colonizers as inferiors, as "wogs." At that point, admiration turns to hatred. The Western settler and official adopts one type of ideology to shore up his self-respect and to justify rule over the colonized, perhaps a continuation of the original nationalism that justified the establishment of the colony. The victims, however, adopt a different ideology, a set of beliefs designed to give them the self-respect and the dignity they lack, an ideology that normally culminates in the assertion of an identity that cannot be content until the colonizer leaves and a new nation-state is created instead. But which nationalist formula shall be used to rationalize the new entity, a liberal or integral one taken from the colonizer's armory of doctrines or a syncretist myth that seeks to preserve aspects of the preimperial culture?

Religion, Civil Religion, and Nationalism

The religious features that are retained in the substantive rationalities that must coalesce or be transcended to result in a fully modern society are very diverse in their effects. Yet these religious themes all try to confer identity and create solidarity among newly mobilized and confused people. Some counterelites define themselves in religious terms even though they no longer fully embrace the religion. Religious themes are prominent in some revolutionary nationalist ideologies that seek to manipulate believers into becoming secularized citizens. Some traditional religions seem even compatible with tendencies toward formal rationality.[24]

How can secular and sacred belief systems coexist in situations in which neither has won a full victory over the other? Do religiously based value systems dominate the secular or the other way around? Are the compromises we can observe to be taken as permanent? Even if, in principle, the two are really deadly enemies, short-term accommodations may nevertheless appear in the outcomes we seek to explain. Thus fundamentalists of all kinds—Protestant, Shi'i, Buddhist—though of course poised against modernity and secular values, may nevertheless be thought of as exercising influence over the eventual shape of a national myth.

For all these reasons, we must consider religion as a serious rival to secular nationalism; even in societies in which the secular seems to have triumphed completely, there are likely to be pockets of belief and behavior that contradict its tenets. Magic and other nonrational forms of belief may flourish among those who are left behind in the modernization process, as antiestablishment values. As such, they may come to dominate a countervalue system, a potential rival nationalist ideology.

In polities rationalized along secular lines religiosity may be alive and well. If so, religion makes no claims on the public weal. Private belief

[24] T. G. Carroll examined four ideal-typical nation-states (liberal, Marxist, social democratic, and conservative) to determine whether each is able to practice formal rationality even though its population is strongly identified with one of the major traditional religions. He concludes that nations strongly identified with liberal and/or Marxist values cannot do so while traditional religions hold sway. He confirms the strong version of Max Weber's incompatibility thesis. However, he also confirms the weak version by showing that modernization can be compatible with Shi'i Islam and Catholicism. Sunni Islam offers more difficulties. Hinduism is neutral, and Buddhism is held to be incompatible with modernization ("Secularization and States of Modernity," *World Politics* 36, no. 3 (1984): 362–82.

and practice following a certain religious ethic, because it is not made the subject of generalized claims on the state, is fully consistent with the victory of the secular that goes with the advent of revolutionary nationalism. The mere fact that many members of the U.S. Congress attend frequent prayer meetings does not make them antimodern or antisecular as long as these meetings remain private devotions and do not give rise to religiously sanctioned political programs. Once they do, as in the American debate over abortion, they challenge the assertion that the secular nationalist is the historical victor. Religion is not an ideological rival of revolutionary nationalism as long as the believer also accepts the legitimacy of public action to improve human welfare on grounds he or she may reject in their private lives. Revolutionary nationalism may also tolerate "civil religions"; it may even seek to foist a "political religion" on its people. Syncretist nationalisms all seek to include some form of official "state religion" into their rationalizing formula.

The very idea of an official state religion is alien to secular nationalists because such a status implies a compulsory, monopolistic, and institutionalized advocacy of key spiritual values that the lay leaders of the state must accept as their own—or at least pretend to accept. On the other hand, secularizing political religions are pseudoreligions: doctrines, rituals, and icons that are modeled on the truly religious but project purely hitherworldly values. Institutionalized Marxism-Leninism illustrates the technique. The "religion" practiced by the Jacobins in the 1790s does so as well, as do the Nazi substitutes for Christian baptism. Rousseau's civil religion was patriotism, expressed in terms suggestive of religious ritual. Citizens of Corsica were to swear: "In the name of God Almighty and on the holy Gospels I herewith, by a sacred and irrevocable oath, bind myself with my body, my property, my will and all my might to the Corsican nation, to belong to it in complete ownership with all my dependents. I swear to live and die for it, to observe all its laws and to obey all its legitimate chiefs and officials in everything conforming to the laws."[25]

The term *civil religion* also is used in a sense not intended by Rousseau, "a belief in a framework of national symbols, rituals, traditions and institutions that, in expressing the common ethic of a people, also reveals

---

[25] As quoted in Salo W. Baron, *Modern Nationalism and Religion* (New York: Harper, 1947), p. 27. Nazi pseudoreligious rites are discussed in George L. Mosse, *The Nationalization of the Masses* (New York: Howard Fertig, 1975). Alliances between syncretist nationalism and religion are illustrated in Fred von der Mehden, *Religion and Modernization in Southeast Asia* (Syracuse: Syracuse University Press, 1986); and Peter H. Merkl and N. Smart, eds., *Religion and Politics in the Modern World* (New York: New York University Press, 1983). The classical piece on political religions is David E. Apter's "Political Religion in the New Nations," in Clifford Geertz, ed., *Old Societies and New States* (Glencoe, Ill.: The Free Press, 1963).

a dimension of purposeful and transcendent ultimacy,'' presumably a divinity and a divine realm.[26] True civil religions represent bodies of religious themes, each legitimated by its own theology, ritual, and institutions, that overlap sufficiently to serve as the common foundation for a culturally pluralistic society. Civil religions rest on genuine, not manipulated, religiosity. The churches forego the temptation to impose their particular preferences by using the state apparatus, in contrast to official state religions. In the United States the acceptance of the Judeo-Christian ethic into the common culture constitutes a civil religion, as does the Catholicism institutionalized in post-Franco Spain.

That leaves us with official state religions, the typical companions of syncretist rationalization formulas. Such religions seek to ensure the coexistence of traditional organized religions with a state that seeks both to introduce and to limit and channel the challenge of modernity. The rulers face the issue of how much secularism to admit, how much of the sacred legitimation of government and public morals to give up or amend. Although dissenters who do not prove too troublesome may be tolerated, an established, official state religion will at a minimum define the pantheon of official values. No separation of private form public religiosity is countenanced. Private worship is expected to include the very value orthodoxy that the official church represents. State and church ally to provide the only acceptable body of ethical doctrine, the only authentic definition of national spiritual self. The clergy are civil servants. They dominate the school system. Established churches are part of the state, and only one church can play this role.

This relationship is most evident when religious fundamentalists dominate state and church, as expressed in restorative formulas. At the reformist end of the syncretist spectrum, however, things are different. Here, hierarchy and bureaucracy make it possible for key individuals to advocate and to lead reform movements that correspond to similar efforts in the secular realm. Organizations provide the opportunities for the authors of new ideologies to seek schools, funds, and missions for the further diffusion of the reformed creed. Research centers may be created to flesh out the ideology and to train acolytes. Moreover, if the religion in question tolerates a number of sects within it, each of these is a potential messenger and missionary for the new ideology, especially if each offshoot in turn has at its disposal, funds, schools, orphanages,

---

[26] S. Bennett, ''Civil Religion in a New Context,'' in G. Benavides and M. W. Daly, eds., *Religion and Political Power* (Albany: State University of New York Press, 1989), p. 151. This conception of civil religion is most clearly articulated by Philip E. Hammond in Robert N. Bellah and Philip E. Hammond, eds., *Varieties of Civil Religion* (New York: Harper and Row, 1980).

Figure 2-3. Transformation of state religions

Activities in or by religious institutions	Spin-off nationalisms

Traditional actions by state-religious
    authorities
     ↓
Reformist forces and movements inside churches ←————→ Restortative syncretism
     ↓
Secular movements retaining civil-religious elements ←————→ Reformist, traditional syncretisms
     ↓
Fully secular forces and movements ←————————→ Liberalism, integralism

SOURCE: Adapted from D.E. Smith, *Religion and Political Development* (Boston: Little Brown, 1973), p. 244.

and easy access to the public school system via some civil-religious mechanism. Secularization may then develop, even if only as an unintended consequence.

I hypothesize that political religions and state religions have typical elective affinities for certain kinds of nationalist ideologies, suggesting a possible progression from the traditional to the secular and modern, as shown on Figure 2-3.[27]

We are now in position to reword in a more nuanced fashion the bland assertion made earlier that a fully rationalized society, under modern conditions, approaches Weber's formal rationality. This conclusion is tenable only if we adopt an evolutionary view of the interactions between Weber's four kinds of rationality, a view that is a function of Weber's (and my) socially constructed reality superimposed on the realities the actors under review construct for themselves.

Practical (or ends–means) rationality is a kind of behavior experienced consciously by actors, subject to actor reflection and correction. Reflection and correction result in what I call *adaptation*. Theoretical (or cause-and-effect) rationality is also experienced and corrected by the actors. Actors who practice this more complex behavior, "higher" in an evolutionary sense, are characterized by me as engaged in *learning*. Next in the evolutionary hierarchy comes Weber's substantive (or value) rationality, bodies of beliefs about causes and rectitude, utopias, and values

[27] D. E. Smith, *Religion and Political Development* (Boston: Little Brown, 1973) is the source of this argument. Catholic Action and its associated organizations illustrate the transformative dynamic demonstrated by Smith. It shows how earlier conservative forms, inspired by the encyclical *Rerum Novarum*, could eventually develop into the liberation theology of Gustavo Gutiérrez and his followers in Latin America and Europe.

that take the form of elaborate ideologies about god, humans, and nature. These are partly experienced by the actors, but rarely so as to be easily changed. Their evolution into different ideologies is usually discerned by the observer.

As Weber showed, behaviors and institutions characterized by these types of rationality conflict; the more highly developed the society in which they are being acted out, the more pronounced the rule of substantive rationality. He argued that the fourth type, formal rationality, is a property of the modern West exclusively. I argue that this type is not perceived by the actors at all. It is a construct inferred by observers steeped in Weberian socially constructed reality. The inference draws on behavior seen by the actors as a changing substantive reality or a conflict among rival substantive realities.

Weber describes formal rationality as involving the institutions we consider as typically modern Western: capitalism, markets, planning, bureaucracy, routinized formal education. I say that there is a strong elective affinity between formal rationality and liberalism. Translated into evolutionary terms, this means that actors animated by liberal ideologies are more likely to behave to bring about conditions that raise their societies from the premodern to the formally rationalized than do believers in other types of nationalism.

But do actors ever get to that terminus? Is it impossible to rationalize societies short of the attainment of the formal-rational pot of gold at the end of the rainbow of change? Our discussion of religion suggests that it is quite possible. But the nagging question remains: For how long can a society remain rationalized, how long can a nation-state remain viable, if it is not launched on the trajectory toward formal rationality, if the conflict among substantive rationalities continues?

WHAT SHOULD OUR CASE STUDIES TELL US?

Is the world moving toward more health, wealth, and peace because it is being formally rationalized under the auspices of liberalism? Our typologies of historical paths, of ideologies, and of myths are now sufficiently imposing, if not overwhelming, to throw into doubt the truth of our informing hypothesis. The logic underlying these typologies suggests the staying power of nonliberal institutions and patterns. It offers a window on disciplined speculation about world order possibilities. How can the coexistence of rival substantive rationalities at the level of states that are, or are becoming, nation-states shape the international relations of the near future?

Are Historical Paths Determined by Original Ideological Choices?

The five paths to nation-statehood refer to the "starting conditions." We now ask: Is there a clear pattern that suggests that the nationalist actors described by each profile typically choose a particular nationalist ideology to fashion a myth? And we must know whether that ideology provides the effective formula for rationalizing the nation-state.

It is likely that the ideology chosen by the counterelite that seeks to fashion a nation-state does not remain unchanged. It may be amended or even displaced before rationalization is achieved. The problem for understanding rationalization, then, is the matter of time. How long does an ideology have to rule before it can have rationalizing effects?

In cases in which the initially ruling ideology is imported or diffused from foreign sources, particularly in late colonial and postcolonial settings, the core problem is different. Here we wonder whether the main counterideology is doomed to ineffectiveness because it did not grow on native soil. And what is likely to happen, again prominently in postcolonial settings, when no single counterideology carries the day?

Who Learns What about Reciprocity in Exchange Relations?

The same question could be phrased: If contradictory substantive rationalities confront each other indefinitely in a given setting, do they prevent rationalization altogether? A corollary question becomes immediately apparent: Are adherents of liberal-nationalist ideologies more likely to learn to practice reciprocity than those who believe in other ideologies?

To learn to practice diffuse reciprocity means that the purity of one's values is subject to reformulation, to compromise. Secular and religious nationalists cannot live peacefully in the same polity unless they learn to slough off values that question the right of the Other to exist. Neither can liberals and integralists.

Nonetheless, is the notion that liberals have a better chance to communicate with the Other than do adherents of other ideologies likely to hold outside the West? Few Third World countries can be considered successfully rationalized. The end of colonial rule left them as independent states, but not as nation-states (with some exceptions in Latin America and Asia). Not many have managed to turn themselves into polities with a clear identity, with a consensual national myth. They hesitate and alternate between a commitment to autonomous and self-reliant development and continued (or renewed) integration into the global economy. They denounce ecodevelopmental notions of economic modernization as hindering the raising of living standards, but they also deplore the rapid exhaustion of natural resources and the destruction of plant and animal habitats in the service of modernization. Liberal, integralist, and syncretist ideologies of nationalism remain in lively competition; of consensual myths there is hardly a trace. And yet social mobilization continues apace!

If liberalism gets in the way of rapid modernization and if it is seen as impeding the dramatic improvement of living standards, it is discredited. Failure to match mobilization with improvements relegitimates beliefs and practices that were questioned earlier; syncretist formulas and religious solidarities reappear, as do integralist ones, possibly of racist hue. Ideologists of these alternatives to liberalism will stress autonomy, cultural integrity, hostility toward the outside world, suspicion of international cooperation, and an insistence on national sovereignty.

Who Is Most Likely to Outgrow the Nation-State?

Most of the important nation-states of the moment may well outgrow their nation-statehood if, as I suspect, continued rationalization within the confines of the nation-state is improbable. Put differently, the leaders of most nation-states will learn to so fashion their policies as to rely less on national and more on cosmopolitan-multilateral modes of action.

Why could they be expected to act this way? The countries of the fully modernized, fully socially mobilized, overindustrialized world—Western Europe, North America, Japan—provide the evidence for my argument. Their citizens consider themselves increasingly entitled to a quality of life and a standard of living that conform to ever-rising expectations. What the capitalist economy does not provide, the state is expected to furnish. When the state, acting alone, seems unable to deliver, multilateral means to provide the desired services must be found. Put differently, the more a desired standard of life depends on economic activities that, in turn, are highly interdependent with foreign trade, interstate flows of money, the deterrence of imported pollution, and desired or undesired patterns of migration, the less a modern nation-state is able to satisfy the wants of its own citizens.

Complex modern societies undergoing change retain a modicum of rational integration by concluding a series of bargains among the major groups into which the citizenry is divided. Sometimes we call such bargains social contract, sometimes an incomes policy, sometimes a "New society." In all these cases the bargains are understandings brokered by politicians that ensure each major group in society a portion of what it demands. The West has prospered as a result of a series or such internal bargains since the 1930s.

A breakpoint for the successful nation-state is reached when no additional internal deals can be struck. Domestic legal-rational formulas

59

for further adaptation that satisfy important groups may no longer be possible when a certain threshold of international technological and economic interdependence is crossed. Though we cannot specify the precise threshold, increasing international interdependence since the 1960s covaries with the inability of the industrial state to conclude such bargains, unless its major trading and financial partners follow suitable supporting policies. Multilateralism is the institution for concluding new bargains under condition of advanced interdependence. But multilateralism implies the loss of the sovereign ability to run ones own economy just as one pleases. The social reality elites in modern societies construct for themselves forces them into rationally choosing supranational means to achieve certain ends. The evidence is plain: the annual summits of the Group of Seven, the power of the International Monetary Fund, the World Bank, and the World Trade Organization, and, above all, the evolution of the European Union and the North American Free Trade Area. Thus, a liberal rationalization formula that ensured the relative happiness of the industrial nation-state is transformed into liberal multilateralism. As a result, the nation-state becomes obsolete for some purposes.

The logic of these ruminations predicts no single outcome. It merely establishes that liberalism and its enemies can coexist on this planet without necessarily subjecting it to enormous conflict and travail. It cautions us that not all historical paths must be walked on forever; that, although some histories may be reenacted, the ideological and institutional affinities revealed by the study of comparative history and politics need not necessarily define the international relations of the future. Neither regional integration nor world government, nor yet a stronger and aggressive nation-state resisting both of these trends, is inevitable. Competition among formulas of rationalization that promise more wealth, health, and peace as the fruits any national leadership must deliver is more likely.

Most nation-states, especially those of types B and D, seem not to stay cohesive. Why not? Social mobilization continues where it has not been completed. Assimilation into elite cultures or into updated folk cultures hardly ever ends. There may always be groups who fail to be assimilated or refuse to make the appropriate adjustments and are discontented and ready to share their discontent systematically with others like them, whether on the basis of language, socioeconomic status, or religion. Even where social mobilization has gone as far as it can, discontent will give rise to new differentiations among groups. Nation-states successful today may be disintegrating a generation from now. Unsuccessful nations, or states not yet nation-states, may never be successfully rationalized. The imperialism associated with nation building in the nineteenth century is obsolete; but this earlier elective affinity with nationalism may well be reinvented in the Third World and in Eastern Europe in the twenty-first century.

Alternative rationalization formulas may imply decentralization as well as centralization, or both at once (though for different demands and issues). All that can be affirmed with confidence is that none of this is likely to happen until the logic of the mobilization-assimilation balance has run its course, until happiness relying on the nation-state has everywhere been tried, until social mobilization is almost complete in most countries. Whether we like nationalism or not, it seems to be a stage through which modern human societies have to pass.

CHAPTER THREE

Great Britain

Nobody invented the nation-state. Rationalizing, centralizing elites evolved in Western Europe, and they succeeded in harnessing their rapidly socially mobilizing populations to the state apparatus, though not all segments of these populations blessed the resulting state with their support and acclaim. We call the result a *nation-state* with the benefit of hindsight; but those who fashioned it acted in the name of other ideas and objectives: restoring ancient liberties, institutionalizing equality and fraternity, making the country safe for private entrepreneurship, uniting the population against alien invaders, or creating a society in which Everyman could live without fear of poverty, disease, and ignorance.

This story began in England toward the end of the sixteenth century. There developed consciousness of a special English identity that became the property of a literate and Protestant landed gentry and urban merchant class. But it took until the 1750s for this narrowly based nationalist sentiment to be diffused to a larger population in the form of a nationalist ideology.[1] Modernity, some might say, was conceived in England

I am deeply indebted to Michael Gorges and Jeffrey Robins for research assistance. I thank Helen Wallace and Sheldon Rothblatt for their help in saving me from making mistakes. I gratefully acknowledge support from the University of California's Institute on Global Conflict and Cooperation and its Center for German and European Studies.

[1] Hans Kohn argues that the sentiment of identity that united Jews during biblical times is akin to modern nationalism, even though Greek and Roman notions of political identity in classical times were not. Other European countries went through quite different experiences. In the nordic countries nationalist sentiment based on cultural rather than political themes was widespread by the eighteenth century; state-induced mobilization soon led to the triumph of liberal nationalism early in the nineteenth century, a liberal nationalism modeled on that of Britain. France served as the model for similar developments in Belgium and the Netherlands. In Belgium a nativist response developed in 1790, a result of

Table 3-1. Some indicators of social mobilization, Western Europe

	Enfranchised population (% of total population)	Literates (% population)	Labor force not in agriculture (%)	Population not living in rural areas (%)	National income per capita (1953 $)
Great Britain					
1840	6	59	77	44	180
1880	9	86	88	68	310
1920	49	95	93	78	480
1960	69	98	95	90[a]	910
France					
1840	1	53	40	24	210
1880	27	83	55	36	380
1920	29	96	71	46	550
1960	62	98	84	63[a]	930
Prussia					
1840	0	91	N/A	27	N/A
1880	20	98	64	41	230
1920	61	99	82	64	380
1960[b]	67	99	90	76	780

SOURCE: Wolfgang Zapf and Peter Flora, "Differences in Paths of Development," in S. N. Eisenstadt and Stein Rokkan, eds., *Building States and Nations* (Beverly Hills, Calif.: Sage, 1973), vol. 1, pp. 193–94 (Table A) and p. 190.

[a]1950.

[b]Federal Republic of Germany.

(Table 3-1). Parliamentary democracy was invented there. Rural life and agriculture were abandoned there first, not on the Continent. Agricultural policy in England was commercialized and subjected to capitalist principles as early as 1688, in contrast to the persistence of policies opposed to the market in France and Germany that lasted into the nineteenth century. Liberal nationalism triumphed early in Britain and was never seriously challenged unlike the experience on the Continent. But when nation-states in Western Europe showed signs of fatigue and supranational European union made its appearance as an alternative, the idea was greeted with some disdain in Britain.

The elites had no model to imitate. Illustrating our Type A, they just did what seemed to come naturally, given their own reflections on the dangers they thought they faced. In fashioning an English, and eventually a British, identity, the elites were "constructing themselves" purely instrumentally. My account will show they needed no British essence to shape the unfolding national blossom and that we can dispense with deeply embedded functions to explain what occurred.

The elites—nobility, landed gentry, rich merchants, and after 1832 the commercial and industrial middle class—acted instrumentally in fashioning a British identity: to protect themselves against foreign enemies—Catholic Spain and mercantilist France. They feared religious civil war and a restive working class.

But the institutions of liberal nationalism characterized their adaptive reforms without serious challenge after 1688. The original national myth survived until today and was used effectively to rerationalize a Britain repeatedly struck by crisis and discontent.

Consistent social learning, however, was not practiced until the 1930s. Until then it was hampered by the absence of consensual knowledge and the sharp ideological distinctions between Whig and Jacobin-liberal conceptions of British identity. But even the adaptations created the tracks of habit that solidified into the institutions of a consensual liberal myth.

Has Britain also learned to outgrow the nation-state? The record is ambiguous as national identity has weakened without yielding to an agreed alternative. Britain remains the analytic prototype of a Type A

---

rationalizing reforms dictated by the Habsburg emperor; after the French conquest, middle-class liberalism took the place of this sentiment when industrial entrepreneurs came to the fore. Nationalism in the Netherlands was confined to the provinces of Holland and Zeeland until the French invasion led to results similar to Belgium's. Dutch "national" sentiment during the long war against Spain was *not* national in our sense of that term. In Spain, there can be no question of a secular nationalism that covered the entire peninsula until the French invasion and its mobilizing consequences. Post-*Reconquista* sentiments posited Catholic universalism, not all-peninsular identity, as the core idea. H. Kohn, *The Idea of Nationalism* (New York: Macmillan, 1943); Arend Lijphart, ed., *Conflict and Coexistence in Belgium* (Berkeley: Institute of International Studies, 1981).

road to nation-statehood, to a society successfully rationalized for long periods under the auspices of a liberal national myth.

England, relative to France and Germany, was physically and economically well integrated before modern times, before she joined with Scotland to become Great Britain. Internal barriers to trade, such as feudal tolls, were abolished by the end of the Middle Ages. Roads were well developed by 1700; inland waterways proliferated during the eighteenth century, as did railroads after 1830. Tariff barriers with Wales disappeared in 1536, with Scotland in 1707. Ireland, gradually conquered and colonized by England and Scotland after 1171, increasingly became part of the English-British economic space. By 1801 there was completely free movement of all factors of production in the entire British Isles.

Moreover, Britain, unlike France and Germany, was a reasonably well-rationalized liberal nation-state by 1800. Its liberalism weathered the strains of the industrial revolution, two world wars, and the Great Depression. Britain's being first on the stage of modernity was responsible for the institutions and ideologies of liberalism serving as a model for admirers elsewhere, although it also furnished the exemplar of evil for opponents of modernity. In that way, Britain, despite its uniqueness, served as a pacesetter for the growth of nationalism and the effort to construct rationalized nation-states everywhere.

NATIONALIST SENTIMENT AND STATE-BUILDING

In 1701 Daniel Defoe in his "True Born Englishman" claimed that "from a mixture of all kinds began / that heterogeneous thing, an Englishman." After enumerating the various ethnic components that produced him, Defoe concludes: "this nauseous brood, directly did contain / the well extracted blood of Englishman." Not only was social mobilization far from complete in the British Isles at the beginning of the eighteenth century, but also the very notion that the inhabitants might be a distinct "people" with a special purpose to fulfill could justify the ridicule that Defoe heaped on those ideas.

Yet the sentiment that there was an English people with a special historical mission had existed among writers and clerics since the Protestant Reformation. Moreover, it had been deliberately fanned by the Tudor monarchs as they built their state on the ruins of feudalism and Catholicism, by destroying local kinship ties and linking the nobility and the towns to the crown. It was Henry VIII and Elizabeth I who made Anglicanism the state church, subservient to the crown, who centralized coinage, transportation, and the law and who systematically created the first internal market in England and Wales free of local tolls and other barriers. They, and their Stuart and republican successors, cultivated the commercial and industrial policies of mercantilism and organized foreign trade and its first cousin, piracy, so as to strengthen crown and state as well as the chartered companies that did the trading and raiding. The Tudors succeeded all too well: their building a centralizing state favored the evolution of a self-conscious translocal gentry, the Puritans, who soon challenged royal absolutism and eased the eventual transition to parliamentary supremacy.

Unlike nationalism, whether as ideology or a myth, these premodern sentiments of identity lacked a mass audience, a popular base. They were the property of the small literate elite in societies in which social mobilization was just beginning. At best, mass sentiments of loyalty were focused on the ruler and on the religion he was thought to personify. This early patriotism, or proto-nationalism in Eric Hobsbawm's phrase, was highly personal in focus; it lacked a territorial or an ideological content other than personal loyalty of subject to king. More abstract ideas were the sole property of the people who self-consciously referred to themselves as "the nation"—the gentry and the nobility.

This elite-based sentiment of identity focused on the preservation of protestant religious values and institutions against the perceived iniquities of Catholicism—"papism" in the popular rhetoric of the time—as personified by Spain. During the long reign of Elizabeth I a self-aware literature dealing with the English language and English culture grew, celebrating the uniqueness of England as the prophet and agent of Protestantism. The word *nation* came into use, prominently in the language of Parliament after the Stuart accession in 1603, although it was not clearly differentiated from the notions of country, commonwealth, and people. Religious rebellion against Rome, the creation of a state church, the confiscation of church property, mercantilist defense, foreign and commercial policies, perpetual war with Spain, and the plundering of Spanish possessions, these were all part of a single syndrome of Englishness. The mission of England was the humbling of Spain for the greater glory of Protestantism.

But whose Protestantism? Here is where the anti-Catholic consensus of Tudor state builders broke down. It was not to be restored until the Orange settlement of 1688 banished the Stuart dynasty's lingering Roman sympathies from public life. The sentiment of being uniquely English (or Scottish) was troubled by the long struggle between Puritan radicals and their Anglican opponents. The Puritans disdained centralized ecclesiastical authority, canon, and institutions, and yet they were passionately committed to state-organized commerce and industry. Parliament was their most cherished political institution, not kinship. Levelers among them claimed that Britons were "free born" because of the practices and rights inherited from the ancient Saxons. There was much talk under the Commonwealth of the specially favored English country-side, climate, industry, and virtue. Some argued that England "is the kingdom that, of all the kingdoms in the world, is the most like the kingdom of Jesus Christ."[2]

Between 1660 and 1720 English elite opinion was a maelstrom of competing ideologies. Anglican sympathizers during the civil war identified true Englishness with the church and the king, specifically with the House of Stuart. Many of them sympathized with or reverted to Catholicism. Those among the elite who called themselves Whigs held the Orange and the Hanoverian rulers as being representative of truly English ways, odd as this notion sounds in ethnically more aware times. These foreign rulers were "English" because they fought "Stuart corruption" and restored the historical freedoms of Englishmen by acquiescing in parliamentary supremacy. Republicans favored "the country" and its representatives in Parliament; Anglican nobles favored a centralizing crown anxious to escape parliamentary scrutiny. Cromwell thought of England as a nation of the elect. The post-1688 Whigs justified their rebellion against the Stuarts by simply claiming to be restoring the ancient liberties of Englishmen. The figure of Britannia became their symbol after 1700; she personified the triumph of ancient liberties over royal control. For others, however, Britannia merely personified the right to enrich oneself. For Tories, such as Lord Bolingbroke, to be a patriot meant to fight against the Whiggish corruption of the English constitution, against the dominance of the House of Commons. For Tories liberty meant not toleration or personal freedom from state intervention so much as the preservation of balance among political institutions. Yet many nobles believed, after 1688, that "God is English."[3]

How could a consensual liberal nationalism emerge from this welter of opposing notions about what it meant to be English or Scottish? The establishment of political freedom and mutual toleration among Protestants (toleration for Catholics and Jews had to wait for another 150 years), as well as the final subordination of the monarch to Parliament (the settlements of 1688 and 1712) came about by default, not as acts of liberal affirmation, as they did in 1789 in America and in France. English politicians were tired of strife, of civil war, of uncertainty because no faction seemed to be able to win a full and final victory. Mutual toleration was the lesson learned from the failure to vanquish one's an-

[2] The statement dates from 1671. Peter Furtado, "National Pride in Seventeenth-Century England," in Raphael Samuel, ed., *Patriotism*, vol. 1 (London: Routledge, 1989), p. 46.

[3] Hugh Cunningham, "The Language of Patriotism," in ibid, p. 58. In Scotland and Ulster, where Presbyterianism played a role similar to Puritanism in creating a sense of identity, God might have been Scots.

tagonist. John Locke's elegant justification of liberalism provided the Whigs with the ideology they needed but it does not explain why Whigs and Tories, former supporters for the Stuart monarchy and former adherents of Cromwell's republic could agree on a constitution. Religious and political toleration was the result of reciprocally learned lessons about internal strife. As Hans Kohn noted, "from its origins, English nationalism preserved its peculiar characteristics; it has always been, and still is, closer than any other to the religious matrix from which it rose, and is imbued with the spirit of liberty asserted in a struggle against ecclesiastical and civil authority."[4] Parliament won out over the crown because of the enmeshment of ideas about personal liberty with lessons learned about the need for religious toleration.

England and Scotland merged by negotiation in 1707, thus creating the United Kingdom of Great Britain; previously England and Scotland had conquered Ireland and England had absorbed Wales. The United Kingdom entered the eighteenth century while undergoing ever-accelerating social mobilization. The peasantry was transformed into a shrinking population of landless wage earners; many former peasants migrated to the burgeoning cities. Noble landowners became agricultural entrepreneurs, protected by the mercantilist policy, that kept out imported food. As the century unrolled, nobles and bourgeois began to intermarry as both began to invest in industrial undertakings, particularly the textile trade. Commercial and industrial activity developed rapidly. Imported cotton became the mainstay of the new factory-based textile industry, and exported cotton cloth became the main income earner. Under mercantilism, foreign colonies were considered highly desirable for both purposes: for obtaining home-owned raw materials and offering guaranteed foreign markets as well. The navigation acts guaranteed metropolitan shipowners a monopoly on intra-empire trade. The American colonies were to rebel against them in the 1770s, thus challenging the chief instrument of mercantilist policy.

The strong elite national sentiments that prevailed since Elizabethan times were augmented during the eighteenth century by a number of populistic trends, enough to lead some commentators to think that the full-fledged nation-state had been achieved by 1745. The 1700s were decades of almost uninterrupted war with France (and its ally Spain) over spoils made valuable by mercantilist principles of statecraft and fueled by the desire to prevent the global hegemony of Bourbon power. These wars were fought in India, the Mediterranean, the West Indies, and in North America, as well as in Western Europe. Waging war was the main business of the government, whose budget increased fifteen-

---

[4] Kohn, *Idea of Nationalism.*, p. 178.

fold between 1702 and 1815. The increase was due almost entirely to military expenditures and debt service. More important, mass-based patriotism was stirred up by warfare. Most of the popular symbolism of nationhood—emblems, anthems, hymns, and flags—originated during the century. The creation, by way of pamphleteering, of myths of national identity went on apace. People were mobilized, physically and emotionally, by the campaigns. The crushing of the last pro-Stuart rebellion in Britain stirred up similar feelings of popular identity with king and country as voluntary militias sprang up in many communities and people organized to defend the Hanover dynasty.

In the eighteenth century, England and Scotland were one source of most of the ideas that, in retrospect, were to be called "liberal." These ideas contained many of the propositions about humankind, religion, progress, freedom from tyrannical government, the rule of law, and the reign of unregulated entrepreneurs engaging in untrammeled trade that flooded the Western world after 1789. David Hume and Adam Smith legitimated the economics of unfettered trade and industry; John Locke had already offered the core arguments about liberty and law. These were the initial ideological ingredients of what toward 1800 became a full-blown liberal nationalism.

British liberalism was a branch of the intellectual revolution we know as the Enlightenment. English and Scottish contributors knew and profited from the work of their French contemporaries. Yet the relationship between the new belief in science and reason with political liberalism was ambiguous; some of the thinkers believed in reason without also subscribing to political liberalism. Still, there was a clear elective affinity between these modes of thought because the practice of liberal politics facilitated the kind of discourse favored by the advocates of reason.

Its flowering resulted from the shock of the American Revolution. The secession of millions of Britons living abroad demonstrated the bankruptcy of mercantilist imperial and foreign policy concepts. The most important emigrant colonies refused to live by the doctrine. The revolution also demonstrated to British politicians that emigrants rejected rule from Westminster, which was seen as royal arbitrariness, in favor of liberty based on a constitutionally limited government and an enfranchised male population of property owners. Whig politicians and middle-class businessmen soon came to clamor for precisely the same reforms in Britain. Liberalism by the end of the eighteenth century came to mean that being British was to be a voter who could conduct his business without interference by the state and who is not to be victimized by arbitrary officials. Excepting the unquestioned need for Britain to rule India and Ireland, liberal Britons also began to think that an overseas empire was not a great blessing after all. It took the French Revolution and the quarter century of wars with France that followed to transform this elite sentiment into a popular movement. Liberalism came of age as another act of adaptation to failure.

Rationalizing an Industrial-Capitalist Society: Liberalism Learns to Adjust

Pangs of Social Mobilization

Britain, in the first seven decades of the nineteenth century was the model for a new world desired by much of Europe; but it also was an unhappy land, beset by intense internal conflict even as the industrial and commercial revolution gathered strength. The rich unquestionably got richer and the urban poor possibly got poorer until about 1850; certainly the poor did not then share in the rapidly increasing national product. The poor also demonstrated their resentment by striking, rioting, emigrating in large numbers, and by coming close to revolution in the form of Chartism. Britain then was neither neatly rationalized nor safely liberal.

The early British capitalists were very insecure about their way of life. The rate of profit earned was modest. Pressure for higher wages exercised by the newly urbanized work force was seen as potentially disastrous for the economy because nobody yet thought that higher profits could result from growing domestic consumption. Surpluses were to be exported. A crisis, the collapse of capitalism, was expected by many in the first four decades of the nineteenth century.

Much unrest at the beginning of the nineteenthth century was triggered by accelerated social mobilization. The last wars against France were one cause. These hostilities created unprecedented needs for manpower forcibly impressed when volunteers were scarce. During the Napoleonic wars probably one out of five Britons of military age served in the army or navy, voluntarily or not; most saw service outside the British Isles. The serious riots and mutinies of 1796–97 were protests against harsh discipline and impressment. More disaffection was triggered when, after 1815, the government did little to provide for invalid veterans or reward demobilized troops. Nor was British unity symbolically shored up after the French enemy collapsed.

The industrial revolution was the major cause of unrest. Spinners and weavers hitherto employed in the putting-out system were increasingly made obsolete by the advent of steam-fueled factories. The government responded with a draconian poorhouse system designed to force people into factory work, which triggered more unrest and protest. On occasion, during the 1830s, the government resorted to armed repression.

During the 1840s private and public agencies faced these sources of disharmony with incrementally adaptive reforms. Tories as well as Liberals saw the need for reform. Factory legislation limited child labor and began to regulate work conditions. Some private entrepreneurs made reforms more generous than those demanded by law. Municipal governments humanized relief for the poor and took other measures not yet mandated by London to aid the working class. The liberal state, despite its principles, entered the field of public health in 1836 by offering mass vaccinations. Most important, the repeal of the Corn Laws in 1846 lowered the price of food. Repeal was aided by the Chartist movement, which ran out of steam and lost its appeal at about the same time. Yet trade unions remained illegal until the 1860s.

Other sources of disaffection were directly political, though they also stemmed from the mobilization of ordinary people. The Chartists demanded not only relief for the victims of the industrial age and poor law reform, but also agitated for the widening of the franchise to include all British males, sometimes by threatening violent revolution. The movement carried forward the agitation of reformist Britons who had sided with the French revolutionaries in the 1790s. These British radicals had worried the government enough to make it launch a deliberate propaganda campaign that pictured a consistently "bad French nation" as seeking to thwart a virtuous, hard-working, freedom-loving and tyranny-hating Britannia. Britons, the government said, are the chosen people who love God, whereas the lackeys of Bonaparte were all atheists.

One argument in favor of the Corn Laws (and against the extension of the franchise) was "that the landed gentry was the class which had the most consistently protected the traditional institutions of the country and their strength must not be destroyed."[5] The ruling establishment learned to pay no heed to these sentiments. Rightly worried about the ability of the country to remain a coherent nation-state during these decades, the political establishment enacted a series of reforms despite loud and bitter opposition from traditionalists. Even though the electorate was not dramatically enlarged by the reforms of 1832, much of the disaffection was removed because the principle of allowing urban middle-class people to vote was granted. The full and final emancipation of Catholics in 1829 was felt to be necessary to still some of the bitter discontent of the Catholic Irish population that was denied any role in

[5] H. Hearder, *Europe in the Nineteenth Century,* 2d ed. (New York: Longman, 1958), p. 184.

public life although it had strongly contributed to the defeat of Napoleon. On the other hand, the ending of slavery in the empire in 1833 was undertaken not for economic or opportunistic reasons but as an affirmation of Britain's liberal mission, to light the West's way toward a civilized future defined by British values.

The success of these measures was shown by the relative political peace that prevailed after 1850. A Reform League was created by the Liberals in 1865 to arouse working-class support for further electoral reform. After the enactment of the reform in 1867 working people did not take the opportunity to organize a radical or a socialist party and dutifully voted for the existing parties of their betters. Prosperity and successful cooptation ensured a relatively low level of political participation; the "labor aristocracy" seemed motivated to demonstrate its respectability, its conformity to middle-class values, rather than any spirit of revolt against it.

From England toward Great Britain

Social integration also manifested itself in the blurring of the contrast between England on the move and the more traditional Celtic societies of Wales and rural Scotland. Despite a modern literature of "internal colonialism," Welsh and Scottish societies were closely integrated with England's on terms of equality, but Ireland remained a plantation colony in the south until the middle of the nineteenth century and a settlement colony in the north until much later. Gaelic Scotland had been colonized and anglicized by lowland Scots after 1745, who had themselves been anglicized hundreds of years before. Some called themselves North Britons after 1707. Few Scots thought of themselves as an oppressed non-British minority. Unlike the Irish and Welsh, they were not the targets of English disdain and discrimination. Of the Welsh a parliamentary commission could say in 1846 that "because of their language, the mass of the Welsh people are inferior to the English in every branch of practical knowledge and skill. The Welsh language distorts the truth, favors fraud and abets perjury. In sum, Welsh was a 'disastrous barrier to all moral improvement and popular progress in Wales,' [made worse] by 'sexual incontinency, the besetting sin . . . the peculiar vice of the Principality.' "[6] On the other hand, the Welsh were not subject to legal

---

[6] Michael Hechter, *Internal Colonialism* (Berkeley: University of California Press, 1975), p. 75. Hechter summarizes the expansion of the English language and culture into these areas as "the struggle of pious protestants to extend English religion and English civilization, first to the 'dark corners' of England and Wales, then to Ireland and the Highlands of Scotland, as a struggle to extend the values of London, and so to reinforce England's national security" (pp. 77–78).

discrimination, as were the Irish, who also suffered from negative stereotyping of the worst kind when they emigrated to England to seek work in industry. The Welsh and Scottish middle class was quite willing, without encouragement or compulsion, to assimilate into English ways, to anglicize itself voluntarily. The more extreme regional dialects were disappearing in England by the 1830s, despite poor school attendance and the persistence of much illiteracy. The Welsh and English nobilities were intermarrying frequently by then. In Wales and Scotland, much as in areas on the Continent where minority languages persisted, the intellectuals among the minorities accepted the superiority of the majority's elite language and conformed to it voluntarily for purposes of daily and official life, while reserving respect for the minority's language for literature and festivals, and in Wales for Methodist church services.

"The Irish problem" was seen differently by various groups in England. A small minority saw English rule as colonial oppression and agitated for Irish home rule, a position that did not win out in Westminster until 1914. A larger group of Protestant conservatives and Orangemen saw nothing wrong with the post-1801 status quo. This group had much support in the working classes of the Midlands. "There was a striking consensus among Englishmen who adhered to this view that the major problem of Ireland was the character of its people and that prosperity and tranquility would never be achieved without a prior moral reformation of the native Irish."[7] Most Liberals opposed home rule but favored reforms that would relax the economic and cultural yoke imposed by the Anglo-Irish establishment in Ireland because they were genuinely committed to increasing democratic participation and social welfare.

The victory of laissez-faire thinking was only too manifest in Westminster's response to the great Irish potato famine of the 1840s. That disaster resulted in the emigration of one million people, mostly to the United States, and in the death by starvation of one-and-one half million. Much of this could have been prevented by timely state intervention. However, it was felt by the Whig politicians that the market should be

---

[7] Richard Ned Lebow, "Ireland," in Gregory Henderson, Richard Ned Lebow, John G. Stoessinger, eds., *Divided Nations in a Divided World* (New York: David McKay, 1974), pp. 30–31. Lebow also argues that as the century wore on, more and more English people developed a guilty conscience about the colonial status of the Irish and that the victory of home rule sentiment at the turn of the century was due to the emotional and intellectual victory of liberalism as *the* British ideology, as the national myth. Catholic emancipation in Ireland also weakened the political role of the Church even though the number of enfranchised Irishmen was actually reduced by the act of emancipation, thus protecting the colonial hegemony of English property owners in Ireland. The repeal of the Test and Corporation Act in 1828 ended the monopoly of Anglican communicants to military and civil office, a monopoly that had been resented, especially by Scottish Presbyterians.

permitted to take its course and that intervention was inconsistent with market principles. The relief that was eventually organized came too late. The public works programs that were to provide an income for destitute Irish peasants so that they might buy the grain introduced by Westminster failed to take off because they were supposed to be financed from bankrupt local sources. Liberal economics triumphed, but British politicians of all parties also learned that colonial rule over Ireland was problematic and could not continue unchanged.

Even before strife and travail gave way to optimism, prosperity, and national integration, changes were being instituted between 1820 and 1850 that would be greeted by later reformers as absolutely essential for a liberal welfare state. Benthamites constituted something like an epistemic community in post-Napoleonic Britain. They and their adherents gave the initial impetus to the creation of a professional police force, in no small measure due to the rapidly rising crime rate in early Victorian times. Face-to-face hierarchical influence was not a feature of impersonal urban life as it had been in a rural setting. Public order seemed to be threatened by the rise in criminal and agitational activity. Even though Britons had always feared a strong state, they welcomed Sir Robert Peel's bobbies. The development of a public health and a factory inspectorate from a corps of devoted physicians and engineers was another tentative step toward a stronger administrative state. It was recognized that there could be no defense of personal liberty without making these concessions to collective welfare. Both developments suggest the early influence of epistemic communities in demonstrating the possibility of a new consensus derived from serious analysis.

Still, after weathering the threatening year 1848 without having suffered a revolution, confident Victorians could explain their success to themselves as being due to their protecting both prosperity and security by avoiding reliance on a strong state, by depending on "freedom." By this they meant the minimizing of bureaucracy, of keeping government expenditures under a tight rein, of avoiding excessive regulation of private choice—in short, classic liberalism, or what at the end of the twentieth century came to be called libertarianism. This attitude could explain the draconian poor laws under which Britain operated and the neglect of the Irish famine. Freedom also meant tolerating dissidents without much repression because 1848 had shown that they were too weak to challenge the existing order successfully. "It was not just that Britain had been strong enough to withstand the storm despite the fact that she had no defenses against it. She was strong enough *because* she had no defenses against it," because people were rational beings who avoid extremism.[8] Ideology made possible piecemeal adaptation.

[8] Bernard Porter, *Britain, Europe and the World* (Boston: Allen and Unwin, 1987), p. 4.

The Triumph of the Liberal National Myth

The mid-Victorian period was mostly one of international peace. The government opposed war and intervention as core instruments of foreign policy. Imperial rule was being widely questioned and inconsistently practiced (except in India). Armed forces were considered an undesirable burden. Free trade, Liberals thought, would make standing armies and navies, imperial administration, colonies, and war totally unnecessary. British capitalism and democracy, they thought, would show the world how to get along without war and without the balance of power. When governments resorted to war and intervention anyway, these steps had to be justified in liberal terms, as aiding democracy, ensuring the eventual predominance of free trade, or safeguarding access to a cherished economic "partner," especially India. By 1850 Britons felt more than ever distinct from other Europeans because they saw themselves as having jumped a major development hurdle: Britain was the most prosperous, advanced, and politically progressive nation on earth. Britons thought of themselves as having discovered the formula for being both free and rich, the quintessential qualities of liberalism.

Still, a sense of collective identity emerged from the political and ideological strife of the first half of the century, not from deliberate policy. Liberalism emerged as the definer of this identity, but not because it ever frontally defeated other ideological claimants. Liberal values emerged victorious as a result of the accretion of separate events and arguments.

Syncretist ideas lost out without having been defeated electorally or displaced by conscious manipulation. During the Napoleonic wars the Tories claimed to be the true Englishmen, the patriots, because they not only opposed the French usurper and tyrant but also defended the true (unreformed) British constitution. Nobody then offered ethnic definitions of British identity; Tories and most Whigs argued that the common purpose of "the people" is their zeal for a particular kind of society. The Tory governments were extremely reluctant to encourage any kind of popular patriotism or nationalism. They deliberately avoided creating a cult of national heroes to celebrate victories over the French. They did nothing about stressing service to the nation for fear of encouraging egalitarian and meritocratic ideas. Anglican ministers preached sermons stressing loyalty and service to king and country, not to political principles and to British society. Nationalist enthusiasm, as practiced across the Channel, was seen as a Pandora's box the nobility was wise to keep tightly shut. Such efforts to celebrate Horatio Nelson as a national hero and to reward war veterans of humble status as were made owed their success to the efforts of commoners, rich members of the middle class.

Conservatives, until the time of Benjamin Disraeli, remained unconvinced of substantive liberal values. Some professed a nationalism that extolled preindustrial British values, saw the genius of Britain in landed property and patriarchal relations between squire and peasant/tenant, and in the Church of England the font of values to be cherished in common by all. Utilitarian morality, the city, the factory, electoral equality, political rights for non-Anglicans—these notions were anathema to people who followed Sir Walter Scott, Samuel Coleridge, and the elderly William Wordsworth. These Conservatives professed a traditional-syncretist nationalism that was made obsolete by the success of a nation whose policies *were* liberal.

One new institution the syncretists endorsed was the protection of the working class, especially women and children, against the abuses of the early industrial system. The tradition of *noblesse oblige* was taken to mean that the well-born had a special duty to protect their weaker dependents against the rigors of modernity. Hence a modern dimension of social service was introduced into political dialogue by the very defenders of an antimodern view of national identity, a view that despised progress and excoriated reason. It is true, of course, that this brand of conservatism was that of Sir Robert Peel and his followers, whose nationalism was of the reformist-syncretist variety, not the traditional or restorative. These Conservatives accepted some liberal institutions and techniques, such as free trade and the enlarged franchise, as well as the anticolonial and isolationist foreign policy. They also subscribed to some of the liberal values, such as rights for the urban middle class and equality for Catholics. Peelites also agreed with the Liberals in opposing reforms favoring workers other than factory legislation. All Conservatives defended the Church of England and the monarchy. Sharp divisions into competing visions of the British "nation" continued into the 1860s. No consensual national myth came into being until the disappearance of romantic conservatism under the blows of Benjamin Disraeli's Tory Democracy.

Liberal values and policies carried the day piecemeal. The victory of the liberal myth is symbolized by Disraeli's appropriation of its core themes for his party. Liberalism triumphed in industry and commerce, in the growth of dissenting mass-based religion, in the decay of Anglican institutions. Liberals believed that knowledge, thrift, and conscientiousness in this life are more likely to benefit people than faith in the rewards of the next. Hence they advocated utilitarian educational and civil service reforms. They advocated further electoral reform, although they opposed the more egalitarian Chartist demands for annual elections and land reform. Even though no new elementary schools were built until the 1870s, socialization of the working class was advanced in

Sunday schools, public baths, evening courses, and by religious foundations, where the values of hard work, competition, and self-reliance were taught.

Liberals viewed the decline of the state religion with indifference in the face of the rising popularity of evangelical Anglicanism and democratic-participatory dissenting churches. These popular movements asserted their Britishness by advocating social reform. These attitudes and activities betoken increased individual religiosity, a closer link between religious conviction and political advocacy than had been seen in Britain since the seventeenth century. However, they also betoken a reduction in the role of the state religion as the definer of civil religion.

Liberal Conceptions of Foreign and Colonial Policy

A consensual foreign policy, a popular commitment to build, or not to build, an empire are powerful indicators of the existence of a rationalized society. Seen in these terms, Britain after 1815 was well integrated. The policies of first safeguarding the status quo and then blessing the world with free trade and national self-determination were seriously challenged by few.

In the first fifteen years following the Vienna settlement, when Lord Castlereagh and George Canning made foreign policy, Britain remained a member of the Concert of Europe Castlereagh had largely fashioned. London participated in the system of regular conferences of the five large powers to maintain the European status quo or to decide jointly on changes to be made. The Concert legitimated Belgian and Greek national independence and the suppression of revolts in Spain. But, with advent of the Liberals and Peelites, the interventions required to maintain the balance of power, in the language of the times, came to be resented and attacked. Victorian politicians mostly took the British national interest to consist of opening the world to British trade and investments. There was more than altruism at stake: in 1860, Britain's foreign trade amounted to 25 percent of the world's total; one third of woollen manufactures were exported; so was 40 percent of her steel and two thirds of her cotton goods, whereas many of the necessary raw materials were imported.

The Liberals had a strong preference for British isolation from continental European theaters of conflict. But they also supported national self-determination and constitutional democracy elsewhere in Europe, provided support did not involve major hostilities and British expense. How, then, do we account for the Crimean War? Britain went to war against Russia to keep the tsar from truncating the Ottoman Empire and thereby threaten access to India. Opposition to the Crimean War devel-

77

oped as soon as it became clear that the war would not lead to a cheap and easy victory. Preference for peace did not mean unwillingness to wage war in defense of a major commercial and strategic interest. Belief in nonintervention did not imply reluctance to use force when this proved both moral and easy, to stop the slave trade, to enforce free trade, and to collect debts, as was done in China, Argentina, and Mexico.

Why did the Victorians think critically of the Empire before the advent of Tory Democracy? "Empire" and "imperialism" were bad words between 1850 and 1870; they described, to the mid-Victorians, the grandiloquent antics of Napoleon III, plebiscitarian pseudo-democracy, not popular freedom rooted in parliamentary government. The labels implied a foreign policy of narcissistic self-assertion, warlike strutting, expansion for the sake of expansion. Britain, after the consolidation of the territorial gains of 1815, no longer followed a deliberate policy of imperial expansion, except in India where conquest continued and the state asserted ever more control over the private firm that had been its agent, the British East India Company. Moreover, a kind of creeping expansion in the South Pacific and South Africa continued because local settlers and military outposts, without authorization from London, continued their conquests.

Although deliberate expansion of the Empire was in abeyance for many decades, not everyone lost interest in maintaining the overseas colonies that had already been acquired. In fact, several very active groups came into being who argued for the retention of a reformed Empire in the service of liberal values. Evangelical Christians joined with secularists in advocating that colonial administration be used deliberately to civilize non-Western "natives," to spread the gospel of Christianity and of secular progress. Missionary societies of all religious persuasions made this argument in establishing their outposts in Africa, Asia, and the South Pacific. The Anti-Slavery Society succeeded in persuading Whitehall not to abandon naval outposts on the coast of Africa so as to be able to combat the slave trade and even acquire a few additional bases. Lord William Bentinck, upon becoming governor-general of India in 1828, said that Britain's task "is the moral regeneration of the immense mass of our fellow creatures" as he initiated the first major efforts at Western education on the subcontinent.[9] The idea of a professional civil service, uncorruptible experts not beholden to a dispenser of patronage, originated in the desire of administrators in India to improve the lot of the colonized.

The most interesting link between British liberal nationalism and co-

[9] Anthony Wood, *Nineteenth Century Britain* (Harlon, England: Longman, 1982), p. 215.

lonial policy lay in the thought and works of the "colonial reformers," a small group of thinkers and administrators who saw in settlement colonies one solution to the ills of industrialization. Led by Lord Durham, this group advocated the massive settlement of people in Canada, Australia, and New Zealand, displaced by urbanism and industrialism, thus alleviating crime, crowding, and disease in Britain. These overseas Britons, however, ought not to be ruled as natives, but as men carrying on the British heritage of freedom. Hence the colonial reformers advocated not only massive overseas settlement but also the phased introduction of full self-government with local parliaments in European-settled colonies. Their establishment in Canada in 1840 was the first fruit of this line of thought. Spreading the gospel of parliamentary government was to remain a theme in British imperialism when the policy of active expansion was resumed after 1870.

How Much Rationalization?

Whatever we may think, English and Scottish elites by the 1850s thought they had successfully integrated Britain, had put it on an irreversible road to progress and contentment. Their success in blunting the most serious sources of discontent—exclusion of the middle class from political participation and reduction of the hardships of early industrial life— made them optimistic. Still, as the score on Table 3-2 shows, they had a long way to go. Liberal politicians were getting skilled at defusing radical agitation with modest reforms. The middle classes assumed control over Britain without having had to resort to the guillotine. The working class, though not happy, at least had not hung their betters from lampposts. The factory legislation and the elimination of subsidized farming had given workers something without alienating factory owners. Even the vindictive "reform" of the poor laws, which had the effect of forcing paupers to work, only led to the ineffective Chartist demands.[10] And, although Disraeli's "two nations" most assuredly remained very different and did not share equally in the fruits of industrial modernization, the difference was not enough to undermine the liberal myth that had begun to persuade the millions of English and Scottish ordinary people to

---

[10] The Chartists had demanded universal male suffrage (fact by 1884); equal electoral districts (never completely established, but the grosser inequities were eliminated in 1884); removal of property qualification for MP's (not completely gone until 1948); the secret ballot (instituted in 1872); salaries for MP's (approved in 1911). The only demand never granted called for annual parliamentary elections. All the demands had been considered outrageous by the establishment when they were first advanced in 1838 (Hearder, *Europe in the Nineteenth Century*, p. 183).

79

Table 3-2. Extent of rationalization, Great Britain

	1800	1850	1900	1930	1950	1970	1990
Political succession	Yes	Yes	Yes	Yes	Yes	Yes	Yes
National myth in education	N/A	N/A	Yes	Yes	Some	Some	Some
Religious institutions	Some	Some	Yes	Yes	Yes	Yes	Yes
Civil religion	Yes	Some	Yes	Yes	Yes	Yes	Some
Cultural uniformity	Yes	Some	No	Yes	Yes	Some	No
Official language accepted	Yes	Yes	Yes	Yes	Yes	Yes	Yes
Income distribution	No	No	Some	Some	Yes	Yes	Some
Workers' organizations	No	No	Some	Some	Yes	Yes	Yes
Farmers' organizations	No	No	Some	Yes	Yes	Yes	Yes
Payment of taxes	Yes	Yes	Yes	Yes	Yes	Yes	Yes
Conscription accepted	N/A	N/A	N/A	N/A	Yes	Yes	N/A
Fighting wars	Yes	Yes	Yes	Yes	Yes	Yes	Yes
Administrative cohesion	Yes	Yes	Yes	Yes	Yes	Some	Yes
Foreign Policy	Yes	Yes	Yes	Some	Some	Some	Some
Peaceful change	Yes	Yes	Some	Some	Yes	Yes	Yes
Legitimacy	Yes	Yes	Some	Yes	Yes	Yes	Yes
Total (%)	75	68	77	87	94	88	80

Legend: Yes = 1; Some = .5; No = 0; N/A = not applicable.

see themselves as members of a very successful nation. But there is also good evidence that large sections of the working class remained alienated and would remain so for a long time. Radicalized workers in some parts of England and Wales rejected the social reformism of the established parties as inadequate even after 1850. In Wales, even during the heady patriotic days of World War I, miners continued to strike until Parliament outlawed the practice, even though the ban could not be enforced for fear of a violent worker response.

Liberalism won by default, not by design. It muddled through to become the successful myth of Great Britain. Elites did not learn to integrate the nation in any systematic way. They adapted piecemeal by heading off discontent as it arose, and they profited from the fact that Britain then had the world's wealthiest and fastest growing economy. Liberalism greased the wheels of progress and contentment and its values justified the halting steps politicians took to satisfy their followers, but it did not provide the reasoned blueprint for learning that its adherents thought they were applying in the United States and in France. And in the event, by 1880 these adaptive measures no longer seemed altogether successful.

RATIONALIZATION RESCUED: LIBERALISM MARRIES IMPERIALISM

The popular historian J. A. Froude foresaw Canada, Australia, the Cape, and New Zealand as British-settled colonies consolidated by a common cord of patriotism. The Empire, after 1867, became a positive symbol of nationhood, synonymous with such terms as Greater Britain, the United Empire, Federated Britain. It connoted a global brotherhood of Britons, committed to the perfection of their free political institutions and to the retention of their industrial prowess, as well as to the diffusion of the blessings of democracy and of Anglo-Saxon culture to "the lesser breeds beyond the law." Liberal nationalism now claimed a global civilizing mission. Why should it take this turn after decades of downgrading expansionary visions?

Imperialism became the ideological synthesis and the practical policy that was seen by many as being able to resolve a number of new tensions in the British polity. Democratization and continuing social mobilization of the working class occurred in a setting of declining economic performance relative to Germany and the United States, setting off serious domestic strife and triggering the introduction of modern social security and other major domestic reforms (Table 3-3).

Overseas expansion and a British civilizing mission corresponded to the prevalent ideologies of "social imperialism" and social Darwinism. They satisfied the nobility's search for honorable employment in the age of commercialism and industrialism in the form of military and administrative service overseas. They promised to reduce unemployment and underconsumption in opening up new protected markets overseas (not, as Lenin claimed, to export surplus capital). Middle-class Liberals, upper-class Conservatives, and working-class Socialists could all identify with such a doctrine. It, along with the outbreak of war in 1914, probably saved Britain from disintegration, while providing one reason why that war broke out in the first place.

Halting Decline: Imperialism, Education, Civil Religion

Though Britain was still seen as the world's premier industrial power, her actual performance was not impressive in the decades before 1914. Gross domestic product grew at a rate of 2 percent per year between 1870 and 1913; GDP per man-year grew at 0.9 percent per year. By 1913, Britain's share of world manufacturing had shrunk to 13 percent. A long depression began in the 1870s. British industrialists failed to respond to the lower prices by energetic policies of technological innovation (though their competitors in Germany and the United States did), and some complained about the relative decline in the skills and energies of

81

Table 3-3. Decline of British dominance in industrial production (% of world output)

	1840–50	1911–13
Coal	65	22
Pig iron	52	19
Steel	70	8
Cotton	48	20

SOURCE: E. J. Hobsbawm, *Industry and Empire* (New York: Pantheon, 1968), vol. 2, p. 24.

British workers. Instead of modernizing the economy, British industrialists merely sought to sell more of the goods produced in their obsolescing plant by relying on the gospel of free trade. Even though living standards clearly improved for everyone, the newly legalized trade unions turned to democratic socialism after the turn of the century, thus indicating their lack of satisfaction with capitalist society. Many contemporary appeals called attention to the decline in productive power, the loss of skills, and the inevitable inability to sustain the military might needed to remain a great nation. This lament about imminent decline and the need to do something about it by means of imperial expansion was the theme on which the political career of Joseph Chamberlain was built after 1890. Imperialism became the adhesive preferred by British leaders concerned about the future of the country.

In late Victorian and Edwardian Britain state efforts to socialize the population to accept nationalist-imperialist principles by means of the educational system came incrementally. Moreover, these efforts were made more difficult by conflicting religious claims to define values. Until the twentieth century, there was no public national system of secondary education at all in Britain. Primary education had been entirely the responsibility of counties until 1870; a national policy came very slowly after that. Education in England and Wales was not free and became compulsory until age 12 only toward the end of the nineteenth century; in Scotland, after 1872, it became free, compulsory, and universal under the control of the Presbyterian churches. The modest act of 1870 was seen by all as a step toward state-sponsored homogenizing secular socialization and therefore supported with reluctance by the Church of England. The rich were being inducted voluntarily into the white man's burden in their "public" schools; the poor had to be inducted by means of compulsory public national schooling, so as to create the skills thought necessary in an industrial-imperial polity. The school reforms also had the purpose of contributing to the equalization of opportunities in later life. While state support for denominational schools survived, after 1902 these institutions were subjected to state curricular standards.

Even though the Anglican church enjoyed a revival in the second half of the century (after having been threatened with disestablishment in the 1850s) and Methodism continued to grow as well, there is no doubt that religion underwent considerable secularization in late Victorian days. In the early parts of the century many people thought it impious to treat the cholera epidemics of 1831 and 1848 by cleaning up the cities. By 1866, "the response was no longer prayer and fasting but—in Disraeli's phrase—sanitas sanitatum, omnia sanitas—the construction of drains and sewers."[11] Methodism became identified not with the millennium, but with the organizing of trade unions and the defense of workers' rights in factories. Anglicanism overcame the irrelevance with which it was perceived by many by becoming concerned with social reform, caring for the poor, compassion and service in this life rather than salvation in the next.

Rerationalization: Incorporation, Social Security, Cultural Homogenization

Social mobilization was completed in this period. Enfranchisement and public education combined with increasing social services after the turn of the century went a long way to turn Britons into citizens, not inert subjects. Class privileges declined. The exclusiveness of classes diminished. Life chances for the poor improved. Neither government nor the economy remained the hereditary property of the well-born. Moreover, Britain's commitment to laissez-faire economic practices also suffered some chinks with the introduction after 1905 of state-financed social security arrangements. The overall increase in the electorate brought about by the successive enfranchisements was not staggering, but it was disproportionately important in democratizing Britain and in incorporating common people into the system because certain previously underrepresented areas (the large industrial cities and the Celtic fringe) received enormous increases in electoral might. Because of these events, the middle classes remained fearful of the power that, many thought, had been given away to potential revolutionaries.

Democratization and incorporation were especially significant in the Celtic fringe. Scotland and Wales became more English, but not uniformly so. The industrialized-urban areas lost their linguistic uniqueness first as Englishmen moved into Welsh industrial areas in large numbers and as lowland Scotland became part of the British market. Welsh speakers, as the century wore on, switched to English as London's administration, state schools, and east–west rail links made Wales part of Britain.

[11] Boyd Hilton, "From Retribution to Reform," in Lesley Smith, ed., *The Making of Britain* (New York: St. Martins, 1986), p. 44.

However, in both Scotland and Wales, many rural areas remained outside the anglicizing vortex. Ethnic opposition to London's dominance after 1900 was diluted because voters had to choose between two parties catering to local resentments, the Liberals and Labour. The Labour Party, being in favor (while in opposition) of home rule everywhere, identified with Scottish unions who claimed to have interests quite different from those of their English colleagues.

Ireland's fate proved to be an issue over which Britain approached civil war by 1914; Ireland tested the Liberals' commitment to national self-determination and the Conservatives' consistency in espousing the virtue of imperialism. Social mobilization occurred in Ireland as well as in England. Irish voters were enfranchised as were their English and Scots rivals in Ulster. The Irish contingent in Westminster increased, and so did its radical alienation from Britain. Yet all efforts at handing administration in Ireland over to the dominant Catholic population were stymied by the opposition of Protestant settlers and their friends in England and Scotland. Conservatives considered concessions to home rule close to treason. When the Liberal-controlled Parliament voted to grant it on the eve of World War I, army units and civil administrators in Ulster were on the point of staging a mutiny, averted by the outbreak of war on the Continent. Liberals were so divided on the issue that one wing, the "Unionists" under Joseph Chamberlain, bolted the party in 1886 and joined the Conservatives. British politicians, as a collectivity, did not learn that imposed rule over Ireland involved unacceptable costs to them until the tragedy of World War I made them weary of continued violence.

Foreshadowing the Welfare State

Although the incorporation of the Celtic fringe into the national fabric was certainly uneven, there can be no doubt that the establishment realized that averting a working-class revolt demanded the abandonment of unflinching policies of laissez-faire. By 1880 a wide range of regulations governing industrial pollution and municipal sanitation had been adopted in an effort to fashion a centralized public health policy. Working hours were controlled more extensively. Compulsory registration of births and deaths led to a system of national statistics. The powers of the police to establish surveillance over potential revolutionaries were augmented. By the early twentieth century, railway fares were controlled by the government. The state felt compelled to intervene in certain strikes. Yet, even though relief of the poor was being rethought, most middle-class people "still assumed that the function of the state was to supplement individual initiative, not to replace it, and they left the structure of the Poor Law to act as a safety net for those too poor or unworthy to benefit from the welfare legislation."[12] That legislation included efforts to provide unemployment insurance (after 1905), old age pensions paid by the state (implemented after 1909), and health insurance paid in part by beneficiaries, private organizations, and the state (established in 1911). All such benefits had been previously provided, mostly to the skilled trades only, by such nonstate agencies as friendly societies, trade unions, and insurance companies. These opposed state entry into the social welfare field and in some cases had to be brought into partnership with the state bureaucracy. It took many decades of study and debate to translate the idea of a systematic social welfare policy into law. How did this occur?

The core step toward a more rationalized Britain was the improvement in the administrative coherence of the state made possible by the creation of a professional civil service in the 1870s. Foreshadowed by the earlier professionalization of the Indian civil service and advocated for Britain since the 1850s, professionalization based on educational attainment became a reality only after the Franco-Prussian War. Two impulses combined to make it possible. The prime minister was eager to undercut the remaining powers to dispense patronage by parliamentary back-benchers to professionally unqualified administrators. All parties were impressed by the efficiency of the Prussian state in crushing France in a few months in 1870. They sought to create a similar British capability largely for reasons of external security. The security argument for administrative coherence was also made in the realm of educational reform in the effort to fashion a national school system.

The advent of social legislation in Britain is a case study in the interplay between expert-reformers, civil servants, and politicians. It illustrates the role of epistemic communities in collective learning. The story begins in the 1830s with the studies of a number of medical specialists, associated with the work of Sir Edwin Chadwick, on the subject of public health and poverty. These investigators established statistically the close association between poverty and unsanitary housing. In the 1880s, Charles Booth and Benjamin Rowntree had conducted celebrated surveys of the London poor to find out who they were and what caused their poverty. Many people were led to abandon the former distinction between the "deserving" and the "undeserving" (or lazy) poor and to see poverty as a cyclical phenomenon associated with industrial development and business dynamics. Specialists interested in these studies also devised measures to combat poverty. Moreover, the investigators themselves engaged in social work and in active advocacy. They allied themselves with a number of young civil servants who respected their

---

[12] Edward Royle, *Modern Britain* (London: Edward Arnold, 1987), p. 201.

methods and shared their values and objectives.[13] This group advocated the proposition that poverty was a solvable ill and that it was the state's responsibility to solve it because previous private efforts had failed. It was this insistence that brought the scientific social reformers into conflict with the organization of private reformers active since 1869, the Charity Organisation Society, a coalition of church groups and friendly societies.

No epistemic community succeeds unless it convinces important politicians of its claims to knowledge. The scientific reformers found allies among both Liberals and Conservatives. The latter had always been ambivalent toward laissez-faire policies and accepted the responsibility of the propertied classes to extend help to the deserving poor even if this involved the state. Liberals wanted to avoid revolution, to incorporate the working class in the nation. It was said of David Lloyd George, one of the politicians (along with Winston Churchill, Joseph Chamberlain, Herbert Asquith) who favored social insurance, that he "spiked the socialist guns with essentially conservative measures from the liberal arsenal."[14]

These measures did not suffice to incorporate workers into British democracy. The institutionalized inclusion of trade union representatives in national economic policymaking, along with representatives of industry and finance and the state bureaucracy, is the most common modern mechanism for achieving full incorporation (neocorporatism). This type of rationalization was never fully achieved in Britain. Liberals opposed it, and so did the trade unions as long as they remained allied with them. However, the dire needs experienced during World War I by the British establishment to maintain the patriotism of the workers resulted in steps leading toward neocorporatism. Trade union participation in the setting of policies relating to war production was institutionalized at the plant level. The welfare reforms were now augmented by rules for protecting worker safety, making collective bargaining more routine, and closing bureaucratic eyes when unions violated legislation banning strikes in war-related industries. The government also paid

---

[13] Sidney Webb developed the idea of a national minimum standard of living in 1901. Thomas Green, the Oxford philosopher, as well as Beatrice Webb and C. F. G. Masterman, were well-known members of this group. Their allies in the Civil Service included William Beveridge (brought to prominence by Winston Churchill) and Llewellyn Smith.

[14] Royle, *Modern Britain*, p. 203. The Lloyd George reforms were apparently also linked to declining industrial performance and to imperialism. Working-class welfare was being endangered because underconsumption led to an outflow of capital that then further undermined industrial adaptation and innovation and, therefore, wages. In the absence of underconsumption and capital outflows, some of the reforms would not have been considered necessary by a liberal government.

pensions to survivors of war casualties and family allowances to wives of servicemen. Conscription, which had never been used before in Britain, was thus made more acceptable. Rent and price controls were introduced.

Social Imperialism as Rationalizer

Such policies define the content of liberal nationalism in this century. They would not have become part of British identity around 1900 unless the work of the scientific reformers had been seen as useful by politicians worried about the moral and physical fiber of the British nation. When large numbers of working-class Britons volunteered for military service during the Boer War, it was realized that the health of the poor was as much a cause for concern as industrial decline. Between socialism, industrial decline, tubercular soldiers, unemployment, and the perception of being faced with a powerful rival in the form of German navalism and imperialism, some British leaders around the turn of the century advocated a dramatic reconciliation among classes and the rejuvenation of British pride and identity. The doctrine that emerged was a fruit of Social Darwinism. It was espoused by left-wing reformers, Unionist Liberals, as well as by Tories.

The story starts with Benjamin Disraeli's Tory Democracy in 1867. Under the label of "Tory Democracy" Disraeli claimed credit for the massive enfranchisement of the working class brought about by the electoral reform of 1867 and led his party to a subsequent victory on the strength of working-class support. This conjunction persuaded many politicians that at least some of the skilled workers were now reconciled to the British nation, that rationalization was progressing. Yet Disraeli took no chances. He deliberately used the pomp and circumstance of the monarchy to make the empire seem part of the British nation, thus giving each humble Briton, seemingly, a stake in the large parts of the world colored red on the map. In the early 1870s the Conservative Party also founded workingmen's clubs in which cheap beer was dispensed in order to turn the minds of workers away from class conflict, to rejoice instead in the British Empire, with India its jewel and Victoria its empress. Under Conservative rule Britain "rediscovered" her stake in India and symbolized that recognition by making the queen Empress of India. By 1880 the Conservatives gloried in confirming the imperial role with Britain's activity in safeguarding the Ottoman Empire (and the road to India), taking over Egypt and presiding over the partition of Africa. By the 1890s territorial expansion was a consensual policy, embraced by the Liberals as soon as the leadership passed from Gladstone to Lord Rosebery. The

87

issue of Irish home rule had divided the party; Gladstone's wing endorsed the reform, but many other Liberals opposed it because they were not sure that national self-determination ought to be practiced that close to home and at their expense. By the end of the century, imperialism had been democratized in the sense that its presumed benefits were no longer confined to industry and shipping, the army and the navy; it was seen as a good in which all Britons gloried and shared. To many politicians imperialism was the glue that held an otherwise badly divided society together. It had become a popular creed, hence "social imperialism."

In 1906, fifty representatives of the new Labour Party were elected to the House of Commons, the first major electoral success for a party opposing the ruling establishment. By 1918, partly because union leaders had been given prominent roles in running the wartime economy, Labour had confirmed its embrace of democratic socialism as the basis for the reforms it demanded; it called for nationalization of the coal mines. Its electoral strength grew after women were given the vote at the end of the war.

How did Labour respond to imperialism? Labour ideology proclaimed belief in national self-determination; it held imperial rule and democracy to be incompatible. Some Labour leaders argued that improving democracy in Britain must mean the end of imperial rule abroad. Others, however, embraced a more cautious reformism and suggested that the democratization of all policy could also be used to turn colonial policy into welfare policy by using imperialism to improve the lot of the colonized. This became the stand of Labour's think tank, the Fabian Society. Such well-known Labour-identified writers as John Hobson, Norman Angell, H. N. Brailsford, and Bertrand Russell, however, preached the absolute incompatibility of democracy and colonialism.

By no means did all workers accept this line of argument. The number of working people who joined in the social imperialist consensus was probably much larger than those who opposed it. Cecil Rhodes seemed to understand the appeal of imperialist nationalism when he wrote in 1895:

I was in the East End of London yesterday and attended a meeting of the unemployed. I listened to the wild speeches, which were just a cry for bread, bread, bread. And on my way home I pondered over this scene and I became more convinced than ever of the importance of imperialism. . . . My cherished idea is a solution for the social problem, i.e., in order to save 40 million inhabitants of the United Kingdom from bloody civil war, we colonial statesmen must acquire new lands to settle the surplus population, to provide new markets for the goods produced by them in the factories and mines. The

Empire is a bread and butter question. If you want to avoid civil war you must become imperialists.[15]

The social imperialist program combined domestic reform with imperial expansion and consolidation, a single project justified by the pseudo-Darwinian notion that only those who fight for their survival have a right to survive. Imperial rule and resisting the German threat would provide the appropriate arenas. The program catered to industrialists who wanted massive naval modernization and an enlarged army. It catered to reformers who wanted to democratize education and make it available to all. For social imperialists Irish home rule was anathema. And they wanted to jettison free trade in favor of an imperial protective tariff. Full implementation was blocked by Liberal governments who favored retention of free trade and the conferring of home rule.

Perhaps the most popularly appealing part of the social imperialist project lay in the democratization of the army.[16] Democratic army reformers led by Lord Roberts, the hero of the South African War, demanded peacetime conscription and the creation of a mass army to weaken the hold of the nobility over the officer corps. Their organization, the National Service League, also demanded the augmentation of peacetime Volunteer Forces, a militia originally made up of bourgeois weekend soldiers trained to put down Chartist revolts. The Volunteer Forces in the early 1900s were made up mostly of working-class members who not only drilled but also engaged in patriotic rituals and in demonstrations designed, in part, to support egalitarianism and democratic forces elsewhere. Workers volunteered by the hundreds of thousands when war broke out in 1914.

It is doubtful that all these reforms, the ones carried out as well as the ones that were blocked, would have prevented drastic derationalization if war had not broken out in August of 1914. A fully revolutionary labor movement did not develop. Nor was the working class as completely alienated from the system as were the king's Irish subjects. Even though full legitimacy seemed in doubt, a mighty wave of patriotism swept the country when war broke out. Now the social imperialist theme, linked to domestic democratization and reform and to the defense of the realm against "the Huns," appeared as a successful rationalizing formula. The trauma of the war, and the institutional adaptations to the need for winning it despite appalling losses and costs, completed the process—for a time. Service in the trenches and the equality bestowed by death

---

[15] Quoted in Bernard Semmel, *Imperialism and Social Reform* (Cambridge: Harvard University Press, 1960), p. 16.

[16] Prominent people in this camp included William Cunningham, Sir William Ashley, Halford Mackinder, Robert Blatchford, and Lord Alfred Milner.

and suffering went some way toward diminishing class distinctions. Full employment in war-related industries increased incomes. Institutional innovations in industrial and economic administration resulted in important new forms of interclass collaboration. Liberal nationalism, under the pressure of social unrest before the war and under the quite different imperatives of that war, showed itself capable of adaptation. But real collective learning did not occur until the trauma of the Great Depression.

How Did Liberal Nationalism Survive the Depression?

Britain only appeared to be a winner in the first Great War. The mood of national unity survived for barely a year; in 1926 Britain again seemed to be on the brink of civil war. The 1920s and 1930s were hard times. Class divisions turned to class hatred, as great as during the days of the Chartists. The aura of inter-class cooperation that had prevailed during the war and the unity engendered by social imperialism disappeared during the travail of the Great Depression and the struggle over the containment of fascism. The survival of liberal nationalism clearly owes a good deal to the totalitarian challenge; World War II became the very challenge to Britain's greatness of which Winston Churchill spoke and wrote so eloquently. It reaffirmed the values and the institutions of liberal nationalism because almost all Britons came to share in them. Between 1919 and 1932, Britain slid toward chaos. Rerationalization began slowly thereafter; full rerationalization, however, demanded not only the defeat of Nazism but also the great Labour electoral victory of 1945. Rationalization is always a matter of degree. It is temporary.

Derationalization Despite Victory

The victorious government in 1919 made very little provision to ease the reentry of millions of servicemen into civilian life. A severe depression greeted the demobilized victors whose faith in an equality and service-oriented Britannia received a rude shock. The Treasury wanted to practice prudence; government spending was made contingent on war reparations to be paid by Germany, an expectation that turned out to be mostly vain. However, these trends were belied by the superficial gains of the war. The British Empire reached its greatest size by acquiring new lands in Africa and in the Middle East. But social imperialism lost its emotional appeal in the mud and blood of the trenches; the expansion of the red-colored portions of the global map did nothing to ensure social peace in Britain.

Muddling through for British politicians and civil servants seeking to cope with the postwar depression meant making small adjustments to orthodox capitalist monetary and fiscal policies. This was as true for Labour as for the Conservatives. The Tories distrusted Keynesian technocrats; Labour, like the Conservatives, felt compelled to listen to the bankers of The City who advised them not to run government budget deficits so as to be able to protect Britain's role as financier for the world's private trade sectors. The "Treasury View" tended to prevail, a view committed to figuring out how to protect a convertible pound sterling based on gold and how *not* to spend public money. The Establishment practiced "the cultural hegemony of orthodoxy," the complacency of those who had succeeded first.

The twenty interwar years were dominated by the Conservatives. By the end of the first war the electoral base of the Liberals was fast eroding as Labour took away the alienated working-class voters and the Tories took the middle-class ones. But Labour's ideological base was heterogeneous and self-contradictory, ranging from doctrinaire Marxists to pragmatic reformers who were not even certain that the nationalization of key industries was the key to utopia. The trade unions, the core of the party, were also divided. Many Labourites favored increased social services, selective nationalization (notably coal mining), home rule for colonies, disarmament, an isolationist foreign policy, if not actual pacifism. The party was radicalized by the failed general strike of 1926 and by massive unemployment after 1931. It actively opposed fascism and policies of appeasing fascist demands while tilting toward pacifism. Unionists were at once class conscious, hostile toward the state, and in favor of international working-class solidarity. Even though the concept of socialist planning was endorsed by some Labourites, the majority in the party continued to believe in free trade even as the government finally put in place the Commonwealth tariff that had been demanded by imperialists since the 1880s. Attitudes toward Scotland and Wales were equally confusing. From an initial position of favoring more self-determination for the Celtic periphery, Labour, once it had achieved the respectability of governing, lost interest in devolution particularly as the Depression triggered a revival of the Scots Nationalist party.

Even though it was Conservative-led governments that began to rerationalize Britain in the 1930s, the Tories' foreign policy of appeasing the fascist challengers of the international status quo exacerbated domestic dissensus. Their prime ministers, Stanley Baldwin and Neville Chamberlain, wanted to avoid a new war so badly that they were willing to make territorial concessions (at the expense of other countries) to Germany and Italy. They also favored arms control. Britain repeatedly rebuffed French overtures for a stronger antifascist stand and had worked for the early rehabilitation of Germany into a status of political equality and economic viability. Appeasement, which was interpreted by the British Left as part and parcel of a policy of active hostility to the Soviet Union (because it seemed to leave Germany free to fight communism), was also opposed by a minority in the Conservative Party led by Winston Churchill and Antony Eden. Labour advocated a strong policy of opposing fascism by relying on the League of Nations, but was just as reluctant as the Tories to rearm. In fact, Marxist-led British scientists, united in the British National Union of Scientific Workers led by J. D. Bernal and J. B. S. Haldane, agitated for a scientists' strike to prevent war-related research, and Oxford undergraduates took an oath to refuse to "fight for king and country." Foreign policy was less consensual than at any time in British modern history.

Renegotiating a National Consensus

The Conservatives invented the muddling-through economic policies that got Britain over the Great Depression. In 1933 unemployment had reached the level of one-third of the work force. In 1900 the government had spent 21 percent of the national budget on housing, education, public health, and social security, considered together. In 1930 it spent 4.5 percent on housing, almost 10 percent on education and science, 6.3 percent on public health, and 21.4 percent on social security! Political liberalism was alive and well even as economic liberalism went into decline. Thoroughly secular in their views by now, Conservative governments disestablished the Church of England in Wales and downplayed all religious values and symbols in public life.

The Tories, painting Labour as dangerous revolutionaries, presented themselves as the party of the British national tradition of compromise, fairness, and freedom. They accepted the need for increasing social services and for regulating markets. They abandoned in turn the gold standard, the commitment to balanced budgets, and free trade. A few industries were nationalized, and managed exchange rates became acceptable after 1931, even though the Conservatives did not accept Keynesian macroeconomic steering until 1941. Stanley Baldwin's "New Conservatism" was very reminiscent of Disraeli's in its emphasis on the reconciliation of class differences. Labour's stress on economic democracy, that is, nationalization and union participation in the running of the economy, rather than on the new economics of Keynes, was not inconsistent with the New Conservatism. After 1941, when Keynesian policies of demand management became more acceptable to Labour as well as to Tories, a compromise on economic policies became realizable in principle, although individual politicians remained slow to pick them up. It required a serious setback for direct planning after the massive Labour electoral victory of 1945 to institutionalize the Keynesian scientific consensus in Whitehall. Keynesians did not become a successful epistemic community until then; they cannot be credited with preventing revolution in the 1930s. Pragmatic Conservatives, who used the Empire as if it were a common market and a monetary union, can claim some success in halting the process of derationalization that set in during the 1920s. Adolf Hitler, however, deserves most of the credit.

Muddling through included the creation of advisory committees to Whitehall for dealing with the new tariff and the Commonwealth preferences scheme as well as the other measures taken after 1931 to regulate formerly free markets, especially for agricultural commodities. The spokesmen for private interests were actually institutionalized in these advisory committees. Moreover, expertise was added in the form of a more scientifically organized scheme of national accounts, invented by John Maynard Keynes and introduced into government by his associates during the 1930s.

These measures suggest adaptation, not learning. The interwar years, however, also saw the beginnings of the process of decolonization, even though the physical expanse of the Empire was greater in 1930 than ever. The paradox is more apparent than real. Colonial rule during these years grew more expensive and more difficult as the Indian independence movement took off in full force. Even before the outbreak of World War II, a quiet consensus developed in London that India must be given her freedom sooner or later; both parties agreed that their own ideologies demanded no less, and that, in any event, Britain lacked the means to use force to prevent a concerted Indian revolt. Imperial bonds with Egypt, Iraq, and Ireland were loosened in the wake of actual or threatened revolts. The British-settled dominions became sovereign states in 1931 by general agreement. True, the consolidation of the Empire through the preferential tariff system was a major symbol of national greatness for the Conservatives, whereas Labour was more concerned about making democratic and welfare reforms in the colonies. It appears that the general public had lost interest, that World War I and its aftermath had reestablished the primacy of local and European concerns over the feelings Rudyard Kipling had sought to evoke. Britons realized that the simultaneous striving for military security, democratic values, and the comforts afforded by the welfare state involved priorities that were not compatible with running the world's largest empire. Perhaps they even *learned* that lesson.

93

THE FATE OF THE LIBERAL WELFARE STATE:
A CASE OF INCOMPLETE LEARNING

In Britain, liberalism defeated mercantilism in the eighteenth century because mercantilist policies discredited themselves by failing to perform, not because better political economy vanquished a worse variety. Systematic knowledge about policy did not defeat adaptation by trial and error. Mercantilism lost because the American Revolution succeeded, not because Adam Smith and David Hume proved persuasive in Whitehall. Social reforms staved off revolution in the 1840s because Tories had a residual feudal sense of *noblesse oblige* and because some Liberals had a guilty conscience. David Lloyd George's reforms in the early twentieth century compensated for the failings of capitalists to invest adequately in British industry, but not because the Liberal Party learned to apply economics and sociology to the making of policy. These measures were highly successful adaptations, no more.

Things after 1945 were different. British politicians and bureaucrats seemed really to learn to reason in innovative ways about cause and effect in policy. Apparently, they knew they had to do better than in the past, that muddling through would no longer do. Nevertheless, by 1975, it became clear that the innovations were just another series of adaptations. They were succeeded by the advent of monetarist economic ideas and policies and by measure to cut back the social democratic welfare state. First "joining Europe" and then distancing Britain from the European Union were justified as measures to halt economic decline. No single idea, no economic civil religion took the place of the post-1945 consensus. Britain, seemingly well rationalized by the 1960s under social democratic and Keynesian principles, slowly slid toward internal strife during the 1990s. Had everything been adaptation? Had nothing solid been learned?

From Socialism to Thatcherism

Patriotic enthusiasm and hatred of fascism were not the only forces holding Britons together during World War II. We now know that the decline in interclass hostility also had to do with the expectation that, once the war was won, the British common people would receive their reward in the form of sharply upgraded living standards. It was known during the war that the major motivation of Britons to the war effort was a commitment to the better material life that was to come after "Jerry was licked." Moreover, it was taken for granted that class differences would decline and that social equality was as important as political equality.

94

Working-class Britons expected the "new Jerusalem" as a reward for keeping up the fight.

Labour became the vehicle for the articulation of the proposition that the essence of the modern British nation was social-democratic. Still, Labour's voice was diluted by internal disagreements. Some were Marxists, and many believed, at first, in central economic planning under state auspices and in the nationalization of most industries. Others were Keynesians who preferred less direct forms of state intervention and more tolerance for private property and for market forces. One group wanted to use the school system to bring about social equality, another was content to let the traditional political class (to which many Labour members of Parliament belonged) continue unscathed. The Labour Left was pacifist, anti-American, and opposed to nuclear weapons; the moderate social democratic center accepted the same foreign and defense policy positions as did the Conservatives, who were in power continuously between 1951 and 1964, and again after 1979. There were ups and downs in the fortunes of both wings, but by 1985 the moderate social democrats had won out. Nationalization lost its fetishlike status, as did pacifism, opposition to nuclear weapons, and resistance to European integration.

The New Conservatives who won control over the party after 1945 were determined to institutionalize the measures of state direction over the economy that had been introduced in the 1930s and during the war. While opposed to nationalization of industry and leveling of the educational system, the Tories also became convinced Keynesians in economics and acquiesced in most of Labour-initiated welfare legislation, including policies ensuring full employment. Class harmony was stressed along with industrial innovation and the upgrading of human skills. It was this kind of Conservative who lost interest in the Empire, who wanted to "join Europe" after 1961, and who eventually lost out to the Thatcherite Tory Right in the 1980s. During the 1950s and 1960s, however, the widespread national consensus favoring the egalitarian welfare state was aptly labeled "Butskellism" (after Tory leader R. A. B. Butler and Labour leader Hugh Gaitskell). Tories accepted comprehensive national health legislation that socialized medicine in Britain, a very generous and comprehensive social insurance scheme, unemployment compensation that wiped out the last remnants of the Poor Laws. Most everyone agreed to the huge funds invested in the construction of new state-owned housing. Most forms of discrimination on the basis of gender were outlawed in 1967, and abortion on demand became legal. Unemployment rarely exceeded 3 percent between 1948 and 1973, in part because of a very active labor market policy involving ambitious training and retraining schemes and tax rebates for workers and employers to avoid layoffs or reduce their impact.

Neither Keynesian nor monetarist policies were able to make the British economy flourish. By 1950 demand-management policies and its econometric models were institutionalized in the Treasury soon after Labour abandoned early attempts at full economic planning. However, even during the reign of Keynesian epistemic communities, economic growth never reached the consistency and rate achieved by the continental countries. Instead, the British pattern was one of "stop-go," a pattern attributed to the absence of the neocorporatist institutions that worked so well in Germany, Austria, the Benelux, and the Nordic countries. British unions were decentralized; they resisted the call of government, employers, and their own leaders for wage restraint. No incomes policy would work. The government seemed to lack many of the monetary and fiscal instruments that would make industrial policy, or even concertation, a practical possibility. This lack is attributed by many to the role of the City because of its commitment to international openness.

Keynesianism was discredited by 1975 because it was unable to cope with "stagflation," the simultaneous workings of recessive and inflationary trends, that heightened trade union militancy and put new pressure on wages. These trends were reenforced during the 1970s by the successive oil shocks and by the increasing international mobility of capital. Investment capital left Britain searching for a more hospitable wage environment. The very success of Keynesian policies in rebuilding Europe and stimulating the miraculous decades of growth also proved a source of its demise because it had made possible the mobility of capital that then undermined the effectiveness of domestic Keynesian instruments.

Since 1979, for almost twenty years, the radical-monetarist Conservatives have ruled. They claimed to be engaged in dismantling the welfare state, though the deed lagged much behind the rhetoric. Keynesianism was abandoned; monetarism was celebrated. Nationalized industries were sold to private investors; government-owned housing was sold to its occupants. There was little difficulty in finding buyers for either: a 10 percent increase in home ownership occurred, matched by the unprecedented situation in which 20 percent of the electorate owns shares in denationalized industries. Labour no longer challenges these changes. After the 1987 elections, the party jettisoned its nostalgia for state-owned industries, planning, and even unilateral disarmament. Inflation was stopped, the pound permitted to float freely, and taxes slightly reduced. Competition and innovation were the virtues to be rewarded, not reliance on state-financed entitlements. The rustbelt in the Midlands grew redder and unemployment there rose to levels not seen since 1931. But the economy of South England and parts of Scotland boomed as a result of these policies. By the 1990s much of resurgent Britain was inhabited by successful yuppies, or would-be yuppies, while the impoverished grew more alienated.

Beyond the Class Society? Imperfect Inclusion

The lot of almost all Britons improved after 1945, but the integration of the country did not. Contradictory trends prevailed, setting the scene for the successful challenge to the social democratic welfare state mounted by the Conservatives after 1979. Upward mobility clearly improved as the educational system was democratized by Labour. By the 1970s union members identified far more strongly than in the 1930s as British nationalists who expected their nation-state to deliver desired services; they paid scant regard to ties with the international or European trade union movement. Class conflict seemed to abate in some ways, but not in others. The number of manual workers shrank from 64 percent of the working population in 1951 to 46 percent in 1986. Union membership declined massively. The Labour Party, seeing the sign of the times, stopped presenting itself as the party of the working class by 1990.

Overall, administrative cohesion was impaired by the failure of corporatism, only to improve markedly under Margaret Thatcher. Both parties attempted to imitate continental corporatist practices when they created a series of tripartite institutions in the early 1960s designed to overcome stop-go limitations to growth by "concerting" policies among all interested actors, public and private. Incomes and industrial policies relying on selective state supports were to be used. These efforts failed. Incomes policies—workers getting additional social insurance benefits in exchange for practicing wage restraints for contractually determined periods—did not outlast pressures from inflation and the devaluations of the pound. Increasingly militant trade unions refused to observe their contracts. Industrial policy, another attempt to imitate a French success, also failed because of the unwillingness of unions and industry to use state-provided incentives to improve productivity. Corporatism did not take root in Britain. The Labour government of the 1970s was unable to innovate, improve productivity, or stop inflation. Nor was it able to control its own supporters. Trade unions, some of them controlled by Trotskyite revolutionaries, struck at will. The left wing of the party again urged radical nationalization measures and withdrawal from foreign alliances. Threatened with chaos and confusion, the nation elected Margaret Thatcher's Conservatives in 1979. The event appeared to presage the end of the earlier consensus on policy and the resurgence of class warfare.

Institutional and administrative shortcomings were largely responsible

97

for the failure of governments in the 1960s and 1970s to overcome stop-go growth and stagflation. The diversity and decentralization of the business sector matched that of the trade unions, who could afford to be truculent because there was little to stop them. The interests of the City diverged from those of the many small highly specialized manufacturers. The latter lacked investment capital to modernize, and there were practically no large investment banks. The state apparatus was used to macro-economic management through fiscal and monetary policy adjustments, not to the practice of industrial policy that requires direct intervention in the economy, even if it no longer sought nationalizations and full planning. The Keynesian bureaucracy dispensed development funds for backward regions and subsidies to failing industries, rather than seeking strategic investments for new industrial products.

Spending on welfare, however, proved very resilient. In 1988, British tax revenues still amounted to 37 percent of the GDP (the average for all OECD countries was 38.7 percent), which was only slightly lower than the 1979 ratio. Although entitlements were reduced somewhat, the main pillars of the social and medical insurance system remained intact, so much so that devoted followers of the New Right have blamed Margaret Thatcher for betraying her own ideology. Funds devoted to retraining the work force actually increased dramatically.[17] In 1990, 56 percent of the people still asked that higher taxes be levied on the wealthy to pay for upgraded social services, despite a decade of deregulation and privatization. The Thatcher governments centralized educational administration and weakened the power of local authorities. They cracked down hard on the power of the unions to defy the state.

Is There Still a British Cultural Identity?

Decolonization clearly did no harm to the average Briton's self-confident perception of being somebody special and different, a citizen of a nation with a superior culture making a unique contribution to the creation of democratic and harmonious societies. Shedding the empire may have enhanced this sense of nationhood. The failure of Britain successfully to practice planning, Keynesian fine-tuning, or corporatism, however, seems to have had a derationalizing effect, engendering a sense of internal distrust. The short-run economic successes of monetarism did lit-

---

[17] Kenneth R. Hoover and Raymond Plant, *Conservative Capitalism in Britain and the United States* (London: Routledge, 1989). They show that, although tax revenues have declined, overall government expenditures have not because of money earned from the sale of formerly nationalized industries. Peter A. Hall argues that the learning took place in the Conservative Party and the associated interest groups, not in the bureaucracy that remained overwhelmingly Keynesian in its cause-and-effect beliefs.

tle to counter this sense of failure. Now members of the European Union and formally committed to a course of pooling national sovereignty with the Continent, do Britons still think of themselves as belonging to a distinct and homogeneous culture, as different from other Europeans, as special and superior?

Events seemed to have torn Britain's identity apart. In the 1970s Scotland and Wales threatened to go their separate ways as Ulster suffered a bloody rebellion. Race riots took place in London during the 1980s. Islamic Britons from South Asia demanded a special legal status. A huge mosque arose in Regent's Park, a gigantic Hindu temple in North London. Some people again demanded a Christian education for their children. The two-party system is under challenge. The Catholic revolt in Ulster is due to the experience of suffering discrimination on several dimensions all at once: religion, class or status, and economic difficulties. The Catholic working-class Irish were disproportionately hit by the decline of Ulster industry, as compared to Protestant descendants of the largely middle-class Scottish immigrants. Just how people differed about their identity, on the eve of the revolt, is shown by these figures: 43 percent thought of themselves as being of Irish nationality (20 percent of Protestants, 76 percent of Catholics), 29 percent as being British (39 percent of Protestants and 15 percent of Catholics), but 21 percent thought of themselves as having Ulster nationality (32 percent of Protestants and 5 percent of Catholics).[18] Little seems to have happened since then to alter people's fragmented sense of identity or to lessen their mutual hatred.

During the 1970s the breakup of Britain into its constituent cultural units (many call them "nations") was widely predicted; in the 1990s Welsh and Scottish separatism is hardly discernible. What was going on? Industrialization undoubtedly succeeded in all but eliminating local and cultural differences within England, just as poverty (i.e., the absence of industrialization) linked to active religious discrimination fueled the secession of southern Ireland in 1921. Before the downturn of the mid-1970s, it is also true that industrialization brought about the almost complete economic and political integration of England and Scotland, although the Scottish Nationalist Party had also kept alive the feeling of cultural separateness of a minority of Scots. In Wales things were more complicated. Rural Welsh tended to be poor and to speak Welsh rather than English and to be Methodists rather than Anglicans. Welsh cultural separateness was kept alive by Plaid Cymru and by demands that the Welsh language be protected and nurtured in the state school system,

---

[18] Richard Rose, *Governing Without Consensus: An Irish Perspective* (Boston: Beacon Press, 1971), pp 208–209. Rose's figures are based on a survey of 1,291 respondents done in 1967–68.

radio, and television. Neither nationalist party was electorally successful before 1970 because Labour monopolized the effort to stimulate compensatory regional development programs and also gave lip service to Welsh demands for cultural autonomy and political decentralization.

The Celtic revolt of the 1970s was the protest of those who were left behind in the process of industrial modernization (i.e., in Wales) and those disproportionately disadvantaged by the decline of British industry (i.e., the Clydeside area of Scotland). Plaid Cymru and the Scottish Nationalists began to win elections because there was "a new awareness that no state-wide political party will commit sufficient resources to achieve development in the periphery. Nationalism has reemerged in the Celtic periphery largely as a reaction to this failure of regional development."[19] In Scotland the discovery of North Sea oil seemed to make possible Scottish economic independence; in Wales support for Labour declined because of the party's neglect of its Welsh constituents. A few cultural concessions and an upturn in economic fortunes, it seemed, could stem the tide of secession and separatism.

And so it came about. In 1973 a Royal Commission on the Constitution recommended some administrative devolution in Wales and Scotland, without touching the economic integration of the United Kingdom, and the establishment of local legislatures with restricted powers. Both proposals were defeated in local referenda, and no constitutional changes at all were made, probably because reindustrialization funds were lavishly invested in both regions. As it turned out, majorities of both regions, despite some remaining local sentiment of a separate self, were unwilling to abandon their British identity and their ties to the larger entity. Britons today no longer worry about being Celts.

If this episode confirms the continuity of British identity, the growing controversy over multiethnicity and multiculturalism as definer of Britishness strongly suggests the opposite. The immigration of Blacks from the Caribbean and of Pakistanis and Indians from South Asia and East Africa became a flood after 1960. Resistance and resentment about the influx of non-Western groups were widespread, especially in working-class circles, a resentment of which such European immigrants as Italians, Spaniards, and Portuguese were not victims. By 1990 about 4 percent of Britain's population was nonwhite. This development was heavily concentrated in a few cities;

---

[19] Hechter, *Internal Colonialism*, p. 265. Milton Esman, "Scottish Nationalism, North Sea Oil, the British Response," in M. Esman (ed.), *Ethnic Conflict in the Western World* (Ithaca: Cornell University Press, 1975). There never was a serious basis other than economic dissatisfaction for Scottish separatism. There never was any discrimination against Scots in employment, subsidies, or any other benefits, though successive governments had reneged on promises of more home rule. The high point of separatism was in 1974 when the Scottish Nationalist Party received 30.4 percent of the vote in a parliamentary election.

94 percent of the nonwhites were born in the United Kingdom. Most of the Blacks and South Asians were, by then, British citizens, but their legal equality by no means guarantees social equality.

Intellectuals and the Labour Left have concluded that the permanent presence of non-Western and nonwhite Britons must mean a redefinition of Britishness as multicultural and multiethnic, thereby in effect making an argument for a global rapprochement between the cultures of the First World and the Third World. That argument has been pursued further by Islamic officials claiming to speak for Muslim South Asian immigrants (though in fact subsidized by Saudi Arabia and Iran). They insist that in a multicultural Britain Muslim citizens ought to have a separate legal status exempting them from many obligations of British law and giving them new religiously sanctioned rights. Militant sentiments and movements of this kind, of course, exacerbate tensions between whites and immigrants. Generous civil rights legislation enacted by Parliament has done little to change matters toward greater intercultural harmony because the laws lack the enforcement mechanisms familiar in America. Would a multiethnic Britain fit into a united Europe better than the traditional British nation? Ethnic tensions created a new line of cleavage among Britons, particularly in a few major urban areas, just as the overall gulf between the classes was perceived as lessening.

Educational reforms also threaten the cultural consensus. The creation of the system of comprehensive secondary schools had the immediate consequence of fudging the distinction between classes, a feature that made this Labour innovation a subject of deep resentment by the upper middle class. Nevertheless, the system was extended even further in 1976 as educational policy was increasingly centralized. But the Thatcherites reversed this egalitarian trend with their school reforms. They relaxed central control over education by allowing parents more choice in where to send their children and by increasing parental involvement in school administration. Upper-middle-class parents can take their children out of the comprehensive schools. The nationalist content of curricula is to be stressed again. So are Christian values. The tone of these changes in the educational system is to combat the sense of egalitarian multiethnic British identity. None of these controversies, however, have challenged the monopoly of English as the sole language of communication. Technical and vocational training programs run by tripartite commissions have increased. For the first time in British history a national school curriculum was decreed. Subsidies to education and support for universities were put on a competitive basis by rewarding only schools and programs for which there is the most demand. The relevant interest groups, far from defending the status quo ante, liked these innovations as they, and various administrative agencies, fought lustily for pieces of the new pie. As a result, past practices were jettisoned as the old ideology justifying the social democratic welfare state was questioned.

It is hard to find a civil religion in today's Britain. Secularism and religious toleration are pervasive. The social democratic welfare consensus of the thirty years following World War II is being shattered by the rebirth of competition and the culture of self-regarding personal advancement of the yuppies who form the backbone of the Conservative Party. Moreover, the modern Labour Party of centrists retains too few stark core values to count as the advocate of a distinct ideology.

But the inability on the part of traditional churches to mobilize their diminishing adherents for political purposes has left the field open to others who are willing to use religion for instrumental—and divisive—ends. Small, overlapping networks of activists urge a return to officially sanctioned Christian values and prominently oppose publicly financed abortions. Left-wingers within the Church of England want to separate from the state better to criticize its policies, while right-wingers wish to retain the church–state tie better to use Christianity to revitalize civil religion.

Immigration and naturalization again trouble Britons. Until the advent of Thatcherism, race and immigration had not been an issue that divided the parties. The inflow of Irish peasants during the 1850s and of East European Jews in the 1880s had given rise to no anti-immigration sentiment—although it did beget a great deal of ethnic stereotyping and widespread discrimination—but the postwar massive inflow of migrants from the Caribbean and from South Asia did. A small group of Tories actively campaigned against allowing further immigration, and they succeeded in getting both parties to restrict the right of people from the Commonwealth to enter Britain freely. Eventually, the status of commonwealth citizenship (with the right to settle in Britain) was abolished and all immigration restricted. Under Thatcher the Conservatives again made terminating immigration a visible issue, whereas Labour showed much more tolerance for a multiethnic Britain and further immigration. Naturalization, however, was made simple for all immigrants; any alien may be granted British citizenship, irrespective of origin, and with a minimum of conditions. This very tolerance seems to enrage underemployed working-class youth whose main pleasure is to beat up and stigmatize nonwhite Britons. Ethnic hatred—polite Britons claim it is merely impatience at the slowness of immigrants to assimilate—is clearly rising.

Britain's Uncertain Tie to the World

In 1939 the British Empire and Commonwealth was still the largest centrally ruled polity in the history of the world. By 1970, the empire consisted of a few island outposts peopled mostly by British emigrants. In the overwhelming majority of cases the separation from British rule occurred without violence and with little acrimony. In a few cases protracted revolutionary warfare took place, almost always when an immigrant white population sought to perpetuate its rule over a majority of indigenous peoples. The Empire, the pride of British nationalism early in the century, had ceased to interest Britons. With the exception of a minority in the Conservative Party, nobody wanted to fight for the colonies or spend money to retain them. How can we explain this massive indifference?

It had cost very little to acquire colonies. For the most part the colonies paid for their own administration. During World War II, however, social mobilization of hitherto inert colonial populations accelerated greatly, as had happened in India before the war. So self-evident had the need to free India become by 1945 that Parliament never even debated the separation. Britain had granted various measures of democratic self-government to several colonies during the war. The Colonial Office had also committed itself to the enhancement of a variety of economic development and social service programs. Confronted with active demands for independence in Africa and Asia by the late 1940s, as well as by unrest in the Middle East and the Caribbean, Britons, rebuilding the home economy and weary of war, were in no mood to fight and pay for retaining the empire. It was simply too expensive to construct a welfare state at home and maintain an empire abroad.

Labour had no trouble at all in making up its mind; its leadership never hesitated. Basil Davidson came out of World War II thinking that a social-democratic Britain could be built only if she got rid of the Empire, that self-liberation necessitated liberating subject peoples. The Conservatives had a little more trouble, but not much. Determined to shed the image of being reactionary defenders of unemployment and the status quo, impressed by the fact that both superpowers were actively anticolonial, the Tories also were less and less willing to bear the burden of empire. Their last hurrah was the aborted invasion of Egypt in 1956, a farcical effort to act like a great power that misfired so badly that "withdrawal from East of Suez" soon became a disorderly rout.

It would be wrong to blame this radical act of learning purely on the unwillingness to fight and pay. World War II, and the general aura favoring human rights and national self-determination fostered by the victorious United Nations, had the additional effect in the West of associating human progress with the liberation of colonies. Britain was not immune to these ideological trends.

There was never full agreement on foreign policy in post-1945 Britain. This is evident when we review the range of opinions within the Labour Party.

103

Those interested only in the socialist welfare state were simply indifferent to foreign affairs, including colonial matters; they were and are isolationists, who also opposed nuclear weapons and British membership in NATO; their anti-Americanism is only a bit less strident than that of a second group, the Labour Left of Marxist inspiration. This group was and is interested in global revolution, in the overthrow of capitalism everywhere. Whereas the first group objected to any intervention in the former empire, the Labour Left argued for active intervention on behalf of revolutionary forces.

Neither group ever achieved control over policy, although the annual conference sometimes endorsed the antinuclear and anti-NATO stance. Attitude toward the colonies was dominated by a desire to turn the Empire into a socialist Commonwealth of Nations, independent states devoted to democracy, equitable economic growth, and the enjoyment of human rights—in short to liberal nationalism. These Labourites were therefore committed to link decolonization to the fight against communism, as in Malaya, Guyana, and Cyprus, to combat the "wrong" kinds of independence movements. The mainstream of the Party accepted the "special relationship" with the United States, so cherished by the Conservatives, and insisted on Britain's remaining in NATO as a nuclear power.

The Tories took pride in their unflinching alignment with NATO, the United States, and with the liberal principles of the Bretton Woods system. Nostalgia rather than interest kept them committed to the Commonwealth as long as it cost little. They were also willing to downgrade the special relationship with Washington when that claim failed to produce anything special for Britain. It was the conservative Macmillan government that, in 1960, reluctantly decided to break with all foreign policy tradition by "joining Europe." Britain was rebuffed twice by Charles de Gaulle, in 1963 and 1967, because he thought of Britain as a European stalking horse for an America he suspected of wanting to dictate the fate of France.

British public opinion reflected this diversity of views. Hundreds of thousands demonstrated against nuclear weapons, though only 27 percent of the adult population strongly opposed them by 1986 (as compared to 13 percent in Germany and 18 percent in France). Only 28 percent strongly favored peace above all (as compared to 23 percent in Germany and 29 percent in France). About as many people identified with NATO as Britain's guarantor of security as opted for alliances with *everybody*, including the Soviet Union! Very few identified specifically with Western Europe. When Britain fought Argentina over the Falkland Islands, the center and right displayed a frenzy of patriotism, whereas much of the Labour party elite and constituency opposed the war.[20] Even though flagging patriotism had fueled opposition to conscription—which was abolished in the early 1970s—the armed forces fought tenaciously in the Falklands and in Ulster.

DID BRITAIN JOIN EUROPE?

Curing the British Disease

In 1973 the Heath government succeeded in getting Britain admitted to the European Community. That new tie to Europe, even though supported by large majorities in both parliamentary parties, remains contested to this day. Economically, Britain is being integrated into Europe, but nothing like a clear European identity is actively competing with the still-prevailing, albeit confused, British nationalism.

Harold Macmillan and Harold Wilson had sought membership because they sensed that something had to be done to cure the British disease of slow growth and failure to innovate. They had realized in an unsystematic way that Britain was no longer able to play the role of a global power, not even in partnership with the United States. They were willing to weaken economic and emotional ties with the Commonwealth and downgrade commitment to a global free trading order in exchange for the more protected competition within the European common market. Unlike early applications for membership, however, the Heath initiative was based on systematic economic analysis that led to the conclusion that British industry required the shock of competition to regain its productive momentum. The failings of liberal nationalism in Britain were to be compensated for by aligning Britain with the seemingly more successful liberalism of continental politics. British self-confidence had taken some bad blows because of poor economic performance. The public had grown aware of these stigmata of decline

---

[20] *Eurobarometer*, vol. 25 (1986), published by the Commission of the European Union, Brussels. British samples usually contain 1300 respondents. Britons displayed less tendency to join social movements advocating these causes than did Germans, but more than the French. Actual as a percentage of possible membership in such movements, 1986 (ibid.):

	Britain	Germany (West)	France
Antinuclear	16	22	6
Peace	17	40	9
Ecology	18	26	10

Also see Peter Byrd, "The Development of the Peace Movement in Britain," in W. Kaltefleiter and R. Pfaltzgraff, eds., *The Peace Movements in Europe and the United States* (London: Croom Helm, 1985).

vis-à-vis the European Community (EC) countries, reminded by the spate of books on "the British disease." The European common market was seen less as a substitute for lost global political glory than a cure for economic backwardness—a distinct instance of collective learning shared by the mainstreams of both parties.

Margaret Thatcher's Instrumental Europeanism

The Tory victory of 1979 was due to the public perception that Thatcherism had more to offer for long-term change: the ability to be competitive, to modernize industry without pity for the losers, reeducate and remotivate the work force, and deregulate and reduce the role of government. Individual initiative was to be rewarded, failure and laziness punished.

The Thatcher government's approach to Europe was most unsentimental. It embraced membership because it saw the British interests in a revitalized laissez-faire capitalism as being more readily advanced through the Community's "1992 Program" for completing a fully competitive continental market. The government even embraced the European Monetary System because it saw it in a strong incentive to follow domestic deflationary policies. However, a total change occurred as soon as the 1992 Program took the form of a more supranational European Union. By the early 1990s, the Thatcher government indicated its total opposition to European monetary unification, reregulation of commercial and industrial standards by Brussels, a European social policy and institutional changes undermining continued national sovereignty. Margaret Thatcher wrongly believed that the lesson about a reborn capitalist-individualist spirit learned by many Britons could also be sold to Europe. Her disillusionment took the form of a reiterated British nationalism, a rejection of Europe. However, her fall and the survival of her successor, John Major, also suggest that the Conservative Party remains as instrumentally attached to European Union as she had been originally.

From Instrument Choice to European Identity?

British impressions of the EC have changed dramatically since Britain joined. In 1973, 31 percent thought the EC was a good thing, and 37 percent said they favored European unification; in 1990 these figures were 52 percent and 71 percent, respectively. In 1983 a mere 32 percent thought Britain had benefited from membership, but by 1990 that number had risen to 45 percent, and 33 percent thought they would regret the disintegration of the Community, and many more pronounced themselves as indifferent. Fifty-eight percent thought that the EC would influence their lives positively, and over 50 percent advocated EC decisional authority over environmental, foreign aid, scientific research, and foreign policy matters. Life since Britain joined the EC seems not to have suffered: 85 percent of Britons pronounced themselves as satisfied with theirs in 1973 against 87 percent in 1990. British democracy was seen as functioning well by only 44 percent in 1973, by 51 percent in 1980, and by 49 percent in 1990. Around 60 percent are content to reform their society by gradual means, whereas 25 percent in 1990 wished to curtail freedoms to protect society from "subversives."[21]

Public opinion about belonging to the EC had fluctuated wildly in Britain since 1960. At times almost half of the public seemed to oppose subordinating British economic choices to European multilateralism. Yet, when the negative mood (especially strong among trade unions and small businessmen) was put to the test in a referendum in 1975 that asked Britons whether they wanted to remain in the EC, only one third voted no. The major banking and industrial firms were always advocates of joining Europe. Still, 71 percent of the public never think of themselves "sometimes" as being European in addition to being British, whereas a mere 12 percent "often" do. Labour voters also favored strong regulation of hours, working conditions, and social security rights by Brussels. When asked about specific government policies and programs *after* the ratifica-

Table 3-4. Preference for EC or EU rather than national decision making in Great Britain, 1991–94

	I	II	III	IV	V	VI	VII	VIII	IX	X	XI
1991	—	—	—	72	41	75	68	44	—	27	34
1992	33	38	—	69	28	68	63	37	40	23	35
1993	36	32	63	66	29	64	60	44	31	21	26
1994[a]	32	32	—	61	31	66	60	39	32	21	30

Note. I to XI refer to the following question: "Some people believe that certain areas of policy should be decided by the (NATIONAL) government, while other areas of policy should be decided jointly within the European Community/European Union. Which of the following areas of policy do you think should be decided by the (NATIONAL) government, and which should be decided jointly within the European Community/European Union?" I refers to "immigration policy," II to "Dealing with unemployment," III to "fight against poverty," IV to "protection of the environment," V to "currency," VI to "scientific and tech[nological] research," and VII to "foreign policy towards non-EC/EU countries," VIII to "defense," IX to "industrial policy," X to "education," and XI to "rates of Value Added Tax." The figures indicate those who answered "European Community/Union."
SOURCE: *Eurobarometer*, samples included about 1300 respondents.

[21] These public opinion data are taken from *Eurobarometer*, no. 33 (June 1990) and no. 34 (December 1990). Ernst B. Haas, "The Limits of Liberal Nationalism in Western Eu-

tion of the Maastricht treaties, however, the dramatic decline of interest in supranational integration is striking, as shown on Table 3-4.

BRITAIN ADRIFT

Around World War I, even Labour thought of Whitehall as the embodiment of the social service state, of the civil service as one of the best components of the British identity Labour intellectuals hoped to fashion. The Administrative Class of the civil service was the idealized image of the good state, a vision surely lost by the 1980s, with its rising contempt for the state. Being British used to mean being white and English-speaking, albeit being devoted to the service and to raising up the non-white lesser breeds under British rule. Being British was seen as being a member of the world's premier trading nation, of a nation devoted to manufacturing quality goods and rendering reliable service, a nation able to back up its overseas commitments and interests with adequate military force when this seemed required.

Few Britons today still entertain this self-image. They are used to multiculturalism, though many resent it, relative weakness, and economic decline. Most no longer expect the state to set things right again. On the other hand, being British is also seen as being easy-going, tolerant of the peculiarities of others, respectful of privacy, and Britain is seen as a society protecting these virtues. Democratic-populist identification with a past tied to industrialism and its questionable advantages is being fostered, at the expense of the older notion that Britishness is incarnated in the green countryside and spacious country houses. It is now just as worthy to discover that one's ancestors were miners or weavers rather than country squires. Patriotism is no longer taught by the schools; it no longer appears prominently in history curricula, assemblies, ceremonies, and "chapel." Voluntary organizations, such as Scouts, no longer consider it their duty to instill respect for British virtues. "Schools no longer provide liturgical space for the worship of nation or state" as one contemporary student notes.[22] Anglicanism used to be the embodiment of British nationhood; Anglican prayers were part and parcel of many secular events. Today the Church of England has been disestablished in all but name. Religion has lost its identification with nationalism, being ei-

---

rope," in Beverly Crawford and Peter Schulze, eds., *The New Europe Asserts Itself* (Berkeley: Institute of International Studies, 1990), pp. 344, 346, 348. Data for trends after 1990 come from *Eurobarometer*, nos. 35, 38, 39, and 41.

[22] Raphael Samuel, "Exciting to Be English," in Samuel, *Patriotism*, 1: xxvi. The entire paragraph draws on this fine essay.

ther a private affair, expressed in sectarian settings removed from politics, or it is supranational, devoted to universal service.

Despite this evidence of a weakening identity, Britons remain attached to peaceful means of changing the political order. The procedural aspects of liberal nationalism remain in place unscathed even if there is contention about the values of liberalism. Only 15 percent believe that it is acceptable to occupy building and damage property in pursuit of one's political values, though 24 percent also accept unsanctioned strikes for the same purpose.[23] The political succession is not in contention, even if the royal family's foibles are fair game for the press.

The institutions of government remain legitimate in people's eyes despite the failings of government to make everybody content, though probably less so than in the 1960s. Football hooliganism and the doings of skinheads do not add up to revolutionary discontent. Still, intellectuals of the Left deplore what they see as the loss of autonomous state intervention in the economy, the erosion of the welfare state, the growth of selfishness in place of a devotion to the common weal, the corruption of politicians, and the failure of the electoral system to represent public opinion fairly. For the Left, Thatcherism embodies the worst of British liberal nationalism, the ultimate betrayal.

Intellectuals of the Right, on the other hand, find the root of Britain's decline in the failure of Winston Churchill to save the Empire and stave off socialism; he should, they argue, have made peace with Hitler instead of weakening Britain by fighting him. For the Right, joining Europe was the final blow, the greatest act of treason to the Britain they adore. Thatcherism could have saved Britain if the pro-Europe Tories had not betrayed it.

Both groups believe that nothing has been learned. More detached analysts, I included, however, believe that several true paradigm shifts in thinking have occurred since 1945 that betoken the ability of British elites to redefine the basic objects of collective life and to discover new policy instruments for reaching them. In the realm of macroeconomics two such episodes of learning occurred: the shift to Keynesian neoclassical economic doctrine and its associated policies from the effort to plan

---

[23] In the mid-1980s, attitudes on the acceptability of unconventional political action were as follows (in percent):

	Lawful Demonstrations	Boycotts	Unsanctioned Strikes	Damaging Property	Occupying Buildings
Britain	41	35	24	3	12
France	52	43	32	4	28
West Germany	44	34	13	2	11

SOURCE: Russell Dalton and Manfred Kuechler, eds., *Challenging the Political Order* (Oxford: Oxford University Press, 1990), p. 77.

the economy; and the abandonment of Keynesianism in favor of monetarist ideas in the late 1970s. Both engendered a true national consensus. Keynesianism represents a learned change because the state became less intrusive and the private sector more prominent, which proved acceptable to moderate Conservatives. Monetarism also shows learning because it tamed inflation and got rid of much obsolete industrial plant; it began as anathema to Labour, but it no longer is. Both are instances of creative acts of rerationalization, though monetarism was a less successful idea than Keynesianism.[24]

Another instance of learning was Britain's abandonment of a great power role between 1956 and 1960. A major shift in one's self-image was required to abandon an empire, drastically cut the armed forces, redefine one's security interest to focus on the Soviet Union and Europe, make peace with and rearm the archenemy, and abandon one's cherished sovereignty for the supranationality of the European Union.

I hypothesized that such dramatic shifts in how one defines the national interest occur only when the elite's ability to fashion bargains at home is exhausted, when no conceivable coalition of groups can come up with policies that work. Elites are willing to abandon the nation-state as the chief arena of action, as the only source of identity, the only repository of ideas, only when they have run into very deep trouble.

In Britain this hypothesis seems to have been borne out by events between 1970 and 1990. How, then, can we account for the emotional withdrawal from Europe, for the dramatic cooling of public enthusiasm? Only the Labour government of the last years of this century will know—and demonstrate—whether our hypothesis will stand up, whether new bargains can be invented for exclusive national action that will also rekindle a less ambiguous sense of British national identity.

In the meantime we can only note that despite significant episodes of social learning, overall rationalization has declined. How can that be, if learning leads to rerationalization and more happiness, even if this involves more reliance on extranational forces? Perhaps without the learning that did occur the slippage would have been much worse.

---

[24] See Peter A. Hall, "Policy Paradigms, Social Learning, and the State," *Comparative Politics* (April 1993): 275–96. Hall uses the term *third order change* for what I call *learning* and *first* and *second order change* for degrees of what I call *adaptation*. Otherwise his conceptualization is very much the same as mine, though he confines it to macroeconomics. See my *When Knowledge Is Power* (Berkeley: University of California Press, 1990) for a fuller treatment of this theme.

CHAPTER FOUR

United States

America did not achieve the status of a rationalized nation-state during the first ninety years of its existence. It originated in the secession of thirteen colonial elites, each ensconced in its own potential state, from Great Britain. The nationalist sentiment professed by the seceding elites differed only marginally from the elite culture of the metropole. The revolt had its origin in the perception of systematic discrimination, of inequality vis-à-vis Britain, not in the assertion of a different ethnicity or culture.

While nationalist sentiment sufficed to inspire the liberal institutions and values that characterized American society ever since, it was not strong enough to give the new country a strong consensual national myth. Liberalism came to dominate American life only after civil war. It was that event that launched the country on the trajectory of liberal rationalization, not the events associated with revolution and independence.

Internal crises were always overcome by way of new political bargains that allowed for compromises among organized interests and groups. Social mobilization was accompanied, for most citizens, but not for people of color, with upward mobility and increasing political partication, with the practice of diffuse reciprocity on the part of elites. Social learning became more pronounced after 1930; it triumphed over clashing notions of national identity, until the trauma of Vietnam and the sub-

I am deeply indebted to Susan Overdorf Siena and Karen Adelberger for research assistance and to my colleague Jack Citrin for intellectual stimulation. Nelson Polsby and Henry Nau criticized the manuscript and kept me from making mistakes. I thank them both, even though I was unable to accept all their comments.

sequent conflict over multiculturalism. America is still trying to rerationalize, to find a national identity to bridge the deep divisions from which
it suffers at the end of the twentieth century. The old individualist liberal
nationalism seems no longer to serve as rationalizing formula.

AMERICAN EXCEPTIONALISM: A VAGUE IDEOLOGY
INFUSES A WEAK STATE

Americans, noted Alexis de Tocqueville in 1831, thought of themselves
as "exceptional" because they considered themselves different from the
West Europeans who were their recent ancestors. (He was not concerned, any more than any other political thinker, with African and Native Americans.) This exceptionalism—which spokesmen for the
rebellious colonists proclaimed often and loudly—lay in their passionate
rejection of what they saw as the European cultural stigmata of snobbery,
hierarchy, and deference to one's betters. Americans were exceptional
in wanting to be free from these cultural burdens, as well as from the
allegedly tyrannical rule of a monarch and a parliament in which they
were not represented.

Independence-minded Americans thought of themselves as inventing
their own novel culture in 1775. As President Woodrow Wilson told a
group of newly naturalized citizens in 1915, they had just sworn allegiance "to no one," only "to a great ideal, a great body of principles,
to a great hope of the human race."[1]

There were many reasons for disaffection with Britain: resentment
about taxes imposed by London; heavy-handed repression in Boston; the
determination of New England merchants and shipowners to defy the
British Navigation Acts; British restrictions on the sale of western lands.
But the sentiment that unified the dissatisfied people of substance in the
colonies was the feeling that they were Englishmen mistreated and un-
respected by their cousins in Britain. The socially mobilized merchants,
lawyers, planters, and clergymen were no longer willing to defer to London because they were not being treated as equals.

Yet the idea of American exceptionalism was far from being shared by
all colonists. It was not strong enough to serve as a national myth. The
idea of a national culture had to be fostered by writers and clergymen
decades after independence was achieved. It would take almost one hundred years and a bloody civil war before a consensual notion of American

---

[1] As quoted by Rogers M. Smith, "The 'American Creed' and American Identity: The
Limits of Liberal Citizenship in the United States," *Western Political Quarterly* 41 (1988):
225.

identity was to emerge that could rationalize the country into a cohesive nation-state. In the 1770s and 1780s the notion of exceptionalism was no more than a nationalist sentiment held by a very influential portion of the socially mobilized, not a consensual ideology.

Trends in trade and communication added to the sentiment of exceptionalism in setting the scene for secession. America was more democratic than Britain because the franchise for voting was more populistic; even poor farmers and artisans were enfranchised in the North. The Anglican church dominated in few places. By 1770, 37 percent of all ships sailed for colonial ports (25 percent of tonnage), 33 percent sailed for the Caribbean (40 percent of tonnage), and only 8 percent sailed for British ports (18 percent of tonnage). by 1765 twelve out of thirteen colonies had their own newspapers, a total of twenty-three; by 1775 there were thirty-seven, published in twenty different towns. The Boston *Gazette*, the most radical paper, had a circulation of two thousand.

Still, half a million colonists remained loyal to Britain. Nearly twenty thousand fought in the king's armies and in Tory militias. The war for independence, thus, was also a civil war between colonists loyal to the British traditions of liberty, as expressed by king and parliament, and those who saw liberty as a set of universally valid natural rights. It pitted people who preferred an egalitarian and highly individualistic version of liberty to the hierarchial and communitarian one that prevailed in Britain. It is doubtful that the masses of farmers and artisans cared much about the distinction. To judge by the numbers of desertions from the continental armies and their fluctuating strength, the common soldier was not significantly motivated by any of these ideas. Soldiers fought because of a sense of being oppressed and out of loyalty to individual commanders.

In fact, there was considerable reluctance about seeking independence even among people who later became prominent patriots, a reluctance expressed by the Continental Congress as late as 1776. The oft-cited reasons for secession did not seem universally compelling. The Lockean view of the British constitution espoused by the patriots was shared by many in Britain, just as the more historicist view of the same constitution was accepted by American Tories. American patriots preferred an explicit list of liberties, justified as universal natural rights, to constrain the state and keep it weak, as opposed to the Tory notion that liberty is expressed in a way of life, in a set of historically evolving institutions.

The rights of Englishmen advocated by the revolutionary elite, thus, were derived from a particular interpretation of English constitutional history. The elite also professed faith in its ability to design political institutions much better than the ones inherited from their British cousins, who were seen by the 1770s as corrupted and oppressive.

The Congregational divines of New England who wrote much of the revolutionary creed saw America as the new Israel, the people chosen by God to spread the word about purity, simplicity, and of liberty based on natural rights for all. Religious and political rhetoric became indistinguishable. Sermons were a vital vehicle for the advocacy of libertarian values. Early American nationalist sentiment contained much Protestant symbolism, a source of unease to many prominent patriots who professed deist views rather than sectarian beliefs. Unsurprisingly, Anglicans also tended to be British loyalists, but to descendants of Puritans it seemed to be taken for granted that Protestant values defined the essence of the American identity to be called into being. Rousseau might almost have felt at ease in the America of 1776 because this sentiment came close to being a civil religion.

Many early American liberals were committed to keeping the central government weak and small. The Articles of Confederation did not even provide for an executive. Hence, if commitment to weak government defines conservatism, American liberalism contained conservatism within it. But this also meant that the conservatives—soon to become known as Federalists—would try to strengthen the central government after 1787. They did so in part because they feared attack from Europe as well as war among the thirteen states, a fear shared by their Republican rivals who opposed a strong union.

The American liberal civil religion insisted on a particular American set of virtues: simplicity of manners, moral purity, forthrightness in personal relations, energy, and uncorruptability—all virtues juxtaposed to European vices—as the hallmark of the new world. Such prominent patriots as Benjamin Franklin and the Adamses, people of cosmopolitan experience and taste, stressed that they preferred American to European manners.

Americans also saw themselves as exceptional because of the country's economic abundance. Unlike the poverty of Europe from which the ancestors of the colonists had sought to escape, the new continent was seen as containing inexhaustible riches in virgin lands, streams, and forests, never mind the fact that Native Americans already made use of them. The promise of abundance was added to the armory of arguments for independence because stolid Britain was held incapable of taking full advantage of it. Only American energy and ingenuity could do justice to the promise of wealth, whether on the basis of individual competitive enterprise or of the autarky-seeking mercantilism preferred by the major merchants of New England and New York. The idolizing of abundance characterized those thinkers who considered America a whole new civilization, not just a new country. They saw an American character that was abundant in generosity, freedom, equality, individualism, and competition. Clearly, conservative Americans, more in tune with the more settled and hierarchic institutions of the Eastern Seaboard, might find other aspects of abundance more to their taste.

The population of the United States was just under 4 million in 1790, 700,000 of whom were slaves of African origin. Native Americans accounted for, perhaps, another 100,000 people. By 1950, 40 million people had emigrated to the United States, 85 percent of them from Europe and 11 percent from other western hemisphere countries. Between 1718 and 1760 about 135,000 indentured servants were imported from Europe. Who would partake of liberty and abundance as a full-fledged citizen?

Ethnic origin was a matter of indifference as long as people were of Caucasian stock; acceptance of the ideology of liberty alone made one an American. The Naturalization Act of 1790 enabled any white immigrant to become a citizen after two years' residence. Thereafter, Federalists wanted to rig the law so as to keep French republicans out, and Jeffersonians wanted to alter it to prevent emigré French nobles from entering the country.

America became independent by following the historical sequence of events I label Type C. That path featured diverse elites dissatisfied with the existing polity for diverse reasons, even though the mobilized/differentiated were agreed on the sentiment of exceptionalism. Still, these unhappy elites were identified with quite different local conditions and interests; they did not share a single elite culture. New England shipowners saw things differently from southern planters; hard-scrabble farmers in northeastern and mid-Atlantic rural areas differed from both; Philadelphia merchants did, too. Not all of them were Lockean liberals. Acceptance of a common nationalist sentiment and a shared set of grievances did *not* mean agreement on a constitutional formula for the post-Secession state. Should it be strong, as communitarians urged, or weak as the Lockeans preferred? What emerged was a compact negotiated among the elites of thirteen existing and functioning states who had no intention of submerging themselves in the weak new union.[2] The scene

---

[2] There is a tradition of constitutional interpretation, beginning with Alexander Hamilton and prominently featuring Justice Joseph Story, Daniel Webster, and Abraham Lincoln, that held that the Constitution was not an interstate compact but an act of the entire American people, represented in the state legislatures that ratified the document, and therefore more significant than the opinions on acts of later state legislatures. Moreover, the Declaration of Independence was considered logically and legally prior to the Constitution, thus enshrining popular equality as a core American value rather than the rights and equality of states. See Gary Wills, *Lincoln at Gettysburg* (New York: Simon and Schuster, 1992). Not only did this doctrine not prevail before the Civil War, but also its persuasiveness was belied by the difficulty encountered in the ratification of the Constitution in 1789 and the fact that normally no more than one-sixth of eligible voters bothered to cast their ballots in the first years after 1789.

was thus set for the first major conflict of the independent United States: the argument over the power of the central government that was to pit Federalists against Jeffersonian Republicans. America began independent life without a national myth and a state so weak as to make the appellation "nation-state" inappropriate. All politically active people were liberals, whether Federalist, Jeffersonian Republican, Jacksonian Democrat, or Whig, but their liberalism proved inadequate for holding the country together.

Before we can tell the story of the victory of the weak-state Republicans and the escalating regional differences that led to the breakdown of the polity in 1861, a number of other questions must be covered. How fast and how soon was modernization completed? Table 4-1 suggests that the transition to modernity was completed around 1910. How rapidly did social mobilization occur? According to Table 4-2, it was substantially complete by 1900. There was little deliberate learning before the turn of the century despite the liberal national myth that took hold after 1865.

FROM INDEPENDENCE TO DERATIONALIZATION: REGIONAL DIFFERENCES DEFEAT LEARNING, 1790–1861

Summary of Events

"In the 1840s and early 1850s," wrote Robert Dahl, "political leaders who might have quarreled over slavery agreed on so many other key questions that they were impelled toward compromise on slavery. By the late 1850s, however, the chances were that a Northerner and a Southerner not only disagreed about slavery; they disagreed about a great many other key questions as well . . . slavery in the territories, the admission of Kansas, the tariff, government aid for the roads, harbors and other internal improvements, the need for the route of the transcontinental railways, federal land grants for educational institutions, homestead laws, banking laws, constitutional theory, ideological views on aristocracy and democracy. By 1861 . . . a senator from South Carolina privately observed 'No two nations on earth are or ever were more distinctly separate and hostile as we are here.' "[3]

Sharp disagreements over all these issues divided not only North from South, but both from the growing western states and territories as well, and all these issues penetrated and were penetrated by the poison of slavery. In 1820 and again in 1850 major compromises were struck in

[3] Quoted in Robert Dahl, *Pluralist Democracy in the United States* (Chicago: Rand McNally, 1967), pp. 313–14.

Table 4-1. The modernization process

	1790	1840	1880	1910	1940	1990
Workers in manufacturing (%)	0.1 (1800)	8.8	25.0	32.1	33.1	18.5
Workers in agriculture (%)	73.7 (1800)	63.8	50.6	32.1	18.3	2.7
Workers in services (%)	2.3 (1800)	5.0	12.5	16.8	23.4	38.1
Manufacturing (% GDP)	5	10	15.7 (1869 and 1879)	22.2 (1904–13)	30.1	18.6 (1989)
Agriculture (% GDP)	—	—	20.5	17.0	7.5	2.1
Services (% GDP)	—	—	*19.1	*14.3	21.2	30.5
Coal (million metric tons)	—	—	65.1 (1885)	378.4	418.0	830.3 (1987)
Raw Steel (million metric tons)	—	1.6 (1867)	1.7 (1885)	25.7 (1910)	60.7 (1940)	80.9 (1987)
Railways (miles)	—	2,000	200,000	352,000	406,000	254,000
Surfaced roads (miles)	1,000 (1800)	7,000 (1850)	—	204,000	1.4 million	2.3 million (1989)
Newspaper circulation (millions)	—	0.8 (1850)	3.5	24.2	43.0	62.3
Telephones (per 1,000 population)	—	—	1.1	82.0	165.1	760 (1987)
Radios produced (millions)	—	—	—	—	11.8	28.3 (1989)
Television sets produced (millions)	—	—	—	—	7.5 (1950)	21.0 (1989)
Post offices	75	13,468	42,989	59,580	44,024	28,959

Note: Dates in parentheses are actual dates for which data were obtained.

SOURCES: Data on workers: 1880, 1910, and 1940; Lance E. Davis, Jonathan R. T. Hughes, and Duncan M. McDougall, *American Economic History* (Georgetown, Ontario: Irwin, 1969), pp. 341–42 (services data include government); 1800 and 1840, *Historical Statistics*, p. 139 (service is defined as "teachers and domestics"; 1800, manufacturing is defined as "cotton/textile and iron/steel"; 1990, *Statistical Abstracts*, p. 396. Manufacturing, agriculture, and service (includes government): 1869 and 1879, 1904–13, and 1940, B. R. Mitchell, *International Historical Statistics* (Detroit: Gale Research, 1983), pp. 908, 911, 930; 1790 and 1840, James F. Willis and Martin L. Primack, *An Economic History of the United States*, 2d ed. (Englewood Cliffs, N.J.: Prentice-Hall, 1989); 1990, *Statistical Abstracts of the United States* (Washington, D.C.: Bureau of the Census, 1992), p. 429. Coal and raw steel: Thelma Liesner, *One Hundred Years of Economic Statistics* (New York: Facts on File, 1989), pp. 80–81. Primack and Willis, *Economic History*, p. 249. Railways: 1890–1940, *Historical Statistics of the United States*, 1975, pp. 727–28 ("total track operated," includes an estimate of Class II and III railroads); 1990, *Railroad Facts* (Washington, D.C.: Association of American Railroads, 1988), pp. 42–43 ("total track owned" by Class I railroads; Class II and III railroad track included). Surfaced roads: *Historical Statistics*, p. 710, and David, Hughes, and McDougall, *American Economic History*, p. 291. 1990, *Highway Statistics 1989* (Washington, D.C.: U.S. Department of Transportation, 1989), p. 111. Newspapers, telephones, radios, television sets, and post offices: *Historical Statistics*, pp. 810, 783, 796, 804–5, and *Statistical Abstracts*, pp. 551, 835, 849.

Table 4-2. The social mobilization process

	1790	1840	1880	1910	1940	1990
Population (millions)	3.9	17.1	50.3	92.4	132.1	248.7
Population growth rate (%)	35.1 (1800)	32.7	26.0	21.0	7.2	9.8
Urban population (≥ 10,000 inhabitants, in millions)	0.1	1.3	10.8	34.1	62.7	124.9
Illiteracy (%)[a]	—	22.0	17.0	7.7	2.9	14.4
Institutions of higher education	—	—	811	951	1,708	3,535 (1989)
Enrollment of school-age population (%)	—	47.2 (1850)	57.8	59.2	74.8	93.4 (1989)
Newspaper reading (% population)	—	3.3 (1850)	7.1	26.2 (1909)	32.4 (1939)	25.9 (1987)
Radio ownership	—	—	—	—	80.3% households	2,122 per 1,000 population
Television ownership (% households)	—	—	—	—	8.9 (1950)	93
Voter participation (%)	11.4 (1789)	80.3	80.6	59.0 (1912)	62.5	55.2 (1984)

Note: Dates in parentheses are actual dates for which data were obtained.

Sources: *Historical Statistics of the United States* (Washington, D.C.: Bureau of the Census, 1975), pp. 8, 11–12, 382, 365, 383, 369, 796, 42; and *Statistical Abstracts of the United States* (Washington, D.C.: Bureau of the Census, 1992), pp. 89, 8, 35, 165, 835. Data for 1990 school enrollment column are from *Projections of Education Statistics* (Washington, D.C.: U.S. Department of Education, 1991), p. 9 (actual figures). Newspaper readership data are from Harold W. Stanley and Richard G. Niemi, *Vital Statistics on American Politics*, 2d ed. (Washington, D.C.: Congressional Quarterly Press, 1990), p. 51. Voter participation data are for presidential elections and are from Walter Dean Burnham, ''The Turnout Problem,'' in *Elections American Style* (Washington, D.C.: Brookings, 1987), pp. 113–14.

[a]Estimates for 1840 rely on head of household reports, which may not be comparable; 1880 and 1910 data refer to the percentage of the population 10 years and older; 1940 data refers to the percentage of the population 14 years and older. Jonathan Kozol provides the figure in the 1990 column for 1984, defining ''illiterate'' as having no reading ability or ability under a fifth-grade level (*Illiterate America* [New York: Plume, 1985], p. 10).

Congress that had the effect of dividing the new western states into slave and free, but the compromise was undone by the Dred Scott decision of the U.S. Supreme Court and the Crittenden Amendment to the Constitution, which, had it been ratified, would have made the introduction of slavery a matter for each state to settle for itself. The debate over states' rights and the right to nullify congressional legislation was partly a cover for a debate over slavery. So were the arguments over the tariff, over federal subsidies to infrastructure construction, over federal as opposed to private and state banking, as well as over access to cheap western lands; all these involved sharp disagreements over whether the Union should aid the southern plantation (i.e., slave) economy, the nascent northern industrial economy based on free white labor, or western homesteading farmers and ranchers who used either servile labor or their own families.

When Jefferson doubled American territory in 1803 through the Louisiana Purchase, the Northeast and the South worried about losing voting strength in Washington. The Northeast opposed the War of 1812 because it might strengthen the slave states and because it interfered with commerce. Much of the North opposed the secession of Texas from Mexico and the Mexican War of 1847 because they were thought to favor the South by extending the number of slaveholding states. In terms of literacy, the diffusion of property, social equality, and participation in public affairs, pre–Civil War America was more highly socially mobilized than any other country despite its overwhelmingly rural character. That, clearly, was not enough to give the country a sense of common purpose, a single identity, a national myth. Only a systematic examination of the indicators of rationalization can make plain why a sentiment of exceptionalism married to liberalism failed to hold the country together.

Sectionalism and the Diversity of Economic Interest

By 1840 manufacturing still did not account for quite 9 percent of the gross domestic product (GDP), and agriculture still dominated at 63 percent. There were no large factories, except a few New England textile mills. But population doubled between 1840 and 1860 because 4.2 million Europeans immigrated to America in those two decades (Table 4-3). Per capita gross national product (GNP) rose by 11 percent between 1834 and 1853 or by 22 percent between 1839 and 1858, depending on what measures are used. The bulk of this growth owed little or nothing to governmental efforts, as most proposals to have the federal government take the lead in industrial and commercial development were defeated.

The lion's share of this growth occurred in the Northeast, where almost all industry was located. The Northeast called for high tariffs to protect infant industries against British competition, although the industry got its start on the basis of imported British technology. It also stood for regulated banking, for a centrally administered monetary system. Northeastern financiers held title to much of the mortgaged land in the South and West. The much-vaunted Yankee business sense and commercial energy took form only in the Northeast, in sharp contrast to very different economic cultures in the South and West. Businessmen

Table 4-3. Immigration, 1851–1987 (% of total by region of origin)

	Northern or Western Europe	Central Europe	Southern Europe	Eastern Europe	Asia	Canada	Mexico, Caribbeans, Central and South America	Africa, Australia, New Zealand	Total (in thousands)
1851–60	56.9	36.7	0.8	–	1.6	2.3	0.6	1.1	2,598
1881–90	44.3	35.4	6.3	4.2	1.3	7.5	0.6	0.3	5,246
1901–10	17.8	28.2	26.4	20.1	2.8	2.0	2.1	0.2	8,795
1921–30	21.2	20.8	14.0	4.3	2.4	22.5	14.4	0.4	4,107
1931–40	15.9	30.8	15.9	3.3	3.0	20.5	9.8	0.9	528
1941–50	25.4	26.3	7.7	0.6	3.5	16.6	17.7	2.1	1,035
1951–60	17.7	26.0	10.6	2.9	6.1	10.9	22.5	3.1	2,515
1981–87	4.1	3.3	2.4	1.7	46.1	2.3	36.9	3.3	4,067

SOURCE: Harold W. Stanley and Richard G. Niemin, *Vital Statistics on American Politics*, 2d ed. (Washington, D.C.: Congressional Quarterly Press, 1990), p. 340.

favored federal investment in infrastructure and held out for high prices for western lands. By 1850 the Northeast was probably as developed industrially and technologically as Britain, excelling particularly in the application of water power. By 1860 the Northeast's per capita personal income was 39 percent higher than the average for the United States: that of the South was 28 percent lower. The restoration of full federal monetary control during and after the Civil War was consistent with northeastern economic preferences.

Things were different elsewhere. Homesteading to conduct commercial agriculture dominated in the Northwest where the free family farm was the preferred institution. Settlement and farming in the Southwest, however, depended somewhat on slave labor. Both areas grew rapidly during these decades. They stood for low tariffs and either opposed all banking as evil, whether done by private bankers or the government, or favored the prevailing system of unregulated private banking under which each bank could issue money without control from Washington. In short, along with free or cheap land, the western farmers embraced inflation. In the Northwest they also favored government investment in railroad and canal construction. In Texas, Kansas, Missouri, Arkansas, Tennessee, and Kentucky farmers remained tied to the use of slave labor.

The South differed from everywhere else. Its economic culture favored a more relaxed and aristocratic mode of doing business, even though the planter class amounted to no more than ten thousand families in the 1850s. Cotton ruled the economy after 1830. Still, most cotton was grown by free white family farmers, some of whom owned a few slaves;

25 percent of all slaves were owned by planters who owned more than fifty slaves. Southern politicians were determined to keep the tariff very low, opposed a centralized monetary system, and regulated banking. Nor did they see any need for an active federal policy of aiding industry and commerce.

An Imperialism That Divides

These same sectional differences in large measure explain the deep division of opinion that prevailed over the conquest of Canada and Florida in 1812, the annexation of Texas after 1835, and the seizure of California, Arizona, New Mexico, Nevada, Utah, and Colorado from Mexico in 1848. The Northeast opposed the War of 1812, even though it was ostensibly fought in defense of the right to trade and ship unrestricted by the British-imposed blockade of Napoleonic Europe. Western farmers and their spokesmen in Congress—the "Warhawks of 1812"—wanted to drive the British from Canada; Southern planters wanted the Native Americans removed from the Spanish-held lands we now call Florida. Federalist-controlled New England states came close to seceding in 1812! Yet President Madison saw the attack on Canada merely as a way to coerce Britain to abandon its restrictions on American shipping.

The Mexican War of 1847 was seen in the North as an effort to acquire fresh agricultural land on which cotton could be grown with slave labor, thus incidentally ensuring southern (and southwestern) control of the federal government, a fear that had persuaded some New Englanders to oppose the Louisiana Purchase, too. Just before the Civil War several State Department officials of southern attachment plotted the conquest of Cuba as another potential slaveholding state; other southerners sought to do the same in Central America and Mexico.

These events prove that imperialism did not unite the sections of the country in a common vision of an American mandate to improve the world. Yet there were such visions even before the onset of serious imperial expansion overseas in the 1890s. The Monroe Doctrine was an expression of one such ideology. In interposing America against any return of European colonialism in South America, it asserted an American mission to improve the Latin and Catholic political cultures, to wean them away from the corruption of Europe, while glorying in an alleged affinity among all republics. This view was asserted by the Adamses and by Jefferson, among the New England and Virginia elites who effectively ruled the country before 1828. There was a more populist basis for American expansionism, as well, as articulated in the 1840s by the Young America group within the Democratic Party. It claimed a "manifest destiny," a divinely sanctioned right to rule North America and the Caribbean in order to bestow the blessings of white civilization on these regions. Married to a geopolitical doctrine that asserted that geography ordains American rule over these lands, the populist imperialism professed here, although disproportionately found in the South and Southwest, also claimed a distinct civilizing mission for the white, Protestant, capitalist, republican institutions that American exceptionalism had produced. This sentiment reappears in many guises in later American history; in the 1850s it was not sufficiently popular to save the Union.

Diverging Social Institutions

Once we etch the North's (and the Northwest's) features concerning state and religion, education, equality, and democracy and match them with those of the South (and of the Southwest), the cascading derationalization of the country becomes very plain despite a veneer of agreement concerning the continental mission of the Exceptional People.

State and religion remained intertwined in the North until the 1840s, and new and passionately devout Protestant sects multiplied in the West. Keeping the sabbath, banning the whisky demon, and for the abolitionists freeing the slaves were things the state was to accomplish. Abolitionists were prominent in public life, although they remained a minority; most Northerners were willing to accept slavery in the South, if that was the price of preserving the Union.

Because the genius of America was thought to be divinely ordained family farming, embedded in the fraternal ties of small-town and rural life, Americans also had the task to solidify and perfect this lifestyle. The abolitionist clergy presented this program together with the defense of industrialism and the practice of egalitarian democracy as the duty of Christian America. Owning slaves was totally incompatible with this duty because it corrupted the slaveowner (not only because it might be unpleasant for the slave). Abolitionists taught that slaveowning was a sin against God, democracy, and the American way.

Even without abolitionist arguments, the prevailing tone of life in the North and Northwest became egalitarian and populist by 1850, althought at first the inroads of Jacksonian egalitarian ways had been resented by the New York and New England elite. Still, members of that elite called for the creation of specifically American culture, especially a literature that could rival Britain's. The North pioneered the creation of free, compulsory and wholly secular schools after 1840, after centuries of church-managed schools and universities. Such education, said Horace Mann, "is the great equalizer of men. . . . It does better than to disarm the poor of their hostility toward the rich; it prevents being poor."[4]

---

[4] Quoted in Carl N. Degler, *Out of Our Past* (New York: Harper and Row, 1984), p. 171.

Things were very different in the South. Life was more secular from independence on; fewer sects developed because fewer non-Anglo Saxon immigrants arrived; the established churches took their religion more lightly than their northern counterparts and made no claims on the state. Government was not much interested in educating the public, and private schools tended to prevail. Southern elites identified strongly with British culture and felt no need to create their own. Southern planters saw themselves as highly successful agricultural entrepreneurs, as the pioneers of a new lifestyle.

Jacksonian populism soon ran its course in the South as the planter aristocracy, which controlled almost all political offices, saw itself as a divinely sanctioned oligarchy, a meritocracy of virtue that has the right to rule because of its earthly success. Managing wholesome relations among the races was the South's big contribution, relations under which the rules of reciprocity dictated ties between the white master race and the black primitives it had the duty to civilize. America, far from being egalitarian and fraternal, was really an aristocratic republic ruled by the fittest. The South was the proper interpreter of the U.S. Constitution, the compact that defined this arrangement authoritatively. Southerners saw themselves as "the better Americans, more faithful to the original idea." Hans Kohn thought that these beliefs add up to a true Southern national myth and that New England never developed a parallel exclusive identity for itself.[5]

A Weak State Hinders Rationalization and Identity Formation

Within a few years the very people who had written the Constitution began to chip away at each other's civil rights. Federalists and Republicans sought to persecute each other, to dispute each other's right to participate freely in politics. A smooth succession in 1800 was ensured only by the deliberate forbearance of Alexander Hamilton and John Adams. The takeover by the Jacksonian egalitarians after 1828 was seen as a catastrophic event by the elite in Boston and New York. Until then the long rule of the "Virginia dynasty" had guaranteed institutional continuity at the center, although it did little to control the turbulence of local politics.

The franchise in the Northeast remained quite restricted until the 1820s, although in the West it had been liberal from the beginning. Universal white manhood suffrage was not achieved everywhere until about 1830. In the West ordinary citizens could expect to be elected to legislative and local executive and judicial posts; in the South and Northeast only their betters stood a chance for political prominence until the

[5] Hans Kohn, *American Nationalism* (New York: Macmillan, 1957), p. 114.

1850s. But by this time the practice of judicial review had been generally accepted, and it usually served as a vital institutional glue. Much the same role was played by the transterritorial political parties that emerged in the 1790s.

Administrative practice, however, could have no such effect because of the paucity of administrative activity. Alexander Hamilton and Albert Gallatin had tried and failed to make the Treasury the administrative and managerial hub of the country, much as the federal budget became later. Even their efforts to create something resembling a central bank were only a temporary success abandoned by Andrew Jackson. Appointments to all administrative posts were determined exclusively by party loyalty and only went to party stalwarts, irrespective of merit or ability. The presidency, prior to the Civil War, was viewed less as a nation-building institution than as an agent of Congress, the repository of the views of the states. Prior to the Civil War the federal executive consisted of the war and navy departments (both presiding over practically nonexisting services), a treasury not in control of the money supply and charged with collecting the only major source of revenue, the customs tariff, a small State Department, and the post office! As small and weak governments were still seen as protective of liberty, the executive departments of the states were not much more elaborate. Jurisdictional disputes between state and federal authorities were common.

The years before the Civil War saw the beginning of a major shift in the views of people about what constitutes the American identity, although the cleavage was not exclusively along the familiar sectional lines. The predominantly Anglo-Saxon Protestant composition of the population changed rapidly after 1840 with the large-scale immigration of Irish and German Catholics, as well as Scandinavian Lutherans. Were these newcomers to be considered potential American citizens, as had all prior European immigrants? Many people associated with the Know-Nothing Movement and its political party thought not. They felt that Catholicism was incompatible with republican egalitarianism, with the kinds of populist values that came to the fore in the North after the Jacksonian revolution.

Mere Adaptation Could Not Save the Union

Successive compromises over slavery, over the tariff, over the mandate of the federal government and the right of states to "nullify" federal legislation managed to postpone the development of a full-fledged southern nationalism and the secession of the South. They did not succeed in halting the steady decline in the cohesion of the country from a high point about 1820, as shown on Table 4.4.

Table 4-4. Indicators of rationalization, United States, 1777–1900

	1777–80	1810–20	1840–50	1860–70	1900
Political succession	N/A	Yes	Yes	Yes	Yes
National myth in education	N/A	N/A	No	No	Yes
Religious institutions	Some	Some	No	Yes	Yes
Civil religion	Yes	Yes	No	No	Yes
Cultural uniformity	Yes	Yes	No	No	Some
Official language accepted	Yes	Yes	Yes	Yes	Yes
Income distribution	No	Some	Some	Some	No
Workers' organizations	N/A	N/A	Some	No	No
Farmers' organizations	Yes	Yes	Yes	Yes	Yes
Payment of taxes	No	Yes	Some	Yes	Yes
Conscription accepted	N/A	N/A	N/A	Some	N/A
Fighting wars	Yes	Some	Yes	Yes	N/A
Administrative cohesion	N/A	No	No	No	Yes
Foreign policy	N/A	No	No	No	Yes
Peaceful change	No	Some	Some	No	Yes
Legitimacy	Some	Some	No	No	Yes
Total (%)	60	65	40	40	89

There was always a big gap between the rhetoric of American exceptionalism with its claim to the moral leadership of the Western world and the readiness of people to endow government at any level with the power to act on these values. The moral mission claimed by the intellectual and commercial elites who broke with Britain was carried into practice by sectional interests, not by a whole "nation."

The very act of negotiating and writing the Constitution as a replacement of the Articles of Confederation must rank as a major act of collective learning. But after the constitutional convention was completed, there was very little deliberate application of experience and knowledge to the design of new policies and institutional routines. The only instance of later collective learning that leaps to mind is the invention of judicial review of legislative and executive acts; without it, the writ of the federal government would have been even weaker than it was.

Americans' learning to live with judicial review implies a change in the meaning we, as observers, should impute to the notion of liberal nationalism. The liberalism professed by all American political elites (other than the pre–Civil War Southern political class) stressed the values of being different from Europe, of equality and fraternity, with a disdain for strong government, a rejection Americans equated with the value of individual and communal liberty. American liberalism did not then profess any explicit admiration for tolerance, discussion, reciprocity, and public services for the weak and poor. American liberalism did not then espouse the *procedures* implied by the First Amendment as constituting the core of liberalism. The acceptance of judicial review, however, constituted a first step in the recognition that full and fair routines of decision making are of the essence of liberalism. It meant the recognition that *procedure* appropriate to the making of all public decisions, rather than a set of substantive values, is the essence of liberal nationalism. The acceptance of judicial review in America illustrates how elites learn to amend their civil religion.

RERATIONALIZING AMERICA: INDUSTRIALISM, IMPERIALISM, AND INDIVIDUALISTIC LIBERALISM 1865–1930

"The Civil War," Henry James wrote in 1879, "marks an era in the history of the American mind. It introduced into the national consciousness a certain sense of proportion and relation, of the world being a more complicated place than it had hitherto seemed, the future more treacherous, success more difficult. At the rate at which things are going, it is obvious that good Americans will be more numerous than ever; but the good American, in days to come, will be a more critical person than his complacent and confident grandfather. He has eaten of the tree of knowledge."[6] The knowledge evoked by James eventually helped America to become an industrial giant, a global military power, and gave her a claim to being the world's conscience.

Rationalization by Adaptation or by Learning?

Between 1865 and 1932, America might have succumbed to intense class struggle, to ethnic strife, to conflict over imperial expansion and war. Instead, despite crises and domestic conflicts, the country was better integrated by 1930 than at any time before. By 1890 it had become a full-fledged nation-state. Did the leading politicians learn to put better knowledge about economics and politics to work in fashioning new institutions and policies? Or did they merely respond to ideological and interest groups pressures in finding new means to old ends? Did they learn or merely adapt?

The evidence is not clear. There was a good deal of labor–management cooperation before 1900 when unions were weak. Thereafter, as

---

[6] Quoted in Degler, *Out of Our Past*, p. 211.

unions grew more powerful, class conflict also intensified as the earlier cooperation was abandoned. In other words, nobody learned then to accept unions and to refashion ways of working with them. The major economic reforms that followed the passage of the Intersate Commerce Act and the Sherman Anti-Trust Act can be explained as mere adaptation by politicians to interest group pressures and the presence of the Populists and Progressives. The creation of the Federal Reserve System was due to the preferences of tight-money advocates in the banking industry who sought to stop the enthusiasm for silver championed by soft-money Democrats and farmers, not to an improved understanding of macro-economics.

Yet Charles and Mary Beard argue that the immense improvements in democratic governance achieved after the creation of the federal civil service constitutes learning to co-opt and channel popular pressures on the part of leading politicians of both major parties.[7] The secret ballot was generally in use by 1888; direct primaries became common after 1903; referenda, recall, and initiative elections were introduced at the state level during the 1890s. The direct election of senators became law at about the time of the introduction of the progressive income tax. Women's suffrage, on the national agenda since 1890, became reality in 1919. To be sure, each of these measures had been the subject of passionate ideological advocacy. But the fact that a majority of legislators eventually accepted them must mean that people were persuaded of the need for the reforms as a means for assuring the legitimacy of American institutions. Learning to perfect decision-making procedures is the supreme hallmark of understanding how to bring about institutions that enjoy legitimate authority.

Whichever interpretation is the more persuasive, it is undeniable that by the beginning of the twentieth century there had grown up an intellectual tradition that thought of public policy as a "science," a systematic body of lore from which "good" policy could be culled. Led by John Dewey, Herbert Croly, and Walter Lippman, among others, these writers advocated knowledge-informed government guidance of the economy and worked for the reform of urban administration. Their first test came in the successful non-market management of the economy during World War I by the Washington bureaucracy that established a corporatist scheme in which top businessmen coordinated production, transportation, and consumption. The system was scrapped in January of 1919 by a president who feared great concentration of power, even if it served a benign purpose.

---

[7] Charles Beard and Mary Beard, *The Rise of American Civilization* (New York: Macmillan, 1933), chap. 27.

The main lines of development need little recapitulation (see Tables 4-1 and 4-2). America grew into an industrial and agricultural giant by 1900 that equaled Britain and Germany, and even surpassed them in technological originality. Massive immigration, from southern and eastern Europe primarily, brought in 22 million people between 1880 and 1914. But not all of these developments, neither in the domestic nor in the international realms, necessarily contributed to the rationalization of the country under liberal-nationalist auspices.

I now examine in greater detail the manner of administrative centralization and rationalization after the Civil War, when the issue of "states' rights" all but disappeared. I then proceed to describe the growth of the liberal nationalist myth. The uneven process of integration undergone by labor and farmers in their effort to tame unrestrained capitalism, the sputtering of social reform after 1913, and the travail of integrating millions of new immigrants test the success of that myth. I survey the struggle between rural-cheap-money advocates devoted to a silver-based currency and the urban-industrial-tight money defenders of the gold standard. Finally, I examine the imperial expansion of the United States in the Pacific and the Caribbean. In 1917 and 1918 the effort was made to civilize Europe, by preaching collective security, democracy, and national self-determination for ethnic groups. That effort failed, in part because of sharp conflicts among internationalist and isolationist, liberal nationalists, cosmopolitans, and nativists.

Rationalization as Administrative Centralization

Alexander Hamilton, John Marshall, Daniel Webster, and Joseph Story had failed to institutionalize the supremacy of the federal government as a truly national ruler rooted in the entire American people; Abraham Lincoln and most of his successors prevailed brilliantly.

Constitutionally, the process of centralization was anchored in the Fourteenth Amendment, which the courts interpreted so as to make the Bill of Rights binding on the states, thus creating enormously expanded procedural rights for all citizens. However, until they were reversed after 1914, the courts at first interpreted these new powers restrictively enough to undo much of the forced "reconstruction" of the South and deprive nascent labor unions of the benefit of some legislation passed for their protection. Administratively, the institution of presidential budgeting by way of the Bureau of the Budget in 1921 was a key innovation. Monetary policy gradually became a federal prerogative as a result of reforms undertaken during the Civil War. But the demise of state and private banks as issuers of money did not become final until the establishment of the Federal Reserve System early in the twentieth century, which signaled the acceptance of modern central banking.

The growth of nationally organized interests groups had a great deal to do with administrative rationalization because of the demands for regulating private business they put forward. With the outlawing of contract labor recruited in China and Europe, trade unions started to develop in earnest. The American Federation of Labor was born in 1886. The European immigrants who arrived just before 1914 were willing recruits and organizers, clamoring for protective legislation that was first enacted at the state level. Farmers' organizations multiplied after 1880 to demand protection against railroads, banks, insurance companies and, after 1920, asked for price supports as well.

Regulation was expressed in a series of antitrust laws designed to curb the power of large corporations. It also took the form of subsidizing and regulating the building and operation of railroads. The federal government subsidized the building of universities and provided incentives for western agricultural development of water resources. It subsidized port and road construction. It paid for pensions for war veterans. The power of the federal legislature was enhanced by its ability to provide entitlements to various groups of constituents, including—prominently—the tariff on imports. State militias came under federal control in the form of the National Guard.

The core of rationalization, however, was the introduction of a federal civil service recruited on the basis of merit and skill alone, a process that took forty years, from 1883 to 1923. Prior to civil service reform, officials were supporters of the winning presidential candidate, appointed by him, thus causing massive turnover every four years. Little attention was paid to specialized training; there was no life-time career in government service. By 1881 there were over 100,000 federal officials recruited in this manner. The reforms gradually enacted after 1883 ended by eliminating patronage as a basis for recruitment in all but the highest ranks and by creating the system of specialized, skill-specific examinations as the sole mode of recruitment. The notion that public administration ought to be treated as a science—and public service as a form of knowledge—was crucial in legitimating change away from the patronage system.

Liberal Nationalism as a Civil Religion: The Politics of Inclusion

The liberal nationalism that took hold in America after the Civil War continued to rely heavily on Protestant religious themes; it also carried on the belief in American exceptionalism, especially as the waves of immigrants that sought refuge from the shortcomings of life in Europe and China seemed to provide proof for the creed. However, the majority of the immigrants were not Protestants. As the free, compulsory public school system developed rapidly, Catholics and others sought refuge in their parochial school from the daily scriptural readings that opened the public school day until late into the nineteenth century.

Redemptive Protestant theology furnished the vocabulary for much of domestic reformist politics, as well as justifying imperial expansion. In the first decades after the Civil War Catholicism and religious indifference gained in urban industrial centers as Protestantism remained the central cultural force in rural areas and in small towns. Later, the adoption of the social gospel by many Protestant churches marked a return to the cities and a search for believers among immigrant workers. Protestant thought justified free republican institutions, the capitalism of individual self-reliance and hard work, and a foreign policy of proselytizing self-assertion.

Protestant hegemony shaped the evolving debate over immigration and the assimilation of immigrants into American society. The failure of the Know-Nothing Movement by 1856 to curtail or shape immigration along Anglo-Saxon, Protestant, and anti-Catholic lines did not prevent similar nativist ideas from reappearing after 1890. Overt rejection of Chinese and Japanese immigrants as not fitting the ideal American identity was added to the original list of objectionable features. The national myth professed adherence to the ideal of the melting pot. Still, some thought assimilation would occur almost automatically, with time, and that traces of remaining non-American ethnic peculiarities were quite tolerable. Others, however, advocated the deliberate Americanization of immigrants: they were to speak only English, be conversant in civic lore and in American history, be sober and clean, work hard, and, after World War I broke out, be untainted by European socialism, communism, and anarchism.

The Americanization movement carried the day after 1915. It was inspired by the Progressive Movement and its hopes to tame capitalism with communitarian norms and institutions, its belief in social engineering to improve education, public health, and the conditions of work, and its endorsement of prohibition. Progressivism was a nativist liberalism in that it wanted to make America safe for the new industrialism. It therefore wanted a working class that was truly American or Americanized, not made up of Jewish and Catholic radicals untutored in the virtues of personal health and cleanliness. The Progressive impulse was largely responsible for the restrictive immigration legislation of the 1920s and for the network of voluntary and governmental agencies seeking to bring about the Americanization of immigrants through special service and training programs that sought to implant core American values by means of explicit teaching.

The 1920s saw more rationalization in the hardening of attitudes against ethnic pluralism. Theodore Roosevelt and Woodrow Wilson opposed dual nationality in law and continued toleration for ethnic diversity in daily life. Both practices had prevailed before 1900. But opposition to participation in World War I was advocated disporportionately by Marxists and anarchists among recent immigrants. This fact gave rise to strong sentiments for accelerating the melting process *and* for limiting and biasing immigration in favor of northern and western Europe. The appeal to cultural pluralism spearheaded by Horace Kallen came to nought. It went down before a renaissance of rural Protestantism in the 1920s. This movement pressed for limits on immigration, but it also featured prohibition and the need to protect Anglo-Saxon institutions against such heresies as Darwinian evolutionism and the sinfulness of large cities. This stance culminated in the racism of the Ku Klux Klan.

By the early 1930s these sentiments were swamped by the evident staying power of cities and of cultures other than the Anglo-Saxon. Instead, we saw an acceleration of the integration of white ethnic minorities into the American mainstream, a process concluded during World War II, just as America's hitherto almost invisible black and brown minorities began to become more prominent.

Remarkably, the country became more rationalized despite the growth of inequality among its citizens. Farmers moving westward did not necessarily improve their living standards as a result of moving because federal land grants favored large holdings. The first generation of European immigrants failed to find gold in the streets. Railroads and banks were perceived by poor farmers as oppressors, especially after agricultural mechanization made the Midwest part of the world economy. Farmers organized the National Grange in 1867 to defend their interests and supported the populist Progressive Party by 1900. Trade union organization proceeded more slowly, but also gathered steam by the 1890s by means of a series of large-scale and violent strikes. Labor became the mouthpiece for social democratic reforms and for the rights of women. Yet Labor also opposed immigration by then, and most of its leaders made their peace with progressive capitalism. Despite—or perhaps because of—these developments, the American national myth continued to stress the virtues of hard work and personal achievement as certain to result in upward mobility and in acceptance into a society perceived as seamlessly middle-class. In any event, the domestic reforms introduced by Woodrow Wilson and supported by the populist wing of the Republicans went some way toward making the perception into reality, especially with the introduction of the progressive income tax and the enfranchisement of women.

*Liberal Nationalism as a Civil Religion: Between Imperial
Self-Assertion and Isolation*

After the Civil War, militant liberalism contained a diverse collection of
themes. It pitted cosmopolitan liberals against nativists, individualistic
liberals who defended untrammeled capitalism against communitarian
liberals who argued for a stronger state to rein in the capitalists. And it
opposed imperialistic liberals to isolationists. By 1900, the national myth
came to stress an imperialistic nativism that justified itself as democratic
social darwinism. But by 1918 this had given way to an individualistic
cosmopolitan liberalism that sought selective engagement in world
politics. Isolationists won only short-lived victories, though they never
disappeared from public and elite opinion because their nativist communitarian liberalism never lacked a constituency.

There was opposition to almost all wars fought by the United States.
Yet the Spanish-American War of 1898 aroused very little, perhaps because it was short, did not require conscription, and involved few American causalities. Most of the public accepted conscription during World
War I; they also accepted repressive measures against pacifists and immigrants from Germany who expressed their opposition to American
entry into the fighting.

*All armed forays were justified by appeals to Jacobin nationalism expressed in
the language of social Darwinism.* Cultural evolution ordained the American
mission to democratize and civilize, especially in the Caribbean area and
East Asia, but also the Europe of 1917. About the Caribbean, President
Theodore Roosevelt remarked that "the manifest mission of the Teutonic nations" included the imposition of public order by force of arms
among the politically immature peoples of Latin America. In 1915 when
President Woodrow Wilson ordered marines into Mexico to topple a
military dictatorship, he justified intervention in very similar terms.

Yet no single plan and no single coalition of interests stood at the base
of American expansion. In each instance of imperial self-assertion there
was a unique coalition in which Republicans predominated, although
Democrats did not always oppose. In each instance the same set of arguments for expansion was heard, but not all imperialists made the same
claims at all times. It is difficult to tell who acted for purely instrumental
reasons and who really believed in the right of the "progressive and
democratic Teutonic nations" to expand.[8]

[8] The confluence of social Darwinism with imperialism and the Anglo-Saxon "racial"
mythology was expressed in works such as these: Sharon Turner, *History of the Anglosaxons*
(1841); George Perkins March, *Goths in New England* (1843); Madison Grand, *The Great
Race* (1916), who advocated literacy tests for immigrants to screen out non-Nordics; after

The set of arguments favoring self-assertion commonly included the duty of America to advance Christian civilization and to realize American's manifest destiny to rule over lesser breeds, to restore order where there was chaos and financial mismanagement. Intervention was justified also to forestall military measures by European powers in the Caribbean and China and to acquire, or protect, naval bases allegedly needed for the realization of any of the other objectives. The U.S. Navy, under the doctrinal tutelage of Admiral Alfred Mahan, developed a strategic rationale for expansion that applied to most situations abroad and featured cultural and historical arguments as well as purely military ones. Many, around the turn of the century, were apparently convinced that the closing of the western frontier presaged social and economic chaos, because it eliminated the safety valve of westward migration and settlement for poor urbanites; hence, expansion was considered necessary to compensate for this loss if class warfare was to be averted.

Unlike the divisive and disputed policy of continental expansion followed before 1861, the militant policy initiated by Secretary of State William Seward thereafter commanded general support. Economic reasoning and manifest destiny justified American insistence that France abandon her Mexican adventure. The same reasons were invoked in President Grant's failed effort to annex the Dominican Republic, Panama, and the Virgin Islands. Anti-imperialist Democrats blocked Republican efforts in 1895 to annex Cuba.

A greatly expanded interpretation of the Monroe Doctrine was used by successive American administrations after 1895 to justify American hegemony in the Western Hemisphere, whether to arbitrate territorial disputes with European powers or to keep European navies from collecting overdue debts. "The United States is practically sovereign on this continent," Secretary of State Richard Olney informed Great Britain.

But anti-imperialism was also prominent. President William McKinley said that only divine revelation persuaded him to annex the Philippines for Protestantism in the face of considerable opposition from organized anti-imperialists who had earlier delayed the annexation of Samoa and Hawaii. The opposition, especially strong among workers, argued that overseas expansion detracted from much-needed domestic reforms, implied the creation of a second-class citizenry among the colonized, interfered with free trade, and prevented the peaceful settlement of international quarrels. Anti-imperialism was taken up by the Socialist Party, which opposed entry into World War I and garnered almost a

---

the Civil War similar arguments were advanced by such writers as Edward A. Freeman, John Fiske, Herbert Baxter Adams, and Josiah Strong.

133

million votes in the presidential election of 1920, even though its candidate, Eugene Debs, was serving a jail term for opposing Wilson's policy.

The peace treaty with Spain that confirmed the annexation of the Philippines and of Puerto Rico passed the Senate with a one-vote majority! As President Theodore Roosevelt announced his policy of self-assertion in uncompromising terms, a strong domestic peace movement developed that focused on compulsory arbitration as the sole acceptable means for resolving international disputes. Its leader, William Jennings Bryan, became Secretary of State in 1913.

It was the vision of President Woodrow Wilson after 1917 to have America shed her provincialism and become the leader of the world, to guide it toward peace based on democracy, collective security, and national self-determination. In so doing he sought to make the world apply beliefs that were almost consensual in America, an outgrowth of the same militant liberalism that had also informed imperial expansion a few years earlier. But the effort to apply lessons allegedly learned from studying history did little to advance rationalization at home. The more perfect integration of American society was the result of growing wealth and the successful Americanization of immigrants, the invention of adaptive institutions, and the credibility of the Jacobin liberal myth.

American Jacobin liberalism rejected power politics, balancing power, and alliances. President Wilson's reasons for going to war in 1917 included the aim of ridding the world of these practices by concluding a new kind of peace. He had wanted to aid Britain and France before Germany launched unrestricted submarine warfare; he only made a half-hearted effort to mediate a compromise peace in 1916. Some believe that he used the submarine warfare issue in 1917 to force a peace (which seemed to require Germany's defeat) that would end all war and bring about democracy in all of Europe. Wilson pitted all his hopes for a democratic and peaceful world order on his proposal for a League of Nations, which would have substituted collective coercive action based on legal procedure for alliances and the balance of power. Postwar borders based on the principle of national self-determination were thought to favor the institutionalization of democratic regimes. Under these conditions, no elaborate American policy of national security would have been required. Wilson also wanted to enmesh an ascending Japan into his structure and thus contain her. In addition he desired to isolate and defeat Lenin's communist revolution in Russia and therefore authorized American intervention in that country's civil war. Wilson inaugurated an anti-Soviet policy that was not fully reversed until the outbreak of World War II.

National defense policy remained ambivalent after 1918. The failure of the

Senate to accept the League of Nations doomed Wilson's initiative; a minority of senators was unwilling to tie American security to the collective will of a concert of the powers. Hence traditional national defense remained an issue. The size of the Army was fixed at 280,000, unprecedentedly high for peacetime, the size of the National Guard at 400,000, and the General Staff was strengthened.

By 1914, the American navy had grown to be the second largest in the world. By 1918 it equaled Britain's. Should it remain that strong even though nobody threatened the United States or challenged its dominance in the Western Hemisphere? President Harding was not worried about any European power but feared a rising Japan. Japan bashing became quite popular in the early 1920s; there was even talk of war over Japanese encroachments in China. The U.S. Navy, on the other hand, was divided over whether to consider Britain or Japan as the main enemy to be feared in the future. Many officers thought that commercial rivalries with Britain were bound to lead to war. The U.S. Navy opposed the outlawing of submarines in order to retain a special offensive capability against Japan, and it also favored the use of limited blockades, in order to be able to harass Britain. Other officials and leaders wanted to get rid of submarines and outlaw blockades as inhumane.

The upshot was the American proposal at the 1922 Washington conference to limit naval strength, to freeze the British and American capital ship strength at parity, while allowing Japan a ratio of 3.5 to 5 each for Britain and the United States. In exchange, the powers accepted the East Asian territorial status quo as final and undertook to construct no additional bases and fortifications there. The Coolidge and Hoover administrations were less concerned about Japan and allowed the reduction of American naval strength below the Washington limits. They also sought to extend the agreement to cruisers, although the other powers would not agree.

America's national security policy, however, brooked no challenge in the Caribbean and in Central America. Financial instability in these countries, as before, was seen as intolerable and, when diagnosed, led to several armed interventions and the installation of subservient governments. The right to dictate core policies to Cuba was not given up until 1934. Washington insisted on retaining its extraterritorial rights in China; it gave no assistance to the nationalist forces there until Chiang Kai-shek broke with the Communists. Instead of relying on collective security, the United States sought the formal outlawry of war as a means of national policy and fostered recourse to conciliation and arbitration as the sole legitimate means to settle disputes. In 1931, when Japan was condemned by the League of Nations for seizing Manchuria in violation

135

of the Washington treaties, the United States pioneered the doctrine of nonrecognition of the seizure as its substitute for the collective security nobody else was willing to practice.

Even though this national security policy was one of "isolationism," America's actual immersion in world affairs remained greater than before 1917. In no field was this more evident than in trade and finance. Before World War I the United States followed a foreign trade policy of taking advantage of other countries' low tariffs while maintaining a high rate of protection for herself. By 1912 interest in exporting had developed to such an extent that a lower tariff was enacted to forestall the adoption of higher tariffs by a restive Britain. Congress sought to raise tariffs in 1921 to protect particular manufacturers, although the resulting bill was weakened by providing for unconditional most-favored-nation treatment of trading partners. The onset of the Great Depression resulted in a reversal of this policy: except for agricultural commodities, higher rates of protection were seen as furthering domestic prosperity.

Until the early 1930s the United States actively supported the interests of American investors in extractive and agricultural enterprises in the Caribbean, especially oil interests. Such support ensured dominance over oil production in Mexico and Venezuela and, by 1928, provided an entry into exploration and production in the then-Dutch East Indies and in the Middle East. American bankers had lent unprecedented amounts to the allied governments during World War I; repayment, they were assured, was not possible without Germany's paying the enormous reparations imposed after the war. Germany's inability or unwillingness to pay resulted in great economic and political instability that Washington wanted to counteract. Financial stabilization in Europe, however, called for a new infusion of American funds. This in turn persuaded the Coolidge and Hoover administrations to back two new large private lending programs that had the effect of enmeshing American banking inextricably into Europe's financial network, which collapsed in 1931.

MILITANT LIBERALISM: "LEADERSHIP OF THE FREE WORLD," 1930–1975

Adapting to Leadership, Not Learning to Lead

By 1932, even though the country and the world were in the trough of the greatest of all depressions ever to have struck the capitalist economic system, America was the world's largest financial and industrial power. In the following forty years, the country engaged in institutional, economic, social, and technological innovation at breakneck speed, remain-

Table 4-5. Indicators of rationalization, United States, 1930–90

	1930	1950	1970	1990
Political succession	Yes	Yes	Yes	Yes
National myth in education	Yes	Yes	Some	Some
Religious institutions	Yes	Yes	Yes	Some
Civil religion	Yes	Yes	Some	No
Cultural uniformity	Yes	Yes	Some	No
Official language accepted	Yes	Yes	Yes	Some
Income distribution	Yes	Yes	Yes	Some
Workers' organizations	Some	Yes	Yes	Some
Farmers' Organizations	Yes	Yes	Yes	Yes
Payment of taxes	Yes	Yes	Yes	Yes
Fighting wars	N/A	Yes	Some	Yes
Conscription accepted	N/A	Yes	No	N/A
Administrative cohesion	Yes	Yes	Yes	Yes
Foreign policy	Yes	Yes	No	Some
Peaceful change	Some	Yes	Some	Yes
Legitimacy	Some	Yes	No	Yes
Total (%)	82	100	66	67

ing true to its self-image of exceptionalism. Abroad, America practiced Jacobin liberalism by becoming the accepted "leader of the free world," committed to fighting and halting the advance of fascism before 1945 and of communism thereafter. First, however, America passed through a short period of partial withdrawal from the world, the period of isolation, as the New Deal of President Franklin D. Roosevelt began a domestic revolution in economic and social policy, somewhat indebted to what passed for social scientific knowledge.

A look at Table 4-5 makes clear that American society was as well-integrated, as content, as confident of its future as it could be; the same table also shows that by 1970, derationalization had taken over with a vengeance. What accounts for the decline in legitimacy, for the loss of national self-confidence? Had nothing been systematically learned about how to perfect a society?

The successful rationalization of America had featured two core ideas and their associated institutions: the welfare state and global leadership to contain totalitarianism. American identity and America's version of a liberal national myth melded these core ideas. Was such a melding possible? Are the two themes integrally connected? Were they fated to contradict each other?

There was increasing recognition that knowledge of nature and of human society can provide a crucial contribution to goal attainment. Government support of basic and applied science was first attempted during World War I in order to enhance military technologies. It was resumed on a modest scale after 1932, but reached giant proportions during and after World War II. The impulse underlying the subsidies and the consultative bodies of scientists that emerged during the 1940s and 1950s was usually military; but important civilian spinoffs resulted in applications in the fields of medicine, air transport, electronics, and space communications. More important still, the success of scientific research triggered faith in "the scientific method" outside the natural sciences. Economics was increasingly regarded as a science, a source of knowledge that was institutionalized in the federal government by the 1950s. The core knowledge at first was associated with John Maynard Keynes. Lawyers and judges increasingly cited sociological studies in their arguments. President John F. Kennedy's New Frontier and President Lyndon Johnson's Great Society programs in the 1960s drew on the same presumed revolution in social science. Science-for-policy became a respectable doctrine in government, although it had been urged by some since the 1920s.

The crisis engendered by the Vietnam War triggered a profound derationalization of the country that belies the permanent impact of what had earlier seemed to be consensual knowledge. As we shall see, the occasional and spotty true learning was dwarfed by decisions based merely on the ideological convictions of leaders, which, when shown to be unacceptable, were discarded in favor of new solutions that were, at best, ingenious adaptations to failure, but not a fundamental reordering of values and objectives. This phenomenon did not occur until the 1980s. American political institutions do not easily lend themselves to decision making in which consensual knowledge predictably prevails.

By the early 1970s clever adaptation did not suffice to shore up the U.S. government's legitimate authority in the eyes of its citizens. Social reform on a scale not seen since the 1930s did not suffice to ensure continued rationalization as the foreign policy of militant liberalism engendered more suffering, death, and disaffection than any previous American war. Decline in legitimate authority was accompanied by a weakening and splintering of liberal nationalism as the American national myth.

The City on the Hill: Egalitarianism at Home and Crusading Liberalism Abroad

Until the events connected with the advent of a multicultural society and the Vietnam War shattered it, America after the advent of the New Deal,

Challenged today!

enjoyed a consensual civil religion as never before. Americans continued to think of themselves and their society as exceptional, as being "God's country." They minimized class and status differences among themselves. Most self-identified members of the working class thought that their beliefs were like those of most other Americans. Upward mobility was thought possible, even inevitable, for those who worked hard.

In contrast to their success in other industrial countries, no labor or social democratic party ever succeeded in America. The lack of clearly etched ideologies associated with the two major parties allowed catering to newly mobilized workers and farmers abandoning the land by Democrats and Republicans. Because there were few self-identified conservatives and radicals before 1968, the institutions of American politics facilitated increasing participation for those who otherwise might have become disaffected from the polity. Labor unions grew in membership, number, and influence, as did farmers' organizations, both as a result of institutional changes legislated by the New Deal.

The influence earlier exercised by Protestant churches on the state diminished after 1930, as American Protestants, Catholics, and Jews began deliberate efforts to downplay their differences, a trend related to urbanization and suburbanization and the consequent decline of religious-ethnic segregation among whites. Tolerance toward Catholics and Jews on the part of Protestants increased markedly. Fewer and fewer people challenged the absolute separation of church and state increasingly institutionalized in the United States, partly because they all could profess a general belief in the same god and in the country apparently so blessed by him or her. Until the Vietnam War gnawed away at all these trends, white Americans thought of their country a great and noble community, united by its belief in the uniqueness of its nationality. Lyndon Johnson evoked that myth by choosing "The Great Society" as the label for his domestic reform program that sought to include nonwhites as well.

Continued egalitarian reform at home was matched with two crusades for democracy abroad: the defeat of fascism, followed by the containment of communism. Yet the American civil religion is ambiguous on the use of military force. Many liberal nationalists favor the power of example and of good advice, helped by judicious material rewards—what came to be called foreign aid after 1948, whether dispensed via the United Nations or directly by the United States, as under the Marshal Plan. But other liberals put their faith in large military outlays, of armed forces second to none, of the network alliances forged after 1949, and of the use of the United Nations for collective enforcement.

Soviet communism was every bit as totalitarian as German fascism. Yet nobody ever urged a policy of "unconditional surrender" in the pursuit of the cold war, unlike the fate meted out to Germany and Japan. Why moderate one crusade, but not the other?[9] The answer lay in the strain of "realism" that was introduced by policymakers who differentiated themselves from the anticommunist ideologues. But both urged the containment of the Soviet Union as the source of communist power. Realist statesmen, such as Dean Acheson, Dwight Eisenhower, Richard Nixon, Henry Kissinger, or Paul Nitze, sought to ensure that the Soviet Union did not expand, *but they did not seek the destruction of the Soviet state or of its political system*. Their most articulate spokesman was the man who invented the very "containment" label, George Kennan. He, along with Senator William Fulbright and Walter Lipman, was seeking a negotiated settlement to the Vietnam War, as were President Nixon and Henry Kissinger. They saw no point of continuing the war as part of an evangelical crusade against the expansion of communism into Southeast Asia, where democracy was not threatened because it had never existed there.

Evangelical anticommunists wanted to "roll back" Soviet influence. But more commonly they were committed to prevent the expansion of Soviet and communist influence in Asia, Africa, and Latin America. Harry Truman, John Kennedy, and Lyndon Johnson represented aspects of this view of containment; so did John Foster Dulles, Dean Rusk, and Robert McNamara, as well as many legislators, trade unionists, business executives, journalists, and ministers. Their commitment to containment had to concern itself with parts of the world other than Europe and East Asia if the spread of communism to what came to be known as the Third World was to be prevented.

President John F. Kennedy, in 1961, said "let every nation know . . . that we shall pay any price, bear any burden, meet any hardship, support any friend, oppose any foe, in order to assure the survival and the success of liberty."[10] Jacobin nationalism called for a militant policy of protecting the independence of all states not subject to totalitarian rule and for the encouragement and protection of democratic governance, although there was and continued to be pervasive ambiguity over when and where democracy was to be succored. Defending democracy, actual or potential, required the support of local armed forces and of possibly autocratic

---

[9] Some groups and writers dissented from the domestic and the international aspects of the civil religion, but they did not become significant until after 1973. Religious fundamentalists, mostly Protestant, shared the anticommunism, but not the liberal egalitarianism, of the period. Neither they nor the self-identified conservative wing of the Republican Party and groups to the right of that party accepted "realist" limits on anticommunist crusading; they identified the Soviet Union with Satan and were responsible for supporting such movements as McCarthyism and the John Birch Society. On the left, some populist and socialist elements, led at first by Henry Wallace, wanted to cement an alliance with the Soviet Union and support it to reassure the suspicious Soviet leaders, rather than practice containment. Sentiments less critical of the Soviet Union rose in the mainstream of both parties after 1960 and found expression in the movement toward arms control and detente.

[10] Inaugural address, January 20, 1961.

regimes; it also required an American readiness to wage unconventional counterinsurgency warfare, instead of the full-scale wars fought in Korea (1950–53) and Vietnam (1965–73). Anti-insurgency warfare was conducted or supported in the Philippines, Malaya, Vietnam, Zaire, Cuba, Greece, Venezuela, Colombia, Guatemala, and Bolivia.

But realist and evangelical liberals agreed on many things. They believed that being forced to live under colonial rule, to be kept from practicing national self-determination, to be poor, sick, and devoid of hope for improving one's life—all these facilitate the advance of communism because communists promise relief from these conditions. Something had to be done for the Third World to prevent such a calamity. American liberalism promised that economic development, if helped along properly, would be relatively simple and automatic, that such good things as democracy, capitalism, and economic development go together.

Liberals also believed in the force of example, the likelihood that the promise of military and economic aid programs would keep the communist threat at bay. The containment ideology included a commitment to ending the colonial system, to national self-determination in the Third World, and to systematic foreign aid. It professed belief in the need to protect basic human rights everywhere, but particularly in parts of the world where the argument could be used effectively to make communism look bad. For both varieties of believers in containment, the defense of Western Europe and of Japan were primary, basic goals; realists grounded their belief in the need to control the industrially most advanced parts of the world; evangelists stressed the protection of democratic institutions and values. The sweeping commitment to scientific research and technological innovation that had originated during the war against fascism provided a further spur to the liberal optimism that animated the civil religion of global containment.

Finally, there was a predominance of views after 1945—though challenged by some—that the global economy ought to be as open as possible to allow trade in goods and services and the free flow of capital. Multinational firms were to do as they please, thus presumably aiding the American economy to prosper as well as the Third World's to develop and absorb Western technologies and know-how. Free trade and capital flows, in turn, would create the condition under which democracy would flourish.

Domestic and Global Liberalism in Public Opinion

It was policymakers, officials, and other members of the foreign policy elite who were concerned with the arguments of realists and evangelical liberal nationalists, not the general public. Public opinion about Amer-

141

ican's relationship to the world was shallow and labile; public reaction tended to respond to events as interpreted by the foreign policy elite. However, the power of initiative enjoyed by the elite was circumscribed by certain general moods, certain fundamental value commitments that characterized the public despite the absence of fully reasoned and clearly articulated views. Four such clusters of commitments were delineated by public opinion research.[11]

Hard-liners favored active measures to combat international communism as the main challenge to American values. They also were concerned about possible internal subversion. Of course, they stressed the maintenance of military superiority over the Soviets and therefore opposed arms control measures. They preferred America's "going it alone" over acting under United Nations auspices or defer to allies. Economic policy was of interest only insofar as it affected military strength. Hard-liners had lost most of their appeal by 1970.

Isolationists were preoccupied with preserving American's exceptional institutions and values from foreign contamination and therefore wished to minimize involvement with other countries militarily and economically. They rejected consistently practiced containment of communism and institutionalized cooperation with other nations. In general they opposed an active military posture and free trade. Isolationists were strongest during the 1930s and steadily lost influence after 1950.

Internationalists, by contrast, wanted to spread the message of American exceptionalism far and wide and were perfectly willing to use force in the process. They believed that free trade and free capital flows would help to create an international order in which peace would also prevail as long as communism was contained. Internationalists fostered alliances with like-minded other states and actively built multilateral institutions because they expected these to serve American's ideological, military, and economic interests. All American presidents since Franklin Roosevelt have been internationalists, as have been most of the elites of the nation. Internationalism has dominated American foreign policy since 1940. It, rather than any of the other clusters, represents Jacobin-liberal American nationalism most consistently.

Accommodationists have always been a minority, strong between 1940 and 1950, and growing once more during and since the Vietnam War. They discounted the threat of communism and generally opposed the militarization of American policy, as well as protesting the use of force

[11] The typology was pioneered by Ole R. Holsti and James N. Rosenau, who give detailed statistical information about the correlates of each cluster of beliefs over time in "Public Opinion and Foreign Policy," *International Studies Quarterly* 36, 4, December 1992: 439–66. "The Structure of Foreign Policy Attitudes among American Leaders," *Journal of Politics* 52, 1 (February 1990): 94–125.

in many specific cases. In general, they prefer reliance on multilateral methods and institutions for the pursuit of most American objectives.

The American side of the history of the Cold War can be written, in part, as the story of how the internationalists' version of American liberal nationalism prevailed over their three rivals'. If learning occurred at all in the pursuit of external objectives it did among internationalist elites, who, for the most part were also cosmopolitans when it came to defining American identity. Cosmopolitanism refers to an attitude that defines American identity, a notion that includes views about domestic as well as international matters. Cosmopolitans compete with two other advocates of a liberal identity, nativists and multiculturalists.[12]

A *nativist* believes in the need to maintain the purity of the American creed, to prevent pollution from alien ideas and forces. Nativists usually oppose immigration, especially the immigration of ethnic groups other than European. They insist on the exclusive use of English in public life and in school. They doubt the willingness of immigrants to adapt. Moreover, they look to the state as the agency to keep pure their view of the perfect American identity.

A *cosmopolitan* believes in the superiority of English and of political institutions derived from the Western cultural matrix, but also holds that immigrants can and should be socialized into the mainstream. Some prefer the competitive workings of a decentralized pluralistic society as the authoritative allocator of values; they stress individualism. Others embrace a communitarian view and want the state to take an active role in realizing it.

Multiculturalists stress the cultural autonomy of all self-identified ethnic groups and oppose inclusion in the mainstream. They argue for autonomous political and social institutions for each group on a communitarian basis and look to the state to make available entitlements.

Table 4-6 presents this typology of public opinion in such a way as to differentiate the three views on the basis of whether the argument is couched in individualistic terms stressing liberty, as opposed to communitarian notions that emphasize equality and fraternity. The second corresponds to Jacobin liberalism, whereas the first is closer to the Whig tradition.

American policy, foreign and domestic, was dominated by cosmopolitans between 1933 and 1975. The Democrats among them tended to be communitarians, the Republicans individualists. Nativists tended to sympathize with hard-liners and isolationists; internationalism was

---

[12] This typology is developed and fleshed out with survey data by Jack Citrin, Ernst B. Haas, Beth Reingold, and Christopher Muste in "Is American Nationalism Changing?" *International Studies Quarterly* 38 (1994): 1–38.

Table 4-6. Varieties of American liberalism

Basis for Identity	Basis of Social Organization	
	Liberty (individualism)	Equality/Fraternity (communitarianism)
Cosmopolitan	Market is main allocator; state is distrusted; melting pot culture for all ethnic groups	State is main allocator; culture of entitlements; melting pot culture for all ethnic groups
Nativist	Market is main allocator; state is distrusted; melting pot for Europeans	Autonomous religion is the basis for political action; melting pot for "god's people"; small-town/rural culture
Multicultural		Cultural autonomy and/or separatism funded by activist state

identified with the cosmopolitanism of the militant liberalism of containment. The few accommodationists tended to be cosmopolitans. Multiculturalism was just beginning to acquire a popular base at the end of this period among African Americans and Hispanics.

How Americans Adapted to Using the State to Save Capitalism

Social democracy came to the United States after 1933 in the guise of state-regulated capitalism, later labelled "embedded liberalism."[13] American politicians and administrators learned that agricultural markets do not adjust automatically as one increases the welfare of farmers, that banks do not necessarily aid the consumer and homeowner, that neither monopoly nor competition among industrialists guarantees painless increases in wealth. They came to understand that to retain the loyalty of the poor and unemployed to the American polity more than private charity and local welfare payments were needed. They realized that the flourishing of democracy depended on a well-functioning economy that makes people more equal in power and in wealth, even if the freedom of the rich is curtailed as a result. The New Deal invented the form of governance that put the federal government at the center of national activity for the first time; it has remained there ever since. The New Deal created the American welfare state; no Republican president before Ronald Reagan wished to scrap it. Until then, policy was made preponderantly by cosmopolitan internationalists, fighting rearguard actions

---

[13] The term *embedded liberalism* was coined by John Gerard Ruggie; see his contribution to Stephen Krasner, ed., *International Regimes* (Ithaca: Cornell University Press, 1983).

144

against occasional nativist-isolationist snipers before the attack on Pearl Harbor. Despite intermittent communitarian efforts, the bulk of policy innovation remained in the realm of individualism.

New Deal policymakers learned to package issues substantively, but the thrust of the overall effort remained adaptive effort despite the work of a devoted epistemic community of Keynesians. Many New Deal initiatives illustrate substantive issue linkage. The Tennessee Valley Authority was much more than a program to harness rivers and bring about rural electrification in the South; it also served to increase farm income, stimulate community organizations and local political participation, and help to raise agricultural prices. The federal regulation of banking combined the protection of depositors with encouraging homeownership, with the expansion of lending, and the limitation of bankruptcies. The creation of a comprehensive social security system implied the victory of a communitarian vision of liberalism over a purely individualistic one because it made the state and employers responsible for income maintenance, not the wage earner alone. It taught the lesson that poverty is not necessarily either the fault of the poor or a natural concomitant of capitalism. Social security made income maintenance part of normal business costs for the first time. The New Deal institutionalized the use of monetary policy as an overall regulator of economic activity by again strengthening the Federal Reserve System.

Still, the Keynesian core of the movement never succeeded in implanting systematic policy learning. The hurricane of major institutional reforms that imposed state regulation of capitalist practices was not derived from a consensual and systematic analysis of the economy and society.[14] The Harvard-centered Keynesian economists did not assume control over macroeconomic steering until 1938; their influence grew during the war. Their real impact was felt after 1945 when they launched the full-employment program at home and the Marshal Plan in Europe, where

[14] During the first three years of the Roosevelt administration these economic reforms were enacted: price supports and very generous credits for farmers; a program of service on public projects for unemployed youths; reforms of the banking system; abandonment of the gold standard; massive rural electrification and irrigation/flood control in the South and West; unemployment insurance; old-age pensions for all; state-supported collective bargaining for reinvigorated trade unions; close regulation of stock and bond sales; and abolition of child labor and comprehensive legislation on workers' rights. A major effort to use a corporatist scheme of reviving industry by permanent consultation between the bureaucracy and the largest firms—the National Recovery Act—was held unconstitutional by the Supreme Court. Thereafter, economic recovery was left to private business, with the state regulating and guiding rather than dictating policy. Two groups of intellectually and institutionally affiliated experts acted in crucial roles in New Deal reforms. One group consisted of lawyers trained by or loyal to the social reformism of Justices Louis Brandeis and Felix Frankfurter; the other consisted of devotees of Keynesian economics. See Arthur M. Schlesinger, Jr., *The Age of Roosevelt: The Politics of Upheaval* (Boston: Houghton Mifflin, 1960).

American Keynesians formed close ties with French and British colleagues professing the same beliefs.

Yet there has never been a clear, unambiguous, political commitment to a policy of eradicating poverty, such as exists in the Nordic countries. There have been temporary relief efforts, special income support programs for nonemployable or handicapped persons, and efforts at structural change by means of social insurance programs, which never quite did the trick. In Washington and in industry, opposition to Keynesianism as well as to the idea of a state-managed welfare economy never died. Social democratic liberalism was never fully "embedded," never fully consensual, even before it was successfully challenged in the 1980s. The very fact that the New Deal turned to the right in 1938 when it abandoned its half-hearted efforts at economic planning suggests the staying power of opinion hostile to state guidance. The New Deal system was often revised, sometimes scaled down, sometimes expanded—most strikingly when in the 1960s it was reborn as the Great Society program of President Lyndon Johnson. It certainly created a culture of entitlements by way of its unsystematic accretions. Its adaptations to a mass society saved the country from serious unrest during the Great Depression and succeeded in giving the disaffected—labor and farmers—an emotional and physical stake in their American identity.

Foreign policy too was loosely linked to the New Deal's program of fundamental domestic reform. There always has been an ideologically driven commitment to free trade in America. During the 1930s, however, serious economic studies showed what President Wilson had already suspected: economic recovery, higher domestic living standards, and continuing steady growth demand foreign markets and easy access to needed imports, mostly primary products. Free trade seemed to be the answer, a policy endorsed by the New Deal regime after a brief period of seeking recovery by withdrawing from the global economy. The policy of withdrawal called for the abandonment of the gold standard and a decision to reflate alone, seen as necessary to prevent the feared further infection of the American economy by Europe's depression.

The 1930s also saw the abandonment of economic imperialism in the Caribbean. The nationalization of American oil properties by Mexico and Venezuela (in the 1950s) did not result in intervention because it was considered more important to have these countries on the American side in the war with Germany and in the cold war than to protect private oil interests. In the 1930s occupation forces were withdrawn from Nicaragua, Haiti, and Cuba; but American troops went into the Dominican Republic to "save" that country from communism in 1965. In other cases clandestine U.S. intervention occurred in the Caribbean. In general, however, foreign policy objectives were practically and conceptually

146

tied to the maintenance of the welfare state because foreign aid, international monetary order, and free trade in goods were nested within measures to spur domestic growth.

After 1945 an economically dominant America turned to global economic liberalism: it wanted to abolish all restrictions on the free and competitive flow of goods, services, and money. The United States took the leadership in creating and running the system of multilateral institutions designed to push the world in that direction, the International Monetary Fund (IMF), the World Bank and regional multilateral banks, and the General Agreement on Tariffs and Trade (GATT).

Yet the commitment to economic liberalism was sacrificed when it was deemed more important to use economic statecraft to fight communism. The United States inaugurated the era of massive, focused foreign aid with the launching for the Marshall Plan in 1948. Foreign aid after 1950 became a standard tool of statecraft to induce the kind of economic growth that would limit the appeal of communism in Latin America, Asia, and eventually in Africa. Economic sanctions became a prominent tool of political pressure. The foreign aid and free trade ideas and institutions were also used to advance the fortunes of the large American corporations who began to invest heavily in Third World manufacturing and service enterprises after 1960, though opposed by some Third World countries who preferred to follow more self-reliant development policies depending on protection against foreign firms. Overall, the commitment to fight communist influence led to a totally new set of techniques and institutions of statecraft that were often inconsistent with the welfare-oriented measures to advance free trade and investment flows.

The social programs of the New Frontier and the Great Society sought to extend the welfare state further by making sporadic and unsuccessful attempts at harnessing consensual knowledge to decision making. Nonwhite ethnic minorities were the last to benefit from embedded liberalism; they did not come into their own until the 1960s. In 1944 only 45 percent of whites believed that blacks ought to have as good a chance as whites to get any kind of job; in 1963 80 percent of whites thought so.[15] During the 1950s, residence in suburbs became common for whites, while inner cities became the ghettos of African Americans, Latinos, and unassimilated Asians. Between 1940 and 1960, 2.6 million African Americans migrated from the rural South to northern cities. As the 1960s began, 80 percent of all African Americans lived in de facto segregated metropolitan areas; 44 percent of black families had incomes of less than $3,000 per year;

---

[15] All statistics in this paragraph are taken either from Allen J. Matusow, *The Unraveling of America* (New York: Harper and Row, 1984), p. 211, or from Irving Bernstein, *Promises Kept: John F. Kennedy's New Frontier* (New York: Oxford University Press, 1991), pp. 18–19.

a quarter of the families were headed by women; maternal mortality rates for African Americans were four times those for European-Americans, infant mortality three times; their unemployment rate was at least double that of the whites.

The civil rights program underwritten by the Kennedy and Johnson administrations was designed to correct these conditions and to ensure that African Americans were able to enjoy full citizenship rights, which meant essentially the ability to exercise freely the rights to vote and run for office. Major social reform programs derived in part from sociological theories of equality were launched, designed to improve education, housing, health care, and enhance the employment opportunities and incomes of nonwhite minorities. "Affirmative action" in employment and contracting was to link the reversal of past discrimination to the enhancement of living standards.

The period since 1960 is one in which science and technology became ever more central to political life and technical knowledge gained ever more respect as an important component of decision making. Increasingly, expert-bureaucrats argued that science ought to be used consistently to solve social problems, especially poverty. "If we can put a man on the moon, why shouldn't we be able to end poverty in this country?" was one slogan of the Great Society War on Poverty advocates. By the end of the 1960s the federal government was financing 64 percent of all Research and Development (R&D) efforts and did 15 percent of the work its own facilities; the rest was given in grants to universities and private industry. Expenditures on education increased by 60 percent between 1964 and 1974, expenditure per student by 24 percent, even though the school-age population increased by only 13.5 percent.

None of this secured the institutionalization of learning in policymaking. The Great Society War on Poverty programs owed their birth to the coincidence of the civil rights struggle, the availability of a great deal of expert-generated theorizing about poverty, *and* the political needs of Presidents Kennedy and Johnson. At the core were many separate programs designed to increase the earning capacity of people who had remained marginal to the economy by increasing skill formation in childhood and late adolescence, child welfare, housing, teacher training, medical services, and food stamps. Politically the most radical was "community action," a set of programs designed to enable neighborhood groups to design and administer their own projects, pressure the local political establishment, and serve as an incubator for new leadership of the poor.[16]

---

[16] Whether these programs were "successful" remains very controversial, partly because of the lack of consensus among social scientists about the meaning of poverty and how to

Even though the legislation creating this structure mandated systematic evaluation of results, the exercise proved useless because it was po-
liticized from the first. More important, no single comprehensive theory
informed the War on Poverty, no consensual knowledge informed the
manner in which the dozens of separate programs were tied together.
There was no systematic aggregation, leave alone nesting, of issues. One
observer noted:

> improved education and training may be ineffective in increasing earning
> capacity unless steps are also taken to change the mix of available jobs, and
> efforts to change the mix of available jobs may fail if low-wage workers lack
> training and education. Either taken alone might fail, when both together
> might succeed. Research and experimentation would detect the failures but
> we have no way to indicate the hypothetical potential success. A rather vague
> assumption of such an interrelatedness marked early political rhetoric about
> the War on Poverty but was wholly absent from the precise, but partial,
> analyses of its effectiveness performed by social scientists.[17]

Major questions concerning poverty and its removal were still on the
research agenda of the 1990s because the evaluation research performed
in the 1970s was ideological and ill designed and therefore led to clearly
wrong conclusions while serving the partisan agendas of community advocates, legal activists, and conservative opponents of big government.

A Hot War and Racial Strife Derationalize America

Embedded liberalism shaped America's stance toward the world from
the presidency of Franklin Roosevelt to Richard Nixon's. American foreign policy was designed to achieve a prosperous and expanding world
economy as free as possible from protectionist constraints as was compatible with the perfection of the domestic welfare state; domestic
growth and prosperity, not free trade and capital movements as such,
were always the core economic objectives. After 1945 American liberals

---

measure it. Together, these programs never cost more than 2.8 percent of GNP in any one
year, although income security measures, health, and education expenditures rose from
27 percent of the federal budget in 1965 to 53 percent in 1980; federal R&D on poverty
grew from less than $3 million in 1965 to $200 million by 1980. Community Action programs found their way onto the federal agenda, despite their being anathema to local and
state officials, and they eventually subsidized revolutionary organizations because President
Johnson never understood that the advocacy of Andre W. Hackett and Lloyd Ohlin, who
taught theories of criminology at the University of Chicago, called for local political em-
powerment as necessary for reducing juvenile delinquency (Matusow, *Unraveling of America*,
pp. 107–26)!

[17] H. A. Aaron, *Politics and Professors* (Washington, D.C.: Brookings Institution, 1978), pp.
156–57.

wanted to contain—some also wanted to defeat—communism in general and the Soviet empire in particular, and in the process make liberal democracy the universally prevalent form of rule. The anticommunist objective raised the issue of how much force the United States ought to use in containing the Soviet Union.

Internationalist exuberance for containing communism brought the United States to the extreme fragmentation of the early 1970s. Containment linked geopolitical and military calculations—the security dilemma—to foreign aid and economic development, to the growth of democracy and the protection of human rights, as well as to the countering of "subversion" at home and abroad. Because this nested cluster of policies led to derationalization, decision makers learned to delink these measures, to analyze the causal nexus of insecurity more accurately and deliberately, to tame the obsession with a hostile foreign ideology. These lessons were learned as a result of the failures incurred during this period, particularly the failure in Vietnam. The détente of 1973 represents the start of systematic learning. Until then, the policy of containment, with its associated measures of foreign aid, nuclear deterrence, and encouragement of democracy abroad, had been driven by the ideological commitments of ruling coalitions, occasionally adjusted by acts of ad hoc adaptation urged by realists, such as the abandonment of democratization policies in Latin America as futile during the Johnson and Nixon administrations, a policy of nonintervention reversed by Presidents Carter, Reagan, and Bush. Only early attempts at arms control represented learning behavior.

Political entrepreneurs and epistemic communities were important agents of learning in the arms control field and in the area of development assistance. No such forces, however, arose to switch the United States away from the ideologically driven determination to fight local communism in Southeast Asia. On the contrary, the Southeast Asian war was the logical outgrowth of the militant anticommunism professed by triumphant cosmopolitan internationalists. The same liberals, however, were also capable of fashioning a foreign economic policy that evolved directly from lessons learned during the Great Depression.

Ideology, not consensual knowledge, inspired the march toward egalitarian and communitarian liberalism. The civil rights revolution was fueled by activists and institutionalized by lawyers, not by knowledge specialists. The legal basis of protecting the civil rights of ethnic groups, women, and homosexuals and of eliminating most forms of discrimination against them was in place by 1972. Just as the Eisenhower administration had accepted the New Deal, the Nixon administration continued the egalitarian policies of the Great Society.

Even though these changes were institutionalized by the courts, it cannot be claimed that expert knowledge informed judges' decisions. They forced the reapportionment of legislative districts so that each represents roughly the same number of voters. They also ended segregated education and transportation. The courts determined when a school district was properly integrated, and they mandated federal monitoring of elections to ensure their fairness. Prior to these reforms, in eight southern states, only 6.2 percent of blacks registered to vote, even though they accounted for 38 percent of the voting-age population.[18]

These reforms, and other relating to nondiscrimination in housing and employment, are consistent with an individualistic liberalism. Other reforms, however, supported a distinctly communitarian version of that creed. Lyndon Johnson proclaimed in 1965 that we seek "not just freedom but opportunity ... not just equality as a right and a theory but equality as a fact and as a result."[19] If a certain class of people, most commonly defined by race or ethnicity, was found not to benefit from a right or an entitlement in proportion to its numbers in the overall population, the courts held that such a group, as a group, was entitled to special benefits. "Affirmative action" came to mean policies favoring especially designated groups of people who were historically the victims of discrimination, even though no active intent to discriminate against them now could be discovered.

Partly as a result of programs tailored to the needs of African Americans and Hispanics, there arose by 1970 organized movements who proclaimed themselves as "black separatists" or "black nationalists," demanding state-funded separate facilities and rejecting the core values of the American national myth. La Raza organizations made somewhat weaker claims for Hispanics, and among African Americans the Student Non-Violent Coordinating Committee, the Nation of Islam, and the Black Panthers positioned themselves as separatists. Many white liberals came to accept these claims, now legitimated by the multicultural version of American liberal nationalism.

Even though these measures did not prevent the enormously destructive ghetto riots of 1966 and 1967, there is no doubt that eventually the civil rights legislation improved the lot of members of ethnic minorities in housing, education, and employment when discrimination had been the main cause of lack of access, not poverty. Much of the success is no doubt due to the vastly increased power of the federal government in actively policing and directing continued access to opportunities. The

[18] Statistics supporting these claims are from Matusow, *Unraveling of America*, p. 375, and Hugh Davis Graham, *Civil Rights and the Presidency* (New York: Oxford University Press, 1992), pp. 13–22. See also Bruce Chadwick and Tim Heaton, eds., *Statistical Handbook of the American Family* (Phoenix: Oryx Press, 1992), pp. 165, 224, 232.
[19] Quoted in Graham, *Civil Rights*, p. 7.

federal bureaucracy increased steadily in the 1960s and 1970s, and it was endowed with powers of direct intervention that earlier efforts at regulation had lacked because they relied on adjudication.

As a result of these mainly ideologically driven changes in American institutions, the predominantly cosmopolitan liberal body of values began to erode. As early as the 1950s the movement that ultimately became known as multiculturalism challenged both the cosmopolitan and nativist versions of liberal nationalism. After 1945, the country took pride in the diversity of its *Western* cultural origins, stressing the near-miracle of how so many diverse cultures manage to coexist in peace and profess a single civil religion. At the same time, however, some writers began to criticize the pressure for conformity implied by policies encouraging the melting of diverse cultures. They did so in protest against growing conservatism, in opposition to the dominance of cold war rhetoric in American politics, and in the face of accelerating assimilation. Will Herberg's *Protestant, Catholic, Jew* deplored the growing interdenominational tolerance as representing a growing secular civil religion that advanced, he noted correctly, at the price of weakening real religions. His plea was supported by some social science research that claimed that assimilation was not the culmination—and should not result—in a full merger of all cultures. Whatever residues of cultural singularity refused to melt, it was argued, should be retained at least to safeguard warm intragroup ties, not as principles of national political organization.

These arguments justified the mass-based multicultural nationalism that arose in the 1960s, partly as an unforeseen consequence of national policies fashioned for different purposes. The prophets of black, and to a much lesser extent Hispanic, nationalism were already active in the 1920s and 1930s, though they lacked a mass following at that time. They preached nonassimilation—resistance to those American values thought to have disadvantaged minorities who were denied any opportunity to assimilate because of systematic discrimination. Hence African American music, literature, and religion were lauded. The creation of business enterprises owned by African Americans was encouraged. During the 1960s some ghetto districts of cities sought, in effect, to secede from the municipal authorities. Increasingly, the movement advocated the creation of separate black institutions in all spheres and denied the possibility of a single nationalism to which all ought to be loyal. For these alienated groups, if there was going to be American nationalism at all, it was going to be a set of beliefs in which diversity—buttressed by extensive public entitlements—was to be the norm.

America certainly grew more egalitarian, but equality did not bring about contentment. Popular attitudes changed dramatically in favor of women's rights to enter professions, have abortions, have careers outside the home, and to rely on outside child care services as well as on that supreme technical fix, the "pill." The educational and employment opportunities of ethnic minorities, including African Americans, improved dramatically after 1970. Yet their discontent seemed to increase as did their standard of living, though four times as many followed the nonviolent path of Martin Luther King than the violent one of separatism. But black discontent did not tear the country apart nearly as much as did the Vietnam War.

Whatever economic and arms control lessons were learned, whatever knowledge was accumulated about how to administer a growing welfare state, these lessons did not suffice to improve race relations by the mid-1970s. Many adjustments not based on consensual knowledge came to improve equality among Americans; but they did not suffice to prevent the growth of a communitarian sentiment that stresses ethnic separatism. Many skirmishes and some battles were won in the cold war against communism and the Soviet empire; but none were as decisive to the American nation as the defeat suffered in Vietnam. It was not the loss of the Vietnam War that undermined the legitimacy of the American creed; it was the hatred among rival American factions that was unleashed by the war itself, the deep questioning of the American civil religion to which it gave rise. Together with the growth of ethnic politics and religious fundamentalism it seemed to threaten the very survival of liberal nationalism and a liberal polity.

Changing without Learning Much

The amount of institutional change America has undergone since the 1950s was truly stupendous. Given the decentralization, multifaceted nature, and often self-contradictory character of American institutions, it is not surprising that the actual amount of formal collective learning was not large. Much change was due to adaptation, and a great deal to simple ideological pressure.

Some of the most important changes resulted from ideological impulses not mediated by much learning or adaptation. The origin of the militant containment policy that dominated American life from 1946 to 1973 was of that kind. So were most of the components of President Lyndon Johnson's Great Society and the War on Poverty waged between 1964 and 1980. The American commitment to fostering human rights and democracy as core principles of action originated in 1976 as the ideology-derived demand of newly mobilizing interest groups.

I discuss examples of learning and of adaptation later. Here I merely list some. U.S. officials learned to practice macroeconomic guidance between 1933 and 1973, domestically and internationally; they also learned to causally link elements in domestic and foreign economic policy. After 1963, officials learned that the pursuit of arms control can actually enhance national security. And they learned in 1973 that they ought to scale down the commitment to containment by delinking items of policy previously considered tightly connected in a single causal nexus.[20]

American leaders also practiced much adaptation. One prominent example is the total of economic reforms introduced by the New Deal. Leaders jettisoned the ideological commitment to fostering human rights and democracy abroad when considerations of security and trade were deemed more salient to American interests. And they abandoned the previously learned lesson about free trade when security or human rights considerations dictated a different course.

The outstanding examples of collective learning involve macroeconomic policy and arms control. The determination by Washington at the end of World War II to sponsor a new international economic order was the result of consensual knowledge: the domination in the economic guidance machinery of committed Keynesians, particularly in the Treasury Department. Committed to a policy of guaranteed full employment, these officials were determined not to allow international currency instability to interfere. Hence they negotiated the system of fixed-adjustable exchange rates based on the dollar, as institutionalized in the International Monetary Fund—until President Richard Nixon unilaterally destroyed the system in 1973 as America's debt to foreigners began to threaten monetary stability at the end of the Vietnam War.

Concerned by an ever more dangerous nuclear arms race, partly fueled by himself, President Kennedy encouraged scientific inquiries on how to contain it. By being able to take advantage of partly ideological and partly scientific argument about the serious risks to public health of continuing nuclear weapons tests, he initiated the first serious negotiations toward agreements that, decades later, resulted in the banning of all such tests. These successes were followed by American- (and Soviet-) sponsored global agreements to halt the proliferation of nuclear weapons and to ban the use and manufacture of chemical and biological weapons altogether. Bilateral agreements negotiated with the Soviets by President Nixon began to slow down the construction of strategic nuclear weapons.

Defense policy also illustrates a significant failure to learn, although the effort was certainly made. Policymaking in a democracy militates against the systematic use of consensual knowledge, because "cognitive"

[20] When George Marshall announced his plan for the economic reconstruction of Europe, he insisted that the operation not "be on a piecemeal basis as various crises develop" so as to "provide a cure rather than a mere palliative." Quoted in Richard W. Neustadt and Ernest R. May, eds., *Thinking in Time* (New York: Free Press, 1986), p. 250.

and "cybernetic" modes of decision making tend to swamp systematic analysis. Yet defense policy under the Great Society programs of the 1960s attempted "analytical" problem solving that sought the fullest possible information, optimal solutions when trade-offs and calculation of alternative outcomes became desirable. Labeled Planning-Programming-Budgeting-System (PPBS), the approach forced "explicit statements of assumptions . . . begins with strategic goals, sets up alternative plans for their realization, quantifies costs and benefits."[21] This approach, which featured true theoretical thinking proved to be unacceptable to bureaucracies used to defending their own limited objectives in less systematic terms.

Adaptation prevailed over learning and ideology as sources of change whenever new means were selected to tackle such problems as poverty at home and abroad, although the theories and explanations for those conditions were not examined. Thus American government got used to adding many new substantive programs when social and technological changes created new demands. Republicans, albeit reluctantly, accepted innovations introduced by Democrats; they rarely abolished administrative agencies and routines set up to implement programs of which they disapproved on value grounds. More systematic consultations with citizens groups, sometimes organized initially as a result of government initiative, became routine. At first it was only labor, business, and farmers; by the 1960s spokespersons and organizations representing ethnic minorities, ecologists, consumers, and the poor were recognized as legitimate participants in advisory committees first created by the Eisenhower administration.

Federal–state comanagement of many programs relating to welfare became a standard feature of governance. Even though a verbal commitment to "planning" was routine by the 1970s, very little analytical decision making and thinking actually occurred, at least not in the agencies given core responsibility for general oversight. Yet a diffuse readiness to change, to adapt, and occasionally to adopt new ways of conceptualizing cause and effect were certainly visible in the 1970s. The federal government became the hub of national governance for all issues that matter to people.

In foreign policy, change by way of adaptation was most evident whenever Washington chose a new course that ran counter to some previously learned principle. The abandonment of free trade principles to serve the perceived needs of military security provides many examples. So does the downplaying of human rights and democracy for similar reasons. As

[21] This discussion depends on the material covered in my "Collective Learning," in George W. Breslauer and Philip E. Tetlock, eds., *Learning in U.S. and Soviet Foreign Policy* (Boulder, Colo.: Westview Press, 1991). The definition of PPBS is taken from Otis L. Graham, *Toward a Planned Society* (New York: Oxford University Press, 1976), p. 172.

the part-evangelist, part-realist John F. Kennedy assessed the policy toward the Dominican Republic's long-lasting brutal dictator, Rafael Trujillo: "There are three possibilities, in descending order of preference: a decent democratic regime, a continuation of the Trujillo regime, or a Castro regime. We ought to aim at the first, but we can't really renounce the second until we are sure we can avoid the third."[22] And to show his real mettle, Kennedy did not hesitate to threaten the use of nuclear weapons when he forced the Soviet Union to withdraw its missiles from Cuba in 1963, even though his predecessor, Dwight Eisenhower, had already quietly decided—despite public measures to the contrary—that these weapons were far too destructive ever to be used.

TOWARD MULTICULTURAL RERATIONALIZATION?

When Richard Nixon resigned the presidency in 1974 to avoid impeachment by Congress, Americans were quarrelling with one another, sometimes violently, over race relations, social values, the role of religion in public life, and over America's proper role in the world in the wake of the defeat in Vietnam. During the presidency of Bill Clinton, twenty years later, they argue about precisely the same issues, *but* somehow the citizenry bestows slightly more legitimacy on its tattered myth and its government than in the 1970s. Is it because politicians have learned to analyze issues systematically and fashion more widely accepted policies? Or is it because new leaders and new ideologies have captured new ground? Either road might have led to a liberal nationalism that is less exclusive, less proselytizing, less alarmed by having to coexist with rival nationalisms than was true in the past. Have they?

Let us look first at aspects of American public opinion during these twenty years.[23] In 1974, 77 percent believed that domestic problems were more important than international ones; by 1980 that number had shrunk to 30 percent. In 1990, 45 percent of Americans rated social and moral problems as most serious, whereas the economy and the environment were cited by only 17 percent each; foreign issues were listed first only by 7 percent. Immigration was opposed by 58 percent, even though 86 percent thought that all races were created equal.

---

[22] Quoted in Abraham F. Lowenthal, *The United States and Latin American Democracy* (Boston: World Peace Foundation, 1991), p. 8.

[23] The 1990 statistics come from "The Two Nations Poll," *Maclean's*, June 25, 1990, pp. 50–53. Other statistics are cited in John Mueller, "Bloodbaths and Dominoes," paper written for the U.S. Military Academy, May 30, 1985; David Ignatius, "Reagan Faces Arms Dilemma," *Wall Street Journal*, June 8, 1984, p. 44.

By 1989 the Cold War was over; containing communism became a relic of past concerns as a reformist Soviet Union took the lead in ending global confrontations of word and deed. Keynesian macroeconomic steering yielded to monetarism as the canon of material welfare, triggering a retreat of the welfare state. The world argued over the priorities of sustainable development and resource conservation as opposed to free trade and untrammelled capitalist development.

These events and trends challenged America's liberal national myth. They caused questioning about past verities; they forced a reconsideration of the permanence of the American nation-state. Is the civil religion too fractured to undergird the myth? Is cosmopolitan liberalism losing as the definer of American identity? Is monetarism and reborn private enterprise capitalism undermining social solidarity anchored in middle-class values? Is the devotion to a single global economy hurting the idea of an American community? These are the main questions that now have to be addressed to probe the strength of the American national myth. Put differently, is continuous learning able to maintain the power of the myth despite the challenges?

The Contested Civil Religion

Legitimacy may have improved a bit, but has the authority of government kept pace? Have Americans come to terms with a multiethnic body of values, a civic religion not anchored in individualistic liberalism? Can religion coexist with a secular state, particularly with regard to education and health care? Are Americans committed to *peacefully* changing institutions and policies with which they cannot agree?

It is clear that America remains rationalized with respect to two vital points: the principle of political succession based on fair elections remains unimpaired, and Americans, by and large, pay their taxes. Whether rerationalization is under way on other points, and whether any systematic learning has occurred remains now to be established.

Race relations remain precarious, even though policy and law now favor communitarianism and are moving toward a multicultural national myth. In 1989, 75 percent of African Americans polled believed that they were not achieving equality because whites do not want them to, even though in 1980 about the same number thought that there was little tension among the races in their own neighborhoods. During the civil rights struggles, Martin Luther King expressed disdain for the use of African symbols by African Americans; he did not want to use the phrase "black power." Fifteen years later Jesse Jackson, in rejecting "black" as an ethnic identity, insisted that "to be called African-American has cultural

157

integrity. . . . It puts us in our proper historical context."[24] President Nixon introduced the first legislation using the affirmative action formula; legislators and courts continued the trend by favoring nonwhite ethnic minorities (and women of all colors) in the awarding of federal contracts, admission to higher education, promotion in civil service ranks—in the face of considerable resentment by whites. Similar feelings did not stop the courts from ordering the integration of public schools on the basis of racial quotas when judges deemed the mere abolition of de jure segregation inadequate for the achievement of equality. By the mid-1990s, however, courts and politicians—to the acclaim of the majority—began to chip away at these institutions.

White politicians and cosmopolitan liberals at first favored such policies in the belief that the creation of group rights would, in the long run, overcome the alienation of minorities from the American polity. Ideology inspired these measures, not knowledge. They have not yet bridged the gulf between all the races. Nor have these multicultural solutions healed the value conflicts between the increasingly assertive homosexual and feminist cultures that, in many ways, are constructing separate and self-contained communities. Many leaders are now admitting that affirmative action has undermined liberalism.

For a while it appeared as if massive subsidies and other support payments to the poorest—who were disproportionately nonwhite as well—would reduce the income gap between whites and some ethnic minorities.[25] Probably the number of African-Americans and Hispanics who entered the middle class increased during the 1980s. Differences in standards of living between the races shrank gradually. However, beginning with the Reagan administration, various support payments to the poorest were gradually reduced, though never eliminated. Black alienation from American institutions seemed to increase despite the objective growth in wealth. Poll after poll hammers home the point that African Americans lack faith in the judicial system. They do not believe whites want them to be equal, despite the evidence to the contrary. Every position not consistent with black aspirations is labeled "racist." African American intellectuals delight in advancing arguments about intrinsic

[24] Quoted in Ben L. Martin, "From Negro to Black to African American," *Political Science Quarterly* 106 (1991): 83.

[25] Hugh Heclo, "The Political Foundations of Antipoverty Policy," in Sheldon H. Danziger and Daniel H. Weinberg, eds., *Fighting Poverty* (Cambridge: Harvard University Press, 1986), p. 314. Heclo demonstrates that such Great Society programs as food stamps, child nutrition, liberalization of social security, and medicare/medicaid were intended to be heavily redistributive but that the political spirit of the times prevented the open acknowledgment of that holistic perspective quite consistent with new theories of social equality and harmony.

differences between white and black culture. Of trust, confidence, and the practice of reciprocity there is nary a trace.

Disaffected whites insist on bringing religion back into the state. The Catholic Church has long asked for, and occasionally obtained, marginal subsidies from the state in support of parochial schools. Protestant fundamentalists, long absent from the political arena, returned in force after the Vietnam war. They challenged existing law by demanding public prayer in public schools, the teaching in public schools of the biblical story of genesis as "creation science," the removal of "secular humanist propaganda" from public libraries, and the outlawing of abortion. They also advocated a hard line in foreign policy. By bringing "God back into politics" millenarian fundamentalists believe they can improve the chances of a favorable divine judgment even before the Tribulation foretold in scripture. Living in or just before the "last days" makes urgent the total moral reform of the country.

The unresolved interethnic-cultural conflict leads to the legitimation of norms and values associated with multicultural communitarianism. But the effort of active religious believers to penetrate the still-secular state smacks of a different kind of communitarian liberalism, one closer to the nativist conception of national identity. The current conflict over the content of the American civil religion runs along two fault lines: between secularists and religious fundamentalists, and between people who derive their identity from European culture and those who do not. The number of non-Europeans is approaching 30 percent nationally, although in California it is now 50 percent.

The primary arena in which these two conflicts are fought is the public school system. The religious culture wishes to penetrate and dominate that system if it cannot have its own schools maintained with state support. Self-segregation is also the trend among the main nonwhite minorities. They seek to change the curriculum by giving prominence to themes that stress Africa and Latin America, alongside the contributions of non-Europeans to American life. They rewrite textbooks to "correct" their alleged Eurocentric content. They insist on the use of Spanish in instruction and on languages other than English in certain arenas of public life. They seek to alter the social studies curriculum to highlight events and achievements in which whites were not prominent. And some argue for state-supported resegregated schools in which these objectives can be more successfully pursued. In 1994, the Clinton administration, fearful that the national myth will be further eroded, directed the National Endowment for the Humanities to conduct "national conversations" on the values still held in common by all Americans, a program deliberately fashioned to reassert a special sense of American identity.

Moral questions regarding the use of force by the government continue to divide the nation. After the Vietnam disaster, the Carter administration sought to minimize the use of force in domestic and foreign affairs. During the Reagan–Bush years, however, the emphasis on exclusively peaceful ways went into decline. The danger of communism, to Reagan, legitimated the actual use of overt and covert military power in Central America and in Africa. The use of force in the Middle East, for both Reagan and Bush, was justified as a safeguarding of U.S. military interests. In all cases, however, some prominent members of the Republican administrations opposed the use of force. Reagan stepped up high-tech arms racing in the face of Catholic and Methodist opposition to the continued reliance on nuclear deterrence. Reagan and Bush despaired of the "Vietnam syndrome," a widespread sentiment of popular opposition to the use of force by the United States, but they proceeded to project military power anyway. By the time of the United Nations-sanctioned war against Iraq, President George Bush was able to exult, "we have finally shaken the Vietnam syndrome."

The commitment to peaceful change still dominates. Despite these conflict over the civil religion, Americans by and large continue to believe that it is impermissible to use means other than those sanctioned by the Constitution to work for change. Violence cannot be used to assert one's views. Religious fundamentalists occasionally violate the commitment to peaceful change in their use of civil disobedience; blacks disregard it when they take to the streets in protest against unpopular court decisions. All groups test the limit of the commitment to peaceful change when they threaten violence or suicide in insisting on their way. However, the commitment to the cosmopolitan-individualistic version of liberalism still dominates its rivals. Most Americans still resist the idea of group rights and ethnically defined entitlements; they still reject public life infused by public religious dogma, even if their leaders look for compromises in these cultural conflicts.

Return to the Market-Driven Economy?

Some students of American economy believe that public reliance on market mechanisms prevails during good times, but that most actors demand, or at least accept, government direction in times of trouble. If this is correct, it represents collective learning at work; networks of officials, corporate leaders, and trade unionists arrive at new modes of economic governance as a result of having analyzed past failures or having changed their theories about what ensured prosperity. Economic policy since the mid-1970s supports this interpretation.

Learning occurred in a setting hostile to collective action. Antitrust law forbade many forms of joint operation. The tradition of continuous joint consultation between government, business, and labor was lacking. Interfirm cooperation was not the norm. Instead of pooling knowledge and resources when adjustments were called for, American business leaders preferred unilateral to multilateral action. The kind of industrial policy practiced by France and Japan was given short shrift because of a continuing value commitment to free markets and to the therapeutic power of competition. Only in times of crisis was a departure from these preferences possible in the form of special incentives held out by the state.

Such encouragement came during both world wars, during the Great Depression, and under the stimulus of arms racing (Table 4-7).[26] Even the rabid promarket Reagan and Bush administrations offered subsidies to high-technology firms to make the Strategic Defense Initiative (SDI) a success and maintain the national capacity to manufacture semiconductors. It also encouraged interfirm cooperation in R&D by relaxing the antitrust laws.

Yet the suspension of faith in the market was incomplete and intermittent. Demands for a government-business-labor–determined policy of overall industrial programming found little interest. The substitution of managed trade for unregulated free trade was considered a heresy in the 1980s and 1990s, even though the Clinton administration advocates policies of retraining labor in declining industries by means of quasi-corporatist arrangements. Some of its officials favor managed trade. Bill Clinton, without success, sought to reverse Reagan's dictum that the "government is the problem, not the solution."[27] Government leaders, as well as corporate chief executive officers, are calling for more investment in education at all levels to meet the challenge of global economic competition.

Learning, albeit temporary, is also evident in America's environmental legislation. Beginning in the 1960s, the United States pioneered in the creation of new bureaucracies staffed by environmentalist-experts. It kept

[26] Codings of programs were done by Susan Siena, using Nelson Polsby, *Political Innovation in America* (New Haven: Yale University Press, 1984). The following issue areas were considered by Daniel Weinberg as potential arenas of policy learning if additional good research were done first: relationship between family structure, housing, immigration, standards of living, homelessness; how welfare influences incentive to work; why Congress prefers in-kind transfers to monetary ones; more systematic labor-market studies. See his contribution to Danziger and Weinberg, *Fighting Poverty*, pp. 348–57.

[27] John B. Judis, *The Grand Illusion* (New York: Farrar, Straus & Giroux, 1992), p. 19. The "Monetarist Revolution" of the Republican decade of the 1980s was based on the consensual post-Keynesian knowledge that linked deregulation, free trade, and low taxes with economic renewal and halting decline. Political constraints prevented the systematic adoption as policy of this knowledge; the epistemic community never fully penetrated the policy community.

Table 4-7. Types of policy innovation in U.S. government

Facilitating Condition	Types of Impetus		
	Knowledge-Based Learning	Crisis-Driven Improvisation	Ideology-Driven Policymaking
Epistemic community plus political entrepreneur	Atomic Energy Commission (AEC), Environmental Protection Agency (EPA), National Science Foundation (NSF), arms control	Council of Economic Advisers	War on Poverty
Political leaders' public relations need	Tennessee Valley Authority (TVA), Rural Electrification Administration (REA)		Medicare, Peace Corps
Political leaders' need to meet sudden crisis	Tennessee Valley Authority (TVA), Rural Electrification Administration (REA)	Truman Doctrine, New Deal banking reforms, National Recovery Administration (NRA), Agricultural Adjustment Administration (AAA)	
New political movement, coalition			Strategic Defense Initiative (SDI), civil and women's rights, affirmative action

up a stream of new legislation during the 1970s to ensure water and air quality, species preservation, resource conservation, and the removal of toxic substances from manufactured goods and from disposal sites. The advent of the Reagan/Bush administrations put a stop to these developments as the interests of business and of the economy were considered more important than those of consumers. Implementation of legislation was curtailed as funds were cut. The fate of environmental protection remains in doubt in the 1990s. What appeared as the victory of consensual knowledge dissipated under the blows of a revived market ideology.

Throughout, the administrative integrity of the state increased. Many administrative agencies created by the New Deal were gradually abolished as their surviving functions were given to other agencies. Domestic agencies were aggregated in a White House–based council, in imitation of the National Security Council. Many services formerly performed by government agencies were contracted out to the private sector. The vigorous policies of deregulation followed by Republican presidents and legislatures also contributed to administrative streamlining. Fiscal and budgetary procedures were put on a more analytical basis by virtue of being centralized in the Office of Management and Budget. Congress, to defend its independent power to analyze presidential budget proposals, created the equally analytical Congressional Budget Office. It takes ingenuity to maintain administrative coherence in the face of constitutionally mandated separation of powers, a feat increasingly made possible by highly professional analytical staff work.

Despite intermittent bursts of learning by leaders, the American economy never regained the vigorous growth rates of the 1950s and 1960s. Technological innovation proceeds at an ever more breathtaking rate, but the gap between rich and poor grows rapidly and net increases in welfare are difficult to discern because newly employed people tend to find jobs only in low-wage industries. More and more it seems as if the social disruption caused by technological innovation outweighs its economic boon. The American middle class is growing less content. A vague impatience with both political parties, expressed also by dropping rates of voting participation, finds voice in the movement for third parties with equally vague programs. The state, so often maligned by conservatives and also by centrist members of the middle class, is still seen as the guarantor of entitlements also sought by the state's detractors.

Derationalization is evident in cultural conflict and in economic discontent.[28] It appears to outweigh the demonstrated ability to learn new ways and to adapt instrumentally. The increasing unwillingness of reasonably wealthy Americans to pay the taxes they could well afford to pay is the most powerful indictment of the argument that ideology is in retreat as the engine of change.

The City on the Hill between Internationalist and Accommodationist Leaders

In 1976, at the height of the "Vietnam syndrome," almost two thirds of Americans believed that the United States was losing world power and should not conduct a unilateral foreign policy, intervene in other

---

[28] For similar judgments based on a panel study, see Citrin, Haas, Muste, and Reingold, "Is American Nationalism Changing?" pp. 4–5.

Table 4-8. Distribution of foreign policy orientation (%)

		1974–76	1984–86
Hardliners	mass public	27	25
	leaders	20	17
Isolationists	mass public	24	23
	leaders	8	7
Internationalists	mass public	26	30
	leaders	30	25
Accommodationists	mass public	23	23
	leaders	42	51

SOURCE: Ole Holsti and James N. Rosenau, "The Structure of Foreign Policy Attitudes among American Leaders," *Journal of Politics* 52, 1 (February 1990): 103. Reprinted with permission of University of Texas Press.

nations' civil wars, or give military aid. Almost 70 percent did not trust the Soviet Union but favored the continuation of détente with both Russia and China anyway. These opinions suggest the advent of accommodationism: by the mid-1980s, 51 percent of leaders and 23 percent of the mass public were accommodationists (see Table 4-8).

Which of the many changes and innovations since Vietnam represent true learning, as opposed to finding new means to attain old ends, or mere changes in personnel reflecting alternatingly influential ideologies? It is clear that foreign policy making has been exposed to the same analytical and projective practices as much of public policy since the Great Depression. Nevertheless, the substantive process of learning has been spotty. Old causal patterns have been abandoned for new and more elaborate ones in some issue areas but not in others. I give many instances of the continued importance of ideology and associated personnel changes as triggers of change.

It is almost universally acknowledged that "growing interdependence" among countries, issues, and events is now an everyday experience. This recognition, in Western countries, occurred in the context of liberal institutions. The exposure of more and more people to education creates an awareness of vicarious experiences and ties. So does the spread of the electronic media of communication. The growth of advocacy and interest groups and their participation in decision making allow for the introduction of new bodies of information and new values. In the aggregate, these trends and institutions lead to an appreciation of new means to achieve old ends; but they also offer fora that allow a hearing for values and objectives previously ignored.

Liberal nationalism favors collective learning, even if the lessons remain spotty. Accommodationism could flourish because the lessons included the realization that nuclear war is not to be envisaged, that it was successfully avoided for fifty years, that peaceful change was brought about at certain times, and that the possibility of multilateral conflict management was demonstrated by some United Nations operations.

Collective learning brought about changes in grand strategy. By 1971 Richard Nixon and Henry Kissinger "had laid aside the cold war vision of a world divided between the godly West and the satanic East and were describing the world in classic balance-of-power terms—divided into the five power blocs of the United States, the Soviet Union, China, Japan, and Western Europe, not one of which was predominant."[29] After 1971, over two-thirds of leaders gave up the overriding national commitment to fighting communism everywhere. Though temporarily reversed by Reagan, most leaders realized that America, if it wished to avoid global war, must find a way to coexist with the only other superpower, even if it did represent an ideology abhorrent to Americans. The lesson was that the destructiveness of modern war and the reality of strategic interdependence made a policy of stubborn confrontation irrationally dangerous. Despite lapses under Reagan and Bush, the corollary was that armed conflict ought to be avoided wherever possible. Internationalist cold war fervor was moderated by accommodationist tolerance for ideological diversity and fear of mayhem. It was confirmed when the Soviet Union gave up the Cold War in 1986.

Arms control was prominent among the lessons learned even before Mikhael Gorbachev's "new thinking" took over. Promoted by an international epistemic community of experts and aided by much formal analysis, defense policymakers had given up on reliance on "the biggest bang for a buck" in favor of sophisticated gradations of deterrence. They learned to plan to fight wars much more controllable than those associated with massive nuclear deterrent thinking. They realized that the nuclear arsenal represents unneeded overkill capacity. With the conclusion of SALT I, SALT II, START, and conventions eliminating chemical and biological weapons, defense planners realized that bilateral and multilateral inspection of arms removed and destroyed enhances everyone's security. Ample technical means to ensure compliance became available to both sides, a fact that did not prevent occasional cheating by the Soviets that was not detected until the 1990s. Despite the lessons learned, it remains true that widespread turf battles among the services continue to generate disagreement about the proper defense posture after the end of the Cold War.

Within these large swaths of policy learning there remained many patches of haphazard adaptation or plain instrumental behavior. The advancement

---

[29] Judis, *Grand Illusion*, p. 193.

abroad of democracy and human rights has become a principled policy priority since 1976; prior to that time it was merely a way to bring about the defeat of communism. That emphasis was due to the influence of interest groups backing the Democratic Party and the values of many Democratic politicians. However, actual policy in Latin America, Asia, Africa, and the Middle East forced these principles into the background whenever they got in the way of advancing security, arms control, trade, or environmental interests. Ad hoc instrumentalism ruled the roost of policy in particular regions.

The United States remained aloof from the Helsinki process of softening the cold war in Europe after 1975 until it was realized that détente and security would be served by the confidence-building arrangements even as the human rights portions of the agreement were used to embarrass the communist participants. Their democratization, however, was taken very seriously after 1989. Policy in the Middle East paid scant attention to democratization because it was preoccupied with preventing the emergence of a local hegemon, fighting Muslim fundamentalism, protecting the West's oil supply, and advancing the Israeli-Arab peace process. Arms control and trade trumped democracy and human rights when policymakers had to choose how to respond to Chinese repression and North Korean nuclear threats. Washington frequently accepted reverses in trade policy with Japan when common security interests loomed larger. Commitments to foreign aid always suffered when concerns over security waned.

The case of the Philippines illustrates the process of unsystematic and unprincipled innovation that typically coexists with fundamental learning; internationalists and accommodationists participate in both kinds of behavior. Neither is consistently a principled or an avid learner. Ever since 1946, Washington has managed to influence deeply the affairs of this former American colony by subsidizing politicians and parties, tailoring foreign aid to reward friends and punish enemies, and relaying to the Philippine government, via the U.S. Embassy, which course of action was preferred by Washington. Occasionally this "advice" took the form of actively supporting forces who opposed uncooperative leaders. As a consequence, Philippine politicians of all persuasions lobbied continuously in Washington. Democratic Filipinos advocated U.S. intervention to topple dictatorships, and dictators clamored for help against "communist" subversives. Washington alternated between favoring both, always in deference to the primary American aim of maintaining the two giant military bases on which American operations in East and Southeast Asia then depended. This kind of policy opportunism was responsible initially for supporting the Marcos dictatorship—and for toppling it later. Whenever long-run policies to enhance democracy abroad clashed with immediate

166

security and economic concerns, the Clinton administration has down-played the cosmopolitan-liberal nationalist belief that America lead a world fashioned by capitalism and democracy. As neither consensual knowledge nor united interest group and public opinion undergird this view, it remains as unsystematic as the ideological commitment to a policy primarily informed by a concern for the human rights of foreigners.

In the meantime there is no knowledge-based consensus on how foreign aid, trade, and industrial policy can and ought to be related to the creation of a post–cold war world order. Realist internationalists oppose the idea that the advancement of human rights ought to inform American policy, but they want active policies that control the trade in technologies that threaten to undermine arms control. Accommodationists want foreign aid linked to systematic policies of promoting investment that aid the attainment of sustainable development and to the building of democracies. Accommodationists want the United States to practice military-humanitarian intervention in foreign civil wars; realist internationalists oppose such policies as ineffective and dangerous. The result is the kind of opportunistic inconsistency we have documented.

Beyond the Nation-State?

There is a pervasive feeling that America is a world power "in decline." Intellectuals say so; many in the mass public seem to agree. Some note the loss of economic superiority over Japan and Europe and the tendency to overspend on defense. Others remark on the loss of the sense of global mission, on the reluctance to shoulder military burdens in crises that do not threaten the United States directly. Many opinion leaders deplore the apparent lack of "will to lead," the waning of the belief in American exceptionalism. Many note the erosion of the civil religion of continuous mutual adjustment among contending groups and interests and the heightened domestic clash of cultures as evidence of decline.

In 1990, only 75 percent of Americans were "proud to be American"; in the youngest age cohort the number declines to 68 percent. In 1994, 86 percent thought that young people can no longer take for granted that they will live better than their parents.[30] Wages for blue-collar workers have declined since 1987; those of white-collar males have remained flat. Median income in 1995 is below the level of 1980. Job losses due to industrial mergers, plant obsolescence, and the globalization of enterprises are rising. Only 3 percent of Americans earned more than $100,000 per year in 1992. The gap between the poorest and the richest is widening; the middle class appears to be shrinking.

[30] All statistics come from *San Francisco Examiner*, September 17, 1995, p. A-17.

Derationalization is evident in that both whites and nonwhites resent this situation and blame each other for it. The professional middle classes, increasingly exposed to unemployment because of the pace of technological innovation, resent having to pay taxes to provide a welfare safety net for the poorest, mostly nonwhites. The redistributive aspect of the liberal myth is under great challenge as a result. Pride in American society remains great, but respect for the government is eroding. The fall in legitimacy is patent. Decline and derationalization appear to go together. Says Seymour Martin Lipset: "There has been a definite falloff in political participation, in popular confidence in the political system and other major institutions, and in adherence to the traditional party system as well as a weakening of some of the voluntary institutions of civil society and—perhaps most important of all—of trust in one another. The rise of television and other new technologies appears to be exacerbating the difficulties."[31]

What responses to the evident decline of American nation-statehood can we imagine? There is evidence that isolationism is making a comeback, as people seek to halt decline by cutting back on global involvement. Both nativism and its opposite, multiculturalism, are on the rise and offer prescriptions for recovery. Both offer new authoritative institutions—albeit very different ones—as remedies; nativists want to strengthen the state and weaken social services, and multiculturalists favor more decentralization of power and more social services. All these formulas seek renewal in a revived liberal nation-state. But the source of the prescriptions is ideology, not consensual knowledge.

Cosmopolitan internationalists and especially accommodationists, however, think they learned that irreversible global ties make recourse to multilateral governance imperative. They believe that the solution lies in deeper ties with other countries and more reliance on international institutions that may end up in making the nation-state irrelevant. Finally, some scholars see a general pattern of organizational decentralization that has domestic and global implications. They marvel at the sprouting of large numbers of informal networks among business firms and advocacy groups that exist alongside subnational and supranational political and economic institutions. Such networks, too, throw in doubt the permanence of the nation-state as the answer to people's aspirations.

---

[31] Seymour Martin Lipset, "Malaise and Resiliency in America," *Journal of Democracy* (July 1995): 17. Answers to the question "Is the government run by a few big interests . . . or for the benefit of all the people?" were as follows: in 1964, 29 percent agreed that big interests run things; in 1980, 70 percent did, and in 1992, 80 percent did. The Louis Harris Poll reported in 1994 the lowest level of confidence ever in political leaders. Only one-half of eligible voters bother to cast their ballots in the 1990s. Yet the polls also report a great deal of residual optimism about the ability of individuals to better themselves by hard work.

*Internationalists and accommodationists, no more than isolationist-inclined na-
tivists and multiculturalists, have not come close to garnering the support necessary
to fashion a new national myth, to rerationalize America.* Neither multilateralism, nor massive decentralization, nor the rebirth of a vital nation-state
enjoy the ideological support to make any of them credible candidates
for a new myth. Yet there is evidence that multilateralism, the preferred
mode of behavior for accommodationists, is steadily gaining support.
Few military operations have been undertaken without United Nations
authorization since 1988. Presidents Clinton and Bush insisted that the
United States would not fight to repel aggression abroad, use troops for
humanitarian or peacekeeping tasks, or mount economic sanctions without the support of multilateral institutions. America insisted on the multilateral institutionalization of global trade and investment activities, as
in the World Trade Organization and the North American Free Trade
Association. Though moving more slowly on the ecological front, even
there more deference to multilateral rules and procedures is shown than
earlier.

Still, there is something unconvincing about this interpretation. There
is little evidence that these measures reflect a principled commitment to
a deeply learned lesson about international interdependence. They
smack of instrumentalism, of using multilateralism when it seems con-
venient, and to avoid it when not. The Clinton administration has sidestepped principled commitment to upgraded multilateral security
procedures; it has sought to limit American involvement in United
Nations operations. Yet, we must remember that eventual principled
commitment to new multilateral-institutional constraints on national
freedom of action may well develop as a result of initial steps that were
motivated by opportunism alone. But as long as enmeshment in multilateralism is still seen as a new means to some old objective, as an act of
adaptation, principled commitment is yet to come.

The following list suggests that public opinion is not dead set against
the learned progress of either multilateralization or the growth of decentralized networks. Almost half of Americans are willing to dispense
with the Canadian border; only 46 percent are absolutely opposed to
political union with Canada and/or Mexico; over 40 percent are willing
to get rid of the border with Mexico for economic reasons. On the other
hand, when cultural factors are brought to the fore, the enthusiasm for
abolishing the Canadian or Mexican borders wanes. The fact that 21
percent think of themselves as first and foremost part of the world or of
North America gives credence to the idea that the nation-state may be
obsolescent.[32]

[32] 1981 and 1990 *World Values Surveys*, as reported in Ronald Inglehart, Neil Nevitt, and

Survey item	1981(%)	1990(%)
Yes, proud to be an American	79	75
Youngest age group	—	68
Abolish borders with Canada		
Yes, in general		46
Yes, for economic reasons		42
No, for cultural reasons		60
Abolish borders with Mexico		
Yes, for economic reasons		41
No, for cultural reasons		52
Political union with Mexico/Canada		
Yes		32
Maybe		22
No		46
Belong to North America or world, as		
opposed to town, nation	10	21

The institutional cure for derationalization might be a dilution of familiar territorial modes of governance by turning to more functionally organized fora. If the solution to certain problems does not seem to lie in the hands of even the strongest nation-states, notably issues related to ecologically sustainable economic life, other institutions ought to be designed. In those areas there seems to be no alterative to the multilateralization of political life. America has made adaptations toward that end; but it did not fully learn that lesson as it struggled with reintegrating its own society. Is there some new formula that mixes reliance on national territorial institutions with functional and global nonterritorial ones? Is there a way of combining territorial with nonterritorial governance, cosmopolitanism with multiculturalism? Probably not, unless the types of liberalism that fashioned America's beliefs about its own exceptionalism yield to some new myth about national identity.

Miguel Basañez, *Convergence in North America* (in press). I thank the authors for sharing their manuscript with me.

CHAPTER FIVE

France

In the 1950s every elementary school student in France learned that

> The French nation has a body formed by the soil and the men who live on it; a soul formed by the history, language, tradition, and symbols. When men feel love for their nation it becomes a *patrie.*The State is the nation organized and administered. The Government is the directing organism of the State. A good citizen always seeks to become educated. He respects the law, pays his taxes loyally, accepts the military [service] obligation, and defends his *patrie* when it is threatened. A good citizen possesses the spirit of cooperation and mutual aid.[1]

Today French children are taught differently because these maxims are considered incompatible with liberal values and tight international interdependence. Before 1800 there was no public school system and no standard curriculum to teach any values to be held in common. Moreover, in 1800 more than half of the population was illiterate and unable to speak standard French. How did France come to be a nation-state? Why is it now losing some attributes of nationhood?

Before venturing answers, I restate the leading questions that inspire this book. Did the historical path that led France to nation-statehood— our Type A—determine the ideological choices that came to character-

I am greatly indebted for research assistance and criticism to Michael Gorges and Karen Adelberger. Stanley Hoffmann and Richard Herr read the manuscript and saved me from making some embarrassing mistakes. I gratefully acknowledge the financial assistance of the University of California Center for German and European Studies.

[1] These sentences are quoted from Laurence Wylie, *Village in the Vaucluse* (Cambridge: Harvard University Press, 1964), p. 207.

ize the nation? Did liberalism come to be the national myth *because* the state created the nation? All elites should have learned to practice diffuse reciprocity in their relations with each other to achieve rationalization, Did they? How did rationalization occur in the absence of a universal commitment to liberalism? Are contemporary French men and women outgrowing the nation-state? Are they doing so *because* of their belief in liberalism? If they are, they are acting out the hypothesis of cognitive and institutional evolution that underlies this book.

RATIONALIZATION AND LEARNING IN FRENCH HISTORY

The story shows that a non-nationally conscious elite began to build a centralized state in the seventeenth century and that a mobilized, but excluded, class, adhering to the same complex culture as the state-building elite, rebelled in 1789, took over the state, and centralized it further, thereby accelerating the social mobilization of the bulk of the rural population. That mobilization was not completed until the end of the nineteenth century. The mobilized were assimilated into the elite's culture, *but* that culture contained several political families, several sharply competing ideologies about the character and mission of the French nation. The state created a nation with a contested culture.

Liberalism was only one strain in that culture. It did not become the accepted French myth until the trauma of defeat by Germany and rule by Vichy were transcended, and it was not institutionalized in a constitution and routinized practices until the advent of the Fifth Republic.

France, therefore, was not fully rationalized until the 1960s. Her travail in deciding on a consensual identity is manifested in coups, revolutions, civil strife, uneven development, a bellicose foreign policy, imperial expansion and colonial empire, and two major wars won at such tremendous cost as to be more like defeats. France became a happy country with a relatively contented population when these episodes were found to be deplorable and their repetition unacceptable. The degrees of rationalization are shown on Table 5-1.

True social learning did not occur until the 1950s. All previous efforts at transcending ideological and institutional conflict, at bridging competing senses of the French self—the Restoration, the second Empire, the Third Republic after the Dreyfus Affair—were merely episodes that illustrate political adaptation. The recourse to imperialism and to halting social reform after 1880 were examples of policy adjustments that sought to evade a searching self-examination of why France was not fully rationalized. Only the post-1945 search for fundamental solutions qualifies as learning.

172

Table 5-1. Extent of rationalization, France, 1800–1995

	1800	1850	1900	1940	1950[a]	1980	1995
Political succession	No	No	Yes	No	Yes	Yes	Yes
National myth in education	No	No	No	No	Yes	Yes	Yes
Religious institutions	No	No	Some	Some	Yes	Yes	Yes
Civil religion	No	No	No	No	Some	Yes	Yes
Cultural uniformity	Yes	Yes	Yes	Yes	Yes	Some	Some
Official language accepted	Yes	Yes	Yes	Yes	Yes	Some	Yes
Income distribution	No	Some	Some	Some	Yes	Yes	Yes
Workers' organizations	No	No	Some	Some	Yes	Some	Some
Farmers' organizations	No	Some	Some	Yes	Yes	Yes	Yes
Payment of taxes	Some	Some	Some	Some	Some	Yes	Yes
Conscription accepted	Yes	Some	Yes	No	Yes	Yes	Yes
Fighting wars	Yes	Yes	Yes	Some	Some	Yes	Some
Administrative cohesion	Yes	Some	Yes	Some	Yes	Some	Some
Foreign policy	N/A	Yes	Yes	No	Some	Yes	Some
Peaceful change	N/A	No	Some	No	Some	Yes	Yes
Legitimacy	Yes	No	Some	No	Yes	Yes	Some
Total (%)	46	41	66	38	84	86	81

[a]In 1958 the score was 63.

Most important, French elites—now almost all liberals—learned that the nation-state is not capable of consolidating a fully rationalized society because it cannot simultaneously guarantee military security, political self-respect, and economic prosperity. As they learned to learn, many of them mastered the additional lesson that France is not so different after all from other advanced democratic countries, that all modern liberalisms are very similar. Learning this lesson went hand-in-hand with a reduction in nationalist fervor. One realization reinforced the other rather than causing the other. The supreme irony is that the steps toward European integration, taken for the instrumental reason of safeguarding the nation-state, produced the unintended consequence of demonstrating the weakness of that nation-state. French elites, however, then learned that one can rationalize further by seeking to profit from unintended consequences.

173

State Builds Nation by Generalizing a High Culture

The building of centralized state institutions with jurisdiction over the territory now known as France occurred before there was much social mobilization. When social mobilization accelerated, it took the form of the newly mobilized being assimilated into the flourishing high culture of the ruling elite. Social mobilization was completed in 1880; the older flourishing folk cultures were in full retreat by 1900. Nationalist sentiment among a few intellectuals was discernible by the beginning of the eighteenth century. More broadly based nationalist ideologies were in evidence by 1790. A consensual national myth prevailed intermittently after 1900, and by 1970 that myth was eroding because of the pull of European interdependence! Evidently, the elementary school children who had to memorize the lines quoted attached very different meanings to the words.[2] The history of the state-built French nation is mostly a history of self-doubt and internal struggle over rival identities.

The State as Centralizer and Mobilizer

In the domains ruled by the kings of France—a more accurate way to talk about French history before the eighteenth century than to call it "France"—political life was dominated by a long struggle between locally based nobles and Paris-based royal administrators. The towns generally sided with the king in exchange for being granted rights of self-rule and exemption from certain taxes. Feudal ways of organizing power and property competed with royal ways, with what became known as absolutism after 1600. Absolutist rulers, beginning with Francis I, but mostly at the hands of the Bourbons, built the French state. They dispensed with the services of the feudal deliberative assemblies. They created a corps of civil lawyers-administrators, thus diminishing the role of canon law and of the Catholic Church in government. They also called into being, albeit through the sale of office and not by means of a merit system, a civil service to which non-nobles could gain access. Louis XIV organized a large standing army instead of relying on feudal and mercenary recruitment anew for each war. Colbert's and Louvois's mercan-

---

[2] The lack of complete success of these pedagogic efforts stands revealed in the fact that in the 1980s, in some Protestant Cévennes villages, the Camisard revolt of 1702 is the main event of local importance the people commemorate, not more recent national events in which many villagers participated and some died. Similar stories are told about villages in Provence and Burgundy. James Fentress and Chris Wickham, *Social Memory* (Oxford: Oxford University Press, 1992), pp. 99–102.

tilism sought to centralize certain industrial activity in state hands, created a navy, and conquered foreign lands. Technological innovation was concentrated in state enterprises. Ideological uniformity in the territories conquered in the wars of Louis XIV and his original domains was sought by outlawing Protestantism after 1685 and by making a French form of Catholicism, Gallicanism, the state church. The Bourbons created the mystic hexagon that is today's France. Prior to the eighteenth century there was no France, just a patchwork of contractual relationships lacking any cultural homogeneity.

Centralization of administration is one thing; the assimilation of people feeling the impact of centralization into a common culture is quite another. Francis I in the 1530s initiated the policy of featuring the French of Touraine at the expense of Latin and of local dialects. He encouraged its use in universities and law courts, as he encouraged merchants and bourgeois professionals to resist the feudal claims of the nobility. His Bourbon successors were more concerned with the powers of the dynasty than with encouraging cultural homogeneity. Yet we have reason to believe that the official status of the Gallican church meant relatively little to most peasants.

Religion was of course, felt to be necessary to gain salvation, but it was also experienced as Sunday entertainment, a mode of socializing and escaping the humdrum of daily work, as an affirmation of local solidarity by way of ritual, rather than as an abstract rationalizer of people's thoughts and identities. Catholicism was readily abandoned by millions of Frenchmen, in all but name, after 1789, when more immediate rationalizing principles became available. It was only at the time of the Great Revolution that state-administered education became general, at least in principle. The Bourbons had previously catered to the needs of the state for skilled professionals and to the middle classes by setting up a number of professional schools, some of which later became the core of the *grandes écoles*.

During the eighteenth century the French middle classes were mobilized in the sense that their children acquired a good education and were taught to look to the state for advancement and public reward. They also learned that they had to pay for such mobility by buying their way into office, civil and military. Having done so, they remained the butt of the aristocrats' scorn by being called cobblers and soapboilers. The bourgeoisie in the eighteenth century could make money and could ape the nobility in taste, manner, and pretense; it could not gain equality with the nobility in other ways. It was assimilated into the values of the elite's culture without being able to enjoy all of these values, without being allowed to forget its inferiority.

The Limits of Social Mobilization before 1790

The Bourbons' ministers rationalized French administration by seeking to create a royal domain with uniform rules for all the provinces and towns of the kingdom. Their success was largely confined to paper. Absolutist rule was more rhetoric than reality. The nobility could not be taxed; neither could the Church. The king's need for money (mostly to pay for wars) caused the sale of many redundant offices, with the result that absolutist administration was often a shambles, in addition to being corrupt because incumbents sought to recoup the expenses of the bribes they had to pay to obtain their appointments. Most villagers rarely felt the presence of administrators and resented them when they did. The victory of absolutism did not bring with it the end of local "nations," *pays, seigneuries,* fiefs, and parishes as the major foci of people's identities. Special rights and exemptions once purchased by a town or a guild or a corporation often had to be repurchased, a practice not likely to endear the royal administrators to the populace.

Tocqueville was exaggerating unpardonably in his description of the *ancien régime* as successfully centralized. Turgot, as late as 1775, could write that "neither the king nor his ministers, nor the intendants of the provinces, nor yet their subdelegates, could acquire a knowledge of the country."[3] Social mobilization was confined to those who eventually rebelled in 1789: the educated bourgeoisie of the provincial towns and of Paris, those who had joined the elite culture but had been refused full assimilation into it, and those who considered themselves to be victims of fiscal oppression.

Nationalist Sentiment before 1790

Montesquieu remarked that he was a human being by nature and a Frenchman only by accident. The *philosophes* of the Enlightenment were not French nationalists. They considered themselves the bearers of a message with universal scope, and they thought of their work as cosmopolitan, as evidenced by their widespread service at many European courts, including Russia's. Even though they thought of themselves as the prophets of a new age, the makers of new cognitive tools, and the advocates of political liberalism as the expression of both, they gave no special role to France in the drama. They certainly claimed a civilizing mission for themselves, but the fact that the mission was being carried

[3] Quoted in Reinhard Bendix, *Kings or People* (Berkeley: University of California Press, 1978), p. 338.

out in French and originated in Paris remained, for the participants, an accident of history.

Yet the accident encouraged later aggressive liberal advocates to claim a civilizing mission for France-as-a-corporate-entity, just as the Capetian kings had claimed to be the heirs not only of the Gauls but also of many other revered ancient civilizations. Later French dynasties persisted in claiming the same legitimation. The Physiocrats, while not nationalist either, nevertheless advocated policies of economic development and organizations that implied more centralization and mobilization. Jean-Jacques Rousseau, although he did not make his case for civil religion specific to France, nevertheless furnished a model to those who later did claim it for the French nation.

Evidence of nationalist sentiment, however, can be seen in the political strife of the middle of the eighteenth century that engaged some of the *philosophes* and many of their bourgeois (and even noble) followers. This strife involved the role of the *Parlement* of Paris in ensuring the victory of Gallicanism over papal claims to doctrinal superiority (as well as over the Jesuits) and in protecting some of the claims of the bourgeoisie. The *Parlement* won its fight with the king, the pope, and the Jesuit order in reaffirming the legal superiority of certain Gallican-Jansenist theological claims. It also prevailed on several financial issues. In fact the *Parlements*, though largely staffed by lawyers of noble descent also included some bourgeois judges, functioned as an institution transcending and uniting these classes, using by 1760 such terms as "citoyen, loi, patrie, constitution, nation, droit de la nation, cri de la nation" in its decisions.[4] The mobilized, but politically unassimilated, claimed the legal equality of all French "nationals" (meaning educated and propertied men). Equality, in turn, implied *popular* sovereignty, not the sovereignty of the king, and hence necessitated a method of ascertaining the will of the people; this implied the need for elections and for institutionalized representation of the citizens. The Abbé Sieyès advanced the additional argument that a society free of privilege cannot entrust government to any class that had enjoyed special privileges before: the right to be represented and to govern lay exclusively with the victims of discrimination, the bourgeoisie. The essential formula for liberal nationalism was in place before the actual outbreak of the Revolution. Moreover, the demands were formulated in a state already in existence, for a people already living within the borders of an entity possessing an identity proclaimed by the King *and* his opponents, even though that identity was experienced only by a minority.

Apparently, the example of Britain and of the United States was a

4. Ibid., p. 357.

powerful one for the early carriers of nationalist sentiment. Many members of the nobility, especially Montesquieu, admired the institutionalized parliamentary role of their British colleagues. Yet, influenced by the presence of Jacobite refugees in France, many also deplored what they saw as British factionalism and rule by clique. Turgot admired Britain's political institutions; but he also came to admire America's, as did many others who equated French assistance to the rebelling colonies as identification with liberty and opposition to royal privilege. Condorcet in 1786 praised America as the example that demonstrated the unity of political and scientific progress. As long as the nobility was still widely seen as something to be admired, Britain was the leading exemplar for French dissidents. As the demand for equality and the abolition of privilege became the main theme later in the century, the American example became the paramount one for the dissatisfied segments of the socially mobilized population, and the Marquis de Lafayette was to become a hero of the French Revolution.

CLASHING IDEOLOGIES, UNSTABLE INSTITUTIONS, 1789–1875

Uneven Mobilization and Slow Modernization

The general picture of uneven rates of modernization—and differing perceptions of interest and of grievance—is illustrated by Charles Tilly's study of the Revolution and Counterrevolution in the Vendée. The parts favoring the Revolution were also those that produced agricultural goods for commercial export; these regions were more urban, relied more heavily on merchants and lawyers, were more exposed to administrators sent from Paris than the rest of the Vendée. Here we find the patriotic clubs, the revolutionary committees, the volunteer national guard units, and a clergy rapidly declining in influence. Counterrevolutions occurred in the sections *unevenly urbanized*, where a textile industry was being rapidly introduced and where the weavers also suffered from wildly fluctuating employment; where the bulk of agriculture was of the subsistence variety; where the local curé was in charge; and where nonresident bourgeois bought noble estates *and* claimed the privileges extracted by the former owners. The spark was the introduction of military conscription and the clergy's obligation to swear allegiance to the secular state. When it became a common experience to post mass grievances, to demand redress, and when all this was symbolized by the calling of the Estates-General (and their subsequent transformation into a National Assembly), the more urbanized parts of France responded by turning to Paris, whereas isolated rural districts and areas undergoing contradictory and

uneven rates of changes tended to respond by devoting newly liberated
political energies to local issues alone.

Unevenness was a fact until the end of the nineteenth century,
whether we examine internal communications, education and literacy,
internal trade and migration, and industrial development. The French
state realized early the importance of building national highways, but it
was only after 1860 that the network was extensive enough to ensure the
movement of produce to urban markets, the migration of peasants to
the city and back to their homes, and the ready access of rural children
to schools. Widespread migration from villages to towns did not antedate
the building of railroads, which began in earnest in the 1850s. Only then
could one expect the ready diffusion of political ideas and ideologies,
the spread of urban politics to the rural areas where most of the French
still resided. Far from being inert and unresponsive, peasants took advantage of improved roads and railroads to market their products com-
mercially. Concurrently, nutrition improved. Peasants generally stopped
to take for granted that the order of things was given, that innovation
was impossible. Initially unwilling to accept the metric system, peasants
in central France in the 1880s made the changes because the merchants,
landowners, and notaries they had to deal with insisted on metric measures and monetary units.

Fragmented Liberalism Stumbles

None of the post-1789 French myth making can alter the fact that prior
to the seventeenth century there was no "France" and that before 1880
there was no cultural homogeneity in the state called France. If the completion of social mobilization is to be taken as the benchmark of potential nationhood, that point was not reached by France before the advent
of the belligerently liberal Third Republic. If nation-statehood is taken
to mean the attainment of a rationalized polity, the crucial date is 1962,
the end of the French colonial empire.

The Revolution of 1789, however, was the beginning of the story of
filling the state with national content. It also gave rise to two opposing
interpretations of the liberal ideology that were not reconciled until
Léon Blum's Popular Front of 1936; I call them "Whig" as opposed to
"Jacobin" liberal nationalism.[5] Jacobins stressed that France is a nation
devoted to eliminating inequality by getting rid of the nobility and the

---

[5] The term *Jacobin* normally refers to the Jacobin Party, which vied with the "Mountain"
and the Girondin Party for dominance between 1789 and 1795. More generally, and this
is my usage, it refers to radical egalitarian liberalism as against a more conservative
("Whig") liberalism respectful of private property and of social differences. In French
history the Whig variety is often referred to as "moderate republicans."

clergy, to reason and justice, requiring the creation of popularly elected government at all levels and to a secular religion instead of Catholicism. The secular religion, inspired by Rousseau's writings, soon acquired its own festivals, temples, ritual, and calendar.

Jacobins took their Rousseau to extremes. The general will alone had the right to rule, and the Jacobin Party, after 1793, saw itself as the sole legitimate expression of that will. As for other states, Jacobins believed that the Revolution had the sacred duty to liberate from feudal, monarchical, and clerical tyranny other peoples still afflicted with these historical evils. Jacobins believed in exporting the revolution by force, if necessary. Their centralizing organic vision of France is symbolized by the slogan "The Nation, one and indivisible." It rejects the political legitimacy of all private interests, collective or individual. As the Abbé Grégoire's Declaration of the Rights of Peoples put it: "The only government conforming with the rights of nations is a government based on equality and liberty. Undertakings against the liberty of a people are an attack on all peoples. Leagues with the object of offensive war and treaties which can violate the interests of a people are an attack on mankind. A people may undertake a war to defend its sovereignty, its liberty and its property."[6]

Whig liberals did not share this enthusiasm. They ruled after 1795, and again after 1849 and 1871, in reaction against the excessive devotion to equality and fraternity of the Jacobins. Whig liberals wanted those reforms of the revolutions of 1789, 1830, 1848, and 1870 that also safeguarded middle-class property right, limited direct democracy by preventing the direct election of most deputies, and avoided rule by organized political parties. Whig liberals wanted democracy and liberty for the propertied middle class alone, and they sometimes proved willing to sacrifice democracy when mass-based parties seemed to threaten property rights. Whig nationalists did not advocate wars of liberation in Europe. They shared the Jacobins' radicalism only when a resurgent right would threaten previously acquired political gains; this happened after 1824, when Charles X sought to reverse the Napoleonic institutional compromises and during the Dreyfus Affair at the turn of the twentieth century.

Both brands of liberals, and even some of their monarchist and socialist critics, agreed that France, as a *grande nation*, had a special mission, as representative of the most advanced form of Western culture, to diffuse its genius as widely as possible, the famous *mission civilisatrice*. Being French had nothing to do with language or ethnicity; being French meant being opposed to church and nobility, to institutionalized in-

[6] Articles 8, 15, 16, 17 of the Declaration.

equality and sanctified superstition. To be French was to be a "patriot," to identify with a *patrie* that subscribed to the values of liberty, equality, and fraternity.[7]

Syncretist Challengers

The French right was never a single or simple movement. Before the advent of the Third Republic it included monarchists anxious to undo the changes of 1789 (often dubbed *ultras*); these people professed a restorative-syncretist ideology. There were also more moderate monarchists who subscribed to a traditional syncretism that accepted a measure of equality and popular participation. Moreover, the followers of the Bonaparte family, and later the supporters of Napoleon III, professed a more populist syncretism that accepted a good deal of equality, although they rejected republican institutions. Finally, at times Whig liberals, when sorely tried by their Jacobin rivals, would side with traditional syncretists.

After 1871, all were strongly anti-German and made the recovery of Alsace-Lorraine the centerpiece of their foreign policy. They all spoke of a French essence that antedates the Revolution and that ought to be cherished, particularly in the form of the unity of a decentralized state with the Catholic Church. But they disagreed on almost everything else, as shown on Table 5-2.

Fragile Institutions

The revolutionary overthrow of the ancien régime inspired sweeping institutional changes. State administration was standardized and centralized in Paris, all feudal rules, courts, and fees were abolished, church land was nationalized, internal barriers to trade were scrapped, and all restraints on free economic enterprise (including artisans guilds) were removed. Elections, albeit with a restricted electorate, produced legislative bodies. Napoleon I abolished republican practices and organs but intensified the work of legal centralization and standardization. The Restoration regime—appropriately so named—illustrates the restorative-syncretist institutional design. After 1821, its government adopted a number of measures that clearly sought to recreate the golden prerevolutionary age. Nobles dispossessed by the Revolution were compensated financially. The press was subjected to severe censorship, and sacrilege was made punishable by death. The Church was restored to its

---

[7] The identification of "patriot" with "nationalist" was pointed out by E. J. Hobsbawm in *Nations and Nationalism since 1780* (London: Cambridge University Press, 1990), pp. 20, 87. He also shows that the term had the same meaning in the United States and in the Netherlands in the liberal revolution of 1783.

Table 5-2. Varieties of non-Jacobin nationalism in France, 1800–1944

Variable	Whig Liberalism	Traditional Syncretism	Restorative Syncretism
Core values of the Revolution of 1789	Reject notions of equality and fraternity, accept some liberties	Reject all; restore monarchy, but may be limited monarchy	Reject all; restore feudal monarchy
Role of church	Tolerate church as symbolic state church; limited role in schools	Catholic church is state church its values constitute the civil religion of France; church controls content of education at all levels	
Postrevolutionary administrative organizations	Retain centralization and expert civil service	Decentralize somewhat weakened state	Restore ancient provinces, destroy centralized state
Industrialism	Favor it, if mercantilistic in emphasis	Suspicious about it	Reject it
Foreign policy	Pragmatically anti-German	Violently anti-German after 1871, revanchism is core until 1940	
Imperialism	Strongly in favor for compensatory reasons; associationist after 1900	Social imperialism, seen as supporting key army and church interests	Essentially opposed because seen as hindering above
Social structure preferred	Hierarchic, but accept universal suffrage	Stress on hierarchy, order, limits on popular participation	Romantic feudalism
Examples	"Opportunist" republicans, in Third Republic	Orleanists, 1850–1900; Boulangists and Bonapartists, 1871–1914; Army leadership in Third Republic; elements in Vichy government (except foreign policy)	Restoration regime, 1821–1830; Action Française in Third Republic; elements in Vichy government (except for foreign and imperial policy)

pre-1789 position and put in charge of education. Teachers and professors not approved by the local bishop were removed from office. Throne and altar were truly joined in almost every way. Divorce, legal under the Napoleonic Code, was abolished.

The Restoration of 1815 reversed the practices of generous political participation introduced by the Revolution, thus setting the scene for the intense interclass conflict of the next century. The electorate under the restored Bourbons was a mere 100,000 wealthy landowners and in-dustrialists, both groups the heirs of revolutionary land confiscations and Napoleon I's Continental System, that is, bourgeois who had done well and former nobles. The Orleanist regime enfranchised another one hun-dred thousand (France's population had reached thirty-five million by 1848), but not even members of the volunteer and largely bourgeois National Guard were permitted to vote. The revolutionary government of 1848 suffered from conflict among the representatives of the classes who headed it, pitting workers against Whig republicans, socialists against liberals. The dictatorship of Napoleon III enjoyed the support of many bourgeois liberals and of mobilized peasants afraid of the newly mobilized workers.

Rationalization was slow to come to French society because self-conscious segments of French people continued to define their identities in almost mutually exclusive terms for a long time. Peasant and towns-man, worker and bourgeois, catholic and secularist (Marxist, anarchist, or humanist) continued to oppose one another in bitter encounters as the uneven process of modernization continued.

THE POORLY RATIONALIZED THIRD REPUBLIC

Completion of Social Mobilization, Slow Modernization

By 1855, all prefectures were linked to Paris by telegraph lines. The prepaid postage stamp was introduced in 1849; in 1860 its use amounted to only five stamps per person per year, but on the eve of World War I that rate had gone up to forty! By 1919, one-quarter of French people lived outside the department of their birth, whereas that number had only been 11 percent in 1860. The Third Republic, after 1877, was de-termined to make rural France part of the nation. It launched the Frey-cinet Plan of railroad building, which not only made French steel production grow at 8 percent per year (on par with Germany's rate and much faster than Britain's), but also tripled the number of railroad work-ers to 223,000 by 1881, "steady jobs for steady people—in the long run an influence more subversive of traditional institutions," says Eugen We-ber.[8] Schools were irrelevant for many rural folks until the end of the century because children were needed for farm work. Again it was im-provement of communications and the perceived need to acquire the skills needed for modern life that provided opportunity and motivation to take advantage of the Republic's compulsory and secular school. In

[8] Eugen Weber, *Peasants into Frenchman* (Stanford: Stanford University Press, 1976), p. 210.

1860, one's local native *pays* and the *patrie* was the same thing for most peasants, and everything else was considered "foreign soil." Only in cities did people understand the idea of a larger nation, independent of direct human interaction. But by 1900 that idea had a much larger audience. What had happened to explain the change?

The compulsory, universal, free, and fully secular school, though decreed in principle in the 1790s and redecreed several times thereafter, did not become a reality until the 1880s. The schools established then by a liberal nationalist government, were staffed with loyal liberal nationalist republicans recruited from the new teacher corps. The new Ecole Normale Supérieure had the task of staffing *lycées* and universities with loyal republicans who had the explicit mission of socializing all French people into secular nationalism. These reforms professionalized the teaching corps; they made teachers into role models for what all French people were to become. The language of instruction was French alone, even though it was not the mother tongue of one-quarter of the citizens (1863). In twenty-four of the eighty departments more than half of the communes did not speak French. Apart from German, Breton, Basque, Catalan, Corsican, Provençal, and Flemish, a number of *patois* of French were also spoken. Many more French people did not write or read standard French; nor were they able to communicate any but the simplest thoughts in French, even if they were officially bilingual. The use of patois and of non-French languages was prohibited in the new schools. Familiarity with French spread as a result, especially as girls began to attend school regularly.[9]

Increased mobility spurred the incentives to learn French. So did industrialization. The movement of vast numbers of refugees southward in 1914 diffused a knowledge of French, as did military service in units not drawn from any single locality. Knowing French became a matter of pride for peasants by 1900, as they realized that being confined to patois condemned one to a country bumpkin's life.

Many Nationalist Ideologies, Weak National Myth

The division of liberal republicans into a Jacobin and Whig factions continued after the defeat of the Second Empire in 1870, although the

---

[9] Weber also shows that religious feasts in rural areas fell into disuse after 1870 and that local festivals fade out as July 14 becomes the national holiday and the Marseillaise the national anthem (1880). Oral recitations and singing in patois at nighttime communal meetings fell into disuse, no new folksongs were written as literacy in French increased, itinerant booksellers visited many villages, and the Paris newspapers achieved a provincial readership. Other scholars believe that most of these events occurred somewhat earlier and that rural France had been integrated by 1851.

Jacobin wing was at first discredited by the excesses of the Paris Commune. While disagreeing on the questions of equality and inclusion of all Frenchmen in the polity, they agreed in seeking to displace the Catholic Church as a political force by bringing about the full separation of church and state. They hoped that compulsory, free, and secular education would produce a homogeneous republican culture. They wanted to limit the power of the nobility in the armed forces. They also agreed on the desirability of industrialization, though the Whigs opposed all state intervention in the process. After the Dreyfus Affair, the ideological position of Jacobin nationalism was increasingly taken over by the Socialist Party as it abandoned Marxist internationalism and, after 1918, left it to the Communist Party.

Strongly committed to Catholicism, the traditionalists, during their rule in the 1870s, reintroduced press censorship and gave the clergy the task of stressing proper French moral values in the school system. Train fares were reduced for pilgrims visiting shrines, and the basilica of Sacré-Coeur was built in Paris to expiate for the crimes committed by the Commune. Says D. W. Brogan of the military at this time: "There was a natural connection between the defeat of 1870 and the renewal of colonial activity. As the hopes of immediate revenge grew less, the more energetic Army and Navy officers became bored with a life of preparation for an ordeal and an achievement that never came. It was this boredom, frankly admitted, that drove one of the two greatest of French empire builders to seek service in Tonkin."[10] Traditional nationalist themes were cherished by Boulangists and Bonapartist during the early years of the Third Republic. After that, they continued to be accepted by much of the clergy and the officer corps, as well as by rural notables and some of the urban lower middle class. It was in the Vichy regime that this point of view found its last lease on life.

The most prominent—if unsuccessful—champion of restorative nationalism in the Third Republic was the Action Française. Popular mostly among students, its founder and ideologist, Charles Maurras (admirer of Maurice Barrès), tirelessly inveighed against the four "estates" that conspired to corrupt France: Jews, Freemasons, Protestants, and *métèques* (foreigners). He believed in the uncorrupted loyalties of "the people" while detesting the ruling bourgeoisie, capitalism, and industrialism. The Catholic Church and Catholic values defined all that was truly French. Like the fascist nationalists of the 1930s, Action Française venerated action for its own sake. It also celebrated provincial traditions as the essence of the nation. Along with the Church, Maurras worshipped the army and therefore was a prominent anti-Dreyfusard irrespective of the

---

[10] D. W. Brogan, *France under the Republic* (New York: Harper Brothers, 1940), p. 217.

merits of Captain Dreyfus's case. In 1932 the Action Française—then in decline—still claimed 70,000 members, as opposed to 170,000 Socialist and communist *militants*. For Maurras, "being a Frenchman is, indeed, a matter of heredity, not merely of will, but it is not a matter of blood, of race. To be French is to put France before all else, to feel in the French fashion, to be at home in the physical and mental atmosphere of France and to feel uprooted elsewhere . . . to have a French mind and a French heart."[11]

During the 1930s there grew up in France a large number of fascist leagues, but no single party and no single leader, though Jacques Doriot came close to being one. All preached action for the sake of action, venerated heroism, and aped the style of the German Nazis. Their targets were Jews, capitalists, bourgeois liberals, parliamentarians. They preached defeatism in any struggle with Germany and demanded what Vichy eventually gave them, an alliance with Germany and the extermination of the Jews.

Imperialism as Rationalizer

Even though republican institutions served as a rationalizing glue only intermittently, the ideology and the institution of imperialism clearly did. The Jacobin ideology contained an explicit theme that insisted on the duty to universalize liberal values: France was to be the instrument for establishing civilization and progress among those unfortunates who belonged to lesser cultures, pagan, Islamic, or Buddhist. That theme was reinforced by the republican-secular liberalism of the rulers of the Third Republic who created the new empire. But it was a sentiment that could easily be shared by militarists, monarchists, and Catholics and that eventually took the form of the same kind of social imperialist doctrine we encounter elsewhere in late-nineteenth-century Europe. Today liberal republicans and Catholic reformers oppose imperial rule; but, in the context of France's civilizing mission, they easily made their peace with it around the turn of the century.

But, first, imperialism had to be sold to a skeptic public which was more concerned with revanche against the Prussians. The actual work of exploring and conquering West and Equatorial Africa was done by military commanders and missionaries not really under the control of Paris. Their works tended to be dismissed by middle-class politicians as the toys of aristocrats and priests. It took the systematic propaganda of a group of liberal parliamentary leaders to persuade their followers that the imperial role was a proper one, a role enabling France once again

[11] D. W. Brogan, *French Personalities and Problems* (London: Hamilton, 1946), p. 60.

to show its greatness, its right to lead and civilize, after the humiliation of 1870. It was this group that, in the 1880s, succeeded in equating patriotism with imperial greatness, not with revenge against Germany. Algeria in particular became a symbol of compensation for the loss of Alsace-Lorraine, especially because many Alsatians decided to move to North Africa rather than become German citizens. As economic and clerical arguments favoring colonization became acceptable toward 1900, the earlier liberal propaganda in favor of imperialism found a receptive popular audience. No single political party was the main advocate. There flourished instead an unstable "colonial party" that embraced all these arguments and that cut across regular party lines.

How could Jacobins make their peace with the discrimination and inequality of colonial rule? The policy of "assimilation" provided the answer. Assimilation meant that, even though the present colonial populations might be primitive and poor, under French tutelage they would eventually become black or tan Frenchmen living overseas, but otherwise indistinguishable from civilized whites. The Republic One and Indivisible would acquire a far-flung citizenry who would incorporate the very values that made France great. Assimilation was the French equivalent of Britain's white man's burden.

But preciously little assimilation actually took place. The colonies became important for reasons that had little to do with the diffusion of Jacobin values. Liberals worried about the declining birthrate and industrial stagnation relative to Germany. They distrusted the Socialists and the trade unions because left-wing pacifism clashed with anti-German revanchist sentiments. The left was stigmatized as *apatride*. Therefore, the argument that imperialism and colonialism were necessary to demonstrate the progressive potential of the French nation was popular in liberal circles, as was the companion theme that a colonial empire was needed to reconcile the working class to the nation. The racism contained in social imperialist doctrine served as a justification for jettisoning the policy of assimilation in favor of an "associationism" that allowed for the continued exploitation of "inferior" races, notably in Algeria. After 1914 the need for military and industrial manpower became paramount. Considerable investment had take place in North Africa and in Indochina after 1900. Settlers and planters had moved overseas in appreciable numbers. Catholic schools and hospitals had been established. A mighty colonial military and civil machinery had grown up in which many young Frenchmen who had no promising careers in sight at home were able to find dignified employment requiring little work. After 1918, the mood toward the empire changed. Now the demand was for the *mise en valeur des colonies*, their systematic exploitation for the benefit of the metropole. This appeared to be the political consensus among the elite during the interwar years, but the bulk of the population, apart from deriving some emotional satisfaction from the empire and sending some of its sons and daughters there, seemed to be generally indifferent.

Institutions of National Uniformity

State, Civil, or Secular Religion? The Jacobins made the Cult of Reason into a state religion, but Napoleon I eliminated that innovation in favor of a return to a state-controlled Catholicism. His nephew sought to limit the role of the church in public life without being overtly anti-clerical. The Third Republic liberals dealt ruthlessly with the church, particularly its schools. After the Dreyfus Affair the clergy was tarred with the right-wing brush. Third Republic liberals claimed to represent democracy, and the clergy was identified with militarism and reaction. In 1880 the Jesuit order was again expelled from France, and in 1901 many other orders were banned as well. When the full separation of church and state was decreed in 1905 members of orders were forbidden to teach. Education, particularly the training of Frenchmen to become citizens of the republic, was to be a purely secular enterprise. The elimination of public prayers, secularization of hospitals and cemeteries, and the legalization of divorce were all decreed before 1900. Moreover the military service obligation of priests and seminarians was affirmed. Until 1945, liberal nationalism was by definition anticlerical, a situation aided by the increasing disregard for Catholic rules on the part of a majority of the French. Baptism was no longer being practiced by all; other sacraments were being disregarded, too. Catholicism stripped of its association with the ancien régime, once the church was disestablished, might have become a true civil religion if the republicans' quasi-religious veneration of their secular nationalism had been less strident. As it was, neither succeeded in furnishing the basis for a civil religion.

The Third Republic's universalization of free, compulsory, secular education aimed at more than anticlericalism. Along with instilling respect for hard work, property, duty, order, cleanliness, authority, and other bourgeois virtues, the schools also taught patriotism and devotion to civic obligations, especially military service. Jules Simon, minister of public instruction in 1871, forbade the teaching of nineteenth century history because, as it could not be presented objectively, it would give a platform to monarchists and conservatives. "Restons dans la science," he said.[12] After 1871 geography also was used to teach patriotism and regret for

---

[12] Quoted in Allan Mitchell, "German History in France," *Journal of Contemporary History* (July 1967), p. 83.

the loss of Alsace-Lorraine, a part of what became known as "national pedagogy."

A multicultural liberal republic? The Third Republic's system of secular nationalist education made no concessions whatever to regions of France in which French was not the main vernacular. Education meant induction into French culture by means of the French language. Children who sought to speak Basque, Flemish, or German were punished by their teachers. Government offices in Brittany, the Pyrenees, and Alsace operated exclusively in French. No concessions to local culture were made in Corsica and Languedoc. The liberal state pretended that soon all would be French.

The commitment to the creation of a single French culture by no means precluded systematic discrimination in the administration of the colonial empire. French nationals who moved to "overseas France" retained all the rights of French citizens. Members of the indigenous population, however, could attain fully "assimilated" status only if they received a French education or served the French state in a special capacity, such as military service or membership in the teaching corps. Failing this status, which was attained by very few other than veterans of military service, the local population was subject to the *indigénat*, a legal status of permanent inferiority and special obligations.

Algeria was a special case. Because of the heavy influx of European settlers, it was made part of metropolitan France by the middle of the nineteenth century, organized into three regular French *départements*. In principle, all who lived there—Europeans, Arabs, Berbers—were French citizens. However, this status was denied to Muslims who declined to abjure their religion. Hence the great majority of the indigenous population lacked the rights of French citizens. Even though institutionalized inferiority was decried by the Socialists and Communists in metropolitan France, various efforts to weaken it were repeatedly foiled by the settler delegates in the French parliament in the last decades of the Third Republic.

Institutions of National Inclusion

France did not adopt comprehensive social welfare legislation until the eve of World War II because of sharp class confrontations. Napoleon III attempted to introduce some social insurance, after the French (like the British) discovered that they had a very serious problem of pauperism in the working class. Even many employed workers did not earn enough to feed their families. The Third Republic at first undid these reforms in deference to the argument that the state should stay out of the economy. A standardized system of state-financed family allowances did not come into existence until 1931. Modest medical insurance, private but state-subsidized, appeared in 1893. State-financed pensions for the very poorest strata became law in 1905. But a comprehensive health, accident, and pension insurance system did not appear until the 1930s. Even then, it did not include unemployment insurance because this was still thought to encourage idleness and prevent workers from adapting to cyclical changes. The current system of generous and comprehensive social insurance dates from 1946–56. Until then, the intensity of class conflict kept the state from acting as bourgeois majorities in the legislatures proved unwilling to shoulder the financial burdens. It took the catastrophe of war and fascism to change their minds.

French leaders were slow to incorporate the poor in the process of modernizing the country. During most of the nineteenth century all of the working class and much of the peasantry were excluded from wielding any kind of economic power. Industrial workers were a special target of suspicion for the state and the upper middle class. The governments of the Revolution had outlawed all "associations," a prohibition that remained on the books under successor regimes, although the law allowed the formation of mutual aid societies. Strikes were illegal and were often suppressed by the army until the reign of Napoleon III. The Third Republic did not allow the formation of industrial unions until 1884. The civil code discriminated against workers. Each worker had to carry a certificate that identified his or her place of work. Employers and mayors had to sign it to prove that the worker was free of debt and other obligations. "The law finally ceased to look upon the industrial workers as a dangerous person, needing careful surveillance" as late as 1890.[13]

Things did not truly improve for trade unions until World War I when dependence on the industrial work force and on its happiness was fully recognized by the governing elite. In addition to the beginnings of social legislation, the embryo of what was later to be known as corporatism became discernible. Unions were asked to comanage the new social insurance law by serving on tripartite committees determining benefits. This set the scene for union service on other state-sanctioned consultative bodies. As a result, unions dropped their opposition to various government subsidies to private unemployment funds, even in the absence of official unemployment insurance. By the 1930s bureaucrats, though perhaps not yet employers, were used to the presence of workers' representatives at high-level discussions concerning the economy. The Vichy government practiced corporatism by appointing its own union leaders (and persecuting the elected one); the Fourth Republic inaugurated the

---

[13] Theodore Zeldin, *France 1848–1945*, vol. 1 (Oxford: Clarendon 1973–77), p. 199.

system of formally including representatives of all the major national trade union federations in the planning procedure.

Until the period of postwar reconstruction, French economic life had been dominated by small factories, many small shopkeepers, and a large peasantry tilling many tiny family-owned farms. The core motivation of these entrepreneurs was to survive without having to compete in the market, to limit the workings of the market. Organizations representing the *petite bourgeoisie* and the peasantry functioned as normal interest groups: they sought to influence legislation, especially fiscal measures, to benefit their members. Most governments of the Third Republic catered to these concerns. Formal "incorporation" of the lower middle class was accomplished because it was this class that furnished the bulk of the electors for the ruling parties.

If the economy lacked progressive cohesion, the state administration displayed a great deal of it. Napoleon I introduced a merit-based civil service recruited exclusively from graduates of specialized elite schools in which students were drilled in the spirit of scientific inquiry. His successors retained the system, though they weakened it be stressing the loyalty of appointees to the regime and allowing for a patronage-based "track" alongside the merit system. These features were eliminated by the Third Republic, which, by 1899, completely relied on a system based exclusively on merit and given autonomy from politics by subordinating it to the *Conseil d'Etat.* This choice corresponds to the republican commitment to equality of opportunity regardless of social origin and to efficiency in administration.

Institutions of Defense

The public's commitment to the strength of the state in its encounters with foreign enemies is a strong indicator of rationalization. The revolution of 1789 created rights that did *not* include full electoral equality for all male citizens; that right became real only in 1848. Universal military service became a duty in the 1790s, but before 1873 the middle class could buy exemptions. Until 1848 the middle class served in the voluntary National Guard (a part-time militia used mostly for controlling riots); after the revolution of 1848 the ranks of the National Guard were opened to all classes, but its appeal remained largely urban. Before 1873 only the poorest served in the regular army, which was a subject of general contempt. After the universalization of the duty to serve, however, the army became an object of honor and respect for all classes, even the peasantry, which was mobilized socially in part because of everyone's exposure to conscription. After 1870 the army became a major avenue of social advancement, higher living standards, and a move to urban jobs after the completion of the period of service. Toward the end of the century Frenchmen voted in large numbers and increasingly identified with national political parties. Electoral abstention averaged 23 percent for all of France between 1898 and 1914; but the average was over 35 percent in Corsica, Provence, Pyrenees, and Savoy. Yet we know that the proverbial wisdom about Frenchmen and taxes was correct: tax evasion in France was and remained a major sport. However, the willingness to fight and suffer enormous casualties in the trench warfare of 1914–18 is proof that the civic obligation to defend the *patrie* was taken very seriously indeed. Despite the carping of the monarchists and conservatives and the beginnings of a socialist opposition to liberal republicanism, the ideology of liberal nationalism, as it worked its way into the minds of French people through the major institutions created after 1870, was consensual enough to see France through the trauma of World War I even without a fully accepted national myth.

Something like a liberal-led consensus about foreign policy emerged in France after the end of the Dreyfus Affair, only to evaporate again after 1923. That policy consisted of preparing for the probable war with Germany, not only over Alsace-Lorraine but also competing colonial claims in Africa and Morocco. Preparation for that war justified the imperial policy so criticized by groups that wanted to concentrate on the Rhine. Republican liberals resisted suggestions from the Socialists that domestic social issues be tackled, preferring to rest their popularity on a foreign policy consensus. That policy even justified the otherwise bizarre alliance with a reactionary and tyrannical tsar. The consensus gave France the *Union Sacrée* governments of the World War I period and resulted in peace terms that had as their objective the permanent crippling of Germany as a potential enemy.

By 1923 it was clear that this objective could not be attained, because both the United States and Britain declined to underwrite French security with long-term alliances. At that point the consensus disappeared. The moderate center opted for reconciliation with Germany and reliance on the League of Nations; the right preferred a policy of armed superiority and indefinite confrontation of Germany. As the Nazis took over Germany, the left and center oscillated between policies for resisting fascism (in Spain as well) and appeasing it by negotiating disarmament agreements and rectifying some of the harsh frontier settlements of 1919. Britain's appeasement of Hitler forced France onto the same path, as domestic opposition to fighting another world war became stronger and stronger. When France did take up arms against Hitler's Germany in 1939, it did so with a less-than-modern army and a very divided public opinion. The defeatist right even took the position that France ought to come to an accommodation with Germany.

The Fragile Legitimacy of pre-1945 French Regimes

The history of modern France was a tale of hatred, distrust, rhetorical excess, and instability until 1945. France has lived under ten different constitutions. Prior to the adoption of the basic law that has prevailed since 1958 no single formula for ruling the country enjoyed overwhelming support. France, until very recently, was always sharply divided into opposing spiritual families, right against left, catholic against secularist, monarchist against republican, defenders of a preindustrial tradition against advocates of an industrial future, capitalist, or Socialist. People did more than disagree: they differed so much that they did not seem to wish to be citizens of the same *patrie*. Members of different ideological families did not intermarry, form friendships, or attend the same schools. They distrusted each other so much that they could not extend to each other enough confidence to conclude firm bargains involving delayed gratification.

What held the country together despite these deep divisions? How do we account for the eventual development of a consensual liberal national myth? One reason is the unwillingness displayed by several less-than-legitimate successor governments to undo all the reforms introduced by their predecessors. Louis XVIII and Napoleon III were especially tolerant of earlier changes, whereas the architects of the Third Republic and of the Vichy regime were less disposed to learn. The opening up of public education and the improvement of centralized administration combined to create a basis for popular identification even in a deeply divided nation. The expansion of the compulsory, free public school system throughout the nineteenth century provided civil service positions for members of the middle class, especially the lower middle class. The expansion of business, banking, and transportation created a demand for more graduates of elementary schools, so that holders of the certificate of elementary studies could look forward to positions of higher status and income than those held by their fathers. The Third Republic certainly did not lack for internal enemies, but after 1880 it also acquired a lot of new friends.

However, this state of acceptance did not occur without a great deal of travail. Orleanist, Legitimists, and Bonapartists challenged the legitimacy of the liberal republic during the nineteenth century; Leninist and fascist integralists sought to overthrow it in the twentieth. To the monarchist right, the Third Republic was always *la gueuse*, the slut. Successful revolts occurred in 1830, 1848, 1851; unsuccessful ones in 1870, 1877, and 1888. Neither peaceful succession nor the nonviolent resolution of domestic differences was institutionalized before 1900, only to be upset again in the 1930s.

Third Republic politicians did not accept working-class representatives as legitimate coalition partners until 1902, and then with reluctance. They did not accept them as leaders of the nation until 1936—with even greater reluctance. But, then, it took the working class left some time to accept the legitimacy of the republic, too, and many never did.

Of course, French Marxist intellectuals, such as Jules Guesde, disdained any kind of nationalism until they joined the *Union Sacrée* government of 1914–17. However, their rank-and-file followers, Marxist or not, turned out to be good patriots when war broke out. They did their military duty and died by the hundreds of thousands rather than turn the imperialist war into a class war, as Lenin had urged them to do. Their mood had been captured accurately by the social-democratic reformist Jean Jaurès. Although a cosmopolitan, he had urged French workers to become nationalists even before 1914 because he predicted that it was the nation that would eventually emancipate them. French workers did have a fatherland, and they were obligated to defend it, he said. During the war trade union officials served on government commissions managing the war economy, although many of their followers seemed to have given up revolutionary opposition to the war policy only because of the fear of being conscripted. Working-class leaders were "included" in the nation after 1914, but the masses were far less enthusiastic. Many unions resumed revolutionary opposition to the state after 1919, and, as the French Communist party did, maintained their opposition to the Republic after 1940.

Not so the Socialist party. It was truly included in the nation and became part of the Jacobin liberal nationalist bloc after 1920. It cooperated with the state throughout the interwar years. Having first opposed colonial expansion as contrary to liberal principles, Socialists made their peace with it because, although inconsistent with pacifism, it was instrumental to the defense of republican institutions.

The Vichy Regime

The Vichy government represents the last hurrah of traditional syncretism in France. Although the fascists supported it, they never won a clear victory over Marshal Philippe Pétain and his supporters. All opponents of the liberal-nationalist conception of France felt marginal, almost excluded. The marginalized were groups and individuals who saw themselves as failing to receive "their due" from the Republic. What was "due them'' might be economic or status satisfaction, a material demand or an ideological one. The Vichy regime, once Nazi Germany had defeated the forces of the Republic in 1940, was the revenge of those who considered themselves marginalized by the Third Republic. The fascists among them were unabashed admirers of Nazi Germany and wanted France to emulate Germany; the syncretists were not. They wanted a noncapitalist, nonindustrial, small-town France, devoted to order, discipline, hard work, family values, and Catholicism. They wanted traditional authority, hierarchy, and, had modernization and mobilization not taken their toll, would have preferred a king in earlier decades. The Republic represented none of these virtues, as evidenced by its humiliating defeat. The Republic represented the illegitimate *pays légal*, whereas the attachments of the right were for the France of blood and soil, the *pays réel*. Vichy represented the revival of the real France, the France which Hippolyte Taine, Maurice Barrès, and Charles Maurras had extolled, and that the army had been unable to save.

The features of the Vichy government were unique for the twentieth century. The head of state, Marshal Pétain, had the powers of an absolute monarch. There was no elected body with legislative powers, though there were various advisory colleges, some of which deliberately aped medieval corporations. Notables from various walks of life and the professions were appointed to these councils. Civil rights and liberties were abolished. Catholicism was honored, though not reestablished as the state religion. Most voluntary associations were suspended, one of the few fascist tenets the "National Revolution" adopted. Capitalism was to be abolished and its place taken by an economy reorganized along Christian corporatist lines; the market as decision maker was to be superseded by inter-class compromises. Church values and Church personnel once again assumed a central role in the school system. A paramilitary youth movement became compulsory. Throughout the Vichy years, of course, the institutions of the National Revolution were attacked by the republican *Résistance* (many of whose fighters professed a Leninist integral nationalism, not a liberal one) and harassed by the growing demands of the German occupying forces. Vichy fielded a volunteer SS unit for the German campaign in Russia; it created a militia to aid the Germans in fighting the Résistance forces, and it participated actively in the extermination of the Jews.

Theoretical Reprise

The state that sought to build the French nation after 1789 did not become liberal until much later. The ideological vision of the victorious revolutionaries was murky; it did not define French liberalism for very long, and it did not succeed in rationalizing the nation-state. No single version of the national myth came close to achieving supremacy until the end of the nineteenth century. Nor was France successfully rationalized until that time.

French elites were slow to learn the practice of reciprocity; they hated and distrusted each other too much until the travail of survival in World War I brought about a change in perception. The lesson did not become permanent until 1944. However, it was the practitioners of liberal nationalism who learned to co-opt their integralist rivals and who eventually rationalized France by fashioning consensual institutions and policies.

And it was the same liberals who also came to question the ability of the French nation-state to ensure the peace and well-being of their compatriots by acting alone. They began and fostered the movement for integrating France into "Europe," thus making a future war with Germany physically and cognitively impossible.

The Unhappy Fourth Republic

Charles de Gaulle is considered by many the greatest Frenchman of the twentieth century. However we may respond to this claim, it is clear that he provided a vision and a direction that enabled the forces unleashed after 1944 to culminate in that massive purge of old habits and emotions that resulted in the relatively contented France of our days. He aided in the evolution of a consensual liberal national myth, in the transcendence of many old nationalist passions in favor of merging into a larger Europe. Some of this achievement came about despite de Gaulle's manifest intentions. None of it could have happened without the massive policies aiming at full modernization launched by the Fourth Republic's elites. Nor could it have happened if these very policies of modernization, undertaken in a setting of ideological dissensus, had not led to painful frustrations and disappointments by 1958. Before proceeding further, the achievements and failings of the Fourth Republic must be summarized.

Consider these two paradoxical events of 1957: French industrialists, after having opposed Robert Schuman's 1950 initiative for a supranational West European Coal and Steel Community, embraced the much more sovereignty-threatening European Common Market. At the same time, after three years of an active rebellion in Algeria, the National Assembly could still seriously debate several schemes for increasing the political rights of Algerians without granting them independence. The shift toward the economic integration of Europe is explained by the enormous successes of the first three of the government's economic plans. The failure to see the anticolonial handwriting on the wall was due to the continued feeling entertained by almost all politicians (and reinforced by the recalcitrant *colons*) that giving up Algeria was "an unacceptable solution for France which would become a diminished power of second or third rank, shorn of her world role."[14] The internal economic success of the Fourth Republic did not translate into a willingness to give up nation-enhancing policies, even when the two came into conflict.

The economic success story represents a clear case of social learning. French technocrats and crucially placed civil servants discovered Keynes after 1945 and put his ideas to work unflinchingly, over the continuing opposition of classical economist-technocrats led by Jacques Rueff. Labor productivity rose by 5 percent annually between 1945 and 1960; so did the annual growth rate of the national product. Per capita income rose by 43 percent between 1949 and 1958, as industry and services steadily accounted for more, and agriculture for less, of the national product. The size and scale of industrial operations rose steadily; by 1966 only 20 percent of plants employed fewer than ten workers, whereas that number had been twice as high in 1936. The number of medium-size firms, however, did not shrink much. Industrial and agricultural expansion was achieved because the state assumed the leading role in investment banking through a number of new public lending agencies that took the place of the private investment houses that had dominated French industrial finance. Even though 150,000 independent tradespeople had gone out of business between 1945 and 1970, 900,000 shopkeepers remained. The number of managers of all kinds also increased, thus confirming the trend toward bureaucratization in public and private organizations. Between 1955 and 1975, 700,000 family farms were abandoned or consolidated into larger units while the number of farm tractors increased twentyfold, and agriculture started on its route of tremendous overproduction despite the growth of exports to other Common Market countries. The rural population, of course, decreased steadily.

Ideological Strife, Shaky Legitimacy

The first constitution of the Fourth Republic went down to defeat in a 1946 referendum; the second was adopted by nine million "yes" votes over eight million "no" votes and eight million who abstained. The old

---

[14] The remark was allgedly made by Prime Minister Pierre Mendès-France, the man who arranged the end of the Indochina and Tunisian commitments. Edward Morse reports that one reason for de Gaulle's insistence on nuclear weapons for France was his need to reorganize the armed forces completely to get rid of officers and units likely to mutiny in the future or to stage coups. Such units might also think of using the doctrine of "revolutionary war" (identical to the U.S. counterinsurgency doctrine) against the French state (*Foreign Policy and Interdependence in Gaullist France* [Princeton: Princeton University Press, 1973], p. 3).

ideological families faded in the face of economic renewal and social reorganization, although not fast enough to give the Fourth Republic more legitimacy than the Third one had enjoyed.

The enormous changes introduced after 1945 were the work of a shaky coalition of centrist parties; the Socialists, Christian Democrats, and various groupings of "moderates"—most of them Jacobin-leaning liberal nationalists, though some of the moderates where Whigs. On the left they were opposed by the powerful integralist Communist party, which was excluded from the government after 1947 despite its central role in the anti-German *Résistance*. On the right the main opposition came from the Gaullist party, which supported the economic and educational reforms but wanted more traditional foreign and colonial policies, as well as a stronger executive, than the ruling coalition.

The old brand of fascism was discredited by Vichy. But a milder kind took its place: an antidemocratic movement of small-town and rural lower-middle-class artisans and farmers unable to compete in a modern market economy and determined to seek lower taxes and state subsidies. They coalesced in the Poujadist movement of the 1950s. Similar sentiments inspired lower-middle-class merchants and small farmers who had settled in Algeria and fought any efforts to work out compromises with Algerian nationalists. French integralists of the right bitterly resisted decolonization and European unification as well. Algeria became a "last line of resistance, a new Verdun."[15] The integralist right disappeared from the political scene after 1965, although it has been making a comeback since the mid-1980s in the form of the National Front.

In 1958 the Republic was overthrown in a bloodless coup carried out in the name of General de Gaulle by mutinous army units from Algeria acting in conjunction with members of the Gaullist parliamentary party. The fact that there was practically no opposition to the coup tells us that the Fourth Republic had lost its legitimacy and that this obvious violation of the norm of peaceful succession aroused no great consternation. In fact, the Fourth Republic parliament voluntarily dissolved itself, after its prompt acceptance of the General as the interim head of state and government had made possible de Gaulle's rapidly dampening the army mutiny.

The Fourth Republic failed because the Gaullist party was never reconciled to the domination of the old parties and the weak constitution, because the victims of its successful modernization policies blamed its institutions and politicians for their plight, and, most of all, because of the war in Algeria. However, that failure came in the wake of a great many important innovations in French life.

---

[15] Paul C. Sorum, *Intellectuals and Decolonizers in France* (Chapel Hill: University of North Carolina Press, 1977), p. 188.

Toward a Social Democratic Consensus

In addition to its economic successes, the Fourth Republic put the church–state conflict behind it by achieving a consensus on the victory of secularism, although allowing the church full autonomy in its own realm, including parochial education. The public system of education was modernized, although the completion of that process became a task of the Fifth Republic after the student revolt of 1968. Tolerance for multiculturalism was firmly rejected for metropolitan France, and the supremacy of the French language and culture was asserted unflinchingly. However, as we shall see, less consistency was shown with respect to multiculturalism in overseas France.

Most important, the desirability of interclass harmony was generally accepted. It was expressed in radical policies of redistribution practiced by way of the extensive system of social security installed after 1945 and the changes in access to education. This new consensus was made possible by the fact that the Gaullists, despite their dislike of the Fourth Republic, endorsed these policies.

It was the trauma of the Great Depression, the threat of communist revolution, the actuality of a fascist one, and the need to recover quickly from the ravages of World War II that made French elites question their old ways of ruling. Catastrophe induced social learning. The state took over control of the economy between 1944 and 1946 and guided the economy through systematic indicative planning until the 1980s. It put its impressive statistical services at the disposal of private firms. The Fourth Republic created a Planning Commission that developed incentives whereby publicly and privately owned firms restored and modernized production and trade. The government nationalized coal mining, the railroads, and certain banks, thus ensuring its control over the core economic activities. The Planning Commission mobilized and guided the investment funds necessary for wholesale industrial renovation. The energy and transport sectors, especially, soon responded to central direction as recovery (now aided also by massive U.S. support) proceeded rapidly. By 1952 production exceeded the volume of 1938 by 45 percent, and the Planning Commission proceeded to reallocate resources to the consumer sector. In the 1950s, French industrial production grew at a rate of 10 percent per year.[16]

[16] The origins of French postwar planning for an industrial policy are tied up with the victory of Keynesian economic thought in France. This was the work of a small group of nonacademic economists, in the Inspection des Finances and a few other key government offices, who found students among the engineers of some of the *grandes écoles*, not the universities. This instance of organizational learning also illustrates the role of epistemic communities. The story is told by Pierre Rosanvallon, "The Development of Keynesianism in France," in Peter A. Hall, ed., *The Political Power of Economic Ideas* (Princeton: Princeton University Press, 1989), pp. 170–93. The universities and state-run research institutes were

Among the lessons learned by French elites about the attainment of social peace was the value of corporatism. France never practiced it as consistently as Germany and the Nordic countries, and after 1980 it went into decline. Corporatism took the form of including organized industry, labor, and farmer groups in economic planning. The Planning Commission did its work through a system of modernization committees in which trade unions, farmers' unions, and industry associations, as well as ministries, were all represented. The plans were technocratic in the sense that they were drawn up by economists in the civil service; but their effectiveness depended on the participation of farmers, workers, and employers.

The influence of labor diminished rapidly after 1950 as the role of employers increased. By 1955 industrialists had overcome the disrepute into which their associations had fallen because of their collaboration with Vichy authorities. Conversely, the unions were strong in the early postwar years because of their opposition to Vichy, despite their organizational fragmentation. The firm guiding role of the state was strongly supported by labor. However, as soon as industry recovered, labor's fragmentation resulted in its increasing marginalization and distancing from the planning process.

Dissensus about Allies, Enemies, Empire

The victory of the Allies forced successive governments to come to terms with the fact that an enfeebled France was in no position to influence the postwar settlement. While the strong left clamored for a pro-Soviet policy, the center opted for alignment with the United States, and the Gaullist right sought an independent policy aiming initially at the dismemberment of Germany. In 1945, France wanted to put the left bank of the Rhine under a permanent French protectorate and prevent the reconstruction of the Ruhr industrial basin. As Britain and the United States rejected these demands, France agreed in 1954 to accept the per-

---

organizationally remote from these policy-oriented economists who depended on ready access to policymakers who were themselves mostly graduates of the *grandes écoles*. Morse shows that what distinguished these people from the prewar predecessors was their determination to shape a future different from the past (*Foreign Policy and Interdependence in Gaullist France*, p. 111). Charles Kindleberger, in making the same point, shows how a particular conception of knowledge and knowledge-based policy informed their work (Hall, *Political Power of Economic Ideas*, pp. 152–55). Despite the economic miracle and the increase in upward social mobility that it engendered, two thirds of French workers were still the children of workers. The working classes did not see themselves as sharing equally in the fruits of the miracle in terms of access to housing, education, and social amenities. Their support of the Fourth Republic was labile, and many supported the communists who remained unreconciled to the republic.

manent incorporation of West Germany into a western alliance with which France aligned itself once the Soviet Union came to be perceived as the chief threat to a peaceful Europe. France was too weak not to choose reliance on the United States over the independence de Gaulle (and others of the center and right) preferred. Therefore, the Gaullists never came to share the enthusiasm for NATO and for the unification of Western Europe with which Socialists, the Moderate Center, and the Christian Democrats identified. The powerful Communist party took the side of the Soviet Union well into the 1970s. In short, France enjoyed no consensus on foreign policy.

After 1944, because the resistance to Vichy and the Germans had begun in Africa, retaining the empire became a matter of general interest, as did the economic value of some colonies for French postwar recovery. The empire at first served as an emotional prop to compensate for the shame of Vichy. But things soon changed. Fighting the revolt in Indochina that began in 1946 required colonial troops as French conscripts were not used in Asia for fear that they might prove unwilling to fight, a fear later proved real in Algeria. The costs of maintaining the empire in the face of colonial revolts became severe by 1953; a large majority of French people began to feel that fighting a war in Indochina was incompatible with raising living standards in France, a much higher priority in people's minds.

Morocco and Tunisia regained their independence in 1956. The Indochinese territories succeeded in expelling the French in 1954. Neither event caused much anguish in French public opinion. Yet how the empire was perceived after the war provided a litmus test of how the French felt about modifying their cultural hegemony. As on much else, they proved to disagree with one another. The difficulty was illustrated by the divisive debates that raged between 1945 and 1947 over the future ties between the metropole and the colonies, the debate over the shape of the French Union.

Consistent assimilationist believed in the Republic One and Indivisible, at home and overseas, provided it was francophone. Jacobin liberals were believers in equality for all, everywhere, provided those who were equal spoke and thought in French. But others downgraded the idea and policy of assimilation in favor of association, a policy of multicultural tolerance and decentralized administration that carried with it continued inequality and discrimination in favor of French settlers and investors. Successive Third and Fourth Republic governments actually practiced associationism as it called for fewer investments in schools and hospitals and other measures that would raise the living standards of the indigenous peoples.

The renaissance of liberal nationalism in France in 1945 demanded some redefinition of relations with the colonies that also implied a clarification of the idea of multiculturalism. The parties of the left and the elected representatives of the colonies in French deliberative bodies favored a French Union of "free consent," a quasi-federal constitution freely linking the metropole to the colonies to which far-reaching autonomy would be granted. A multicultural definition of identity was implied.

This position lost out to a school made up of the parties of the center and right. They believed in a French Union of "tutelary subordination."[17] The Union was to be made up of metropolitan France, the overseas departments, and associated states; it was to be ruled by the president of the republic and the French council of ministers, who appointed the administrators of the "Associated states," as heretofore. "The Union . . . relied upon and sought to protect hegemonic beliefs about the indissoluble ties between continental and overseas France and the special French vocation to humanity expressed in that relationship." Of recognition for multiculturalism there was hardly a trace. The French Union that came into being, although it granted some representation in the French parliament to overseas populations, did not greatly change the earlier relationship of association either in spirit or in practice.

France's peculiar and unresolved relationship to Algeria illustrates the conundrum and killed the Fourth Republic. Legally, Algeria was part of metropolitan France; its Muslim population, however, was denied the rights of French citizenship to enable the European settler population, which amounted to over 10 percent of the total populace in 1954, to rule as it liked. Various efforts after 1945 to redefine the status of Algeria to enhance Arab and Berber equality were defeated because of the influence of the *colons* in parliament. The creation of an Algerian legislative assembly proved meaningless because rigged elections preserved *colon* domination.

Although giving up Indochina, Tunisia, and Morocco had aroused little dissent among the mass public, the Algerian revolt tore France in two, pitting the right identified with settler insistence on the status quo against the left searching for formulas giving equality to Muslim Algerians. De Gaulle was thought to support the imperialistic right. Draftees destined for service in Algeria began to evade service. Conscientious objectors sought to stop troop trains. As the liberal nationalists in France increasingly abandoned identification with the empire as antidemocratic, settlers in Algeria and their supporters in France organized groups that resembled the maneuvers of the fascists of the 1940s. Keep-

---

[17] The term is Ian S. Lustick's. See his *Unsettled States, Disputed Lands* (Ithaca: Cornell University Press, 1993), pp. 98–99. Quotes on this page come from the same source.

ing Algeria French appealed to diverse ideological families, including liberals who wanted to extend equality to Arabs and Berbers by means of French citizenship, and syncretists who wanted to keep them subservient.

LIBERAL NATIONALISM RATIONALIZES FRANCE

The Gaullist Vision of a Harmonious France

Charles de Gaulle enjoyed almost immediate legitimacy when he stepped into the Elysée Palace. His message stressed France's oneness with its pre-1789 past *and* the Jacobin insistence on popular sovereignty and a global civilizing mission, past grandeur as well as future renewal. Algerian *colons* loved him because he announced oracularly "je vous ai compris," but Socialists and Christian Democrats accepted him because he stood for orderly reform and modernity. The army leadership regarded him as the modern equivalent of a classic traditional nationalist only to see some of its key officers cashiered within months. He saw the need for very close links with a resurgent Germany as the only way to contain it.

The Gaullist vision unfolded incrementally between 1958 and 1962. It consisted of three interrelated propositions. (1) Foreign policy is the most important state responsibility because it asserts the identity of the nation. Incidentally, it can be used to overcome the intense strife among political parties that the General wanted to transcend. (2) French culture is the world's most developed; France is the best spokesman for Western civilization. Therefore, France must be a great power, and that demands an independent foreign policy, not integration with others or subordination to an alliance. (3) If the resource base for an independent great power policy is lacking, then France must find speedy alternatives and compensations. She must also avoid expending energy and treasure on such secondary fripperies as colonial empire and devote herself to industrial innovation instead. That, in turn, demands the possession of nuclear energy and nuclear weapons. The program enjoyed widespread support from all but the remnants of the Poujadist and racist right, as well as the Communist party and the workers' and student organizations close to it.

Institutions of Modernization and Inclusion

The Constitution of the Fifth Republic is less accommodating of corporatist practices of consultation and participation than the Fourth had been. Conversely, technocratic predominance became greater than before. But trade unions suffered much more from the decline of corporatism than did farmers and artisans' organizations.

The Fifth Republic intensified the large-scale measures of industrial and agricultural modernization launched by the Fourth. The "threatened" lower middle class responded by violent protests, strikes, and attacks on tax offices. The government's response, the Loi Royer of 1972, "incorporated" the disaffected shopkeepers and artisans through the creation of corporate bodies at the local level to control the rate of change, especially the establishment of supermarkets. The administration of rules affecting the manner of doing business was decentralized by giving appropriate powers to local commissions that accorded permanent representation to the interest groups that spoke for the lower middle class. The state successfully co-opted this opposition, but the opposition also penetrated the state. Both sides learned that they could not prevail without each other—and modernization of the economy continues with the participation of these erstwhile opponents.

The peasantry had succeeded as early as the 1890s in extracting a position of special solicitude from the state by being granted very favorable tax treatment. Partly because of the demographics of elections and partly because of a widespread belief that the welfare of the peasantry determines the fate of France, successive French governments subsidized agricultural production quite generously. Nevertheless, the farm population often rioted and used violence to keep farm subsidies from being lowered. In fact the protests increased as Fifth Republic policy sought to decrease the number of farms while augmenting their size, and also lower the amount of agricultural subsidies (and surpluses). Successive French governments sought to co-opt rural dissatisfaction in various ways, each representing a different variant of corporatism.

The Fourth Republic had allowed various farmers' organizations to elect delegates to regional committees managing state subsidies, but the Fifth found it desirable to practice corporatism by favoring one single union of peasants, the one most disposed to back the government's program for agriculture. That union has exclusive powers to comanage with the ministry of agriculture all structural adjustment, land concentration, migration, and retraining subsidies. Continued opposition to government policy, therefore, has fallen to other peasant unions that do not have official recognition, and such unions enjoy less support because they lack access to the favors dispensed by Paris.

But economic change came at the expense of the inclusion of the trade unions, although their influence increased temporarily in the early 1960s as the result of centralization. Government efforts at full economic "concertation" that was to involve them, farmers', and business organizations failed in 1964, although sectoral indicative agreements were concluded thereafter with employer participation alone.

Even though some comanagement councils were created after the students' and workers' revolt of 1968, they never amounted to much and did not satisfy an increasingly restive working-class population who benefited little from economic growth after 1970. Things changed dramatically after the Mitterrand government abandoned its policy of "socialism in one country" in 1983. By legally strengthening the power of local unions to bargain collectively with employers, the state actually weakened corporatist inclusion because the local unions lacked the strength to bargain. By then the Socialist party and many of its allied technocrats had foregone any intention of building up working-class power. They had learned that capitalism was not going to disappear just because it had changed institutionally in becoming multinational. Hence they also learned that corporations had to become more flexible and labor more adaptable and more efficient if firms were to remain competitive internationally.

The Fifth Republic's administrators and politicians displayed a great deal of learning. They asked themselves why France was not as rationalized as other industrial countries, why no consensual national purpose had evolved. And, as they compared themselves with the United States, they decided to make science and technology serve the nation directly, using the methods of industrial policy and indicative planning already in place. This involved making up for the "science and technology gap" from which technocratic elites thought France was suffering, improving state directives to private industry regarding priorities in investment and innovation (industrial policy), upgrading state-directed research and development activity (R&D), and improving the system of higher education. I now describe the institutional aspects of collective learning.

The dominance of technocracy and the marginality of parliament in the 1960s did not mean that planning sidestepped politics. French planning is said to be flexible because it moderates technocratic control with bargaining. The Plan favors aid to innovative investors who follow state direction; but that does not mean that noninnovative and even redundant sectors fail to receive aid from the state. It is true that administrators ally themselves with innovative representatives of large firms; but it is also true that this alliance is moderated because treasury officials ally themselves with representatives of small and medium enterprises in order to hold down fiscal burdens. True, trade unions are not favored negotiating partners in these coalitional procedures, but even they can be valuable allies in certain situations. In short, democratic participation moderates the rigid logic of optimal resource allocation, though not all participate equally.

Planners increasingly made use of systematic forecasting methods and formal models. Science and technology were being applied to the planning of the future of science, technology, defense, and the economy. Planning increasingly took into account access to foreign markets, including the European Union, and to foreign imports. The terms of liquidation of the colonial empire ensured France continued preferential access to African primary commodities and export markets, in return for generous administrative and economic aid to the newly independent countries.

Planning also came to include the French military-industrial complex that included the major aerospace and electronics firms. Industrial policy under Gaullist governments aimed at creating a nationally self-sufficient computer and microelectronics industry, an aerospace industry, a nuclear power industry large and complex enough to export electricity, nuclear enrichment and reprocessing equipment, and an oil production complex relying on former colonies. All of these industries were to be capable of producing military equipment for French use as well as for sale abroad. Industrial policies of this magnitude required enormous increases in state-financed R&D. Funds devoted to reorganizing state research institutes were sharply increased, to levels approaching R&D per capita expenditures in the United States. The status of researchers was upgraded. Close links with private industry were formed. Periodic inventories of scientific manpower were done. More elaborate equipment was bought. Organization and group effort were stressed over individual genius. Managerial tools involving science and technology were increasingly used to plan future scientific and technological efforts. Most important, the isolation of French universities from R&D efforts was overcome, as was the concentration of technical training and applied science in a few of the *grandes écoles*. The skills and facilities needed to practice an effective industrial policy were successfully decentralized and deconcentrated, diffused over the entire society.

Success proved elusive. France did not arrive at independence from the world oil market. Its computer and electronics industries fell behind Japanese and American firms despite industrial policy. In the aerospace and nuclear sectors, however, enormous successes were scored. De Gaulle had wanted industrial modernization and military independence without sacrificing traditional French social values. He wanted to avoid the growth of a consumption-oriented society. The revolt of 1968 demonstrated his failure on that score. It also shattered the hope that a foreign policy of independence and grandeur was possible for a modern, wealthy, and welfare-oriented France.

Toward a Multicultural Conception of French Identity?

If we discount the rhetoric that harks back to the France of Chrétien de Troyes and focus instead on the performance of Fifth Republic governments and on its constitutional practices, even General de Gaulle comes off as a liberal nationalist, not just his party. This becomes clear when we examine the beliefs and institutions that have prevailed in France since 1960.

Religion and the role of the Catholic Church have ceased to be major issues. The Church no longer claims a privileged status and accepts the fact that most French people are not religious. Society and polity are secular. Religion becomes politically salient only when the state seeks to control the parochial school system instead of leaving it to its users. Draft resistance ceased being a problem when no unpopular wars were waged. Conscription remained an accepted *rite de passage*, though nonmilitary forms of service became available in the mid 1990s. It was discontinued, not because of popular opposition but because the armed forces preferred highly trained professional personnel. Even tax evasion is no longer the indoor sport it once was.

Rationalization is also manifest in the educational reforms begun under the Fourth and completed by the Fifth republics. The school-leaving age was raised to 16 years in 1959; access to secondary schools was made easy. By 1970, after a massive reform of the baccalaureate examination, almost 70 percent of the 210,000 students who took it each year actually passed. With the construction of new universities and technical schools, the number of students enrolled in higher education increased by 11 percent per year between 1958 and 1970. Access to the elite became easier in Fifth Republic France.

The reform of the educational system accentuates the movement toward a professionally trained work force that is no longer self-employed. Dubbed by some "elitist egalitarianism," it seeks to combine universal access to public schools with a later school-leaving age and with a rigid process of selection in the upper grades, resulting in the sharp increase in those receiving the baccalaureate degree and in increased attendance in the technical *lycées*. Local governments were given much larger powers concerning school construction and curricula. The issue of state subsidization of private (i.e., largely Catholic) schools, formerly so contentious, ceased to be salient. By 1974, only 23 percent of the population opposed subsidization; even the Socialist party, always in the forefront of anticlericalism, no longer evinced much concern after a massive show of parental concern forced it to cancel plans for further laicization. Some parents seem to prefer Catholic schools for pedagogic rather than religious reasons; evidently the state is no longer seen by all as the hegemonic definer of values. Nor is the status of the Catholic religious values very significant in public discourse. The Giscard d'Estaing government legalized easy divorce and legitimated state-financed abortion and contraceptive services. Non-Christian religions are growing in France almost as rapidly as in America; some claim that they have 500,000 members.

Decolonization apparently encouraged non-French-speaking minorities in France to assert themselves. The movement for Occitania, led by *lycée* teachers eager to legitimate their native tongue and their jobs, had been dominated by fascists; left-wingers assumed control after 1960. The long-lived Breton movement for autonomy also came under left-wing control in the 1960s, even though earlier it had been led by Catholic corporatists, fascists, and romantic ethnicists who had fought the Jacobin nationalism of the Third Republic leaders. These movements opposing a homogeneous French culture and nation were animated by a feeling of having been left out of the prosperity and growth of modern France, of being a neglected periphery that was also the victim of cultural oppression. Peripheral mobilized but unassimilated elites were reabsorbed readily enough during the 1980s once additional regional developments funds were channeled in their direction. The Fifth Republic sacrificed a little of its rigid French ethnocentrism once the Algerian monkey was off its back when it granted some of the demands for cultural and linguistic concessions made by its own minorities, to the Basques, Bretons, Occitanians, and especially in Corsica.

Even though patois disappeared, most non-French languages are still in evidence today. Moreover, they have been given official recognition by the Fifth Republic in the form of radio and television time. They are taught in schools as an optional subject (but not used as languages of instruction) and are featured in folkloric celebrations. None of this has diminished the commitment first expressed in the school laws of the 1880s by Jules Ferry that the language of France is French and that French alone will be featured in nationwide communication. The Fifth Republic merely added the toleration for a limited bilingualism which the Third and Fourth had denied.

How was it possible to retain a civil religion after 1962, even though pride in the empire had once been a core part of the French national identity irrespective of one's ideology? Prosperous and consumption-oriented people, apparently, have no need for social imperialist ideologies and notions of a civilizing mission to shore up their self-esteem. "By 1962," says Edward Morse, "one of the important changes in French foreign policy was its orientation to the future and to change in the international society, rather than maintenance of the preexisting order. French society, in short, reached the age of high mass consumption at the same time that the colonial legacy was eliminated and that a political foundation of the Fifth Republic was laid.''[18] Others argue that de Gaulle could justify French withdrawal from Algeria and Africa because it clearly did not mean a loss of status, given France's march into prosperity, high technology, and presumed military independence.

Administrative cohesion has been diminished as the result of a great many reforms that add up to achieving the opening of the state to civil society that François Mitterrand had hoped to achieve after 1982. French citizens now file complaints against the state before a supranational tribunal for violations of right covered by the European Convention on Human Rights. Socialist Prime Minister Michel Rocard in 1988 spoke of "unlocking" French society to make it more adaptive, to reduce the role of the state to guaranteeing the rules of competition in civil society and the economy. Judicial review, long considered a state-enfeebling American oddity, is now practiced. Specialized functional courts are proliferating, thereby watering down the clarity of centrally made law. Prefects are now called "commissaires de la république," and their powers are no longer as awesome as those first defined by the Jacobin Republic. City councils can impose taxes. Citizen participation at the local and regional levels is a reality. Elected officials, unlike earlier practice, are restricted to two simultaneous mandates. Political parties are actually expected to seek compromises with each other. Everyone is supposed to be "liberal," an adjective that now means respecting civilized reciprocity in public life and toleration of dissent, rather than retaining its historical meaning of constitutional rules, free markets, and untrammeled capitalism.

Administrative cohesion suffered further as a result of the enactment of the Loi Defferre in 1982, which gave wide-ranging power over public works, education, and social services to regional governments and municipalities. This devolution certainly encouraged democratic inclusion and participation at the local and regional levels, but it did not automatically improve the quality and cost of services. Devolution encouraged regional autonomy, even interregional cooperation, at the expense of control from the central ministries involved. However, it did not diminish the desire and the capability of exercising control from Paris, thus in effect creating multiple and competing administrative bodies.

The clearest test of a tendency to accept a multicultural identity for French women and men is the changing nature of French practices regarding citizenship and immigration. The Jacobin version of nationality was decidedly nonethnic: one was French by virtue of being born in France or by naturalization, which was made easy. There was one explicit assumption that went with naturalization: being French means assimilating fully into French culture, into republican secular culture. This as-

---

[18] Morse, *Foreign Policy and Interdependence in Gaullist France*, pp. 111–12.

sumption is largely unchanged today. Socialists, Gaullists, and moderates accept it, but it is given poignancy by a growing xenophobic sentiment that denies the innate ability of immigrants to assimilate.

The traditional and integral-nationalist versions of French citizenship were quite different: they stressed gallo-germanic descent and Catholicism as the core ingredients. Even the xenophobic National Front has abandoned this conception, rooted in a pure ius sanguinis, by admitting that other Europeans are potential French citizens. Nevertheless, it argues that non-Europeans immigrants cause unemployment, inflate the social service budget, pollute French culture, and cause social decay by increasing crime and destroying the organic unity of France-as-a-family. Moreover, they argue that Muslims are unable to assimilate because they cannot shed their religion.

These concerns appear to be widely shared in the 1990s. But before the lean 1980s, immigration was welcomed. The free access of Algerians to the French labor market was guaranteed in the settlement with Algeria. There was no discrimination on the basis of national origin, and a generous interpretation of the right to asylum prevailed. Millions of people streamed into France, more and more, legal and illegal, nonwhite. One million naturalizations were granted since 1948. As various governments sought—ineffectively—to stem illegal immigration, a number of voluntary legal aid and human rights societies sprang up to help nonwhite immigrants, a development hard to conceive under the hegemony of the Republic One and Indivisible.

Nonetheless, the coming into being, in fact, of a multicultural society of unassimilated aliens and of young Arabs and Africans born in France, has not brought with it the abandonment of the principle of assimilation or the acceptance of multiculturalism as a permanent state of affairs. After several failed attempts during the 1980s to restrict the right both to immigration and to naturalization to penalize Muslims, the Loi Pasqua of 1993 accomplished both aims. It makes it harder to enter France, facilitates deportation, gives a very restrictive interpretation to the right of asylum (which required a constitutional amendment), and makes it harder for the children of North Africans to become French citizens (unless their fathers fought in the French army). The law, as well as the widespread opposition to Muslim immigrants, challenge frontally the nonethnic Jacobin theory of citizenship. Not unexpectedly, there are now organized groups of immigrants who demand collective rights for themselves, a trend that makes it more difficult to advocate continuing assimilation on the part of Jacobin liberals who defend immigrants.[19]

[19] *L'Express,* 16 September 1993, reported these results of a public opinion survey: Immigrants believing French are racist, 30 percent; immigrants believing they are treated

How Legitimate Is the Fifth Republic?

De Gaulle staked the legitimacy of his republic on France's role as a major power on the success of a foreign policy independent of the Western alliance in general and of the United States in particular. This theme resonated convincingly with French intellectuals of the left and right; it did not seem to interest the average French voter very much.

Successive presidents and prime ministers wavered in their application of the General's vision. They unflinchingly resisted the pressure of other Western governments to join a fully liberal international economic order when liberalism appeared to threaten the interests of French farmers and of the entertainment industry. They fought for the international recognition of French culture. They refused to adhere to the restraints on nuclear weapons preferred by Washington, even though 62 percent of the French public thought in 1995 that the government ought to stop nuclear testing. But on the big issues of war and peace, of German reunification, and the future of postcommunist East Europe, they acted as loyal members of NATO. At no time did de Gaulle's successors push the policy of independence to the point of no return in relations with other Western countries.

Nor did the French public want such a course. Except for the rapidly shrinking Leninist left, the French public always considered itself part of the West, despite the stylish expressions of sympathy for Third World causes that leftist French intellectuals voiced after the disappearance of the colonial empire. Grandeur and foreign policy independence did not appear to be necessary ingredients for lending legitimacy to the institutions of the Fifth Republic.[20]

The Republic seems to please most French people, 77 percent of whom pronounced themselves satisfied with their lives in 1973, 80 percent in 1990.[21] Satisfaction with democracy is less stable. In 1990, 23

---

equally with the French in looking for housing or work, 56 percent; immigrants believing they should not live in immigrant areas, 91 percent; immigrants very interested in the politics of their countries of origin, 53 percent; immigrants very interested in French politics, 68 percent; immigrants opposed to restrictions on family reunion, 41 percent; immigrants favoring crackdown on illegals, 80 percent; immigrants fearing deportation, 18 percent; French believing that immigration contributes to insecurity, 53 percent; immigrants must shed their non-French customs, 83 percent; immigrants should live among French people, 75 percent; immigrants take jobs away from French people, 52 percent. In 1990, 6.3 percent of the population consisted of foreigners, or 3.6 million in a population of 56.6 million, of whom 2.9 million were aliens. The Front National has received about 12.5 percent of the national vote in recent elections, though it did much better in some localities.

[20] In three surveys (1989–90) on attitudes concerning German reunification the opposition in France never exceeded 15 percent.

[21] All survey figures in this and the next section are taken from *Eurobarometer* (Brussels:

Table 5-3. Satisfaction with democracy at the nation-state level in France and Germany, 1990–94

	1990	1991	1992	1993	1994
France	53	61	40	41	47
Germany	75	74	61	51	52
Germany (western)	81	66	66	55	57
Germany (eastern)	49	34	44	36	35

percent wanted to limit freedom to protect society against "subversives." The economic malaise of the 1990s has left its mark, as shown in Table 5-3.

Despite labile mass support for democracy, the party elites learned to practice it by transcending their historic ideological confrontations. When the Socialists took control from the Gaullist-UDF coalition in 1981, they planned massive nationalizations of industries, banks, and insurance companies, extensive popular participation in governance at the plant and neighborhood levels, and reinvigorated central planning at the expense of institutionalized economic cooperation with trading partners. The commitment was to "Socialism in One Country." By 1983 the experiment was abandoned because of huge losses in nationalized industry, inflationary pressures, weakness of the franc, and disruption of trade relations with neighbors.[22]

France seems to have stumbled into an almost two-party system, in which the two large parties alternate peacefully and agree on marginalizing the remaining antisystem groups. The Socialists today play the role of Jacobin liberals, the Gaullists and their permanent ally, pro-business UDF, that of the Whigs. The rump Communists, the Ecologists and the proto-fascist National Front—the most threatening challenger of the Republic's legitimacy—remain unreconciled to liberal nationalism as now practiced.

In 1982, 55 percent thought that the welfare state reduces inequality,

---

Commission of the European Union), annual volumes since 1974. French samples usually contain 1000 respondents.

[22] The amount of gross domestic product devoted by the state to supporting the standard of living of citizens amounted to 42.5 percent, the highest among the six largest industrial economies, in 1980. The new government proceeded to raise entitlements still higher for housing, pensions, health insurance, and family allowances. The minimum wage was raised by 15 percent, as the number of hours per week to be worked was reduced. The nationalized banks were forced to lend the necessary funds to keep obsolete industries going. High-technology industries were to be developed rapidly alongside those in the northern rust belt, which were to be saved. All this was done to retain national wealth in the face of what the left considered an incompetent capitalism, a flawed market system unable to lead France into the twenty-first century.

75 percent considered that the welfare state helps those most in need, and 77 percent accepted remaining levels of inequality as unavoidable. These expressions of satisfaction with the welfare state were exceeded by thoughts that France would do better if she cooperated more with her common market partners; in 1985, 70 percent felt that more European cooperation to fight unemployment and inflation was in order; 72 percent were willing to transfer more sovereignty to the European Union within ten to thirty years. In 1981, only 28 percent of respondents expressed themselves willing to make personal sacrifices to help another Community country experiencing economic difficulties, but in 1985 that number had risen to 83 percent. The consolidation of the liberal nationalist myth clearly did not prevent a growing identification with Europe. It confirmed that France was not unique as it came to resemble more and more the attitudinal and institutional landscape shared by almost all democratic, pluralistic, industrialized countries that practice welfare capitalism.

The sputtering of the socialist program demonstrates the death of the old political ideologies. The Communists lost all relevance. The working class became more of an interest group than a movement for radical change. The Socialist party, like most political parties in liberal-nationalist states, decided it would rather remain in power than adhere to doctrine. It made its peace with market economics in a welfare state, and it accepted cooperative policies with conservatives who also cherish their stake in the status quo. However, workers' self-government and a more active role for workers in the management of industry became a casualty of the grand compromise. Although more corporatist bodies exist than in earlier decades, the demise of planning weakened the practice of corporatism at the center. The Gaullists abandoned their former concern with state autonomy in favor of *désétatisation*. When the Socialists returned to power in 1988, they accepted the Gaullists' confirmation of commercial and industrial competition, the regulation of financial markets, environmental legislation, and still more radical reform of the educational system in the direction of the American system. They sacrificed declining smokestack industries to heavy investment in the R&D needed for a successful microelectronics sector.

FROM FRENCH TO EUROPEAN IDENTITY?

Policy toward Europe

Since 1970 France has inexorably become less self-centered and more a part of a larger West European political identity. De Gaulle succeeded in fashioning a consensual French identity, only to lose it to a more encompassing one, even as he was overcoming the competing ideologies that had animated the French. His very success in attaining the rationalization of France proved inconsistent with an exclusive French identity. How success at home could not be combined with the retention of French autonomy abroad is the story now to be told.

The movement toward a federal union of Western Europe was essentially a French movement, sparked around 1950 by politicians looking for a non-military method of containing a Germany expected to recover its industrial prowess. Led by Jean Monnet and Robert Schuman, proponents of the movement sought noncontroversial tasks that would deeply enmesh the economies and societies of the Western European countries with one another. They hoped that new interests and perceptions of common needs would arise as a result of such ties. These perceptions would then lead the people so enmeshed to leave behind feelings of mutual exclusiveness. New transnational ties were expected to form and lead incrementally to permanent peace between Germany and France because both would cease being self-contained nation-states. The means chosen for the realization of this dream were first the construction of a common market, a full economic union later, and a federal political union at the end of the trail. Most of the scheme worked, as we now know, but it took a great deal longer than these brilliant visionaries had expected.

The entry into force of the Treaty of Rome in 1957 was a milestone on that trail. Its intent was to strip the member states of sovereignty over their economies and to pool economic sovereignty instead in the collectivity, the European Community. A year later the Fourth Republic collapsed; de Gaulle had no desire to give up any sovereignty over anything, though he, too, sought permanent reconciliation with Germany. He was also content to use the Community to advance his ideas about French interests if he could eliminate the federalist component. He used the threat of French secession to force decision making by unanimity. However, his efforts to shoulder the common market institutions aside in favor of a new intergovernmental West European political directorate (the Fouchet Plan) died as a result of everybody's opposition.

Internal French imperatives also conspired to complicate the General's policy. The need to cater to domestic agricultural and export interests compelled the government to seek special arrangements, especially for farmers, with the other European states that had the effect of deepening regional interdependencies. De Gaulle gave up independence to make economic policy to consolidate the rest of his program, which required support from foreign governments. Still, until the late 1970s, French enthusiasm for supranational European integration went into hibernation.

The 1970s and early 1980s were the years of stagflation in Europe. Economic growth came to a halt, revenue declined, inflation soared, as energy prices quadrupled because of the perfection of oligopolistic pricing practices on the part of oil-exporting countries. The French economy was as hard hit as any other. France, however, was no longer ruled by a charismatic nationalist but by sober conservatives who did not regard economic health as a mere means to finance political grandeur. France turned to the common market and to more perfect economic union, though *not* to political federation, under Presidents Georges Pompidou and Valéry Giscard d'Estaing.

After 1977 the renewed interest in Europe took the form of fashioning with Germany the European Monetary System. At first, the Mitterrand government sought to reverse the course by attempting to practice socialism in one country. As we saw, the right-wing socialists learned to seek France's future by means of a renewed interest in European unification in 1983. Mitterrand launched the "1992 Program" of perfecting the single European market by initiating integrative steps that covered all economic regulations and activities, not just trade. He committed France to full monetary union, a single European currency, and sought to persuade his partner nations to take important steps toward political unity by the end of the century, including a single European foreign and defense policy, the so-called Maastricht Program. A referendum was held on the Maastricht amendments to the Treaty of Rome; a razor-thin majority approved the treaty as a bitter opposition containing both Jacobin and Whig liberal nationalists denounced it. The single market continues to flourish, but monetary unification stalled after 1992 for economic reasons. France's failure to persuade her European partners to adopt a single foreign and defense policy is manifest in the debacle over the former Yugoslavia.

Why and how did successive French leaders decide to link the future of their country to that of a unified Western Europe? How much of French identity remains intact after forty-five years of intense European integration? Is French liberal nationalism being pooled with a European liberalism just as it reached fruition in France?

The Possible Obsolescence of Liberal Nationalism

Placing one's national identity into a larger pool of a more extended identity need not require selflessness, altruistic motives, or even a sharply poised choice: such a shift may be purely instrumental, and it may lack any concern with a final commitment. Seventy-two percent of a large French sample thought in 1980 that advancing European unity was the only way to defend national identity and economic interest against the "big powers."

National identity, I hypothesize, wanes in proportion to people's realization that their nation no longer helps them to better themselves. Nationalism declines whenever the nation-state is perceived at not being able to secure the economic future or the physical security of its people. Inability to ensure a wholesome environment, monetary stability, or industrial innovation may engender similar frustrations with one's government. Put slightly differently, elites learn to turn to non-national resources and authorities to help them to solve problems that can no longer be removed by means of internal coalitions of interests and of bargains among them. Nationalism weakens when elites run out of domestic bargains.

France Learns to Depend on Europe

Giscard d'Estaing's government learned to control inflation and restrain budget deficits by forcing the franc to remain within the limits dictated by a West European regime of monetary stability that was based on Germany's, the European Monetary System (EMS) installed in 1979. No domestic bargain was possible to attain these macroeconomic objectives; only Germany seemed able to force the necessary monetary and fiscal discipline on France once the government had decided to liberalize financial markets and to float the franc. The EMS allowed France to share some of the costs of stabilization by enlarging the number of currencies that would bear the burden of international realignment.

Because that policy implied the end of French monetary autonomy (as well as that of all the other members of EMS except Germany), the left wing of the Socialists rejected this externally imposed discipline only to be overruled by Mitterrand's decision to hasten the process of European economic integration. Said his prime minister: "Quite simply, a real left-wing policy can be applied in France only if the other European countries also follow policies of the left. . . . I want to change the habits of this nation . . . [of resigning] themselves to living with an inflationary disease."[23]

If Mitterrand had tried to stick with socialism in one country, he would have paid a heavy price in domestic support. As Peter Gourevitch summed it up:

[23] Quoted in Hall, *The Political Power of Economic Ideas*, p. 87. This episode is fully analyzed in Peter A. Hall, "The State and the Market," in P. Hall, J. Hayward, and H. Machia, eds., *Developments in French Politics* (New York: St. Martin's Press, 1990); Wayne Sandholtz "Choosing Union," in Michael Loriaux, ed., *France after Hegemony* (Ithaca: Cornell University Press, 1991).

There were strong sanctions that social groups could have employed had he tried. Despite extensive nationalizations, the French economy remains deeply integrated into the international market economy. . . . It was clear to Mitterrand and his advisers that to take the left Socialists' route in 1982–83 would have wrenched France away from the track followed by the other countries to which France is linked, thereby provoking intense hostility from French and foreign capital alike. Capital would have left the country, trading partners would have imposed sanctions for treaty violations, domestic protest from all sorts of groups would have intensified. . . . Only vast internal support could have overcome this kind of pressure . . . but when the decision was being made, Mitterrand did not have that kind of support.[24]

French leaders were in the forefront of those who, by the beginning of the 1980s, felt that some energetic new measures were required to lift Europe beyond inflation, recession, stagnation, and the loss of even the internal market to extra-European multinational firms with advanced technologies. France at first responded by creating "national champions" that with state subsidies would produce the desired technological innovations. This worked only in a few sectors; nor did it stop the decay of the steel industry, though it kept out some American and Japanese multinationals. The scale of neither the needed investments nor the potential market sufficed. Moreover, any deliberate industrial policy had to face the facts of an already established Western European common market because the European Union determined the rules of competition and limited national subsidies. France, however, was willing to subordinate her industrial policy to supranational rules as long as French objectives were attained as well.

The most striking supranational solution to national problems came in the area of European R&D policy, resulting in the early 1980s in two major institutional innovations, the European Strategic Program for R&D in Information Technologies (ESPRIT), and the European Research Coordinated Action consortium (EUREKA), along with several similar minor operations. ESPRIT, though unreservedly supported by France and French industry, is a program of the European Union, drawn up as a result of joint planning by the Union and industrialists. EUREKA, however, is the result of Mitterrand's initiative, designed to avoid supranational control and explicitly directed against American penetration of the European R&D scene. Individual firms decided to participate in one or more of almost three hundred separate regional research projects in the microelectronics field. Industrialists and bureaucrats who know that neither socialism nor capitalism in one country is feasible have no need to love Europe and favor European federation to conduct EU-wide

[24] Peter Gourevitch, *Politics in Hard Times* (Ithaca: Cornell University Press, 1986), p. 189.

industrial policy. French firms are associated with 71 percent of the projects funded by ESPRIT and with 67 percent of those under EUREKA's wing.

Learning, clearly, can take the form of saying "when you can't lick 'em, join 'em." French industrialists convinced the bureaucrats and politicians to do just that when the strategy of nurturing national champions failed to bear fruit. Major manufacturing firms began to create an extensive regional network of bilateral and multilateral ties by joining forces on distinct projects of research and product development. Leaving behind the framework of the nation-state went hand in hand with a disenchantment with corporatist practices of consultation and consensual decision making, with state planning and direction. Leaders of business preferred industrial policies fashioned cooperatively by themselves, obtaining eventual state and European Union support.

Liberal nationalism, whether played out at the level of the existing state, below the level of the state, or above it, is indissolubly linked with democratic rights and institutions. Seeking to solve difficult problems that plague the nation by shifting them to the European plane implies the need to make supranational institutions more democratically responsive than they were designed to be. Moreover, once it had been determined that the welfare state can prosper only in collaboration with other welfare states united in a true common market, it became necessary to assure that the core institutions of the Union could decide matters quickly. This, in turn, persuaded the Mitterrand government to abandon the Gaullist insistence on the right to veto important EU decisions. France led in the reform of the Treaty of Rome that introduced voting by majority in the Council of Ministers and in widening the mandate of the European Parliament. France also led in the movement for enlarging the jurisdiction of the European Council to include foreign policy, to make the Council into an organ of the Union, and to push Europe along the path of political unification after 1992.

The commitment to improve welfare policies and to democracy can also undermine the nation-state "from below." The EU disposes over relatively large funds to encourage the economic development of underdeveloped and deindustrialized areas in member countries and to support the retraining and reemployment of workers and farmers made redundant by economic change. The administration of these funds calls for local participation, for a measure of corporatist representation sidestepping national democratic institutions. In France, Spain, and Scotland such subsidies tend to go disproportionately to minority-controlled areas whose political claims are thus supported and enhanced. In short, the Europeanization of economic policy entails some delegitimation, via new participatory institutions, of the national government.

218

France Has Second Thoughts about Europe

Right-wing Socialists, the UDF, and the center of the Gaullists tied the future for France indissolubly to that of a united Europe. The unification of Germany seemed to make the project ever more urgent, leading to enthusiasm on the part of the government for the economic and the political portions of the Maastricht program. But their voices were challenged by a new wave of opposition by 1992.

Left-Socialist and Gaullist intellectuals were one in defending the purity of French identity against Europe's by arguing that in a united Europe France's exceptionalism would drown in European liberalism; France would lose the ability to preach Jacobinism to the world all by itself. Trade unions joined them in demanding a return to protectionism and in denouncing the neoliberalism of business. Monetary union with Germany was presented as yielding to the *diktat* of the Bundesbank. The outflow of capital to Third World production sites was condemned at the same time.

Although the government did not yield to the economic nationalists, its restrictive immigration policy did. Moreover, the insistence on protecting French cultural products shows sensitivity to these fears about the future of French identity. Voices in Parliament, and not merely those of the National Front, spoke up in dread about France's open borders, its openness to foreign goods and influences of all kinds. But center and right-wing politicians who have expressed sympathy for an exclusive French nationalism also have sought remedies by raising the common external tariff of the EU in preference to unilateral French moves: Fortress Europe, not isolationist France.

French public opinion during the 1980s favored the turn to Europe; since 1991 support has become much shallower. In 1990, 57 percent of the French thought their country had benefited from membership in the EU; in 1994 that number was 39 percent. In 1990, 50 percent said they would be sorry if the EU disintegrated, though an equal number appeared to be indifferent. Forty-eight percent thought that the EU will influence their lives positively; 60 percent favored enlarging the powers of the European Parliament, and a similar number wanted a sharp increase in the powers of the EU over social welfare policies; that support had shrunk to 49 percent in 1993. In that year, 5 percent said they thought of themselves as having European nationality, 32 percent said they were French exclusively, and 60 percent combined both identities in their responses to the question "in the near future do you see yourself as. . . ."

One of the most interesting tests of the continued strength of national as opposed to European identity is summarized on Table 5-4: how do

Table 5-4. Preference for joint EC or EU rather than national decision making in France, 1991–94

	I	II	III	IV	V	VI	VII	VIII	IX	X	XI
1991	—	—	—	69	71	82	71	47	—	42	70
1992	58	58	—	70	61	82	70	53	66	34	68
1993	57	52	62	62	56	70	71	43	57	26	61
1994	61	62	—	68	67	79	74	52	56	29	68

SOURCE: *Eurobarometer,* June 1991, December 1992, June 1993, July 1994. Samples included about 1000 respondents.

Note: I to XI refer to the following question: "Some people believe that certain areas of policy should be decided by the (NATIONAL) government, while other areas of policy should be decided jointly within the European Community/European Union. Which of the following areas of policy do you think should be decided by the (NATIONAL) government, and which should be decided jointly within the European Community/European Union?" I refers to "immigration policy," II to "dealing with unemployment," III to "fight against poverty," IV to "protection of the environment," V to "currency," VI to "scientific and tech[nological] research," VII to "foreign policy towards non-EC/EU countries," VIII to "defense," IX to "industrial policy," X to "education," and XI to "rates of Value Added Tax." The figures indicate those who answered "European Community/Union."

people respond when asked to choose between national or supranational governmental compentences?

Those who feel that France's submersion into Europe is final can take comfort in the finding that public opinion continues to favor an EU policy for almost all governmental tasks except measures dealing with industrial policy and the currency, as well as education. Those who see a resurgent nationalism will point out that the tasks for which support has eroded are crucial for the maintenance of a national identity. In the meantime, the overall support for European unification has slipped from 80 percent in 1990 to 72 percent in 1993.

France appears a bit less rationalized in 1995 than it had in 1990, when it had not yet been appreciated that the *trente glorieuses*, the thirty years of economic and social success, had come to their end. Public distrust of politicians is on the rise, the impatience with official corruption is more lively. Disillusionment about the evident limits of French power and influence abroad is widespread. Liberal nationalism is fraying from blows originating from the right; no pervasive attachment to a liberal nationalism derived from a European identity is evident. There are indications, however, of a liberal attachment to sites of governance smaller than the nation-state, although they can hardly be called "national" in their own right.

Yet most French citizens clearly no longer care about past passions, historical grandeur, and the mystic beauty of the hexagon. Few are likely to continue any lingering belief that to be fully human means being French, though these beliefs were once surely useful in rationalizing France. Says Stanley Hoffmann: "There are signs that the present day French are, more or less prosaically, ready to give up on the inspiring myths of universality, exceptionalism and the mythical views of the past."[25] French intellectuals despise vague notions such as "pooled sovereignty"; they remain ill at ease with forms of governance that lack a federal constitution or a strong unitary one; they fear an immersion of the French self in the German and find it difficult to imagine modes of rule that are not tied to clear ideas of territoriality. Once they get used to these things, once it is appreciated that the possibility of domestic bargains for rerationalizing a fraying polity is exhausted, the reality of an untidy, uneven, and incremental weakening of the national identity will sink in—and be shrugged off.

[25] Stanley Hoffmann, "The Nation, Nationalism, and After," in Grethe B. Peterson, ed., *The Tanner Lectures on Human Values*, vol. 15 (Salt Lake City: University of Utah Press, 1994), p. 279.

CHAPTER SIX

Germany

During the 1980s German historians were debating whether German history is an aberration from the West's, whether Germans had trod a *Sonderweg* because of they had jettisoned liberalism and the Enlightenment for the murder and repression of the Nazis. In the 1990s some German commentators harped on another aspect of German uniqueness: Germany's unquestioned lack of constitutional and territorial continuity (its present borders date from 1991), and the concomitant fact that Germans disagree with one another as to what it means "to be German." During the nineteenth century, other German historians held that German history was uniquely different from the West's because Germans had to fashion a common state—which never included all Germans—long after a "German nation" had come into existence.

This chapter is devoted to the proposition that neither the history of the formation of the German nation-state nor the racist-integral nationalist interlude is unique. Both events have occurred elsewhere. All such episodes are instances of the multifaceted character of nationalism and of the difficulties of achieving a happily rationalized society while contending nationalist ideologies are fighting one another. Germany did not finally achieve rationalization until the 1950s. Mere approximations to integration were attained by quasi-authoritarian means in the Wilhelmine era and by totalitarian measures under the Nazis. Liberalism was crucial to the final stage, not the earlier approximations.

I gratefully acknowledge the research assistance and acute criticism of Michael Gorges and Karen Adelberger. Peter Katzenstein and John Leslie read the manuscript and saved me from making many mistakes. I am grateful to the University of California's Center for German and European Studies for financial support.

I hold that the rationalization of a polity is manifested by the acceptance of a consensual national myth in a modern or almost modernized society and economy. I also hold that successful rationalization may be upset and disrupted and that a rerationalized polity may either be patched together by adaptive steps or firmly cemented by acts of social learning. Rationalization, derationalization, and rerationalization have elective affinities with variable combinations of these features: the sequence of steps that led to the nation-state, the extent of social mobilization at the inception of the process, the degree of prior cultural homogeneity of people being integrated, and the gulf between the elite and the folk cultures.

Germany, along with many other countries, represents the combination of these factors I label Type C, which suggests that the early victory of a liberal-nationalist rationalization formula is doubtful. In Germany such a formula was struggling for acceptance before 1949 without ever succeeding. Social mobilization was almost complete when Bismarck began the process of fashioning a German nation-state, always a factor that complicates the victory of liberalism over competing syncretist formulas that inspire various articulate segments of the public. Weimar and Wilhelm II sought to fashion a patchwork of liberal and syncretist institutions; one fell victim to World War I, the other to the Great Depression, a fact used by contemporary German historians to justify their *Sonderweg* argument. Only the elites of the post-1949 Federal Republic (FRG) exhibit true social learning. As they succeeded in rationalizing modern Germany under liberal auspices, they also seemed to be running up against the limits of their nation-state's ability to satisfy all the demands of the German people. Hence continued rationalization is seen by many as depending on the successful integration of the FRG into a united Europe. But others see a secure future in a renewal of German national hegemony over *Mitteleuropa*. Different people learned different lessons from the failures, crimes, and tragedies of German nation-statehood. Which is the final, the true lesson? Which mode of reasoning is consistent with theories of progress and reasoning linked to liberalism?[1]

A Brittle Polity Comes into Being

French Invasion Triggers German Nationalism

Nationalist sentiment among the numerous German literate elite during the eighteenth century lagged far behind similar attitudes in Britain and France, a condition due to the peculiarly apolitical situation in which

---

[1] For a full explanation of these concepts, see Chapters 1 and 2.

the German bourgeoisie was placed. The well-educated and numerous German members of the *Bürgertum* of the eighteenth century were certainly mobilized. They were by no means assimilated as equals into the ruling nobility and autocracy, but they did not seek equality and the right to participate in political life. The reigning ideology of *Bildung* taught people to seek a moral life based on education and hard work, but it discouraged them from engaging in public affairs. As there were 2,000 political jurisdictions in the pre-Napoleonic German polity, each practicing cameralism, there was ample opportunity for well-educated commoners to find administrative careers. Prussia, the most developed bureaucratic autocracy, employed many non-Prussians in that capacity because most of the native nobility, the *Junker*, disdained education and entrepreneurship until well into the nineteenth century. The socially mobilized middle class of eighteenth-century Germany was composed overwhelmingly of state-employed members of the free professions, not of merchants and manufacturers or agricultural entrepreneurs. Such professionals still accounted for almost 90 percent of the elected delegates to the revolutionary parliament of 1848. Unlike their counterparts in Britain and America, they lacked many opportunities for civic participation. "Obedience is the first duty of citizenship," said a Prussian minister of the Interior.

German *Bürger* remained indifferent to the idea of a German nation until after 1810. The courts aped French institutions, whereas the bourgeoisie admired Britain's. The major writers of the period considered themselves cosmopolitan adherents of the French Enlightenment, not as Germans. Only the excesses of the French Revolution caused many of them to reconsider their position and, like Fichte and Hegel, take seriously the possibility of a syncretist German nationalism anchored in the Prussian state.[2] The triggering event was the military humiliation of Prussia by France in 1806, followed by France's truncating and occupying Prussia. This trauma gave rise to the period known as reform and liberation, the ending of cameralism and of serfdom, and the admission of commoners into an army now based on universal military service. *Bildung* was now reinterpreted to include patriotic service to a "fatherland." The mobilized bourgeoisie was officially assimilated into a state that made itself into a mouthpiece of "the people" for the first time, even though

---

[2] German intellectuals, in general, despised Prussian absolutism prior to 1806. The Enlightenment triggered an interest in patriotism (which was identified with individual liberty) and in natural rights but only very rarely a specifically German sense of political identity. Among the exceptions were Klopstock who revived and popularized the "Hermann der Cherusker" myth of German primordialism. On the other hand, Herder's use of primordial arguments about language and national genius were *not* used by him to justify German nationhood, though they were so used by Fichte a little later.

the sole purpose of this pseudo-populism was the expulsion of the French. It was unclear then and later whether the proper focus for this populist German identity was to be the existing state (as tended to be true in Prussia and German Austria) or an as-yet nonexistent all-German state. Prussia and Austria made no constitutional changes after the defeat of Napoleon, but some of the southern German states did enlarge the ability of the *Bürgertum* to participate in politics. In general, after the initial reforms were made permanent, the French shock was followed by policies that safeguarded the aristocratic order while strengthening the administrative power of the rulers.

The Failure of Liberals to Fashion a German State

The so-called liberal revolution of 1848 was in fact not so liberal; it also failed because the King of Prussia was compelled by the Emperor of Austria to forego the crown that the Frankfurt Assembly had offered him, thus dooming the birth of an all-German state. Before being forced to decline, he had expressed his reluctance to accept the crown of Germany because it was offered by popularly elected delegates and not by his fellow rulers. In any event, the offer was made only by those delegates who favored a German state that excluded Austria; the Assembly had been divided on the question of whether Austria was or was not German.[3]

Following this debacle, the liberals were reduced to working at the level of the thirty-nine German states. All along, a syncretist nationalist movement existed alongside the Liberals. The Syncretists generally wished to retain vestiges of the system of estates and guilds in their opposition to free-market industrialism. They were unabashed monarchists and admirers of premodern Germanic folkways. Student organizations and protestant clergy were prominent among them. Some Catholics felt ambivalence over the national question, identifying with the Catholic ruling dynasties of their states rather than with an all-German polity that was going to be ruled by Protestants. Nonliberal ideologies were represented among the parliamentary delegates in 1848; they tended to favor the confederal "great German" (or pro-Austrian) constitution for the new state, whereas the Liberals tended to advocate the more centralized "small German" (or pro-Prussian) solution.

[3] All-German liberalism before 1867 was represented by the Nationalverein, the Prussian component of which was the Progressive Party. The Nationalverein always stood for the federal parliamentary constitution opposed by Bismarck. It also stood for keeping the working class and its unions out of politics and for an assertive German foreign policy. The Nationalverein never gained much strength south of the Main. The confused character of German national symbolism is described by George L. Mosse, *The Nationalization of the Masses* (New York: Howard Fertig, 1975).

The Liberals' commitment to constitutional freedoms was tested during the 1860s in Prussia and shown to be hollow by Bismarck. They had fought him tenaciously in 1862 when he disregarded the constitution, but they capitulated when their economic demands were met. Successive Prussian governments had brought about the economic unification of Germany by 1867 by means of the gradual creation of a customs union north of the Main river and the abolition of all internal tolls and fees on trade. After 1867 German Liberals were agitating primarily for the completion of German economic unity in the form of the standardization of weights and measures and of money, of company law, a common postal system, credit regulations and patent rules. By the end of the 1870s, they were asking for a protective tariff for the Reich and for more aggressive government assistance in foreign trade. Upon gaining all of these goals, success seemed to sap their interest in also pursuing a liberal political agenda.

Bismarck Fails to Fully Rationalize Germany

German unification in 1870, in form, came about as a confederal compact among the rulers of the German states, who proclaimed the King of Prussia as their Kaiser. In doing so, however, they also accepted a protoliberal confederal constitution drafted by Bismarck, used after the war of 1866 to integrate the northern German states with Prussia. This constitution was endorsed by the chastened all-German Liberal Party. The Liberals also hailed the acts of Prussian conquest that created the North German Confederation that in turn became the German Reich when the south German states joined. But its confederal character and monarchical sheen pleased the reformist and traditional syncretists as well.

Unification happened against a backdrop of almost-completed social mobilization in a setting in which there was no conflict between elite and folk cultural values. This meant, of course, that there was a large, literate, and aroused public to contest the content of the all-German nationalism that was to endow the new state.

By 1871 only 4.8 percent of Germany's population lived in cities that had a population of over 100,000, and almost 64 percent still lived in towns of 2,000 people and less. But only 43 percent still made their living from agriculture, 98 percent were literate (though this included a fair number of functional illiterates and people who knew little or no German), and 20 percent of the population was able to vote (as opposed to 27 percent in France and 9 percent in Britain).[4] By that time the rate

---

[4] All statistics dealing with social mobilization and public expenditures in this chapter

of industrialization, urbanization, and modernization in Germany was a good deal faster than in Britain and France. Just under 5 percent of the labor force was in government service by 1895, almost twice as many people as in Britain and France. The Germans spent 34 percent of the federal budget on defense in 1872, almost 11 percent on science and education, and 9.6 percent on public health and social welfare. But still there was no national myth, even after the creation of the Reich, though Bismarck sought to create one. His government used the schoolroom and the churches, as well as the academic community and the army to create the symbols, tradition, and values needed to buttress a national self-consciousness focused on the Reich. These efforts were only partly successful. Poles in the east resisted German-language schools; Catholic Bavarians objected to the attempt to introduce Hohenzollern-oriented patriotism into theirs. The peasantry elsewhere objected to compulsory extended school attendance laws and reforms of the curriculum that seemed to threaten patriarchal family life, indeed to any kind of secularization. Catholic and social-democratic subcultures with their own organizations retained their existence alongside those of the new state that sought to extend downward the reformist-syncretist nationalism that characterized its elites.

The most painful evidence of the lack of a nationalist consensus was the so-called Kulturkampf, Bismarck's and the Liberals' effort during most of the 1870s to strip Prussia's Catholic population of its subculture by means of state-sponsored discrimination against Catholics and their institutions. In the East this also took the form of enforced Germanization of Poles and the settlement of Germans in these lands to create family farms at the expense of both German and Polish-owned large estates. The Kulturkampf "amounted to a centralist drive for the primacy of the citizen-state relation in the organization of public life, with radical implications for other traditional ideas of social order and the Prusso-centric version of federalism. . . . For liberals the Kulturkampf meant exactly what the term said, a struggle to unlock the potential for social progress, freeing the dynamics of German society from the dead hand of archaic social institutions."[5]

The Kulturkampf represented an effort on the part of the National Liberal party to enforce its notion of a modern secular German citizen against groups that remained hostile to this conception of solidarity and identity. In that it ran counter to the Conservatives' more traditional

---

come from Wolfgang Zapf and Peter Flora, "Differences in Paths of Development," in S. N. Eisenstadt and Stein Rokkan, eds., *Building States and Nations* (Beverly Hills, Calif.: Sage, 1973), 1: 190, 193–94, and from Peter Flora, ed., *State, Economy, and Society in Western Europe, 1815–1975* (Chicago: St. James Press, 1983).

[5] Geoffrey Eley, *From Unification to Nazism* (Boston: Allen and Unwin, 1986), p. 69.

preferences; Bismarck supported the Liberals only because he considered Catholic institutions as rivals to those of the Prussian state and therefore subversive of the loyalty to be expected of a subject of the Hohenzollern rulers. In any event, they lost the battle against the Catholics and against Social Democrats whom they branded enemies of the nation. But as they proceeded to make the new Germany safe for industrial capitalism, they never managed to make friends of those who remained attached to a premodern view of politics, the many reformist and traditional syncretists, particularly in the parts of Prussia that were conquered in 1866. The traditional syncretists insisted on the christian foundation of the fatherland, on rulership based on divine grace rather than on popular consent, and they objected to the free market capitalism of the Liberals and the government.

Traditional notions of German identity were represented by the patriotic historians, notably by Heinrich von Treitschke, their dean. He recast the telling of German history—and this became official curricular policy—so as to make the founding of the Reich the natural and only possible culmination of all previous events, and the Hohenzollern dynasty the agent of providence and of destiny. The German Volk is an organic body with a will of its own. One motto of the new state, as if to cover over the brittleness of its ideological underpinnings, was "one Volk, one Reich, one God." Yet that people could not agree on a national holiday or national anthem!

The fragmentation of German society was extreme. Conservative nobles saw themselves as the sole authentic carriers of German nationality, just as Liberals insisted that they alone deserve being called the German nation. Artisans spoke of themselves as the historically true Germans, and salaried employees, in identifying with the National Liberals, were insisting on their special status to avoid any possibility of confusion with the despised manual workers.

As Table 6-1 shows, modernization, urbanization, and industrialization progressed rapidly during the 1880s and 1890s. This entailed a rapid increase in the working-class population and a drive to organize trade unions. It also implied the growing appeal of the Social Democratic party that espoused a Marxist-revolutionary ideology, though the unions were far less revolutionary than the intellectuals who led the party. The Social Democrats were the chief advocates of universal male suffrage in Prussia (it already existed for Reich elections) and of rigorous respect for civil liberties. They were feared by the bureaucracy and the National Liberal party. Hence, upon failing to vanquish the Catholics, Bismarck began a decade-long persecution of the Social Democrats and of their trade unions as potential subversives.

But he also sought to preempt their appeal. The German government

Table 6-1. Public expenditures of all German governmental entities by major function, 1872–1975 (% of total expenditure)

	Defense	Housing	Education Science	Public Health	Social Security[a]	Economy/ Environment
1872	34.0	0.2	10.8	3.0	5.8	1.1
1881	25.6	0.3	17.6	3.9	3.8	1.6
1891	26.3	0.5	17.4	4.1	3.6	1.7
1900	25.2	0.7	18.1	4.5	3.9	2.0
1913	26.6	0.7	19.5	5.0	5.2	2.4
1925	4.4	7.8	16.2	5.2	21.6	2.1
1932	4.9	2.3	15.0	3.3	33.7	3.2
1935	24.8	2.0	10.7	2.5	18.7	4.0
1948	24.7	5.9	11.2	5.0	21.2	4.7
1955	11.9	7.9	9.8	3.7	26.8	5.6
1960	12.9	7.4	10.5	3.9	24.4	7.0
1970	10.1	2.2	15.1	5.2	20.6	7.3
1975	9.1	2.2	17.3	6.0	24.0	4.3

SOURCE: Peter Flora, *State Economy and Society in Western Europe, 1815–1975* (Chicago: St. James Press, 1983), vol. 1, p. 391.
[a]Figures do not cover all social insurance benefits, only federal and *Lander* subsidies to social insurance institutions.

that persecuted Socialists and trade unionists and presided over the West's most thorough industrialization process also invented the compulsory state-operated, state-subsidized social security system. This was no coincidence. Before the great innovations enacted in the 1880s, German employers and local governments had provided poor relief and paternalistic services for workers (such as housing and childcare), but coverage was spotty and entitlements uncertain. Academic social reformers had advocated a more consistent policy of state-supported and regulated social services since the 1870s to mitigate the impact of drastic industrialization and urbanization and to avoid the marginalization of the working class. Christian conservatives held that the state had an obligation to do these things to moderate the workings of an individualistic capitalism of which they disapproved. Liberals, although far from enthusiastic about measures that would interfere with free markets, acknowledged that pure and untrammeled individualism should not be a German trait and acquiesced in compulsory health and disability insurance, and to pensions to which they, as employers, had to make financial contributions. Bismarck and the bureaucrats with whom he drafted the legislation, moreover, were very concerned with presenting the new Reich as a Christian State, a state with a social conscience, because only thus did he consider it possible to link the worker to the state and make him truly German rather than a rootless proletarian. The bureaucracy wanted to remove incentives for workers to join trade unions, to keep wages, hours, and working conditions from becoming subjects of large-scale bargaining. Therefore, along with the insurance entitlements came corporatist tripartite commissions to administer insurance funds and adjudicate claims, conceived deliberately as substitutes for unions and parliamentary "agitation."

Superficially, however, the polity seemed rationalized after 1870. Catholics and workers, although discriminated against, did not threaten to rebel. Neither did the oppressed Poles. There was little industrial unrest.[6] The principle of succession for the Kaiser was never in doubt. People paid their taxes, and draft evasion was minimal. The war against France had been universally popular, as was the annexation of Alsace-Lorraine. Bismarck's foreign policy was entirely peaceful thereafter. Nobody challenged it even when, after 1880, he acceded to the imperialist requests of the Liberals by becoming interested in a colonial empire in Africa and the Pacific.

FAILURE OF SUPERFICIAL RATIONALIZATION

Between 1890 and 1917 Germany almost became a rationalized nation-state as institutional and symbolic devices began to bring about a rapprochement among the contending claimants to rival notions of German identity and purpose. Superior economic performance certainly helped as well, as did a deliberate policy of making industrialization more bearable for the working class. But defeat in World War I laid bare the brittleness and superficiality of the compromises. We now discuss the reasons for the brittleness: Germans could never agree whether a primordial ethnicity or loyalty to the state defines their collective identity; the adoption of social imperialism and the practice of selective upward mobility did not suffice to mute class conflict; ethnic minorities were not sufficiently assimilated; the "democratizing" reforms of Wilhelm II were all rhetorical.

The mirage of successful rationalization, of pseudo-rationalization, be-

---

[6] The Social Democrats, as the repressive legislation went into effect, polled just over 300,000 votes in the Reichstag elections of 1881; in 1890, just before the legislation was repealed, they polled 1,427,000 and, with 19.7 percent of the vote became the largest party in parliament. Before 1890 the unions were weak, but thereafter they became a major interest group and drew away from the Social Democratic party. The Socialists' Erfurt Program (1891), though orthodox-Marxist in content and committed to the complete overthrow of bourgeois society, nevertheless opted for parliamentary-electoral tactics to achieve this aim.

tween 1890 and 1918, illustrates the limitations of social adaptation, as opposed to social learning. True learning occurs when key elites systematically examine their failures to integrate their society, when they seek to understand why the values they sought to impose failed to catch on. True social learning occurs when key elites realize that institutions fail to represent and affirm desired values. True social learning, therefore, involves the reasoned search for new values and for new institutions more likely to integrate the views of a squabbling people. That search is based on knowledge, on analysis, on reasoning, not merely on instrumental compromises among rival positions and groups. The adjustments attempted in Germany, however, mostly lacked the quality of reasoned search. They were instrumental adjustments, temporary deals among antagonists, adaptations of the moment that only lasted a moment.

People or State as Definer of Identity

One could be a German because of one's descent from German stock—the primordial tie of *Blut und Boden*. In German history this position is known as *völkisch* (ethnic). One could also be German by virtue of being a loyal subject of the sovereign—the state and its constitution define citizenship—which meant that a popular-parliamentary view should prevail. Or one could seek a formula that somehow combined both positions. If so, one had to offer a conception that dealt simultaneously with the cultural roots of identity and the constitutional role of the Kaiser.

If Bismarck's first allies, the National Liberals, had remained united as the mainstay of the new Reich, the formula would have stressed the unitary-parliamentary, secular, and populist aspects. A "liberal" Kaiser was seen by them as a quasi-plebiscitary patriot-ruler of a united Germany cast as an enlarged Prussia. Some called this type of rulership a "National Monarchy." But the Liberals fragmented in 1880, and Bismarck played down the unitary and parliamentary aspect in favor of a confederal formula that camouflaged Prussian hegemony, although he accepted the populist emphasis. Catholic traditional syncretists preferred a Kaiser who symbolized the continuation of the medieval-corporatist-christian ideas, explicitly designed to oppose the Prussian-patriotic view; other traditionalists saw in Wilhelm I the linear successor to the Reich's founder, Charlemagne; both wanted to counter the parliamentary-populist emphasis of the Liberals.

Wilhelm II saw things differently. He sought to legitimate his rule by stressing continuity with the medieval Reich, with the Prussian-dynastic view, and with a quasi-bonapartist populism that allowed him to rule "his people" directly, without chancellor, parliament, or parties. He attempted a kind of democratic authoritarianism that also raised the issue

231

applied only to Reichsdeutsche

of Germany's civilizing world mission. A syncretist *Nationalmonarchie* became a distinct formula for some German conservatives after 1910. As Friedrich Meinecke said of the Kaiser in 1913, "We are not satisfied with the knowledge that our nation is a great spiritual *Gesamtpersönlichkeit*; we also demand a leader for it for whom we would walk through fire."[7]

In the 1910s many commentators linked this symbolism to the introduction of a "democracy" that stressed the citizens' loyalty and devotion to the dynasty as representing the people, not history. The dynasty represented continuity and stability, whereas the parties and parliament evoked the image of confusion and strife. A superficial rationalization was the result. As even Catholics came to accept the Protestant dynasty, Liberals hoped to exploit the populist notion of *Sozialmonarchie* in favor of perfecting parliamentary institutions and instituting new social reforms.

Yet the syncretist parts of this program remained more pronounced than the liberal. The romantic-conservative German youth movements endorsed this pseudodemocratic view of rulership. Love of country was to be a searing personal experience, linked to strengthening Germany against its foreign enemies, to anti-Semitism, to the protection of Germans living outside the Reich. The Kaiser became the symbol of these views, in opposition to parliamentary and bureaucratic institutions, to political parties and interest groups. The target of such groups as Wandervogel, the Pan-German League and the German School League was the Marxist-derived class basis of social and political identity advocated by the Social Democrats and their trade unions. Being German was supposed to mean being part of an organic whole; ethnicity was the ultimate definer of identity. A people (*Volk*) was more important than the state, although the unity of people and state was seen as a desirable situation. Modern secular values were suspect, though not all were rejected, not even all aspects of industrialism. We are witnessing a powerful reformist-syncretist nationalism in these organizations.

Permanently Excluded or Successfully Assimilated?

The *völkisch* assertion of Germanness was expressed primarily in policies directed toward the Germanization of Poles, Danes, and the small group

---

[7] Quoted in Elisabeth Fehrenbach, *Wandlungen des deutschen Kaisergedankens, 1871–1918* (Munich-Vienna: R. Oldenbourg, 1969), p. 91. Efforts were made to represent this view of the monarchy in the school curriculum, in the creation of a monumental architecture and in singling out Richard Wagner's music as emblematic of German culture. The Kaiser's special military role was also an important rationalizing symbol. Wilhelm II was referred to as *Oberster Kriegsherr* and as the special patron of the Imperial Navy being created in the decade preceding World War I.

of French-speaking Lorrainers. The Jewish minority was eager to assimilate. The anti-Polish effort was the most sustained and extensive. Until 1886, Prussia was content to have loyal subjects in its eastern provinces, irrespective of their ethnic identity. Thereafter things changed. Poles migrated to the Ruhr in large numbers to become miners and to East Prussia to seek work on landed estates. The *Kulturkampf* was interpreted by Liberals and Protestants as demonstrating the persistence of institutions hostile to the new German state not only because of catholic identification with Rome but also because so many catholics were Poles. (In 1910, 10 percent of the Prussian population was still Polish.) In 1886 the Prussian government began a systematic policy of settling German peasants in the eastern provinces and of alienating the necessary farm land from the big Polish landowners. Nationalists had urged such policy to create the economic infrastructure for a policy of gradually eliminating Polish culture. Both social Darwinist arguments and geopolitical ones were marshaled in defense of policies that made the German language compulsory in all schools and that urged the creation of a German citizenry with a single culture. After the turn of the century such policies were intensified under the pressure of new associations of German settlers in the eastern provinces, supported by the bureaucracy in Berlin. The speaking of Polish at public meetings was prohibited. Although the events of 1919 demonstrated the failure of many of the Germanizing policies in the frontier regions, these policies were ultimately successful in other parts of Germany where Poles had settled.

On the other hand, German workers became patriotic citizens *even though* the Social Democrats and the trade unions also grew very rapidly; but unions became less revolutionary as they increased in numbers and in power. This was true even though Social Democrats were systematically excluded from the civil service even if they scored well on the entrance examinations; neither were they accepted as officers in the armed services. (Jews and Catholics were equally subject to discrimination in employment in higher civil service and army positions, even though the Reich authorities leaned over backward to provide proportional representation in the federal civil service for candidates from all the *länder*, even at the expense of discriminating against better qualified Prussian candidates.) Other institutions, too, tended toward rationalizing the polity because of their appeal to the middle class. Many could vicariously identify with the nobility because they were given reserve officers' commissions in the army. Student organizations (*Burschenschaften*), in aping aristocratic manners, permitted university students to identify similarly. Many other ways of giving official recognition to middle-class people and organizations gave Germans a status that bound them to the state.

Wilhelm II as Would-Be Reformist Syncretist

The accession of Wilhelm II to the throne in 1890 marked the beginning of a deliberate government policy of inclusion, evidenced most importantly by the repeal of the antisocialist laws, a higher tariff, acceptance of Catholics, and intensified imperialism in Africa and China. The government aimed at the creation of a unified Right to face a restless working class that was to be won over to the nation. As in Britain and France, the ideology of social imperialism was invoked to woo the working class as new colonies and a battle fleet were acquired. The inclusionary course embraced modernity, industry, and science (and was therefore acceptable to the Liberals provided that civil liberties were also protected); it was also opposed by traditional-syncretists who were ill at ease with modernity. Artisans, small businessmen, some professionals, and German migrants to the eastern lands were especially bothered, and thus they flocked to the patriotic and imperialistic associations just described. These became mass organization using modern means of mobilizing people, though devoted to fighting modern values. The Right sought to protect itself against downward social mobility as it saw other segments of the middle class join the upper classes in a marked rise in social status and wealth.

Those who benefited from the pace of modernization accepted the Reich, and those who felt themselves harmed by it attempted to save the Reich from its own modernizing success. Both trends embraced nationalism, albeit different strands, and both accepted imperialism as right and good. Liberal nationalists as well as syncretists gloried in the global spread of German might and culture, although for different reasons. But is was the successful industrialists and their allies who increasingly defined the content of German nationalism; they gave the Right its program, not the landed nobility that held the visible reins of power. Yet, the ideological rapprochement among the various rightist elements never resulted in an organizationally unified conservative party professing a single strand of nationalism.

Derationalization, the War and the Revolution of 1918

Before as well as during World War I, Germans did their military service and paid their taxes; after 1914 they died for the fatherland in very large numbers. That bloodbath also was the high point of what seemed to be a great patriotic coming-together under the legitimating aura of a popularly based imperialism in which even some Social Democrats seemed to glory. The development of the German party and electoral system before 1914 explains the surprising moratorium on ideological confrontation that was to last until 1917.

Federal (but not land-level) electoral participation, a good indicator of legitimacy, rose steadily between 1900 and 1910, as did the numbers and membership of interest groups. The intensity of political party activity, as measured by the number of local branches and their meetings, also rose sharply. Socialists, Poles, and Catholics all voted in record numbers despite efforts to intimidate them. On the other hand, where, as in Prussian elections, voters saw the system as hopelessly rigged against them while favoring the upper classes, they stayed away from the polls in droves.

The 1907 Reichstag elections were interpreted as a plebiscite endorsing Germany's *Weltpolitik*, its policy of assertiveness to secure "its place in the sun": colonies, trade, naval might, as well as recognition of its premier position in central Europe. All parties, including the Catholic Center and the Progressive Liberals (but not the Social Democrats), affirmed the justness of imperialism. The Center became part of the governing coalition. The Social Democrats saw the handwriting on the wall; a major segment of the party affirmed its patriotic commitment, muted its opposition to imperial expansion, and supported Germany's role in the war in the summer of 1914. However, the rift between an emotionally patriotic Right and a "me-too" patriotic Left only grew: "This multiplicity of nationalist conceptions . . . made nationalist appeals as much a source of conflict as unity. Despite its own elevated sense of classless cultural solidarity, nationalist ideology could never escape the conditions of German society before the First World War."[8]

The size and importance of the colonial empire that Germany had managed to acquire were far from impressive, a condition that fueled the demand for more colonies. The Pan-German League continued to articulate these demands, as did the other patriotic associations. But it also stressed, along with the Conservative Party and Friedrich Naumann's Liberals, the need for consolidating a German *Mitteleuropa*, to advocate expansion toward Russia. A strong foreign policy also was equated with a strong culture, a strong national character, all needed in the Social Darwinist–defined struggle for survival among peoples and nations. Social imperialism was a favorite theme of many across the political spectrum. In response to the question, "What is national?," a leader of the Pan-German League replied:

Everything that relates to the preservation, promotion, future, and greatness of our people and Reich is national; that means that national questions of

[8] Eley, *From Unification to Nazism*, p. 76.

the first order are: the army, the navy, colonies, Germanization of the Prussian eastern provinces and North Schleswig, de-Latinization [*Entwelschung*] of Alsace-Lorraine, honorable representation of the German Empire, protection of Germans, preservation of the citizenship and civil rights of Germans abroad, cultivation of the German language and German schools abroad combating the treacherous [*vaterlandslose*] [sic] Social Democrats.[9]

It is still a matter of historical debate whether Germany's entry into World War I was motivated by imperialism or was due to miscalculation about British and French responses to the Russian and Austrian behavior in the Balkans. In any event, imperialist appetite soon developed after the outbreak of war. Those who see German imperialism as the glue that sustained the society can point to the plans to create Polish and Baltic client states in the east, annex parts of French Lorraine, seize more of Africa, and create an independent Ukraine. Continental annexationism became more popular and important than overseas imperialism. *Völkisch* notions of cultural-racial solidarity came into their own after 1914.

The war years also marked the high point of interclass cooperation and government planning. The allied blockade of Germany meant that after 1916 it became necessary to organize the entire German industrial and manpower apparatus into one giant planned war economy run by Walter Rathenau and General Erich Ludendorff. Trade unions, even socialist ones, and trade associations were given administrative and decisional tasks as they were organized to implement decisions of the bureaucracy that they had helped to make. Strikes were avoided until nearly the end of the war, prices were controlled, raw materials allocated, and trade organized by these means. The very difference between government and the private sector was obscured by these corporatist arrangements, even though some employer associations at first balked at joining socialist worker representatives in common bodies of governance. Some industrialists even saw in the war economy "an opportunity to create a German Gemeinwirtschaft under which German capitalism would be organized in the spirit of Prussian discipline and self-sacrifice and under which corporate groups would administer a planned economy in the service of the national welfare."[10]

The revolution that ended Germany's role in the war shattered such dreams. In any case the agricultural sector was never included in the corporatist scheme of the *Burgfrieden*. Germans did not learn to live with industrialism, with ideological conflict, and with inequality after 1890.

---

[9] Roger Chickering, *We Men Who Feel Most German* (Boston: Allen & Unwin, 1984), p. 79.

[10] Gerald Feldman, "German Interest Group Alliances in War and Inflation," in Suzanne Berger, ed., *Organizing Interests in Western Europe* (New York: Cambridge University Press, 1981), p. 164.

But the beginnings of the welfare state, the possibility of electoral coalitions, and the half-hearted revolutionary spirit of most workers might have become steps toward learning to live in harmony—if the lost war had not poisoned the national well. But it is also true that social insurance, like the war economy corporatism, like social imperialism, was inspired by the ideology of a harmonious society ruled by a benevolent state and its bureaucracy, realizing its historical destiny, *not* by consensual knowledge about how such a state of affairs might be designed. Action based on ideological conviction and on instrumental motives is not action justified by rational knowledge.

RACIST NATIONALISM RERATIONALIZES GERMANY

Why Weimar Lacked Legitimacy

Until engulfed by the Great Depression in 1931, postrevolutionary Germany looked like a temporarily stricken industrial giant who was recovering speedily. There was considerably less industrial strife in Germany than in France and Britain, although unemployment rose to one-third of the labor force in 1933. In 1925, 8.5 percent of the labor force worked for the government, a considerably higher percentage than in France and Britain. The state spent only 4 percent of its budget on defense in the 1920s (because of the one-sided disarmament obligations of the Treaty of Versailles), but 6.8 percent went on housing, 13.6 percent on science and education, and a whopping 33.6 percent on social security, even though taxes in Germany were somewhat lower than in Britain and France during the 1920s (14.8 percent of the gross domestic product [GDP] in 1925). Taxes rose to 22.7 percent of GDP by 1937, reflecting the massive rearmament and public works programs launched by the Nazis in their successful effort to spend their way out of the depression.

Yet Weimar Germany was far from happy (Table 6-2). The half-hearted revolution that overthrew the monarchy was carried out by Social Democrats and supported even more half-heartedly by the Catholic Center and the Democratic Party. During the fourteen years of the Weimar Republic, twenty-two cabinets attempted to rule, an average of a little less than eight months per government. Nine elections to the Reichstag were held during this period. The highest vote garnered by any party in any election was the 44.2 percent obtained by the Nazis in 1933. The three parties who refused to accept the liberal Weimar constitution as legitimate earned together 64 percent of the vote in 1933, 27.6 percent in 1928 when things appeared to be going well for democracy, and 34.9

Table 6-2. Extent of rationalization, Germany, 1880–1990

	1880	1910	1930	1940	1970	1990
Political succession	Yes	Yes	Yes	No	Yes	Yes
National myth in education	Some	Yes	No	Yes	Yes	Yes
Religious institutions	No	Yes	Yes	Some	Yes	Yes
Civil religion	No	Some	Some	Yes	Yes	Some
Cultural uniformity	No	Some	Yes	Yes	Some	No
Official language accepted	Yes	Yes	Yes	Yes	Yes	Some
Income distribution	Some	Some	Yes	Yes	Yes	Yes
Workers' organizations	No	Some	Yes	Yes	Yes	Yes
Farmers' organizations	Yes	Yes	Yes	Yes	Yes	Yes
Payment of taxes	Yes	Yes	Yes	Yes	Yes	Yes
Conscription accepted	Yes	Yes	N/A	Yes	Yes	Some
Fighting wars	Yes	Yes	N/A	Yes	N/A	N/A
Administrative cohesion	Some	Some	Yes	No	Some	Yes
Foreign policy	Yes	Yes	No	Yes	Some	Yes
Peaceful change	Some	Yes	No	Yes	Some	Yes
Legitimacy	Some	Yes	No	Yes	Yes	Yes
Total (%)	59	84	68	84	83	83

percent in 1920, a year of considerable unrest. Because they aroused so much critical opposition (as well as praise), the striking scientific, artistic, literary, and aesthetic achievements of the Weimar years contributed to the political and economic turbulence rather than counteracting it.

Germany's population was almost completely socially mobilized, highly urbanized, and dependent very heavily on an industrial economy. In terms of its problem-solving capacity the government seemed to be doing well until it lost a terrible war. However, the tensions the the Wilhelmine elite had been unable to resolve now reappeared with a vengeance. The immediate years following the revolution were beset with communist conspiracies and strikes; these were repressed with some gusto by the rump armed forces, who were somewhat slower to put down the rightist *putche* launched by militant veterans' organizations and the fledgling Nazis. Two monarchist parties were less violent, but no less opposed to the postrevolutionary regime and its trade unionist and bourgeois leadership. Unemployment was a problem even before the Great Depression because general unemployment insurance was not created until 1927 and proved totally inadequate after 1931. The noncommunist workers, tenant farmers, and middle-class supported the Republic, partly because it promised to protect society from Bolshevism and from harsh peace terms. The spotty success of the republican coalition in foreign and domestic policy induced many middle-class voters to turn to the conservative parties, thus further weakening the Weimar coalition, and giving solace to integral nationalists. Farmers who owned their own land opposed the Republic because of low agricultural prices. The German People's Party (right-wing liberal), led by Gustav Stresemann, became the middle-class vehicle for a dignified foreign policy, of rejoining the liberal West while also obtaining less humiliating peace terms; but Stresemann also acted as a member of the anti-Weimar Right; his party would not join a government that included Social Democrats. Nor were the Catholics united, as a separate Bavarian Catholic party arose over its disagreement with the Center's increasing reliance on initiatives from Berlin, where it formed the pivot of almost all Weimar cabinets. On the right, the Nazis and the Conservatives competed for the same electorate, and from the extreme left the strong Communist party attacked everyone (except the Nazis after 1933).

The Weimar constitution was not consistently secular. It sought to please all organized religious interests by offering state salaries for the clergy (though all religions were recognized as official) and religious instruction in public schools, thus undoing the anticlericalism of the Democrats and the Social Democrats. The religious establishments were tax supported despite a rhetorical endorsement of the separation of the churches from the state. Tax-supported denominational schools were tolerated as well. Weimar Germany's civil religion was riddled with contradictions.

Industrial and economic relations in Weimar began with the corporatist war economy system fully intact and endorsed by the unions and by industry in 1919 as the *Zentralarbeitsgemeinschaft*. The system collapsed in 1924 because the deeply divided parliament was unable to adopt legislation to make it permanent, thus reintroducing a sharper class conflict as economic conditions deteriorated. Its downfall also symbolized industry's willingness to seek allies on the Right rather than work with the trade unions. While industrial corporatism lasted it gave major benefits to the workers and successfully circumvented antilabor proclivities in the bureaucracy and in the Reichstag. After its demise the employers renounced many of the concessions earlier made to the unions. Ironically, these developments would later be seized upon by the Nazis in their attacks on capitalism and "plutocracy," even though the Nazis also accepted campaign contributions from industrialists.

The Right despised Weimar. In an excess of devotion to liberal principles of interest representation the drafters of the constitution introduced a system of proportional representation that guaranteed almost all shades of organized opinion a few deputies, thus of course contributing further to government instability and making impossible the formation of stable coalitions anchored in a few large parties. The Right was electorally rewarded for campaigning on the claim that Germany had not lost the war in the field of battle, but as a result of a stab in the back by the Marxist parties (who had indeed been instrumental in organizing the mutinies in the fall of 1918 that broke out after the defeat in France). Syncretist and integral nationalists took solace in this face-saving fable. They blamed the antinationalist "treason" on the members of the Weimar coalition. For the Right, the very democratic features of the constitution were insults to German identity, to the continuity of German history as symbolized by strong, heroic leaders unconstrained by legalistic provisions.

The liberals were further weakened by their acceptance of the peace treaty with its major losses of territory and with the galling placement of Germans under Polish, French, and Belgian rule. Equally galling was the forced acknowledgment of responsibility for having initiated the war (the famous "war guilt" clause of the Treaty of Versailles) and the admission of having committed war crimes. Because of its rigidity on church and school issues, the Center, unlike its Christian-Democratic successors in 1948, never managed to expand its electorate beyond the Catholic core, many of whose members later were to vote for the Nazis. The Conservatives, unlike their pre-1918 predecessors, became a mass-based party with supporters in all parts of Germany.

Versailles and the Great Depression Trigger Racist Integralism

Where then, did the Nazis recruit their supporters? The party entered electoral politics at the federal level in 1924 and garnered 6.6 percent of the vote, apparently from lower-middle-class people especially badly hurt by the hyperinflation just concluded, taking votes from both center and Right. The core clientele, it appears, consisted of small retail merchants, pensioners, artisans, and farmers who blamed large-scale corporate capitalism for their economic plight but who rejected class-struggle explanations and solutions in favor of formulas stressing German organic unity. After 1930, the appeal of the Nazis spread to middle-class voters of all types as all Liberal parties became the main losers in all depression-era elections. In rural areas, moreover, the Nazis gained at the expense of the right-wing conservatives. The Nazis became a party with equally strong foundations in traditional rural society as well as in industrial-urban settings in which socialist and communist power had eroded.

"The NSDAP, after 1930, was well on the way to becoming the long sought-after party of middle-class integration."[11]

Yet the Nazis did very poorly in the last pre-depression elections in 1928. It seems likely that the Weimar coalition might yet have survived if it had been able to master the depression instead of being swamped by it. Liberals and Social Democrats paid no attention to Keynesian demand-enhancement prescriptions in their macroeconomic policies, although Keynes's work was well known to German economists and appreciated by some. Things were complicated by the post-Versailles reparations issue, which had the effect of linking economic with overall foreign policy matters. Thus, the democratic parties wanted to make an effort to pay reparations and keep Germany within the rules of the still-liberal international economic system while also stressing civil liberties in domestic life. Parties to the right of the coalition, however, linked their preference for authoritarian governance with rejection of any obligation to carry out the reparations clauses of the Versailles Treaty. Nor was the Right committed to German participation in a liberal world economy. Heavy industry turned protectionist and hostile to the continued payment of reparations even after they were rescheduled in 1929 and joined others in demanding a revision in Germany's favor of the territorial settlement of 1919. In short, the deterioration of the economy went hand in hand with ever shriller challenges to terms of the Versailles Treaty. Integral visions of German identity and German "needs" successfully challenged more liberal ones.

It was the Nazis who benefited from this vipers' nest of passions, conflicting interests, and failed policies. They found an ideology able to cross the lines of tension and hatred in Weimar Germany to become a myth, albeit for only a dozen years. They catered to the fears of those who felt cheated and threatened by the large-scale impersonalism of corporate capitalist life, by the compassionless tyranny of instrumental rationality and bureaucratic efficiency, by Weber's Iron Cage. They gave solace to those who wanted to defy Britain and France, the "plutocratic capitalist" oppressors of the German people's heroic nature. They promised to save Germany from Jewish-Marxist materialism. The Nazis undertook to give Germans the self-respect of which Versailles had robbed them. To fulfill the promise, of course, Germany was given a revolutionary-totalitarian national myth, not the comfortable small-town *Gemütlichkeit* of the traditional syncretism of which pre-1933 Nazi propaganda reeked.

---

[11] Thomas Childers, *The Nazi Voter* (Chapel Hill: University of North Carolina Press, 1983), p. 178.

241

The Nazi Racist Integral Myth

When Adolf Hitler became German chancellor, his party was clearly the most successful in attracting support from all classes and regions of Germany, from Protestants overwhelmingly but from a good many Catholics as well. The Nazis had made a special appeal to elderly people on fixed incomes despite their youth-dominated self-image and propaganda. By 1932 they had also acquired a large constituency among university students, farmers, and civil servants. They had made inroads into the upper middle class and even among blue-collar workers not organized by the large industrial unions.

This electoral appeal contained many opportunist arguments that effectively camouflaged the truly revolutionary ideology that constituted the core of Nazi beliefs. The Nazis despised the German upper classes, bourgeois as well as noble, as tainted by cosmopolitanism and capitalism. The leadership of the party came largely from the lower middle class, from marginal professionals, from World War I veterans who had been unable to adjust to civilian life, not people likely to inspire confidence in the upper-middle-class–dominated German bureaucracy and industrial circles. The Nazis appealed to all who were, or felt themselves to be, in trouble and who blamed "the system" for their difficulties. It appealed to people unable or unwilling to analyze their difficulties with the help of unemotional and analytic cognitive tools, who preferred the "salvational" means promised by a charismatic leader who demanded full surrender and loyalty from his followers. Nazism was a true political religion not only in its ritual and symbols but also in its psychological appeal. Because the faults of "the system" included not only the capitalism practiced by oligopolistic firms but also the bureaucracy of soulless efficiency, Nazi followers expected that Nazi functionaries would take the place of the old civil servants. When this did not quite happen, Hitler got the support of industry and of large-scale agriculture for Nazi macroeconomic policies in exchange for his promise to destroy the trade unions and to create instead Nazi-controlled unions that would lack the power to influence wages. That promise was kept: trade unionists found themselves in Dachau along with Jews, Freemasons, Marxists, journalists, and members of the Reichstag.

Despite their successful destruction of the old trade unions, as well as of all other voluntary organizations of Weimar "civil society," the Nazis also sought a comprehensive inclusion of the working class in the national community. All *Volksgenossen* were equals. All former trade unionists belonged to the compulsory Labor Front, which, along with several other party organizations, became responsible for the disbursements of social security, leisure time, and vacation benefits. The Hitler Youth took

242

the place of the youth organizations that had been associated with the former political parties. Robert Ley, the head of the Labor Front, noted that "nothing is more dangerous to a state than homeless men. In such circumstances, even a bowling club or a skate club assumes a state-maintaining function."[12] He was right; the working class was indeed successfully integrated into the state, albeit by totalitarian devices.

The Nazis espoused an egalitarian sense of community based on racial purity alone, not status or wealth. They remained ambivalent toward Christianity, that "slave religion," denying it any role in defining German values or—more accurately—Aryan values. Politically engaged clerics were persecuted along with all enemies of the *Volk*. The central importance of anti-Semitism in Nazi ideology was directly linked to Nazi opposition to capitalism and socialism because Jews were held to be the leaders of both. Moreover, they, along with Slavs, were said to threaten the purity, and therefore the survival, of the Aryan race because of the threat of miscegenation. The survival and the revival of the Aryan race, in the form of the German nation, were one and the same thing; they demanded the conquest of living space for the *Volk* and the creation of a new European order under German direction. Racial thinking was used to justify not only genocide but also eugenic legislation, euthanasia, rules governing procreation among the racially most pure and for relations between Germans and non-Aryans.

All non-Aryans were removed from public life after 1933. Capitalism was to be purged and made accountable to the people. The red menace was to be curbed for good. The military glory of Germany was to be restored. The Nazi party was the embodiment of the emotional commitment of the individual to the collectivity—one of the favorite Nazi slogans was *Gemeinnutz geht vor Eigennutz*—and the main instrument of collective action. The rule of the party was to be total. Everything it demanded was licit and everything of which it disapproved illicit. Integralism in ideology and commitment included also integralism in leadership: all governance was totally hierarchical and flowed from the will of the leader, a charismatic person imbued with superhuman powers, who in turn delegated some authority to lower-level leaders.

The leadership principle was the sole constitutional norm of Nazi governance and the preservation of racial purity the core theme of Nazi integral nationalism. In fact, the Nazi party never achieved the monopoly of totalitarian control that it sought because of the survival of pretotalitarian institutions on which the conduct of the war depended, the bureaucracy, the armed forces, and the large corporations. Nazi institutions

[12] Cited in Gregory Luebbert, *Liberalism, Fascism, and Social Democracy* (New York: Oxford University Press, 1991), p. 275.

came into being alongside the older ones, to compete with them. Thus, the Nazis created a party-led army (the SS) alongside the Wehrmacht and party police (the Gestapo) alongside the regular police. They also created their own civil administration, whose competencies were not clearly differentiated from those of the regular civil service. And they set up a system of party-controlled industrial enterprises, eventually staffed with slave labor, of which today's Volkswagen automobile is a survivor. Government made generous use of terror against any putative domestic enemy of the new order.

Racist Ideology in Action

The Nazis aimed at a total remaking of European society, a true continental revolution, though their preoccupation with the war that was being lost made implementation of most of these plans impossible. Still, as one Nazi writer argued, "a new organically structured Europe was coming into being, led by a Reich aware of its heavy responsibility. The peoples of Europe formed a community of destiny, within which each nation had the living space and freedom necessary for the unfolding of its own unique strength and tradition."[13]

That freedom turned out to be defined strictly by Nazi racial thinking. Aryans would rule; the Scandinavian and Dutch peoples were part of the master race along with Germans; Britons were potential allies whom Hitler sought to woo until 1941. Part-Aryan cultures (Czechs, Balts, French) were to be allowed some autonomy as helpers to the master race.

Nazi administration reflected these ideas. Bohemia and Moravia were annexed to the Reich but not treated as colonial territory; a similar fate was planned for the Baltic countries. The conquered "Aryan" western and northern countries were ruled by local Nazi allies, although the Jews in these countries were slated for extermination (as elsewhere) and many people were taken to Germany as slave labor. Slovakia and Croatia were made "independent" fascist states allied with Greater Germany; Italy, Hungary, and Romania already had fascist governments allied with the master race.

The Nazis regarded Slavic eastern Europe as agricultural lands to be stripped of their native population and given over to German colonization. Those Poles, Ukrainians, and Russians who survived the systematic killing of all educated and skilled people were to be confined to menial tasks in the service of German peasants who were to be moved to the East. As it happened, the parts of Poland and the Soviet Union incor-

[13] Quoted in Robert E. Herzstein, *When Nazi Dreams Come True* (London: Sphere Books, 1982), p. 36.

porated into the Greater German Reich proved most unattractive to potential German settlers, and military defeats kept the genocide of Poles and Ukrainians from being carried to its planned completion. Jews and Gypsies were not equally fortunate.

It still seems incredible that this regime, apparently, rerationalized Germany into a coherent nation-state. The economy began to perform very well; Germans accepted the reintroduction of militarism and of conscription with seeming enthusiasm; Nazi racial policies aroused no opposition; terror and police-state methods were not experienced by most Germans, and informing on friends, neighbors, and even parents was accepted as patriotic. Germans fought tenaciously in six years of unprecedentedly violent war, despite suffering enormous casualties. Only one ineffective effort was made to overthrow the Nazi regime, the failed assassination plot of July 1944. We cannot tell, of course, whether the Greater German Reich would really have remained rationalized for even a fraction of the thousand years Hitler prophesied if Germany had not been defeated in 1945. Nor can we be wholly certain of the role of repression in giving us a false impression. As Henry Mason said, the Nazis successfully combined "a messianic and apocalyptic vision of history *within* the political, bureaucratic, and technological system of a highly developed industrial society. What took place within Nazi Germany were interactions between totally heterogeneous phenomena: messianic fanaticism *and* bureaucratic structure, pathological ideology *and* routinized administrative decrees, archaic modes of thinking *and* a highly complex modern society."[14] Integral racist nationalism *is* able to reunite such fissiparous strands, to provide murderous bonds of identity as its acolytes seek to transcend a past they see as tainted. Fortunately, we were spared a test of its staying power.

LIBERAL NATIONALISM RATIONALIZES THE GERMAN FEDERAL REPUBLIC

The defeat in 1945 destroyed the German state and shattered its society and economy. Physically, German cities were in ruins as a result of allied bombing, which killed 300,000, wounded 780,000 civilians, and eliminated 20 percent of residential units; 12,350,000 refugees streamed into the western occupation zones from territories east of the Oder-Neisse line, escaping from the Soviet armies. There was no German government until 1949; the country was cut up into four separate occupation zones, each ruled by a foreign military government. Heavy American aid was

---

[14] Henry L. Mason, "Implementing the Final Solution: The Ordinary Regulating of the Extraordinary," *World Politics* (July 1988): 549, paraphrasing Saul Friedländer.

required to reignite the economy as the Soviet occupation forces stripped away, in the form of reparations, much of the industrial plant still intact. There was little food and less fuel. Interallied commissions made the key decisions for German industry.

The evolution of the Federal Republic started from this low point. By 1970 over 30 percent of the population lived in cities over 100,000 inhabitants, only 18.7 percent remained in villages; 7.5 percent of the labor force was still active in agriculture. The service sector now accounted for over 43 percent of the labor force; 10.6 percent worked for government at all levels. Sixty-seven percent of the population was enfranchised in 1960, 99 percent was literate. In 1950, government still spent 13.5 percent of total public expenditures on defense, and social security took 45.7 percent. Education and science took 7.3 percent, and 4.9 percent was devoted to government-subsidized reconstruction of the housing stock. By 1960, 20 percent of the gross domestic product (GDP) was devoted to government social programs. The fledgling Federal Republic was on its way to continue the German welfare-state tradition with a vengeance. It is especially noteworthy that during the travail of economic reconstruction between 1945 and 1950 German administrators and their U.S. overlords were determined to avoid the economic errors of the Weimar governments, especially hyperinflation.

How Liberal Nationalism Became the Civil Religion

The Federal Republic (FRG) that emerged from the ruins is a much more successfully rationalized state than were Wilhelmine and Nazi Germany, not to mention Weimar. Prussia was dissolved as the hegemonic entity; Catholics ceased being an inner-directed minority, as confessional differences lost much of their earlier salience; the nobility and its base in the armed forces disappeared. Perhaps most important, the terrible moral burden of the criminal Nazi past made any pretension to an assertive foreign policy quite unthinkable before 1989, the miracle year of modern international politics.

Before we can explain how political parties that barely tolerated one another under Weimar learned to practice diffuse reciprocity, we must identify the new actors on the political scene. The Western Allied occupation authorities actively encouraged the forming of parties dedicated to liberal democracy at the local level, with the result that three major parties had emerged by 1949. They, in turn negotiated the Basic Law of West Germany, that became the all-German constitution in 1990, under strict supervision of the occupation authorities who decreed that the constitution could not be as centralized as Weimar's had been, but not as decentralized as Bismarck's. The Basic Law was declared to be

246

"provisional," valid only until the Soviet-occupied eastern zone, later the German Democratic Republic (GDR), would be allowed to rejoin West Germany. The FRG declared itself the sole authentic successor state to former German states, thus stigmatizing the GDR, which was under the totalitarian control of the communist-run Socialist Unity Party (SED), as illegitimate.

No explanation of how and why the FRG is fully rationalized under the auspices of liberal nationalism is credible until we come to the end of this chapter. In this section the institutional elements of the liberal national myth are presented: new political parties who trust one another, a flowering of pluralism and of participatory social movements, the democratization of public education and of the military, the commitment to peaceful change, and the maintenance of civil liberties.

The new political parties encouraged by the occupation authorities remembered the strife of Weimar only too well: they were determined not to reenact it. The only party to emerge from the Nazi era relatively unscathed was the Social Democratic Party (SPD). The SPD at first remained Marxist, committed to a democratic but anticapitalist workers' state, opposed to NATO and European integration as inconsistent with the goal of German reunification. It won no federal elections with this stance. In 1959, the SPD officially abandoned the class struggle, its proletarian orientation, opposition to the Western alliance, and anticlericalism. Instead, it embraced the principles of the "social market economy" and European economic integration in its search for a broader electoral constituency. It also became virulently anticommunist and a staunch defender of the civil libertarian content of the Basic Law. The Free Democrats (FDP) were torn during the 1950s between a pro–free enterprise wing dominated by northern industrialist and a small-enterprise/welfare-state–oriented southern section. Marginalization at the hand of the dominant Christian Democrats (CDU) forced the FDP toward the left. It remained a defender of the social market economy and of Germany's pro-Western bias, and it functioned as a small possible coalition partner for both major parties.

The CDU originated as the former Catholic Center's bid to become a force devoted to basing policy on Christian values; it opened its doors to Protestants and has since lost it confessional coloration altogether. At first torn between conservatives devoted to free enterprise and christian socialists who sought state control over large corporations, the CDU became a center-right party; it invented the idea of the social market economy, an economy owned and managed by private business, including very large corporations, but constrained by the practices of corporatist decision making (which gave the trade unions a special role of importance) and made tolerable to workers by an extensive system of social

247

security and social entitlements. The CDU is otherwise nonideological, devoid of a special program, a catch-all party. It made itself the architect of all of German postwar foreign policy with the exception of the SPD's *Ostpolitik* of the 1970s. Its catch-all character provided a big incentive for the other two parties to downplay their ideological commitments and to become partners in a tolerant consensus that went unchallenged until the advent of the Greens.

No liberal national myth would have arisen unless the Western allied authorities had carried through a program of de-Nazification and reeducation. High-level Nazis were systematically purged from public life, and many were jailed. Communists, accused of being hostile to the practice of electoral democracy, were actively discriminated against in public employment in the West, as were noncommunists in the GDR. The Allied authorities, together with reform-minded Germans at first planned major changes of the educational systems, which were largely shelved under pressure of Cold War thinking. There are major curricular differences among educational systems run by the various *Länder*. In general, however, textbooks were systematically rewritten to remove glorification of the German past and to tone down German nationalism. When a nonaggressive national anthem had to be chosen, Konrad Adenauer substituted the pacific third stanza of the *Deutschlandlied* for the objectionable first. The flag of the 1848 democratic unity movement (also the flag of the Weimar Republic) became the new national colors.

Social studies were deemphasized in primary and secondary schools, although the inculcation of democratic civic values became an important task for the schools. The secondary school system was made more accessible to working-class and lower-middle-class children; no tracking was to take place until a student's sixteenth year. Social mobility was also to be encouraged by the construction of large numbers of new universities, some of which, after 1968, fell under the control of radical antidemocratic groups for some years. Nevertheless, the system of secondary and higher education still seems disproportionately geared to the aspirations of the middle class whose children benefit far more from the secondary schools than do working-class children in terms of success at universities. Although the teaching of contemporary history was neglected in secondary schools, both German states took care to use history texts to vilify each other, to inculcate students with the belief that the "other" Germany lacks legitimacy. The children of immigrants must attend school where they are treated as Germans, though some of the *Länder* offer some work in lower grades in the immigrant's language until the student is deemed ready for instruction in German alone. Most bilingual education is paid for by the country of the immigrant's origin or by private immigrant-aid associations. On the whole, the FRG is not eager to make

248

special services available to immigrants. To the extent that any values are taught in school, the ideals are liberal and cosmopolitan.

The FRG's armed forces were explicitly designed to avoid the practices associated with former German armies, navies, and air forces. Recruitment relies on conscription; however, generous exceptions from service are provided in the form of conscientious objection and alternative public service. Draft evasion has been heavy at times, although it declined as the period of service was shortened and as the Bundeswehr seeks an increasingly professional basis.

Civilian control over the armed forces is absolute and unquestioned. Soldiers are citizens in uniform. The legislature decides on the deployment of forces outside Germany. The first such deployment took place in 1995, following an authorization by the Federal Constitutional Court. The democratic attitude of the armed forces is fostered by a principle labeled "self-guidance," which is used in the indoctrination of all troops. Each soldier, far from being the obedient automaton of earlier German armies, is a "co-responsible citizen" who expresses in personal conduct the liberal German values he or she is to defend. The German soldier need not obey orders that violate the rules of German democracy; he or she enjoys all civil rights. Military legitimacy derives uniquely from the mission to defend the democratic order.

This remarkable act of social learning did not go unchallenged. Self-guidance did not find acceptance without bitter resistance from the center-right. It was widely criticized by the left as inadequate during the 1980s. There continues to be disagreement over the extent to which the Bundeswehr ought to feature, in the names of units, uniforms and ceremonial, the tradition of its predecessor armed forces. The architects of the Bundewehr wanted to minimize such traditions; but the CDU tends for favor their retention and continues to agitate for the restoration of symbols that had been removed. Similarly, while the SPD and Greens want Bundeswehr personnel to be conscious of the crimes of the Wehrmacht and the Nazis, right-wing opinion (prominently including Chancellor Helmut Kohl) wishes troops to identify proudly with their predecessors irrespective of possible political taint.

Civil liberties are widely respected despite the travail of post-1945 nation formation. The police, like the Bundeswehr, was subjected to legal-democratic control as a result of the Occupation. In general German criminal jurisprudence allows for few convictions and even fewer incarcerations. Violent crime was minimal until the 1990s. Thus, when in the late 1960s and during much of the 1970s, a wave of left-wing terrorism struck German society, this policy of forbearance was severely tried. The outbreak of right-wing violence in the 1990s was seen by many Germans as being fueled by an overly restrained police response.

Between 1970 and 1979 there were 649 acts of political violence, including 31 assassinations and 163 hostage takings. Between 1980 and 1985 there were over 1,600 violent acts, now committed by both the left and right. The government responded by creating a federal criminal police and enhancing surveillance techniques, much to the lament of civil libertarians in the Left. Nevertheless, German democracy survived unscathed despite the administrative recentralization in Bonn of Land police forces and the stepped-up interpolice cooperation among European countries.

Despite the presence of many refugees from formerly German areas, now Polish, Russian, and Czech, who wanted to go back to their homes rather than assimilate into the culture of the FRG, most people had accepted the finality of the Oder-Neisse border by the 1960s. When given the choice between the continuation of prosperity in the context of the alliance with the West or efforts to bring about reunification, almost everyone opted for the status quo. West Germans overwhelmingly identified as *West* Germans by 1970, not as the Germans who inhabited the Germany of 1938. Citizens of the GDR were taught that they were the true Germans, the Germans of the new socialist person, the heirs of what was always superior in German culture.

By 1970, the erstwhile refugees had been successfully absorbed into FRG society. Differences between Protestants and Catholics were so lacking in salience that, by 1974, 69 percent of all marriages were cross-confessional. Not only the CDU, but also the chief trade unions, were then interconfessional in membership. All churches receive state recognition and state subsidies paid for by the income tax, although separate confessional school systems are in decline. Churches are prominent in political advocacy, even though they make little effort to impose their spiritual values on a population who, on the whole, is growing indifferent to all organized religion. In Bavaria alone there is a tendency to make Catholicism the state religion.

Legitimacy and Participatory Pluralism

In the mid-1970s, 80 percent of the population said it prefers the FRG to any other historical German state. Konrad Adenauer is voted by over 50 percent every year as having done the most for Germany because he restored German dignity, independence, and friendship with France, while Bismarck was mentioned by only 10 percent. In 1983, only 56 percent of respondents claimed that they felt proud to be German. German history is no longer taught systematically in public schools; when in 1986 the government proposed the creation of two new museums of German history, many objected because they could not agree on which modern events to memorialize. In the mid-1970s only 22 percent of Germans thought they had more in common with other Germans of a different social class then with Frenchmen of the same class. Reunification was actually opposed by 14 percent of West Germans in 1989. Eighty-two percent pronounced themselves satisfied with their lives in 1973, while 88 percent felt this way in 1990. In 1973, only 44 percent were satisfied with the workings of German democracy, but in 1990, 81 percent expressed satisfaction. In 1970, 70 percent were content with incremental reforms in German society; in 1990 the number was only 55 percent, and 39 percent wanted to curtail freedoms to control subversives.

Transitions among governments have been unruffled by controversy. Thanks to the rule that no party receiving less than 5 percent of the national vote may receive legislative representation, no right-wing extremist party has seats in the Bundestag, although such parties sometimes win 10 percent in local elections. The strongly negative reaction to the appearance of violence-prone extraparliamentary political groups bespeaks general respect for electoral and party practices. No call for a strong leader to save the nation has been heard. Voters turn out in large numbers. People continue to pay their taxes and do their national service without going out of their way to sanctify the state they serve. The economic policies and practices that went along with these sentiments surely helped to produce this widespread sentiment of legitimacy. As David Conradt noted:

> While the increase in support for the present system and the decline in positive feelings for past regimes have been the result of both generational changes and the performance of the Bonn system, the important point . . . is that all major social, . . . economic, and political groups ranked high in their support for political competition, freedom of political expression, sense of representation, and the parliament. Support, at least for the liberal Republic established in 1949, has by the 1970s become diffuse, not significantly related to any particular group or policy of the government. These principles and processes have become accepted norms for the conduct of politics in the Federal Republic.[15]

Although most institutions are legitimate and most differences over policies no longer elicit passionate conflict, one major new controversy came to the fore as a result of the government's full-scale endorsement of nuclear energy as the way to achieve energy autonomy: the quality and future of technology and of technological innovation. Grass-roots movements challenged unquestioned adjustment to unbroken techno-

---

[15] David P. Conradt, *The German Polity* (New York: Longman, 1989), pp. 54–55.

logical innovation. The Green Party's emergence in the 1980s is the expression of this disaffection with modernity. Belief in science and progress remains strong, but the previously unchallenged faith that science will solve all problems is gone. The fear of environmental degradation and the desire to foster a wiser use of natural resources pit a "postmaterialist" younger generation against the older people. New extraparty movements challenge the sanctity of the institutions and policies blamed for environmental crises: capitalism, bigness, materialism, arms racing, the cold war, the unconstrained pursuit of private group rather than of the general interest. Although skepticism toward science has not meant the rejection of telematic and information technologies or the wholesale condemnation of innovation many West Germans have indeed rejected a policy of "progress at any price." The ruling parties, however, still believe that technological innovation remains the guarantee of prosperity. The Greens, moreover, pose a much more basic challenge to the German consensus, a challenge that extends to foreign and defense matters.

Social mobilization, apparently, does not stop when all citizens have become literate, most of them vote regularly, the huge majority are aware of events around them, many travel, and all know they are part of a world they experience regularly on television. Social mobilization continues because people who were normally inactive politically are now aroused to action and self-assertion. These newly mobilized were the rebelling students of 1968 who became the Green and extreme left-wing parties of the 1970s and 1980s. They express a syndrome of poorly integrated passions, including radical ecological sentiments, pacifism, antinuclear commitments, condemnations of the cold war and of nuclear deterrence, neutralism, feminism, radical Marxism, and opposition to further technological change. The substantive connections among these themes are weak. In Germany at least, supporters of this syndrome tend to shun the older parties in favor of the Greens, though the left wing of the SPD is strongly sympathetic to some of these causes, to the contempt for bureaucracy and the distrust of the state.

The German Greens made the transformation of capitalism and the abolition of militarism the core demands derived from their analysis of ecological crisis. They question the moral validity of most German institutions and denied, at first, the very legitimacy of the Bonn republic. Electoral successes, of course, made most Greens more accepting of existing institutions, particularly as they attained almost 10 percent of the popular vote in some *Länder*. They reject military preparations in favor of tactics of nonviolent resistance. Some Greens are clearly integralists and protototalitarians (though not nationalists), but others subscribe to a cosmopolitanism in which it is hard to discern a specifically German identity. Were European liberalism to falter, it is quite possible that the Greens would offer the forum in which a new German "nationalism" might take shape, stressing participatory democracy and nonbureaucratic administration, anchored in small groups of the committed. The German Greens so committed would show "the way" to the rest of the world. In the meantime, the Greens fight the foreign policy consensus and the materialist complacency of the majority of Germans.

The postmaterialist trend was an unintended consequence of the reforms in higher education undertaken in the 1960s. These had resulted in a huge increase in the number of young people attending universities, in upward mobility, in expectations of a rewarding professional career. However, the economic crises of the 1970s led to disappointment because of a considerable amount of intellectual underemployment and unemployment developed, fueling feelings of alienation from "the system." Moreover, during the 1980s, admission to universities and to some disciplines was made more difficult as state subsidies to students were reduced.

But the blooming of hundreds of new voluntary movements is far from guaranteeing effective legislation and administration. Prior to the increasing prominence of postindustrial issues, most controversies in the FRG were discussed by corporatist bodies before they were submitted to orderly legislative debate. The new issues on the agenda make this practice more difficult because the clashing opinions jump class and party lines, unlike the older economic differences. Postindustrial issues greatly complicate democratic-corporatist decision making.[16]

By the time reunification came about, citizens of the FRG were smugly self-satisfied, with the exception of the minority of postmaterialists. They had largely forgotten the sentiments and symbols of all pre-FRG all-German formulas of identity. Legitimacy was rooted in a shallow sense of national self, in a weak commitment to the liberal collectivity. Moreover, that legitimacy seemed to have its roots in the corporatist social market economy.

---

[16] Policymaking for civilian nuclear energy illustrates the complication. In 1973 the FRG committed itself to an ambitious program of reactor construction with the full support of all relevant trade unions and industry associations as well as of the CDU/CSU; the SPD and FDP were internally divided, though their leaders pushed the program. The tremendous public opposition sparked the formation of the Greens and of antinuclear groups, but it was all in vain until the Chernobyl disaster reignited the opposition. Thereafter the SPD wanted to stop the program and the CDU/CSU split over the issue, leading to enormous uncertainties as Land and federal governments repeatedly clashed over the issuing of operating licenses, after many billions of deutschmarks had been spent on the equipment. As of 1995, none of the facilities planned in 1973 had come on line.

Democracy, Legitimacy, and the Social Market Economy

By 1966, the FRG's economy had developed from the basket case it had been in 1945 to the world's third largest; Konrad Adenauer and Ludwig Erhard had brought about the "German economic miracle" by means of the social market economy, which

> expressed the balance between the liberal and the social democratic impulses in postwar Germany. Labor—protected by social insurance, formal recognition of its organization rights, political freedom and . . . workers' comanagement [of industry]—was willing to accept the linkage of wage gains to productivity. Germany entered a period of labor peace. . . . German capitalists could thus count on a steady supply of highly skilled, hardworking labor. Government policies encouraged growth and support. Erhard's tax laws encouraged the reinvestment of profits and gave substantial benefits for investment in capital equipment, while tight monetary policy kept inflation very low, which helped provide the necessary stability for foreign trade.[17]

The state created the parameters for and behaviors by the private sector from which prosperity emerged, stressing the prevention of inflation and providing a very generous system of social entitlements. Active management of investment and production was left to the private sector, albeit a private sector that functioned according to corporatist principles of consultation. The social market economy was far from being the unregulated free-enterprise utopia of classical liberals, although Keynesian demand management was rejected at first. Efforts for a more comprehensive form of planning were not made until 1967, when medium-term investment plans for the entire economy were worked out in Bonn, which were then enforced jointly by the federal and land governments by means of an agreed fiscal policy. This form of planning, under SPD leadership, led to a short period of Keynesian demand management in the early 1970s. German methods of economic steering, though they differed from practices elsewhere in the industrialized world, nevertheless proved very effective in legitimating the liberal values that inspired them.

The successful integration of Germans into the FRG is in no small measure due to the economic success of their nation. Conversely, the lack of legitimacy of the GDR had a great deal to do with the economic failures of that regime. By 1990 the German economy was the largest and the most export-prone of the European economies. Its labor force was thoroughly unionized, but the number of industrial disputes remained among the lowest in Europe. In 1979, 10 percent of the labor

---

[17] Peter Gourevitch, *Politics in Hard Times* (Ithaca: Cornell University Press, 1986), p. 171.

force consisted of foreign immigrants, and in 1976, 17 percent of all live births occurred in the families of guest workers. In the mid-seventies, the FRG devoted only 6.4 percent of its public expenditures to defense, but an overwhelming 46.4 percent to social security and, 12.2 percent to education and science. As a result of the pivotal position given the mark under the rules of the European Monetary System (EMS) that came into being in 1978, the FRG became West Europe's central banker in fact though not in law.

Institutionalized interest group participation in the making of policy — societal corporatism, as distinguished from the state-directed variety — is a central liberal value in much of Europe.[18] In Germany, it flowered because economic thinking was dominated by export-oriented industrialists allied with democratic trade unions rather than the coalition familiar from earlier eras of German history, heavy industry, and large-scale agriculture catering to a protected home market. German-style corporatism is expressed in a variety of institutions. German corporatism differs from other European models because the state does not occupy a directing position at all times. Legal frameworks made by the state, nevertheless, shape the institutions of corporatist governance of the economy. Worker codetermination is practiced on the shopfloor as well as in corporate board rooms. Consequently, labor leaders, having access to the firms' books, are well informed about the ability of the firm to pay wages and benefits while remaining profitable. This, in turn, strongly influences the pattern of collective bargaining, which takes place at the level of industrial sectors, not of firms (as in the United States) or the entire economy (as in Sweden). Finally, corporatist institutions include a very large number of advisory councils to government departments staffed by experts representing the major organized interests.

There are limits to participatory democracy as acted out in corporatist institutions even though industrial peace, the smooth functioning of corporatist-run social insurance funds, and overall prosperity are associated with it. Major investment decisions are made by large banks. The state is willing and able to ignore its advisory committees when the bureaucracy

[18] I use the term *corporatism* more loosely than most to denote a mode of democratic governance in which many important decisions are made only after extensive formal consultations among interest groups represented in organs established by law. Many commentators favor more restricted definitions. Some want to confine the term to voluntary decision making in the industrial economy, to collective bargaining in which the state plays a pivotal role. Others take this restricted definition but limit it further to situations in which the bargaining takes place between the state and the national peak associations of labor and industry, which leads to binding decisions for the entire economy. This is sometimes called "strong corporatism," as formerly practiced in Sweden and Austria. Somewhat weaker versions prevailed in Norway, Denmark, and Switzerland. Germany's pattern, for the purist, is a very weak corporatism. See Kathleen Thelen, "Beyond Corporatism," *Comparative Politics* (October 1994): 107–24.

and the ruling parties feel strong enough to do so; they sidestepped the consultative bodies of the health insurance funds when they imposed a law limiting the earnings of pharmaceutical firms and of physicians. The state subsidizes industrial research and the social insurance funds; it has sharply reduced its contributions in the 1990s. Perhaps most important, the Bundesbank, after all, controls the value of money with its bias against inflation, and thereby imposes sharp limits on the range of meaningful collective agreements. After 1973 the bank adopted a consistent monetarist stance and thus reenforced the supply-side emphasis given to the social market economy by the Schmidt and Kohl governments. Nevertheless, Helmut Schmidt felt compelled to retain some demand-stimulation measures as well because of his commitment to the Group of Seven to act as a "locomotive" for the ailing Western economies.

Despite severe shocks in the 1970s and early 1980s, the corporatist social market economy continues to perform well. Keynesian ideas of macroeconomic steering never really won out in German thought, though they inspired policy in Bonn between 1966 and 1973 because the SPD was ideologically predisposed toward demand management. Yet even the Social Democrats subscribed to the lesson learned during Weimar: never let inflation get the better of you. The Schmidt and Kohl governments therefore reverted to an upgraded social market economy with its emphasis on supply-side forces, self-regulated competition, and reliance on exports. More important, German economic analysts, after the first oil shock of the 1970s, persuaded the government of the need for an industrial policy in the form of public assistance to certain key sectors of the manufacturing branches. Even before this decision was made, however, the Keynesians had prevailed to the extent of persuading the *Länder* governments to plan together with Bonn the kind of economy that could adjust continuously to technological change while maintaining full employment, a step that called for more government intervention than the social market economists preferred. But toward the end of 1970s the government once more adopted deflationary measures rather than subsidizing firms in trouble. Committed to wage restraint, the main trade unions prefer to counter declining employment opportunities due to technological innovation by reducing the workweek to thirty-five hours, a decision approved by the government.

Sectorally focused industrial policy was the key measure adopted. The impetus was the perceived need for developing energy sources alternative to oil, and because of the high cost of R&D, of encouraging superfirms that could act as national champions. Public funds for research designed to lead to such guided innovations, including environmentally sound technologies and technologies to humanize the workplace, were voted in 1978. Justified by SPD economists and bureaucrats as *Struktur-*

politik, these measures were fully endorsed by the trade unions. It was taken for granted that in an economy in which full employment was thought to be dependent on high export capacity, it was considered imperative that Germany remain internationally competitive, which in turn called for unceasing technological innovation. The unions, locked into the collective decision-making process by the prevailing corporatist institutions and practices, accepted wage restraint and concentrated instead on safeguarding existing entitlements, strengthening their control over state-financed training and retraining programs, and improving conditions on the shopfloor. Industry did not oppose *Strukturpolitik,* cautioning however that it should not lead to state control over investments or to export cartels. These restrained measures, in which none of the parties seeks to score a full victory, have been especially visible in the troubled steel industry, in which modernization turned out to be less painful than elsewhere because of the substantive consensus on what needed to be done and the procedures for satisfying all the parties (except unskilled and foreign workers). Corporatism protects the most skilled workers disproportionately. Yet it ensured relatively smooth adjustments to an economy as much exposed to the winds of change as any.[19]

Germans also learned how to cope with challenges to their welfare state. In their determination not to slide again into the intense internal conflicts of the Weimar period, post-1945 Germans learned to appreciate the virtues of solidarity and burden sharing. The principles of equity that undergird the social insurance system illustrate this lesson learned. The generous system of pensions was indexed to changes in the cost of living. Richer *Länder* agreed to transfers of tax revenues to subsidize the poorer ones. Unemployment insurance sought to guarantee that joblessness—unacceptable in principle—be made dignified. The myriad of private health and occupational accident insurance funds were subsidized by Bonn.

This system was threatened by serious cost overruns as well as by hard economic times by 1975. Severe cutbacks were made in funds for education, housing, and health care. Additional cutbacks came between 1988 and 1992 in reimbursable health costs, old-age pensions, and oc-

---

[19] Some commentators dispute that the social market economy performed well in the 1980s and after. They argue that it was unable to provide for full employment for these reasons. Fiscal and monetary policies (the latter not under the control of the government) were not synchronized. The unions felt that they were cheated because their wage restraint was not matched by low profits. Unemployment increased despite the commitment to shorten the work week. The Bundesbank was unable to banish all inflationary pressures. Moreover, administrative cohesiveness was undermined by the fact that the necessary close coordination between federal and Land policies was often lacking because of long delays in decision making. See Fritz Scharpf, *Crisis and Choice in European Social Democracies* (Ithaca: Cornell University Press, 1987).

cupational accident insurance. Yet consumers, when confronted with the statistics of early depletion and cost overruns, expressed a preference for curtailment of benefits over increases in their contributions to the funds. Solidarity and burden sharing, it seems, are principles that work in both good and hard times.[20]

The political legitimacy of Germany's democracy, undoubtedly whiggishly liberal but not markedly nationalistic, quite clearly derives from the successes of the social market economy and its corporatist mode of governance. Germans feel they "never had it better"; they experience a sense of pride in their achievements. Polls show that voters express their approval of the parties in response to the size of their pocketbooks. Yet the social market economy functions on the basis of publicly regulated competition; it is not rooted in wholly free markets. Says Wolfgang Streeck: "The German state is neither *laissez-faire* nor *étatiste,* and is best described as an *enabling* state. Its capacity for direct intervention in the economy is curtailed by vertically and horizontally fragmented sovereignty, and by robust constitutional limitations on discretionary government action."[21] It has learned, since being reconstituted by the United States, Britain, and France, to help groups to organize themselves and therefore avoid the extremes of pure market-driven incentives and authoritative central allocation of values.

The Pro-Western Foreign Policy Consensus

Germany could have been reunified in 1952 if Stalin's offer to end the division in return for the neutralization and demilitarization of the united country had been accepted. Rejection of the offer was a foregone conclusion because it was not for Konrad Adenauer to accept, but for Washington. The FRG was not to be fully sovereign until 1955; until then most Allied control powers remained in force. Washington, together with its major European allies, had by then decided on the rearmament of Germany and on its inclusion in whatever western military union was to emerge. The CDU government had decided that the future security and welfare of Germany were wholly dependent on a close alli-

---

[20] Not all commentators agree with this evaluation. Wolfgang Streeck fears that the strain of unification may undermine the ability of the system to perform well. He also fears that increasing globalization of production may undermine the social insurance and codetermination systems ("German Capitalism: Does It Exist? Can It Survive?" in Colin Crouch and Wolfgang Streeck, eds., *Modern Capitalism or Modern Capitalisms?* [London: Francis Pinter, 1995], pp. 14–15). Claus Offe thinks that the shrinking actuarial base of the insurance funds threatens the future of all social insurance. The core of the German system of social insurance is groups of insured *workers;* the shrinking industrial work force results in a much larger pool of uninsured people.

[21] Streeck, "German Capitalism," p. 6.

ance with the West; such an alliance was seen as an absolute prerequisite to eventual reunification.

Between 1952 and 1956, the FRG joined NATO and became a founding member of the supranational institutions from which the European Economic Community (EC) emerged in 1957. The removal of Allied controls was explicitly premised on the enmeshment of the newly sovereign FRG in the webs of regional economic and military integration. This evolution speeded up after the rapid communization of the GDR following the abortive revolt of 1953. The division of Germany seemed to become irreversible after NATO, in effect, tolerated the building of the Berlin Wall in 1961, constructed by the GDR to prevent the continuation of the heavy flow of its citizens toward the West. Everyone understood that the return of the FRG to international respectability was allowed only because the exercise of sovereignty was also curtailed by membership in intergovernmental and supranational organization. Everyone thought that close German association with the West effectively precluded reunification; Moscow was hardly going to agree to augment NATO's power by ceding the GDR to it, at least not before 1989.

The CDU's foreign policy was thought by the government to have a direct relationship to the strengthening of democracy in the FRG. Adenauer and his group sought close association with their occupiers in part because they wanted Western protection against any lingering German hankering after integral nationalism. When forced by events to choose between a Western guarantee for German security and welfare on the one hand, and reunification on the other, the CDU and FDP did not hesitate to choose the former, much to the chagrin of the SPD, which favored neutrality, demilitarization, and aloofness toward European integration until 1959. Conversion to the CDU and FDP position, the formation of a foreign policy consensus of deemphasizing reunification, came only after the SPD decided to shed its Marxist patina. While jettisoning an all-German policy in fact, Bonn nevertheless kept up the pretense of speaking for all of Germany. It did so by refusing to recognize the GDR or have any dealings with it and to break relations with any government that recognized Pankow. The GDR in 1967 created a specific East German citizenship whereas the FRG stuck to Adenauer's policy of considering anyone born within the 1937 borders of the Reich as a (West) German national, including refugees from the GDR.

The SDP's approach made definitive by Willy Brandt and Helmut Schmidt after 1969, confirmed the atrophy of unification efforts and also sought to mitigate its consequences. Technical and cultural exchanges with Pankow were authorized and the policy of absolute nonrecognition abandoned. The policy of paying the GDR for releasing people to the West, begun by the CDU, was intensified along with financial subsidies and symbolic gestures.[22] Brandt, apparently, wished to keep alive the consciousness of an all-German nationality even as he recognized the GDR as a sovereign state and accepted the existing borders as final. He initiated a series of personal meetings with his GDR opposite number and announced the doctrine of "one German nation, two German states." Brandt thus denied the existence of two rival German nation-states while admitting the lack of a single one. Nevertheless his formula suggested the potentiality that a single nation-state might reemerge, a position that ran counter to the popular attitudes that had formed by then. In 1972, the CDU unsuccessfully challenged as unconstitutional the treaty whereby the two Germanies recognized each other formally; the party opposed the agreement to defend its claim that the FRG alone was the German nation-state.

We cannot be sure whether these SPD-inspired measures, continued by the CDU government in the 1980s, helped to bring about the East German vote to merge with the FRG. We can be reasonably certain that the SPD-inspired *Ostpolitik*, launched in 1972 but also continued by the CDU in the 1980s, helped to bring about the relaxation of Cold War tensions in Europe. Institutionalized as the Helsinki Process, a series of military and cultural measures were initiated by the NATO and Warsaw Pact states after 1975 to increase contacts across the Iron Curtain, improve the observation of human rights in the East, advance the control over conventional arms, and relax military tensions. This policy was the cornerstone of German foreign policy; it recognized the finality of post-war political borders (unless changed by popular vote) and forswore the use of violence in interstate disputes.

However, there were voices on the left of the SPD who demanded more: a nearly neutralized FRG and GDR, mediating between the antagonistic cold war blocs, pioneering a postindustrial decentralized society, devoted to principles of ecology and humane industrial life. When the United States, with German approval, insisted on deploying a new generation of intermediate-range nuclear missiles in Germany in the early 1980s, a enormous popular opposition movement sought to block the deployment. Although the movement did not succeed, the Kohl government sidestepped NATO policy by continuing its active policy of détente with the GDR as well as the symbolic recognition of its existence.

---

[22] Between 1963 and 1989, the effective end of communist rule in the GDR, nearly 34,000 political prisoners where "bought free," more than 2,000 children reunited with their parents in the West, and more than 250,000 family reunifications arranged by the Bonn government. A total of DM 3.5 billion was paid to Pankow for these purposes. A single "freedom purchase" after 1977 cost DM 95,847. In addition, DM 2.4 billion was invested by the Bonn government in the GDR. Almost 1 billion in commercial credit was also provided. See Timothy Garton Ash, *In Europe's Name* (New York: Random House, 1993), pp. 146, 658–59, 154–55, 514.

Nobody expected the GDR to collapse in the wake of Soviet withdrawal, an equally unanticipated event. West Germans did *not* learn to conciliate communists to earn reunification. *Ostpolitik* had not prevented the further integration of the FRG into the dense network of the western economic, military, and legal web. *Ostpolitik* contained no effective challenge to the deepening of German enmeshment into the institutions and practices of Western cooperation; German nationalism was no longer assertive enough to challenge the perceived benefits of interdependence. Membership in the EU has meant the FRG's loss of control over its tariff and its agricultural sector; it has compelled the government to subsidize the prices French and Italian farmers receive for their products. The Bundesbank has become the lender of last resort for the other EU central banks. German consumers pay more for their food because of the EU control over agriculture. Environmental regulations are subjected to rules made by the EU; economic policies were regularly reviewed and criticized by OECD. Because German leaders considered themselves more dependent on French support than on British support, they backed de Gaulle in blocking British membership in the EC, but they backed the United States in France's quarrel with Washington over European defense. Any temptation to profess a more highly focused German nationalism than the weak sense of identity that actually prevailed in the FRG was held in check by these regional commitments and responsibilities.

Germans learned to put a sober and considered choice concerning issues of material welfare and security ahead of passionate belief, spirited advocacy, and unbending commitment. They learned to substitute instrumental for consummatory reason in permitting themselves to be tied to Western collective choices instead of insisting on the single-minded pursuit of national unity. When asked in 1969 what freedoms they would be willing to give up in exchange for reunification, only 3 percent were willing to forgo the freedoms of speech, free elections, and multiparty competition, and 10 percent were willing to sacrifice freedom of assembly. In 1951, 80 percent of the adult population opposed the finality of the postwar territorial status quo, but in 1972 that number had shrunk to 18 percent. The days of heroic foreign policy feats were over; the foreign policy of the sword yielded to that of the briefcase.

THE GDR AS A FAILED NATION-STATE

The communist government of the GDR, before and after *Ostpolitik*, tried very hard to make the former Soviet occupation zone into a socialist

261

nation-state.[23] For many years observers were deceived into believing that the leaders were succeeding, despite the massive flights of East Germans toward the West. It took the enormous popular demonstrations of 1989 and their demands for democracy to expose the lack of appeal that the communist nationalist ideology had evoked. As if sensing its isolation from popular feelings, the Socialist Unity Party (SED) had changed the content of the ideology a number of times, although none of the changes had the effect of establishing a separate GDR identity that could have prevented the effortless annexation of the state by the FRG in 1990.

Before 1971, the SED's Walter Ulbricht claimed that the GDR alone could exercise moral leadership over Germans because it was free from the Nazi and imperialist taint of its rival. The SED spoke of the inevitable reunification under socialism after the inevitable defeat of Western imperialism. Until then, however, reunification must be sacrificed to building a socialist nation-state in the GDR. The FRG's *Ostpolitik* was greeted by Pankow with the launching of a policy of *Abgrenzung*, of drawing a cognitive line between the two states in order to emphasize the separate identity of the East German nation. The ideology stressed historical ties between Germany and the Slavic world. References to the all-German past were removed from the constitution; use of the adjective *German* was curtailed. The identity of Eastern Germans, the SED said, lay in their class origins and their socialist mission, not their culture, which, admittedly, did not distinguish them from West Germans.

During the 1980s the SED went out of its way to claim older German symbols and personalities for its own. The leadership argued that such "East Germans" as Martin Luther, Frederick the Great, and Otto von Bismarck were "progressives" in the overall trajectory of German history and therefore were legitimate definers of solidarity for later socialist Germans. The SED did this in the face of FRG efforts to use the same personalities and symbols in its continuing claim to be sole legitimate successor to earlier German states. These themes were advanced without resurrecting the argument for reunification after the demise of "imperialism." The cultural unity of all Germans was now emphasized.

Why undertake these ideological gyrations? The SED leaders, thanks to the extensive opinion polling of the secret police apparatus, knew that there was no real GDR nationalism at the level of the populace. What little there was had declined during the 1980s, notably among youths. This caused them to redouble efforts to create such a sentiment. When border crossings, visits, and economic contact multiplied during the 1970s and 1980s, the model of the successful capitalist German neighbor in which personal freedom had flourished had to be coun-

---

[23] This section is heavily indebted to the work of Susan Siena.

tered. So did the rehabilitation as authentic German heroes of the old Prussian and Saxon personalities. The countering had to take the form of cultural symbols that stressed Germanness rather than the new socialist personality, which was quite obviously worse off than its capitalist cousin. A feeble attempt at maintaining *Abgrenzung* just the same was still made in the form of the claim that the GDR represents the most progressive portion of German history. This claim, as we learned in 1989, carried no weight with those who clamored for reunification, but it did not fall on entirely deaf ears. Neues Forum and the Evangelical Church organizations, the most active proponents of democratization in 1989, rejected reunification in favor of a drastically reformed but still separate, anticapitalist, and anti-NATO East German state, only to be repudiated in the elections that followed Erich Honecker's resignation. The ideological ingenuity of the SED was never able to overcome the example of a successful, if very attenuated, German liberal national myth next door, a myth whose adherents could display their achievements quite effortlessly on the television that almost all East Germans watched.

UNIFIED GERMANY, EUROPE AND THE WORLD

Germany and the Unification of Europe

After a short period of delirium about the new unity of the Germanies, it became clear that nothing like a reborn German nationalism, a hankering after a restored historical identity, a new search for hegemony in central Europe, was in the making. East Germans grumbled about the economic and personal hardship incurred by giving up socialist bureaucracy for markets and competition, dictatorship for democracy. West Germans grumbled about the laziness and inefficiency of their ethnic siblings and about the costs of updating and cleaning up East German industry. The Kohl government felt it necessary to reaffirm its loyalty to European integration in no uncertain terms, to symbolize its leadership in that process by joining France in demanding that the EU become the military and foreign policy forum of Western Europe as it completes the economic and monetary union. In short, it seems as if the reunified Germany is not really a rationalized nation-state any longer, but a state already committed to achieving a new rationalization in a larger European structure. What would account for the shift away from nation-statehood, if indeed it is occurring?

The conviction that Germany's wealth and economic security are inseparable from the ability to export remains unshaken. Therefore, industry and the trade unions share the bureaucracy's implacable commitment to free trade and the free movement of capital, globally as well as on the European continent. However, as German influence over global economic policy has to contend with Japan, with which it often clashes, as well as the United States, with which it is not always in complete agreement, free movement of all factors of production within Europe offers a more attainable objective. German industrialists have been enthusiastic promoters of interfirm cooperation under the direction of the EU Commission for R&D efforts in the fields of computers, telecommunications, electronics, and new materials, and they also have advocated the creation of completely free internal markets for the EU Fifteen. German trade unions, similarly motivated and committed, because of codetermination procedures, to industry programs, also have identified with European integration without necessarily being committed to European federalist ideologies or persuaded by their French and Benelux colleagues. They must seek to compensate at the level of the EU for the loss, after 1992, of economic power they formerly enjoyed by virtue of German law alone. Economic and institutional commitments have induced all major German economic actors to anchor their fortune in a united Europe rather than a sovereign Germany. They have so far been even willing to subsidize the farmers of some other EC countries in exchange for having a nearby market for manufactured goods that accounts for over 20 percent of gross national product (GNP).

It is generally recognized in Germany that the creation of a single economic sovereignty in the EU cannot be restricted to economics. The three governing parties favor the creation of federal or confederal EU institutions, collective decision making that allows for parliamentary participation and denies a veto power to individual governments. In addition, the SPD backs the unions in calling for a very strong EC charter of social rights, the condition that would allow the unions to Europeanize German-style codetermination and corporatist decision making. When it comes to defense policy, however, matters get more divisive. The CDU is willing to have the EU evolve into a defense community and to use German troops for multilateral peacekeeping while a slow process of multilateral arms control continues. The SPD, however, wishes to accelerate disarmament, and it opposes using German troops outside Europe. The SPD agrees with the CDU in upgrading a unified European deterrent force in preference to complete reliance on the American presence.

The Greens, of course, oppose all of this. They lack interest in Europe as a focus of German identity, hesitating between a global vision of humanity and a special vision of a utopian Germany that would become the light of the world. They clearly reject any upgrading of the EU into a military entity because they cling to their belief in nonviolent resistance as the only legitimate form of self-defense. For the majority of Germans, however, the unwillingness to mount a purely national defense against an enemy who is less and less real acts as an additional incentive to seek security in a larger European union, whose need for high-technology arms would fit nicely into Germany's economic calculations in any case.

German popular identification with European integration is permissive, not wildly committed. In 1990, 80 percent favored European unification; 62 percent thought the EU was a good thing; 53 percent thought Germany had benefited from membership; 48 percent said they would regret the disintegration of the Community while an equally large number professed to be indifferent. When asked which policy areas should be handled jointly by the European countries under EU auspices, the results show a clear decrease in interest (Table 6-3). One poll asked whether people would sacrifice membership in NATO and/or the EU for reunification; West Germans answered as follows: 11 percent would forego NATO and the EU; 15 percent NATO but not the EU, and 5 percent the EU but not NATO. But before unification, only 28 percent wanted to give the EU a mandate for defense policy, and 66 percent

Table 6-3. Preference for EC or EU rather than national decision making, Germany, 1991–94

	I	II	III	IV	V	VI	VII	VIII	IX	X	XI
1991	—	—	—	78	54	73	69	54	—	37	43
1992	66	47	—	72	47	70	75	57	54	37	54
1993	72	52	71	77	50	66	72	63	55	41	55
1994	54	42	—	71	45	64	68	62	46	32	50

SOURCE: *Eurobarometer* 35 (June 1991), t. 19; 38 (December 1992), t. 27; 39 (June 1993, t. 24, t. 27; 41 (July 1994), t. 22. Figures for Germany after 1990 are for united Germany.
This table represents the percentage of respondents who answered "for" on the following question: "Irrespective of other details of the Maastricht Treaty, what is your opinion on each of the following proposals? Please tell me for each proposal, whether you are for it or against it. . . . "
Note: I to XI refer to the following question: "Some people believe that certain areas of policy should be decided by the (NATIONAL) government, while other areas of policy should be decided jointly within the European Community/European Union. Which of the following areas of policy do you think should be decided by the (NATIONAL) government, and which should be decided jointly within the European Community/European Union?" I refers to "immigration policy," II to "dealing with unemployment," III to "fight against poverty," IV to "protection of the environment," V to "currency," VI to "scientific and tech[nological] research," VII to "foreign policy towards non-EC/EU countries," VIII to "defense," IX to "industrial policy," X to "education," and XI to "rates of Value Added Tax." The figures indicate those who answered "European Community/Union."

were in favor of a strong European social charter. These attitudes are sufficiently stable and general, if shallow, to allow far more solidly committed policy elites to pursue active integrationist measures.

Elite support for European integration has been unswerving, though based on both instrumental motives and socially learned behavior. Since unification the instrumental side of the support has probably grown in importance. German elites advocate the expansion of EU by giving the Brussels organs additional powers, especially over monetary policy, *and* by expanding the membership to include newly democratic Eastern Europe. But they hedge their support by insisting that the Bundesbank continue its high-interest policy and extend it to the projected European monetary union and that German subsidization of the EU budget be curtailed.

On the other hand, German elites have clearly learned that most major policy problems are not amenable to national solutions, that the national political playing field does not permit the construction of political bargains that will adequately deal simultaneously with economic, environmental, and military security. Perhaps equally important, they have learned that they can play a more important and autonomous role in foreign policy after reunification only if they "sanitize" their initiatives by packaging them as European multilateralism. Only thus can they reassure their foreign allies as well as Germans still reluctant to play an active global role.

Liberal Germany Faces the World: Uncertainties

The liberal consensus in Germany was clearly shaken by the travail of reunification. Violence against non-Western immigrants reached alarming levels, especially in East Germany. There is a revival of right-wing extremism that stresses Nazi racial themes. This expression of an integral nationalism is thematically inchoate because it is found largely among lower-class unemployed youth, again disproportionately from deindustrializing areas of East Germany. After the government made special aid programs available, anti-immigrant violence subsided. The racist-integralist party, the *Republikaner*, is more ideologically circumspect and remains electorally marginal, perhaps because of the institutional barrier posed by the Five Percent rule.

Disaffection from liberal nationalism is expressed more effectively in the vote for the former GDR Communist Party, now reborn as the PDS. In the federal election of 1994 it gathered 4.4 percent of the national vote, but nearly 20 percent of the ex-GDR vote. Its supporters feel that life under the old regime was not so bad after all, that they miss its

policies of guaranteed employment and cheap housing. They disproportionately distrust democratic institutions, especially parliamentarism.
They are recruited from the ranks of students, of former office holders,
former supporters of Neues Forum, from pacifists and workers who lost
out as a result of the introduction of free markets.

We do not know whether this form of alienation from liberalism is
going to flourish in the future. We do know, however, that pro-European
cosmopolitanism—and its concomitant, the weakening of liberalism focused on national identity—is being questioned in postreunification
Germany, though it has not been displaced. Its continued hold on policy,
however, will surely depend on the particular conception of German
identity that will eventually triumph, a point I take up later. At the present, the cosmopolitan consensus is challenged by left-wing pacifism and
by a conservative "revival of German national interest" school of
thought.

*Even before 1990, the pacifist left-wing of the SPD and the Greens considered
any use of military force, especially nuclear weapons, incompatible with German
identity.* These groups were not afraid of possible Soviet aggression, considering the Soviets to be a status quo power fearful of a nuclear Western
alliance. This group spearheaded the pacifist opposition to the deployment of nuclear weapons on German soil and sought to downplay any
military role for the FRG, any overly close involvement with Western
Europe that meant the practical abandonment of additional ties with the
GDR. The Greens, however, are not only pacifists who favor the FRG's
leaving NATO and disbanding the Bundeswehr, but also active neutral-
ists. They favored the demilitarization and neutralization of both Germanies before 1989 in order to remove the military argument against
unification. The very appeal of the Greens' argument, of course, had
the effect of drawing voters who previously had identified with the pacifist wing of the SPD. The Greens' neutralism and advocacy of unilateral
disarmament was a direct result of their concern for the environment;
they argue, not unreasonably, that Germany's ecology is more vulnerable
to a European nuclear war than anyone else's, that humane ends cannot
be attained by using inhumane means. For them, not the unity of the
wealthy capitalist states ought to be the main goal of German foreign
policy, but service to the poor Third and Fourth World countries.

*Conservatives are concerned that there is no adequately articulated German na-
tional interest because of the a priori commitment to multilateral institutions as
fora for thinking about German foreign and defense policy.* They complain that
there is no German strategic thinking. They wish to emulate the American practice of defense analysis carried out by civilian defense intellectuals. They regret that one of Helmut Kohl's advisers could argue that

"the *Staatrsäson* of a united Germany is its integration in Europe."[24] German defense officials anticipate that there will be more ethnic conflict in Southeast Europe. They worry that Germany might have to start worrying about retaining access to strategic raw materials, and, as in the Gulf War, rely too much on allies whose interests might not exactly match Germany's. Some think that the CDU/SPD policy has been entirely too Eurocentric.

Though the core framework of the conservative defense thinkers remains participation in multilateral institutions, they worry about the possibility that the allies lack a consensus for a common decision or will take too long to arrive at one. Germany, therefore, ought to be able to make its own military moves autonomously. Toward that end, the Defense Ministry now favors small mobile rapid deployment forces that may operate as part of a NATO or a United Nations force, or they may not. In short, critics of the past policy of self-abnegation foresee a German diplomatic and military role similar to the one played by Britain and France in the context of multilateral fora.

Mainstream thinking in the SPD favors multilateralism above all. The party supports rapid progress toward full European federation. Its hesitating support for German military participation outside the traditional NATO area is contingent on German immersion in multilateral forces. Mainstream thinking in the CDU is only marginally less committed to European federation and somewhat more willing to mount German military might even if not all foreign countries approve.

The essence of the mainstream view was articulated by Hans-Dietrich Genscher, for two decades foreign minister, a major architect of the Maastricht treaties and of German reunification. But that view is now being questioned even in the CDU and FDP as insufficiently mindful of Germany's true national interests. Genscher considered power politics obsolete, the use of military force a thing of the integral nationalist past. Liberal Germany's special role was to demonstrate to the world what can be accomplished with diplomatic skill and economic prowess alone. But the exercise of this role demanded that Germany assert herself more than she had before reunification, but assert herself *only* in the context of multilateral enmeshment. Once such a role is asserted successfully, Germany would be obligated to contribute more heavily than in the past to collective operations. Checkbook diplomacy would not suffice.

The commitment to multilateralism still dominates as the primary rule of German engagement in the world. If that painfully learned lesson continues to prevail, German liberalism will continue to blend into an

---

[24] Quoted in Hans-Peter Schwarz, "Germany's National and European Interests," *Daedalus* (Spring 1994): 84.

anational cosmopolitanism, opposed only by the alienated but impotent fringes on the Left and Right. Cosmopolitanism, whether focused on Europe or on the world as a whole, is the attitude of the elites. The mass public tolerates cosmopolitanism without strongly identifying with it. But it might come to oppose cosmopolitanism if that stance comes to be identified with economic or strategic failure, with personal and emotional suffering. Hence, the still competing conceptions of the most desirable form of German identity are likely to dictate who will feel comfortable with a squishy cosmopolitanism and who will opt for an assertive national self.

Mastering the Past or Fashioning a "Usable" Past?

In 1986, before anyone took seriously the possibility of a peaceful reunification of the two German states, there erupted among German intellectuals the "Historians' Fight." It was triggered by the argument, supported by Chancellor Kohl and many in the CDU, that the FRG ought to be seen as a fully developed nation-state with its own national character, which had nothing to be ashamed of and ought to take its place among the nations as a proud and self-confident member. Crucial in this argument, of course, was the contention that the crimes of Nazism were exaggerated and ought not be allowed to burden the present generation of West Germans. Modern German identity ought to be "normalized" by the recognition that Nazism was no worse than Stalinist Communism, against which it was a legitimate defense. The German people, to survive as a distinct people, must be given a "usable past."

Left-wing opponents of the "conservative" historians countered that normalization implied going back on the moral benefits of liberal cosmopolitanism. Making up a "usable past" is to master the past by papering it over. The left wanted no new self-righteous nationalism in Germany, even if its ideas were derived from the West European Enlightenment and even if Nazism was to be seen as an aberration (as Kohl repeatedly suggested). In short, the postwar learning to be civilized implies the recognition that Germany remains tainted by the Nazi legacy. A usable past is an unacceptably nationalistic one. To master the past means to live forever with the knowledge of a great crime.

The argument remains unresolved, though several planned symbolic acts endorsing the conservative view of the matter were not carried out. What is the evidence offered by German public opinion as to which view is the more popular? If the conservatives are tapping a hitherto hidden vein of unified opinion, Germany may move in the direction of a strong, reborn sense of national identity, though probably still liberal. It would then provide support for the reassertion of a distinct national interest in

Germany's relations with its neighbors and with the world. If not, the legacy of Hans-Dietrich Genscher will continue to prevail in foreign policy, and the anational cosmopolitanism of most German elites will still dominate public life.

Many in the CDU favor the redefinition of a German identity that buries the memory of the Nazi interlude altogether because, they say, it should not burden generations of Germans innocent of any part in it. Other measures also suggest support for this view. German law governing the acquisition of citizenship strongly favors the *ius sanguinis*: descent, irrespective of domicile, determines citizenship. Naturalization is very difficult. Recent changes in the law allowing the German-born children of immigrants to become German citizens were regarded with some suspicion by the Right. The formerly generous right to asylum was sharply curtailed. Foreigners residing in Germany should not be allowed to vote in local elections. Ethnic Germans who had lived in eastern Europe and the Balkans for centuries were greeted as citizens when they emigrated to Germany in large numbers during the 1980s. But in the mid-1990s they are seen as unassimilable burdens on the exchequer.

Upgrading the position of the military in German life is seen as a direct support for the rebirth of national identity. Germans killed in World War II are to be honored, as are surviving veterans, because Germany ought to be seen as much a victim of the war as its perpetrator. The Bundeswehr ought to be more visible, more honored, frequently on display. Kohl lobbied hard to have German units included in the events celebrating the fiftieth anniversary of the Normandy landings and of the end of the European war. Active participation of German forces in multilateral "out of NATO area" operations is part of this assertion of identity. Half of Germans surveyed support such a policy, but half considers it a violation of human rights. In 1993, a poll of young people revealed that 91 percent would have *no* sympathy for violent riots over the issue of granting asylum to foreigners.[25]

Yet, the evidence suggesting the persistence of an anational mood is there as well. East Germans tend to oppose any kind of adventurous foreign or defense policy; moreover, they remain very confused and conflicted about their own history after being told that the Nazi and Marxist versions were false. In 1992, when asked "are you proud to be German," 69 percent of West Germans answered in the affirmative, but 71 percent of East Germans said yes. In 1993, of a sample of Germans aged between 14 and 27, 47

<hr />

[25] All public opinion figures in this section come from one of these sources: Elisabeth Noelle-Neumann and Renate Köcher, eds., *Allensbacher Jahrbuch der Demoskopie, 1984–1992,* vol. 9 (Munich: K.G. Sauer, 1993); Heinrich August Winkler, "Rebuilding of a Nation," *Daedalus* (Winter 1994): 107–27; *Eurobarometer,* no. 36 (December 1991), table 63. German samples usually contain 1000 respondents.

percent of West Germans professed themselves proud of being German, whereas 68 percent thought so in the East. In 1991, only 47 percent in the West and 45 percent in the East report that they feel close to the country (the average for the EU being 53 percent). Among the young, only 3 percent of West Germans and 17 percent in the East said they could not imagine having a foreign friend.

It even seems as if East and West do not consider themselves part of the same nation. In 1990 almost 60 percent of East Germans felt that the two Germanies share the same culture, but only 33 percent of West Germans felt that way! By 1992, only 35 percent of East Germans felt they were more All-German than East German. A year later, only 22 percent of West Germans and 11 percent of easterners felt "together as Germans"; huge majorities in each section of the country thought they were divided by large opposing interests: 65 percent of West Germans were not eager to pay for upgrading living standards in the East; 59 percent were unwilling to curtail their own living standards to raise that of the East. Western contempt for the perceived laziness, helplessness, and lack of skills of easterners is pervasive.

Upgrading Germany's military role continues to arouse a great of deal of opposition. The Greens espoused an extreme position on this point: they want to get rid of the German state altogether by splitting Germany into self-governing regions. European peace in general is to be sought by radical decentralization of state power. Most people, according to opinion surveys, continue to think of Germany as a nonmilitary country, even if they want Germany to take a more active world role. Most people see such a role as being best played by fostering arms control and humanitarian and development aid in the third world. Many Germans see world peace and global prosperity not in terms of national, but rather as universal rights, the rights of the world community. Such a commitment, then, leads easily away from thinking in terms of unique national interests, as Genscher had urged, to the recognition that there are few solutions Germans can contrive alone to solve even German problems.

Learning to Transcend the Nation-State?

When West Germans were queried in 1989 about what characteristics all Germans share, 91 percent mentioned language, the most obvious and least emotionally charged response, and 68 percent mentioned history; national identity and way of life elicited a positive response from 38 percent and 22 percent, respectively. Yet 55 percent say they never think of themselves as Europeans in addition to being German. These sentiments do not bespeak a strong sense of either national or European identity. The continued insistence on safeguarding a hard-won prosper-

271

ity and technological leadership suggests an underlying sense of fear that catastrophe might still be in store for Germany. The reluctance to give up NATO and the attempt to find a new unity among all Europeans suggest a lingering sense of physical insecurity as well. Have Germans learned a collective lesson, as compared to 1870, 1919, or 1933?

Germans have learned two lessons, almost at the same time, about their national identity: to trust each other and to trust their neighbors. The crimes and catastrophes of the Nazi era taught them the costs of integral nationalism; their dependence on American help in regaining economic security linked to active resocialization gave support to the attractiveness of liberal nationalism. The need to repudiate wholly a criminal past delegitimated integralism and lingering syncretist sentiments, while defeat in 1918 had not delegitimated the monarchy. A polity successfully reorganized under the auspices of liberal nationalism, albeit partly imposed, then prospered and regained its dignity in close cooperation with the former victims of Nazi imperialism, thus further legitimating liberal nationalism as practiced in Western Europe. Thus Germans learned, at one and the same time, to trust each other within a single national myth *and* to rely on their neighbors by engaging in a process of successful collective decision making.

The same paradox that characterized the recent history of France also appears in the German case: just as a previously deeply divided polity achieves integration under a commonly accepted set of rules and principles, just as it is rationalized under liberal auspices, its citizens find it necessary to safeguard their newly found coherence and prosperity by transferring power to regional institutions. Safeguarding successful national integration when achieved under conditions of high industrialism and democracy requires augmentation with a new focus in a larger identity. Confidence in one's power to solve all problems within the confines of a sovereign nation is questioned when one lives with rapid and unpredictable technological change, when one fears technology while hoping for unending progress, when great prosperity is mixed with apprehension that all might end in unemployment and inflation. We have no reason to think a European regional identity is emerging in the minds of Germans, but we have ample reason to conclude that Germany is no longer the focus of many expectations, no longer the core of most people's unthinking loyalty. To seek a more effective forum for satisfying one's perceived needs is to learn.

CHAPTER SEVEN

Japan

"Be filial to your parents, affectionate to your brothers and sisters; as husbands and wives be harmonious; as friends, true; bear yourselves in modesty and moderation . . . always respect the constitution and observe the laws; should emergency arise, offer yourselves courageously to the State; and thus guard and maintain the prosperity of Our Imperial Throne coeval with heaven and earth."

This excerpt from the Imperial Rescript on Education (1890) is thought by many students of modernization and of Japan to symbolize Japan's uniquely successful way of entering the modern world without being swallowed by the West, the ingenious way of a latecomer to achieve not merely survival, but ascendancy.[1] How was it possible for Japan to modernize rapidly without disintegrating, after Britain and the United States, simultaneously with France and Germany, but ahead of Russia?

Successful rationalization is in the eyes of the beholder: to scholars writing long after the event the process seems impressive, but to contemporaries success seemed frighteningly precarious. Later observers point out that there were few rural revolts and that peasant unrest stressed millenarian religious and purificatory themes, not challenges to the political system. There were no political revolts after 1877, no attempted coups until 1936, and no more political assassinations than in Germany,

I gratefully acknowledge the indispensable and critical research assistance of Rudra Sil and Anno Tadashi. Mari Miura collected and translated public opinion data. I deeply appreciate the help of Gregory Noble and Peter Katzenstein.
[1] Imperial Rescript on Education, as quoted by Kenneth P. Pyle, *The Making of Modern Japan* (Lexington, Mass.: D. C. Heath, 1978), p. 99.

273

France, or Russia. We know of no mutinies or of much draft evasion during Japan's many and bloody modern wars. Yet the statesmen who fashioned the modernization, whose policies rationalized post-Tokugawa Japan, always saw themselves on the brink of disaster, fearing class conflict, a slackening of patriotism, an inability to resist Western imperialism, an overly rapid assimilation to Western ways, or inadequate speed in discarding traditional ones.

Scholars disagree whether Japan's success is due to culturally unique features or to processes we can observe elsewhere. When Tokugawa rule was overthrown in 1867, did the change betoken the beginning of a historically unique path to modernization or the continuation of a process of nation building that resembles the global process more than it differs from it?[2] My argument against uniqueness acknowledges the existence in modern Japan of a powerful school of analysts who see Japan's history as the cautious adaptation to modern life of the traditional notions of organic unity. The metaphor that Japan is like a single harmonious household (*ie*), whose members assume roles in life consonant with the smooth maintenance of that structure, dominates this argument. Perhaps it was the disruption of that pattern that fearful Japanese modernizers stressed inordinately. But I deny, along with Ronald Dore and others, that such features were so powerful and so rigid as to prevent the initiation of universally visible processes that are capable of being interpreted with generally applicable categories and concepts. Japan's march toward modernity as a rationalized nation-state is consistent with our Type A, even though the rationalizers deliberately followed somewhat older European models of nation building.

Both schools admit that Japanese modernizers, like those in Western Europe and the United States, did not have to impose an elite culture on competing folk cultures: the traditional elite culture was not challenged from below, but from foreign sources. The country was culturally homogeneous; it had never been conquered; it had been subject to a single, albeit feudally decentralized, regime since 1200, which had easily assimilated Chinese cultural influences, especially Confucian doctrine and institutions. There had been an idea of a "Japanese essence" (*kokutai*) juxtaposed to Chinese influence since the eighth century, reinforced by a general feeling of xenophobia. Literacy and urbanization were high; there was a functioning public school system by the early

---

[2] The authors identified with the "uniqueness of Japanese political culture" thesis prominently include Kawashima Takeyoshi, Nakane Chie, Murakami Yasusuke, Kumon Shumpei, Sato Seizaburo, Ruth Benedict, Robert Bellah, and George De Vos. For a summary of such views, see Takie Sugiyama Lebra, ed., *Japanese Social Organization* (Honolulu: University of Hawaii Press, 1992). For Ronald Dore's contrary interpretation, see his *Taking Japan Seriously* (Stanford: Stanford University Press, 1987).

nineteenth century (earlier than in Europe and the United States.). Even before the arrival of Commodore Perry in 1853, Tokugawa feudal practices and institutions were in an advanced state of decay.

These features suggest the existence of a nascent nation-state even before the Meiji reformers set out to create one after 1867. Other features, however, suggest that Tokugawa rule had certainly created a state, but not a nation-state. There was no suggestion of popular participation in governance above the level of the hamlet. A rigid four-tier class system was maintained; only the top tier, the warrior (samurai) class, participated in governance. Samurai lived according to a demanding code of loyalty and obedience to their feudal masters, even though two hundred fifty years of internal peace had effectively deprived them of a calling and, in many cases, of an adequate income. Central administration depended on the cooperation of local feudal rulers (daimyos); after 1855 the most disaffected among them were to be the focal points of the revolt against the Tokugawa government. There was no official religion; in fact, the whole idea of a centralized religion was alien to traditional Japanese culture. Buddhism played no consistent unifying role after 1192, and Shinto, before Meiji, was merely a decentralized folk religion devoted to the worship of local gods at myriads of local shrines. Officially the emperor represented the Shinto divine hierarchy in his person and in rituals in which he participated, but he remained marginal to the political life of the country. Confucian notions of social order, obedience, and benevolence were stressed by the Bakufu (the Tokugawa "military" government), not the imperial institution.

What lessons or insights, then, is the Japanese story going to yield about our hypothesis of collective learning and cognitive evolution away from the nation-state? The syncretist rationalization formula chosen by the builders of the nation-state proved initially successful, but it also became the victim of its own success at the end. It does show, however, that nonliberal rationalization formulas can be very effective in Type A situations.

An enormous amount of adaptation was accomplished by the syncretist modernizers, although little learning occurred. On the other hand, after defeat and occupation, impressive lessons were learned by the defeated elites, one of which involved the acceptance of a Japanese version of a liberal national myth and the institutionalization of diffuse reciprocity in political bargaining.

Japanese liberal nationalism is not deeply rooted. In fact, the Japanese collective identity is increasingly evanescent, difficult to pin down in attitudes and behaviors. Although policymakers are overtly committed to solving their problems in their own ways, that is, by national means, the reality of policy making suggests that the postnational forces visible in

275

Europe are, in different ways, also making their appearance in Japan. Is Japan really so different from other old nation-states?

Attributes of Late Tokugawa State and Society

The idea of a Japanese nation existed in the minds of certain intellectuals by end of the eighteenth century, although it is doubtful that the bulk of the population knew or cared. Early national self-consciousness was triggered by the increasingly visible presence of the West, an intellectual and technological presence experienced by intellectuals and officials despite the official policy of exclusion of foreigners, the prohibition of foreign trade and travel, and the persecution of Christian converts. Moreover, the looming threat of a technologically very superior foreign military presence became increasingly obvious after 1840, especially Russia's. However, initial national consciousness also arose independently from a desire to sharply differentiate the legitimacy of Japanese political institutions from China's, to assert the cultural autonomy of Japan.

The assertion took the form of *kokugaku*, the study of things purely Japanese, unpolluted by Chinese accretions. Motoori Norinaga and Hirata Atsutane were core contributors. Along with pointing to a national esthetic sense embedded in Shinto beliefs and practices, they stressed the direct descent of the Japanese emperor from the sun goddess Amaterasu (unlike the Chinese imperial dynasties), the identity of political rule with divine sanction, and the absolute loyalty all Japanese owed to the ruler. Hence no mere human could claim that the emperor had lost the mandate of heaven, as men could in China, although subordinate rulers like the Tokugawa shoguns could and did lose legitimacy when their actions conflicted with the divine-imperial edict. However, this accusation did not become prominent until 1853, after America's "black ships" had humiliated the Bakufu.

Devotees of *kokugaku* were opposed by scholars committed to studying Western ways and urging their selective adoption, especially scientific and technological knowledge (*rangakusha*). Some Tokugawa officials encouraged this activity despite the self-imposed isolation of Japan. These scholars and officials did not believe in Japanese cultural superiority over the West or over China; consequently they could easily accept a vision of the world that was not centered on East Asia.

The Bakufu submitted to the ending of Japan's seclusion, the admission of foreigners and of trade, as demanded by the United States. Moreover, the Bakufu had to accept the Western system of unequal treaties, the restrictions on the right to levy import tariffs and to grant foreigners extraterritorial legal rights. It also broke with a number of traditions by

276

seeking foreign military advisers, groping toward a central monetary and fiscal policy, encouraging the manufacture of firearms, building a modern navy, and permitting foreign firms to establish themselves in Japan. Moreover, many Japanese students were sent abroad to study Western subjects, especially science and engineering. Westernizing intellectuals applauded, but traditionalists saw these steps as a terrible humiliation.

The impact of the West, it appears, was merely the last straw that helped to undermine the old order. The Tokugawa civil religion lauded the Confucian values of loyalty to one's superior and the master's benevolent care for the servant. It stressed a martial code of honor and service for samurai and raised that group above all others. Tokugawa beliefs and institutions decried commercial activity and despised merchants as a class. Governance was a mixture of centralized bureaucratic rule and hamlet autonomy.

The trends of the eighteenth and early nineteenth centuries, however, belied the official scheme. Cities grew as peasants moved to the burgeoning commercial centers. Merchants prospered, as did moneylenders. Interurban transportation thrived. Rulers of fiefs far from the capital strengthened their own administrations, schools, and armed forces. Some secretly sent students to the West. And the samurai, unless they managed to find positions in the bureaucracies, grew poorer, more dependent, and increasingly irrelevant to the evolving society because they possessed neither the skills nor the beliefs to prosper in it: loyalty was no longer rewarded with benevolence.

This crisis of the Tokugawa state was met with complex intellectual responses known collectively as Restorationism. Some participants in this movement wished to save the Bakufu while others worked for its overthrow. The Mito school of Confucianists sought to reinterpret Chinese Confucianist doctrine to make the Bakufu seem the most legitimate source of adaptive action against the foreign threat. To be loyal, the Mito scholars said, meant to commit oneself without reservation to a moral goal consistent with *kokutai*, not to obey one's superior blindly. Confucian thought came to the help of the regime in other ways, too. The belated effort to adapt benefited from the stress on education, on a large school system, and from the belief in merit and talent as entitling bureaucrats to rule. More important, these doctrines also legitimated the successful modernization launched from the top down after 1867.

Many of the restorationists who eventually defeated the discredited Bakufu, however, thought otherwise. They disliked adapting to Western ways, even though one of them, Aizawa Seishisai, had advocated a multiclass army and navy, the abolition of the four-class system, the fostering of firearms, and the use of Shinto to rekindle the spirit of *kokutai*. Incarnated in the person of Yoshida Shoin, and rallying under the slogan "revere the emperor, expel the barbarians," these samurai launched a rebellion against the Tokugawa, ostensibly to punish them for their efforts at adaptation and to return to direct rule by the divine emperor.

Their victory in 1867 was ironic in several ways. The restorationist nationalists came mostly from the southwest, the part of the country most deeply influenced by the West and most modernized militarily; they worked for the restoration of centralized imperial rule, even though they had resisted the increased bureaucratic centralization practiced by the Tokugawa. And, although acting in the name of tradition, the majority of the young samurai who fashioned the Meiji Restoration immediately went to work to force Japan to modernize far more radically than the Bakufu had attempted. In all likelihood, many of them had never taken literally the slogan to expel the barbarians. Many of the rebels believed in a restoration that was more a renewal than a systematic return to the past.[3] Although certainly xenophobic in their fear of Western power and influence, these advocates of renewal also heeded the work of the *rangakusha* in wanting to work for selective adaptation.

Such rebels were syncretist nationalists not committed to a full restoration of the past: the restorative doctrine soon turned into a traditional-syncretist nationalism, tinged ever more with strains of reformist thought as the Meiji era unrolled. Moreover, the Restoration, though this had not been the Confucianists', Yoshida's, Hirata's, or Aizawa's intentions, turned populist. The statesmen of 1867 realized that, without massive popular support, they would not be able to modernize, to resist a foreign takeover successfully. The most important innovation was not the restoration of the emperor or the transformation of Shinto into a state cult celebrating *kokutai*, but the fashioning of institutions facilitating mass participation manipulated from the top. All people were to become members of the divinely blessed national family, not just the favored few. All were to be able to contribute to national salvation on the basis of their personal dedication, talent, and skill. The ingredients of the Meiji civil religion were ready to be blended, thanks to the intellectual agitation of early nationally sensitive intellectuals.

---

[3] The Japanese use the word *ishin* to connote "restoration," which means "renewal" rather than going back to a previous dispensation. There is some controversy as to whether the Restoration was the work of the mobilized/unassimilated strata of Tokugawa society, as Type A demands. True, the Restorers were young, lower-rank samurai unable to live a traditional feudal life because of socioeconomic changes that had already occurred; they were rejected and treated poorly by the regime. On the other hand, the Restoration was also supported by some traditional daimyos who sought to settle a very old quarrel with the Tokugawa clan, though all were members of the same high culture. These daimyos were "unassimilated" only in the sense that the Tokugawa treated them as outsiders.

SYNCRETIST NATIONALISTS AS TEMPORARY RATIONALIZERS

From their takeover of the government until the first war against China in 1894, in a little over one generation, the Meiji reformers transformed Japan from a semicentralized agrarian late feudal society devoid of mass national consciousness into a nation-state with modern armed forces and an industrial infrastructure. They mobilized the masses under the slogan "rich nation, strong army." They replaced hereditary officials recruited from the samurai class with a modern civil service based on competitive examinations after abolishing the four-tier class system. They created modern structures of education at all levels modeled on those of France and the United States, a legal system adapted from the German and French based on equal rights of all citizens. The navy was modeled on the British, and the army, including universal military service, on the French and German. Belgium provided the model for the central bank. After 1890 there was a parliament modeled on the Prussian, based on elections featuring a sharply restricted franchise. Local and district administration followed the French pattern of centralized control.

The organization of the economy proved to be the key to the success of breakneck modernization (Table 7-1). From the beginning, the state dictated policy even though private entrepreneurs (often former samurai) were encouraged to start manufacturing enterprises of all kinds. Stress was placed on heavy industry; shipyards and steel mills were begun with government help, and subsequent production was guided by government directive. At the same time, merchants and rich peasants also invested in light industrial enterprises. In 1884 Japan was the first country ever to draw up an economic development plan that used numerical production targets and set growth rates, although the methods used were unsystematic and primitive. The flexibility of the Restorers was amazing. They experimented freely with their Western models and did not hesitate to jettison one in favor of another when they were disappointed with results. They showed no principled attachment to any foreign model, using them all instrumentally in their fear of being taken over by the West, as was China at that time. No European "latecomer" had developed anything like the Japanese method of state industrial guidance by 1900.

At first, popular participation was totally manipulated; democracy was not on the Restorers' agenda, although a dissident democratic movement arose in the 1880s. The drafters of the autocratic Meiji constitution ignored the appreciable pressure for a more democratic charter. After 1900 things became more complicated. Japan had begun its imperialist penetration of China in 1894, although the European powers kept her from reaping the full benefit of her crushing victory. The march re-

Table 7-1. Indices of Japanese industrialization and economic development, 1880–1970[a]

	1880	1900	1920	1940	1960	1980	1990
GDP, current prices (billion yen)	0.81	2.41	15.9	39.4	15,503	240,176	424,537
GDP, by sector of origin (% of selected sectors)[a]							
Agriculture	41	34	27	24	13	3.7	2.4
Manufacture/mining	7	11	18	33	37	28.8	29.3
Construction	2	3	3	3	6	9.4	9.9
Transportation/communication	1	3	10	9	9	6.2	6.2
Output of electric energy (million kwh)	—	—	3,815	34,683	115,472	577,521	857,272
Output of steel ingots and castings (1,000 metric tons)	—	—	841	6,856	22,138	111,395	110,339
Length of railroad, lines open (km)	158	6,300	13,645	25,126	27,902	(27,104)[b]	—
Merchant ships registered to Japanese citizens[c]							
Total number	(210)	(1,329)	1,940	1,819	2,134	8,825	7,668
1,000 tons gross	(41.2)	(543)	2,996	5,683	6,931	39,015	25,186

SOURCE: All statistics for 1880–1960 are from *International Historical Statistics: Africa and Asia* (New York: New York University Press, 1982); all statistics for 1980–90 are from *Japan Statistical Yearbook, 1993–94* (Tokyo: Bureau of Statistics, Management and Coordination Agency, 1995).
[a]Statistics for 1885 have been substituted for 1880.
[b]Statistics for 1970.
[c]Statistics from 1920 onward are for steam- and motor-driven ships only. Statistics for 1980–90 are for steel vessels, except fishing craft.

sumed in 1904 with the victory over Russia and the subsequent takeover of Korea, followed by the economic penetration of Manchuria. It intensified during World War I when Japan took over the German possessions in China and the Pacific and assumed a special economic hegemonial role in China by virtue of the Twenty-One Demands. All these victories depended on the dedicated loyalty of an army based on mass conscription, on popular acquiescence. People were not slow to demonstrate their disappointment with government in 1905 when large-scale riots took place, protesting what people thought insufficient gains at the expense of Russia.

As the economy came more and more to resemble that of any industrialized country, labor unrest also developed, and with it incipient Marxist movements. Japan's rulers, not used to class-based dissent, branded dissidents as "disloyal to the emperor": stepped-up social mobilization was felt as threatening the system.

Finance and heavy industry organized themselves into a few large combines of manufacturing, trading, and banking interests (*zaibatsu*). They functioned in alliance with the powerful state bureaucracy. Rural notables dominated life in the agricultural sector.

During and after World War I democratization was increasingly demanded by the newly mobilized, as Western cultural ways also found much more acceptance, only to be discarded suddenly after the onset of the Great Depression. Significant reforms were made in response: the government introduced universal manhood suffrage in 1925; and it began the peaceful alternation in government of the two parliamentary parties. One was slightly more liberal than the other, although both were anchored in the ruling economic oligarchy and the bureaucracy. Still, the alternation responded to electoral results. Responsible parliamentary government seemed on the point of consolidating as Taisho Democracy.

Yet social discontent accelerated during the 1920s, as both rural and industrial unrest picked up. The onset of the Great Depression in 1931 proved to be the most serious blow yet to the rationalization of Japan: the work of the Meiji Restorers seemed to be coming apart at the seams. It was in this context that discontented elements, mostly in the army, began to articulate the need for a Showa Restoration, a return to an organically unified nation that rejects capitalism, dedicated to the service of an emperor, who was to lead a campaign to expel the capitalist West from Asia. The seed for the Pacific War was planted in the perceived threat to the survival of an organically whole, autarkic Japan. A traditional-syncretist national myth was successfully fashioned by the Meiji Restorers, but the institutions put in place had failed by 1930 to preserve a fully rationalized state and society. Japan's venture into fascism and full-scale imperialism followed this failure.

Nationalist Ideologies and the National Myth, 1867–1931

"The Imperial line, unbroken for ages eternal" and "loyalty to the Emperor and filial piety" were among the slogans used in Meiji times to rally and unite the Japanese people, all the people. These appeals were ideological innovations urged by reformers in late Tokugawa days, but not traditional precepts applicable to common people. As Ito Hirobumi, perhaps the foremost Meiji statesman, explained: because religion is not a strong social force in Japan and because western notions of constitutional monarchy and separations of power were not acceptable, all power and all legitimation for the national essence comes from the imperial institution.[4] Moreover, all Meiji reformist intellectuals agreed that "since the nation includes [in] its 'national polity' [*kokutai*] all internal values of truth, morality, and beauty neither scholarship nor art could exist apart from these national values. They were, in fact totally dependent on them."[5] But, this essence, the myth makers argued, was in mortal danger because of the threat of Western imperialism. The very survival of Japan as a civilization demanded the total integration of the people into a single organic family ruled by the divine emperor.

Still, survival also demanded that some of the tradition be sacrificed to meet the threat effectively. And here some stressed reformists and others traditional-syncretist nationalist themes. The original proponents of "revere the Emperor, expel the barbarians" had been unwilling to sacrifice any tradition; they were concerned with restoring old ways already weakened by the Bakufu, but by 1877 they were dealt out of the political game.

The reformers went out of their way to fashion a new civil religion by making Shinto into a state cult, a distinct and deliberate ideological innovation already recommended by opponents of the Bakufu. In 1868 the new government separated Buddhism from Shinto, persecuted Buddhist priests, and created a new bureaucracy, the Department of Divinity, which designed rites for emperor worship that drew heavily on Confucian themes. During the Great Promulgation Campaign (1870–1884) the government sought to inculcate a new religious creed—the Great Teaching—that stressed love of the Shinto gods and of the country, the link of the emperor and people to heaven, and the need to obey the

[4] Liberal-leaning and syncretist constitutional lawyers in late Meiji, Taisho, and even early Showa Japan disagreed in how to interpret the constitution. The officially taught doctrine (dubbed "exoteric") held that Japan was an absolute monarchy. However, it competed with an "esoteric" doctrine that held that the emperor had permanently ceded many powers to the parliament in an effort to make Japan as Western as possible.

[5] Maruyama Masao, *Thought and Behavior in Modern Japanese Politics*, edited by Ivan Morris, (New York: Oxford University Press, 1963), p. 6.

emperor. The creed was also designed to straddle and subsume the existing religions. Government evangelists interpreted these themes to stress the need to obey the new Western ways being forced on the country. Because of continued infighting among priests of the old religions and of rival interpreters of the new creed, the religious reform effort was reorganized in 1875 as the State Shinto celebrated under the auspices of the great national shrines that prevailed until 1945. Following State (not popular) Shinto rites became compulsory for all Japanese. As the cult was not considered a religion after 1882, it did not infringe on the freedom of religion guaranteed by the Constitution of 1889.

But continuing disagreements between rival syncretist nationalists prevented the emergence of a single and consistent plan of borrowing Western institutions. The lack of a consensual myth facilitated an instrumental and experimental approach to borrowing, but it also left room for arguing about how to legitimate the innovations. It is clear that those who claimed to act in the name of tradition took many liberties with the content of the old way, as in the case of the inventors of State Shinto. Justifying innovation in terms of pseudo-traditions became a major task of Meiji intellectuals.

Some, notably Ito Hirobumi, Okuma Shigenobu, and Itagaki Taisuke, were willing to take over some Western values, not merely borrow institutions and techniques. Thus they brought about the acceptance of parliamentary institutions, although Japan's was the least democratic parliament among major countries when it was created in 1889. They also favored political parties, provided they remained "loyal" to the Emperor, and they were willing to envisage a conduct of public affairs that was not monopolized by the bureaucracy.

Most, however, were more traditional. Personified by Yamagata Aritomo, the father of the modern Japanese army, Okubo Toshimichi, and Kido Koin traditional syncretists were willing sacrifice Japanese values only if they seemed to conflict with the overriding objective of avoiding China's apparent fate. The traditional syncretists favored a national myth that advanced modern industry and a strong modern army and navy. They favored Western education as a technique only to the extent that it aided in the creation of these institutions. Hence they wanted to get rid of such Buddhist and Confucian-legitimated values as quietism, blind and unthinking obedience to superiors, and loyalty to local power hierarchies.

Severe challenges to this myth arose after 1900. As Table 7-1 shows, the success of the Meiji reformers was evident in the growth of education, industry, and urban life. Despite the traditional-syncretist themes that infused education and government propaganda, however, there was evidence of class conflict by the turn of the century. Socialist groups emerged among Christians, workers, and journalists; trade unions were being or-

283

ganized; strikes became common—all trends that challenged the reality of any Japanese essence. Christianity became quite popular; so did manuals on entrepreneurship and personal self-improvement. Social Darwinism was all the rage; it suggested that Japan's drive for progress and survival was merely part of a universal movement, not something unique, though it also justified imperialism! Most socialists attacked capitalist competition as un-Japanese and urged that the future class struggle could be headed off if the state abandoned guided capitalism.

The second generation of the Meiji urban elite, people who came to maturity after 1880 and received a Western education, thought the reforms did not go far enough because they had not rejected enough of the Confucian value system; but the Western values to be substituted were individualism and aggressiveness in the service of the nation, not liberalism.

These proto-Western ideas challenged traditional syncretism. In the rural corners of Japan, an opposing sentiment gained strength. Thanks to a network of army reservist organizations that included special schools, civic action groups, sports events, and indoctrination in kokutai, the rural population was taught to remain faithful to the traditional-syncretist national myth, to regard the critique by urban dissidents as treason. Similarly, the instability of incipient parliamentary party rule and the corruption of politicians became a target of rural disgust. The notion of Japan as a harmonious family seemed challenged by these modernizing trends.

By 1895 all shades of nationalists had become imperialists, although some had harbored ambitions to carve up China since the 1870s. Imperialism united the country *because* disputes among proto-liberals, reformist syncretists, and traditionalists divided it. Dissidents from traditionalism endorsed expansionism because the West continued to discriminate against—and apparently despise—Japan despite its enormous progress. Western governments insisted that, until Japan became "a civilized nation," discrimination would continue, although this sentiment abated somewhat after Britain allied herself with Japan in 1902. The Japanese elite, not unnaturally, equated a policy of imperialism with becoming civilized as the major Western governments practiced expansionism in Asia and elsewhere. Traditionalists, moreover, saw the West as "a pack of ravenous wolves." Emulating the West became essential only to defeat it at its own game, said the traditional nationalists. But what if emulation-via-modernization results in disloyalty and unrest? The answer was: penetrate Korea and China, make their modernization the mission of Japan to limit Western influence in all of Asia. Traditionalists saw Korea as "a dagger pointed at the heart of Japan," a strategic threat if not controlled by Japan. Liberals and socialists thought that it was Japan's civilizing mission to cure other Asians of their sloth and corruption, not eject the West. Social Darwinism became the liberal and socialist justification for imperialism, in contrast to the geopolitical and strategic fears that motivated syncretists. What united all nationalists was the fear that the organic unity of Japanese society was threatened by modernization itself unless the country was given a new collective mission.

Derationalization: Perceived or Real?

Table 7-2 suggests that Japan remained reasonably rationalized even after 1900 and before the onset of quasitotalitarian governance. However, Japanese leaders thought otherwise. Internal dissidence, which in liberal cultures was accepted as normal, was experienced as almost intolerable by many Japanese leaders who continued to idealize Japan as a harmonious familylike nation. Parliamentary institutions that seemed to function reasonably well in liberal eyes were seen as disruptive. In the institutional life of pre-1945 Japan they were never allowed to play their Western role. A severe "peace preservation" law sharply restricting civil liberties was enacted in 1925. But when Japan turned to revolutionary-

Table 7-2. Degree of rationalization, Japan, 1880–1990

	1880	1900	1920	1940	1960	1980	1990
Political succession	Yes	Yes	Yes	Yes	Yes	Yes	Yes
National myth in education	Some	Yes	Yes	Yes	Yes	Some	Some
Religious institutions	No	Yes	Yes	Yes	Yes	Some	Yes
Civil religion	No	Some	No	Yes	Some	Yes	Some
Cultural uniformity	Yes	Yes	Yes	Yes	Yes	Yes	Yes
Official language accepted	Yes	Yes	Yes	Yes	Yes	Yes	Yes
Income redistribution	No	No	No	No	Some	Some	Some
Workers' organizations	No	No	No	No	Some	Some	Some
Farmers' organizations	No	No	No	No	Some	Some	Some
Payment of taxes	Yes	Yes	Yes	Yes	Some	Yes	Yes
Conscription accepted	Yes	Yes	Yes	Yes	N/A	N/A	N/A
Fighting wars	Yes	Yes	Yes	Yes	N/A	N/A	N/A
Administrative cohesion	Some	Yes	Yes	Yes	Yes	Yes	Yes
Foreign policy	Yes	Yes	No	Yes	No	Some	Some
Peaceful change	Yes	Yes	Some	Yes	Yes	Yes	Yes
Legitimacy	Some	Yes	Yes	Yes	Yes	Yes	Yes
Total (%)	59	78	66	84	79	86	82

totalitarian nationalism after 1936, institutional and ideological changes did not quite ape the European model because the innovations were justified in terms of historical continuity with Japan's traditional essence.

Selected traditional political institutions persisted until 1936. One of the most influential Meiji constitutional lawyers, Hozumi Yatsuka, taught that the Constitution was a gift from the emperor, who voluntarily bound himself to obey the law. As the law governs the relationship between everyone, the emperor and heaven, there can be no distinction between a private and a public sphere. Nevertheless, absolute personal power is illegitimate, unless sanctioned by the imperial hierarchy of authority. Revolt against absolute power is licit if it is undertaken in the spirit of the political tradition; revolutionary action that rejects the tradition, however, is unthinkable.

Political parties, once they took root after 1900, were elite organizations composed of local notables; they did not have or seek mass membership, even after universal manhood suffrage was introduced and even though up to 75 percent of the electorate usually went to the polls. Parties had strong ties with "families of influence," local landowners, industrialists, and officeholders. Interpersonal and interfactional competition within parties was common and facilitated the conclusion of new alliances and coalitions of interests. Top leadership was collegiate, never charismatic in all of modern Japanese history, a fact that was to give Japanese fascism its unique character. Competition between the two main political parties was really devoid of deep ideological or even programmatic content.

Moreover, party and parliamentary competition was not of consistent importance to the conduct of government because of the role of the bureaucracy in shaping legislation and budgets. The military services were not subject to civilian control: they reported directly to the emperor and appointed the ministers who served in cabinets, which had a tendency to be short-lived in any case. The military were a totally autonomous institution in pre-1945 Japan, which, by virtue of its control over the conscription system, had direct access to the Japanese masses.

During the Meiji era the *Genro*, a council of elder statesmen, most of whom had participated in the Meiji Restoration, advised the emperor on all major matters of policy. Their power exceeded that of the cabinet, the parliament, the bureaucracy, and the military until about 1910. Acting on the basis of consensus, an imperial opinion backed by the *Genro* ended debate.

Educational policy illustrates the tension between nationalistic socialization and adaptation to modernity. Even though compulsory universal education was instituted in 1871, the spirit of syncretism that emanates from the Imperial Rescript did not always prevail. During the 1880s and even after there was an ongoing dispute between Confucianists, Japanese nativists, and westernizers over the content of the curriculum and the role of moral precepts in defining it. The nativists won most of the points, but by the 1920s the Ministry of Education thought it necessary to reemphasize *kokutai* as the core of the curriculum *because so many of the teachers were too westernized in their tastes to take it seriously.*

The military and the State Shinto authorities defined the civil religion. Essentially the young samurai who animated the Meiji reforms had been unemployed warriors until their capture of the government gave them a new stage on which to act out their ideology of selfless service to the nation. It is hardly surprising that the new army epitomized the novel, but traditional, mandate. The introduction of conscription—everybody could now be a warrior—was justified as part of education for national service and for self-sacrifice. The system of local reserve associations ensured that the demobilized soldiers remained part of the national family. The military took the lead in reorganizing local government. Hamlets were combined into larger clusters of villages, ostensibly self-governing but actually tied closely to the authorities in Tokyo by means of networks of school principals, Shinto priests, village headmen, and prominent landlords.

Religious institutions were made to dovetail this arrangement. When the government persecuted the "old Buddhism" of folk cults centered on local temples, serious efforts were made by religious reformers to modernize and spiritualize Buddhism. The result was a new Buddhism that denounced remaining feudal customs, magic, superstition, and much traditional ritual in favor of an other-directed personal ethic. Once this happened, Buddhism ceased to be perceived as a threat by the government, although Shinto alone became the kernel of the civil religion.

Again, the military proved central because of the importance of Yasukuni Shrine (and its local branches) as the repository of all the nation's war dead, martyrs of service to *kokutai*. Shinto shrines became a nationwide locus for the worship of the Emperor and his ancestors, human and divine, from having once been mere centers of local cults. By this means, "the obligations individuals owed to their families and the local Shinto gods were sublimated and transformed into loyalty to the state. Thus, by grafting its ideology into the traditional folk practices of Shinto and ancestor worship, the state manipulated the people's primitive *voelkisch* feelings of pride, guilt, and conscience, making these the emotional base for a new civil religion."[6] Ise Shrine and its local affiliates became the center of emperor worship. By 1940, almost eight million

---

[6] Winston Davis, *Japanese Religion and Society* (Albany: State University of New York Press, 1992), p. 21.

people paid annual tribute there. Shinto universities were founded, the priesthood was professionalized, and other graduates went on to teach in public schools. These people became the full-time propagandists for *kokutai*.

The economy, too, was often rendered as an organic family. The national myth provided the justification for the close ties between the military, the economic-financial bureaucracy, and the private oligopolistic owners of industry and commerce, the Zaibatsu. Agriculture and small business were heavily taxed to support government budgets that allowed for heavy military purchases from the Zaibatsu. When non-Zaibatsu firms and farmers formed their own groups, these were co-opted by the government-created associations that came to govern each economic sector during the war. These private interests deliberately minimized competition among each other, a policy sanctioned by the state. Even though they had harmonious relations with the state, the Zaibatsu retained some institutional autonomy as partners of the state even during the war.

Japanese industrial relations could be seen as an instance of very ingenious adaptation. The number of trade unions had increased to 973 by 1936, from 107 in 1918; this increase covered a mere 7 percent of the work force. Most Japanese firms considered unionization and collective bargaining as unacceptable class confrontation. Factory legislation was opposed by business; some regulations were slowly enacted between 1890 and 1930, but full-fledged free trade unionism was never allowed. Instead, a socially progressive segment of bureaucracy, the Social Bureau of the Home Ministry, fostered the notion of the factory as a moral community, dedicated to industrial production, and the harmonious coexistence of owner and worker. Coopted workers and reluctant employers were induced to join the semiofficial Cooperation and Harmony Society, which enacted social legislation and mediated industrial disputes in a partly successful effort to head off Western-style confrontational industrial relations. After 1931, the state's role became ever larger as fascist corporatism became the preferred model of industrial relations, a shift that resulted in the shunting aside of the established unions in favor of a new group of "patriotic" labor leaders.

The imperialist foreign policy pleased all interests. The ideological underpinnings of Japan's foreign policy of imperial expansion have very old roots. The notion that Japan also needed a safe market for its industrial goods appeared as early as 1895, although this demand did not trigger the first war with China. But the notion that a protected market for exports and a safe source of rice imports were essential became strong by the 1920s and was used to justify the consolidation of control over Korea and Manchuria. It took the Great Depression, which hit Japan hard after 1929, to make the Zaibatsu into supporters of imperial expansion. Hitherto they had supported the "soft" policy of Shidehara Kijuro, avoiding military conflict in China in favor of peaceful economic penetration and good relations with the West, including arms control and freezing the territorial status quo in East Asia. The "hard" policy, espoused especially by Tanaka Giichi, called for active anticommunism, military control over Manchuria, the Soviet Far Eastern region, and North China, as well as confrontation with Western states opposing this course. Tanaka's Seiyukai party became the pre–World War II advocate of the traditional-nationalist program of imperialism against Shidehara's Minseito, which favored accommodation.

Japanese Fascism and World War II

Neither party satisfied the large number of secret societies that had grown up by 1930, made up mostly of young officers of rural background. They had the support of the "Imperial Way" faction of the army general staff and were in control of the crack army units stationed in Manchuria, who staged the incident that launched the second Sino-Japanese War.

The movement developed in a context of economic stagnation and rising left-wing agitation that was ruthlessly suppressed by the government even during the 1920s, but yet felt as very threatening by the Japanese Right. Exports fell by 50 percent after 1929; the prices of silk and rice reached rock bottom. These trends were met with protectionist measures and antiforeign propaganda. The already weak parties discredited themselves further by inaction, governmental instability, and corruption. In November 1930 a young fascist assassinated the prime minister who had just agreed to another naval arms limitation treaty. During the following twelve months the Kwantung Army took advantage of indecision in Tokyo to conquer Manchuria (without having received orders to do so). Two more ministers and the head of the Mitsui Zaibatsu were assassinated by May 1932. Thereafter, all civilian governments ruled at the tolerance of the armed forces until the army, stopping an attempted coup by junior officers on February 26, 1936, took over the reins directly. Thereafter, even former communists and liberals joined the front of nationalists committed to imperial expansion.

The fascists believed in a Showa Restoration. Japanese integral nationalists maintained that the Meiji Restoration had gone astray because of its toleration of capitalism, political parties, individualist ethics, and its efforts to accommodate Western powers. The prophet of this creed was Kita Ikki; claiming a religious basis for his ideas in both Buddhism and Shinto, he reaffirmed the social equality of all Japanese in selfless devotion to domestic socialist reform and a foreign policy of driving the

289

West from Asia. He wanted to rid the country of the bureaucracy, the Zaibatsu and capitalism, to lead to a return to agrarian values and rural economic pursuits. Just as the proletariat has the duty to cleanse the nation, he taught, Japan is itself a proletarian nation with the mission to cleanse capitalism from Asia. It was this creed that animated the young revolutionary terrorists who challenged the government and took over parts of the army.

Kita's creed both resembles and differs from European fascism. It is less revolutionary than its Italian, French, and German cousins because of the stress on the Japanese religious tradition, despite the striking Marxist accretions. It is in harmony with European fascism in the dedication to spontaneity, action, blind devotion, self-sacrifice, and disdain for cold reason. Institutional differences are also marked. Nothing like a monopolistic party machine holding the state and the armed forces in its thrall ever developed, though existing political parties were proscribed. Compulsory state-run organizations took the place of labor unions and voluntary groups. The Imperial Rule Assistance Association sought to coordinate these state-sponsored associations in all walks of life and economy, but it did little more than propagandize for *kokutai* and determine the content of public education. The economy continued to be run by an alliance of the Zaibatsu with the military and the bureaucracy. There was no leadership principle, no charismatic rule. It would have conflicted with the emperor myth, the established civil religion.[7] The Japanese, despite the fascists' demands, continued to tolerate their brand of capitalism and military populism. Nor was the Showa Restoration supported by a new dependent middle class, as in Europe; its supporters came from the old middle class, farmers, lower-level bureaucrats, and occasionally from the Zaibatsu.

After 1932 governments were run by coalitions of integralists and established traditional syncretists. The "Control" faction of the army general staff, mostly traditional syncretists, assumed control of the country in 1936, when it tamed the "Imperial Way" faction by executing the extreme Showa restorationists, including Kita. Its leader, General Tojo

---

[7] The fascist educational system was dominated by the doctrine of *kokutai no hongi*, a restatement of the Meiji version that stressed making a new Japan even better than the Meiji system, based on the notion that all of Japan is a no-class single organic family. Japan was to be saved from democracy and Marxism. Shinto education was encouraged; Christianity and Buddhism were again persecuted, as were millenarian "new religions." Typical propaganda slogans of the period included: "the eight corners of the world under one roof"; "Japan—the leading power of East Asia"; "Kokutai stands foremost among all nations"; "a hundred million hearts beating like one"; and "Loyalty to the Emperor and patriotism." Taken from I. I. Morris, *Nationalism and the Right Wing in Japan* (London: Oxford University Press, 1960).

Hideki, became prime minister in 1941, after having been minister of war for several years; he accepted a good deal of the program of the integralists, although his civilian predecessor, Prince Konoye Fumimaro, had not. Tojo's group considered war with the West inevitable because it correctly predicted that the West would not accept an Asian order dominated by Japan. Convinced that Japan could not survive unless it dominated East and Southeast Asia, the government prepared for a war with the United States. The military leaders favored a showdown, although some civilians apparently were willing to compromise on the new Asian order. Japan's rapid conquest of the targeted countries was crowned by the creation of a Japan-centered economic and political system called the Greater East Asia Coprosperity Sphere.

Japan's Modernization: Self-Fulfilling Prophecy of Self-Destruction

Japan's schizophrenic modernizers were remarkably adept at assimilating Western techniques and institutions considered useful in ensuring cultural and political survival. The first two generations of modernizers were geniuses at practicing adaptation. But they were poor learners. Their heirs, the rulers of Japan during the 1930s, persistently drew the wrong lessons from their own and others' histories. Because of their own short-sighted adaptations, ideological and institutional, they destroyed the handiwork of their fathers and grandfathers. Of course, all Japanese leaders were blinded by the contradiction between their obvious successes and their pathological fears of failure. Modernization, until the malaise and reverses of the depression years, had seemed almost flawlessly successful. It appeared that the wholesale borrowing of techniques, the more selective choice of foreign institutions, and the outright rejection of most Western values, had saved Japan from the fate of China and catapulted her into becoming the leading power of East Asia and the western Pacific.

But the Western powers never intended to conquer Japan, keep her from becoming an important trading state, or deprive her, on principle, of access to primary commodities. That was the lesson *not* learned by Japan because of ideological blinders; Japanese nationalists mistook deterrent action for offensive thrusts. True learning seemed possible during the 1920s; it was choked off by the nativist responses to the depression and the Western condemnation of Japanese imperialism. Henceforward, the ideological track on which the military and their allies moved furthered the xenophobic responses that led to the self-fulfilling prophecy of global war—and the destruction of the old Japan of brilliant adaptations.

From Defeat to Rationalized Powerhouse

The American Occupation: Triumph of Westernization?

Even during the Taisho period, the heyday of possible liberalism in Japan, the police was used as an active mechanism to repress social and political dissent, to spy on society, to encourage individual Japanese to inform on one another. Police auxiliary organizations mobilized society as they penetrated it, while claiming to act "in harmony" with the community. After 1936, Japan became a full-fledged police state. Today, "thought control is an ancient memory. Dissenters walk the streets freely. ... Dissenters are free to publish their views widely in all of the media without censorship. They hold secure positions in the universities. Opposition parties regularly take about one-half of the vote. The labor movement has declined ... but nevertheless continues to take part in the political process."[8] The police prides itself on not using violence, not even under severe provocation from rioters, and on cultivating cooperative relations with the community, to serve its needs with help and advice (though it also uses these friendly relations for quiet surveillance).

In the wake of the Meiji Restoration, Fukuzawa Yukichi urged his compatriots to "leave Asia," to shed non-Western cultural ways in favor of the West's. The American occupation (1945–1952) was "to insure that Japan will not again become a menace to the peace and security of the world" by making it a "peace-loving nation"[9] inspired and governed by liberal democratic institutions. To a remarkable extent, these objectives were attained.

Japan received one of the most advanced liberal constitutions. Its Article 9 commits Japan never to go to war. The armed forces were abolished. The emperor was remade into the "symbol of the nation and of the unity of the people ... whose position is derived from the will of the people with whom resides sovereign power."[10] Military leaders of the war effort were tried and executed; 100,000 civilian wartime officials were initially purged, but most were rehabilitated by 1955 and many became very prominent conservative politicians and bureaucrats. A sweeping

---

[8] Herbert Passin, "The Occupation—Some Reflections," *Daedalus* (Summer 1990): 124.

[9] Quoted in ibid., p. 110.

[10] Japanese Constitution, Chap. 1, Art. 1. The Constitution remains legitimate in the eyes of the Japanese public. In 1991 82.6 percent thought it a "good" document; the lowest positive evaluation had been 51.3 percent in 1967. Those who pronounce it "not good" reached a high of 27 percent in 1980 and a low of 7.4 percent in 1991. However, opinion is very divided about whether the Constitution ought to be amended with respect to two issues. Those who wanted to amend it in order to remove the pacifist demilitarization Article 9 garnered 16.2 percent of the vote in 1993. Strong minorities also want to amend it because the document was imposed by the United States, not for any substantive reason. The numbers are: 38.2 percent (1986), 45.4 percent (1991), and 23.1 percent (1993).

land reform was enacted and never repealed. Democratic labor unions with the right to organize freely, strike, and bargain collectively were introduced; by 1949 there were seven million union members, almost one half of the industrial work force.

Women acquired equal rights in law. Local government was decentralized and local officials made elective. Education ceased being a vehicle of government propaganda. The occupation authorities opened up the previously very hierarchical school system by creating a large number of new middle and high schools to which poor children gained access for the first time. Educational reforms thus had the effect of accelerating upward mobility, even though other attempted democratizing measures, such as elected school boards, failed to take hold. Even after Japan reneged on some American-imposed reforms, the opening up of the educational system had produced permanent effects.

The most prominent case of backsliding concerned the organization of industry, banking, and commerce. The American effort to break up the Zaibatsu by means of anti-trust laws was soon rendered ineffective by the invention of the *Keiretsu*. These are groupings of firms related by means of interlocking directorates and supplier contracts, usually clustered around a bank that finances them all. Still, the Keiretsu represent a less restrictive and more competitive form of economic concentration than did their predecessors. They also turned out to be very effective engines of economic recovery from the trough of destruction and hunger into which Japan had fallen by 1946.

The Return of Bureaucratic-Oligarchic Rule

Even though a parliamentary system based on competitive rival parties was among the permanent legacies of the Occupation, the meaning of that system differed in each of several stages that characterize post-1945 Japanese democracy. Between 1945 and 1955 several socialist and conservative parties competed ferociously; they alternated in office until 1948, when Yoshida Shigeru, a former imperial official, became prime minister and inaugurated the rule of the group that became the Liberal Democratic Party (LDP), which governed Japan until 1993. The LDP resulted from a fusion of several right-leaning parties, forged by the fear of the business community that industrial recovery would be crippled because of the strong unions and disruptive strikes of the 1950s and the founding of a new Japan Socialist Party (JSP). The peak of unrest was reached in 1960, when opposition to the renewal of the security treaty with the United States resulted in very large student-led riots. Nonetheless, this period clearly saw more competitive politics than what followed.

The LDP formed a deep and lasting link with some major corporations, the bureaucracy, the small peasantry that remains in modern Japan, and the traditional urban lower-middle-class merchants and artisans. The coalition brought about the Japanese economic miracle and made Japan into a global economic superpower even though the LDP was driven by personalistic factions. It stressed industry over commerce, production, savings, and investment over consumption, and exports over imports. The bureaucracy, mostly the Ministry of Trade and Industry (MITI), guided the process with financial incentives and planning. This coalition legitimated the culture of *sararimen* ("salary men"), protected preindustrial sectors with barriers to imports and detailed regulations, made frequent deals with the opposition socialists, and proved to be incredibly subject to financial corruption. It also introduced the system of nonconfrontational industrial relations and the long-lived alliance with the United States. Parliament, until the end of the 1980s, was a front for a coalition dominated by the bureaucracy, big business, and the protected traditional sectors united under the LDP umbrella, although regular elections determined the relative strength of LDP factions allied with these groups.

Increasingly publicized corruption in the form of financial payoffs to key politicians of both major parties discredited parliamentary and party politics by the end of the 1980s. The period came to an end because of increasing mass-based demands that the ruling oligarchic coalition be opened up, that consumption and environmental issues receive more attention. Some of these issues had aroused the public before. Prime Minister Ikeda Hayato had committed the country to doubling incomes after the security treaty riots seemed to suggest that revolution was imminent. Prime Minister Tanaka Kakuei had greatly expanded the social insurance system. Prime Minister Nakasone Yasuhiro sought to reduce protectionism and the power of the bureaucracy to regulate domestic commerce. None of this sufficed to stave off electoral defeat for the LDP, its internal fission, and the ongoing effort to make electoral and tax reforms. Possibly, the crisis of the 1990s will usher in a more democratic Japan because it pits the vested beneficiaries of the old coalition against modern urban groups more interested in consumption and a higher quality of personal life.

After 1973 incomes rose as high-technology Japanese goods flooded the world; but, as Japan proved reluctant to import or allow foreign investors in Japan, a backlash developed in other industrial countries that compelled Japan to look for markets and investment opportunities in Asia and to relax its protectionism somewhat. Until then, Japan had presented a very low profile to the rest of the world, relying for its military and diplomatic security almost entirely on its treaty with the United States. Self-abnegation was abandoned in economic relations by Prime

Minister Nakasone in the 1980s; even in military matters, more voices advocated increasing the Self-Defense Force (as the new army was dubbed), for repealing Article 9 of the Constitution, and going above the hallowed 1 percent of GNP benchmark for military appropriations. And, in discussions about education, culture, and the media, more and more was heard about "Japan theory" or "Japan lore" (*Nihonjin Ron*), a new civic spirit inspired not by the West but by traditional Japanese themes. The advocates of Japan theory expressed the fear that something quintessentially Japanese was being lost in this helter-skelter plunge into Western ways. They saw not a society that had risen from the ashes of 1945 and rationalized itself successfully on pluralist principles but a badly fragmented and bickering family forgetting its roots.

Are There Cracks in the Nation's Identity?

In 1990 Japan still received a resounding 82% rationalization score, higher than that of most other advanced industrial countries (Table 7-2). It was the very pluralist 1950s that inspired the LDP-led coalition's efforts to recentralize political life from the top down. In 1956 the Police Agency listed 1,000 small right-wing groups, with a total membership of 100,000; the Japan Communist Party had a mere 60,000 members; 1.2 million voters supported right-wing authoritarian parties in 1953; 1.5 million voted communist. Both had largely disappeared by the mid-1960s. Voting participation has fluctuated between 76 and 72 percent of eligibles since 1945, down from the prewar rate, as enfranchisement has reach 65 percent of the entire population. These figures compare very favorably with American electoral statistics. In 1978, 89 percent of a national sample professed a preference for gradual methods for changing things of which they disapproved; only 4 percent considered using illegal measures. Why then worry about rationalization?

High voter participation hides a strong feeling of ambivalence toward the parliamentary process. Most Japanese prefer the local to the national level as a forum for action. Feelings of incapacity to influence national events are common, as is contempt for parliamentarians and political parties. Middle-class urbanites especially feel that their representatives do not protect their interests.

Japanese tend to feel that their nation is very special—and yet they also feel that it is inferior to others and that it has something to learn from other nations. Increasingly, and despite the demythification of the pre-1945 institutions, people mix respect with indifference toward the emperor.[11] The marked popularity of the Buddhist Soka Gakkai movement

---

[11] In 1978, 53 percent of respondents thought Japan was not "one of the first-class

is attributed by many observers to widespread alienation in contemporary Japan, particularly among incompletely Westernized lower-middle-class people.

Two illusions etch the identity most Japanese profess: everyone is a member of the middle class, and Japan is ethnically as well as racially homogeneous. Undoubtedly, the economic miracle has engendered a great deal of homogenization of taste and income at a relatively high level, lending some justification to the self-perceived middle-class status of all Japanese. However, the claim ignores the systematic discrimination in employment against educated married women (despite legislation directed against the practice). The majority views the differentials that exist among ethnic groups as a result of lesser individual ability; it believes that fair competition under conditions of equal opportunity guarantees that all deserving people receive their due.

How Liberal Is Japan's Civil Religion?

The Role of the Emperor

Postwar Japanese beliefs about the national culture no longer owe anything to Shinto. *Kokutai* is dead, but many other pre-1945 beliefs are not. Devotion to self-sacrifice and the practice of personal austerity for the sake of national economic well-being took the place of emperor worship in the immediate postwar years. Such devotion, just as did *kokutai*, taps into traditional beliefs about loyalty to the extended family, to the ancestral household. Expressive ritual respect for the nation and for the family look very much alike. After 1945 loyalty to the group, especially the work group, took the place of loyalty to the nation, thus directly serving the goal of achieving national recovery and subsequent prosperity.

Though legally a constitutional monarch with purely ceremonial functions since 1945, the emperor only slowly descended to his present status of public respect mixed with indifference. In the eyes of the mass public he retained a special charismatic role for years after the official demythification of *kokutai* and of Shinto. He retained his appeal because he personified (and may still personify) core Confucian values of social har-

---

countries" and 70 percent thought that Japan had "something to learn from other countries." forty-four percent felt "indifference" toward the emperor, and 22 percent professed a "favorable feeling," but only 30 percent expressed "respect." Murakami Yasusuke, "The Japanese Model of Political Economy," in K. Yamamura and Y. Yasuba, eds., *The Political Economy of Japan* (Stanford, Calif.: Stanford University Press, 1987) vol. 1, p. 78.

mony, duty, and benevolence. Thus, we face the task of judging how much syncretism remains in the officially liberal national myth.

When, during the massive suffering of the immediate postsurrender period, the public was evidently confused by the sudden denunciation of the old national myth, the Showa Emperor left his seclusion and began several years of constant public exposure. He traveled to many parts of the country, encouraged miners and workers, offered condolences to widows of servicemen killed in the war, expressed his gratitude to war veterans who had just been repatriated, and even patted the heads of children. He may have done so to escape charges of being a war criminal, but his efforts were also designed to spur people on to work harder for reconstruction, to sacrifice once more for the national good. Years later, people victimized by environmental disaster or other misfortunes still called on the Emperor to save them or appealed to the Emperor to legitimate their suffering.

Perhaps because he is still seen as more than just a figurehead, there is no uncertainty about political succession. Nor is there any dissent now from the commitment to settle all internal disputes exclusively by peaceful means, though this was not the case until the end of the 1960s and may be challenged in the face of religiously sanctioned terrorism.

Still, the fact that the civil religion also contains many themes that challenge these traditional elements must mean that Japanese identity remains ambiguous despite the acceptance of several core beliefs about society. Japanese civil religion remains ambivalent over the primacy of individualism, over democracy itself if that institution is defined in terms of individual rights. The personal dedication to hard work to ensure the nation's prosperity is now challenged by many. More and more Japanese seem to entertain serious doubts as to their place in the world, their purpose, their mission. They hesitate between seeing and celebrating themselves as unique and embracing global interdependence linked to Western and cosmopolitan values.

Religion and Education as Shapers of National Identity

Even though between 65 percent and 75 percent of Japanese report that they have no religious faith, between 70 percent and 77 percent consider having one very important! Despite the clear decline of religious practice since World War II, it appears that many Japanese retain a religious feeling and seek religious affiliations. State Shinto was abolished in 1945; state subsidies were taken away from the shrines; references to Shinto were removed from the school curriculum, and the Imperial Rescript on Education was rescinded as antidemocratic. Worship at rural shrines, Shinto and Buddhist, declined. Yet, the Shinto priesthood reorganized and still presents its faith as the incarnation of Japanese culture.

But a quite successful challenger arose in the form of the Soka Gakkai, a sect of over four million members, mostly from the lower classes and disproportionately made up of recent women migrants to big cities. Soka Gakkai presents itself as the only authentic Japanese religion because its inspiration, the thirteenth-century priest Nichiren, preached the superiority of a Japanese incarnation of the Buddha. Many commentators believe that both mainstream and Nichiren Buddhism continue to strengthen the civil religion because they legitimate the work ethic and the existing socioeconomic system.[12]

The failure of the major religions to give agreed content to Japanese nationalism has been accompanied by the rise of new religious sects that show much more sensitivity to providing a spiritual and transcendental basis for national identity, of which the Soka Gakkai is merely the largest. Many new sects, in opposing aspects of modern industrial/urban life, stress the collectivist values and institutions that challenge the liberal content of Japanese nationalism.

Still, secularism has won all the symbolic battles. Yasukuni Shrine, formerly a major Shinto establishment, and still honoring Japan's war dead, was stripped of all government financial and symbolic support in 1946. After 1975 successive prominent LDP politicians, including prime ministers, sought to pay official visits to the shrine. They were sharply criticized by opposition parties and the press; the practice stopped or became a purely personal gesture. People were asked between 1953 and 1978 whether incoming prime ministers ought to visit Ise Shrine, especially sacred to the Emperor, which had been the custom; in 1953, 57 percent thought he should, but by 1978 the number had shrunk to 20 percent. Five times, the LDP sought to revive state subsidies for Yasukuni Shrine; five times the concurrent majority norm prevented the legislation from passing.

The system of public education has moved away from the liberalism of the American occupation's reforms. Originally, teachers had been given control over the classroom and locally elected bodies of parents over policy. By 1960, the Ministry of Education had succeeded in recentralizing the system while triggering a major conflict with the powerful left-wing teachers' union, many of whose members are Marxists. So were many university professors until the 1970s, especially among social

---

[12] The Society is organized hierarchically, starting with small therapy-group–like "friendship" units. Group meetings stress self-criticism and self-improvement. It owns enterprises and fields a successful political party, Komeito.

scientists, a fact that apparently did not do much to radicalize permanently the future civil servants and Keiretsu personnel they taught.

The conflict arose mainly over the nationalist content of textbooks, over "whether the teaching of history should concentrate on the miseries of the nation's past or on its glories, whether it should emphasize the doings of the rulers or of the ruled, whether it should inculcate the values of patriotism and dedication to national progress or of resistance to authority and the establishment of individual rights."[13]

Prime Minister Nakasone Yasuhiro attempted a major reform in the 1980s. He sought to reduce the competitive and hierarchical character of the system by liberalizing the admissions examination for higher education, to diversify the curricula, and to weaken the teachers' unions by abolishing tenure and lengthening probationary employment. However, the bureaucracy (and most of the LDP) accepted only the commitment to improved patriotic and moral training, the very theme opposed by the teachers. The teaching of history did not then include discussion of Japanese aggression; it omitted most of the twentieth century and made no mention of war guilt. Cautious references to these events did not find their way into the curriculum until the mid-1990s.

Ethnic Minorities and Citizenship

Obtaining Japanese citizenship is almost impossible for people not of Japanese descent. Unlike most other liberal nation-states, Japan has not found it desirable to accept as its own talented non-Japanese able to make important contributions to the economy and the society. Koreans, people of "mixed blood," and the *burakumin* (Japanese descendants of formerly "unclean" castes) are victimized by systematic discrimination in employment and education.

Burakumin live in de facto segregated quarters, suffer from unemployment and employment in unskilled occupations, high school dropout rates, and social deviance. Many join radical left-wing movements; others join criminal organizations. The government denies the existence of systematic discrimination and buys off more active discontent by offering remedies on a case-by-case basis. Some particularly determined members of the group manage to "pass" into middle class society, but most continue to live on the margins.

Koreans, 70 percent of them born in Japan, are the victims and de-

[13] R. P. Dore, "Textbook Censorship in Japan," *Pacific Affairs* (Winter 1970–71): 550. In 1990, a *Mainichi Shimbun* poll reported that 73 percent of a sample of 2,227 people agreed that the national flag ought to be displayed and the national anthem sung at school ceremonies; in 1992 an NHK poll reported that 60 percent felt that way.

scendants of victims of earlier colonial policies; often they try to assimilate and even succeed occasionally. Over 70 percent attend Japanese schools; 3,000 apply for naturalization every year. Yet those who "pass" are stigmatized by North Korean organizations who strive to retain their separate identity. Though fragmented politically, Koreans coalesce when they see the need to defend themselves against perceived discrimination because trade unions do not help Korean workers. Koreans and Burakumin are more prone to aggressive behavior than the rest of the population, perhaps because they appraise themselves as less worthy. Japanese tend to feel that Koreans do not observe normal norms of cooperative behavior within the work group. The permanent place of Koreans in Japanese society is the subject of much disagreement.

So is the place of other foreigners. Since 1995 the state has taken over the financing of election expenses to limit competition for financial contributions. This has raised the issue of whether the payment of taxes should entitle resident aliens to vote in local elections. Should a positive decision be made it would signal a major step away from *ius sanguinis* as the definer of national identity.

Between Individualism and Collectivism

In the Western experience of nation-state formation an individualistic ethic, a utilitarian approach to economic matters, and liberal political institutions did not, in the end, prevent rationalization; in Japan, the lack of all three clearly facilitated it. It should therefore not surprise us that democratic Japan has maintained a rationalized polity without fully integrating liberalism, individualism, and utilitarianism.[14]

In 1970, 55 percent of respondents to a survey thought that claims made for individual rights were too strong because obligations to others were not stressed enough. In 1993, 45 percent of respondents thought that people ought to be more socially oriented (31 percent favored an individualist orientation). In 1982, 55 percent agreed with the statement "do what is of benefit to other people, whether or not it is what you want to do yourself." In a 1973 survey most respondents tended to characterize Japanese as diligent, persistent, but impatient, quick to be enthusiastic, and quick to cool off; somewhat fewer thought Japanese were

---

[14] The Japanese word for "individualism" (*kojinshugi*) connotes selfishness and immaturity; the word for "individuality" (*kosei*) connotes personal development and the ability to function well. See Joy Hendry, "Individualism and Individuality," in Roger Goodman and Kirsten Refsing, eds., *Ideology and Practice in Modern Japan* (New York: Routledge, 1992), p. 56. In 1973, almost 90 percent of respondents endorsed as "important" or "quite important" freedom, religious feeling, love of country, revering one's ancestors, and filial piety.

insular, imitative, and vindictive.[15] Japanese children are taught young to defer to the face-to-face group and not to assert themselves as individuals. They are socialized to believe in harmony within the group, in respect for superiors and older people, and in the need to practice reciprocity. Conflict among loyalties is reduced by favoring the face-to-face group. Law, and the insistence on principle, are minimized in the resolution of disputes in favor of compromise and conciliation.

Japanese business and industry, too, is slow to adopt formally rational operational norms regarding personnel when these conflict with such Confucian values as *wa* (harmony), *on* (debt), and *giri* (obligation). Despite the emphasis on individual property rights in the Meiji and the postoccupation civil codes, notions of collective household property survive along with remnants of the Confucian norm of benevolence in the use of property and the conduct of commercial relations. The Confucian norm of the authoritative role of parents, heads of households, and officials of firms as heading a structure of hierarchy is still visible, though much weakened. Business firms respect their past practices of reciprocity even if it is to their present financial disadvantage, as in their preference for Japanese goods and services even when imported ones are cheaper and better. On the other hand, the much-vaunted small-group relations among networks of politicians, bureaucrats, and business leaders are in no way unique to Japan; they are commonly found in liberal societies.

But there is also evidence of a trend toward a liberalism that stresses individualism. The marked increase in social mobility after 1945 has contributed to a growth of individualism and individual opportunities for advancement and to a concomitant decline in hierarchical patron–client relations. Many more Japanese express interest in norms of citizenship and of public life that downplay harmony and consensus. The post-1993 political reform movement stressed both transparency in bureaucratic and parliamentary procedure and elections untainted by corruption. Until the demise of the old LDP there was little public expression of unhappiness with either economic or foreign policy; criticism of both is becoming common. The influence of the bureaucracy over business had been declining, though the confused parliamentary scene since 1993 has put it back in the saddle. In short, the democratic aspect of pluralist politics may be gaining at the expense of the manipulated aspect. Public opinion polls confirm that people worry less about the "un-Japanese" aspects of their constitution and put less trust in "good political leaders," preferring popular participation instead.[16]

---

[15] Data taken from Hayashi Chikiio et al., *Nihonjin no Kokuminsei*, vols. 3, 4 (Tokyo: Idemitsushoten, 1975); government surveys, 1970, 1993.

[16] See Prime Minister's Office surveys of 1955 and 1965, and NHK survey of 1975; see also Hayashi et al., *Nihonjin no Kokuminsei.* Note also the practical disappearance by 1970

HOW LIBERAL ARE POLITICAL INSTITUTIONS?

Liberal Democracy or Nativism?

There is little doubt that the domination of electoral politics by the LDP for almost forty years contributed greatly to a rationalized Japan. How can this domination be squared with our claim that parliamentary democracy has gained greatly since the late 1960s?

During the first fifteen years of parliamentary rule debates were confrontational; fistfights in the Diet and obstructionism by the minority parties were routine. The LDP often prevailed by means of procedural chicanery as the opposition used other rules to block action. As LDP and JSP strength declined, both sought to form tacit coalitions with other parties and the other parties consequently entered the parliamentary game on more civilized terms. Minority party support for legislation climbed from 43 percent to 70 percent between 1975 and 1977. The Speaker of the House became a powerful and respected arbiter. The norm of concurrent majority consensus took hold under these conditions.

Moreover, the LDP was never a monolith, as proved by its fragmenting in 1993. It was always a coalition of separate factions, each of which mediated between grassroots followers and their representative in the Diet. Each faction was a client–patron network that tended to satisfy its constituents. All groups of voters, except labor and citizens groups, favored the LDP. Even this limited form of democracy ensured that the state was no longer run entirely by the bureaucracy, as before 1945.

On the other hand, some traditional collectivist themes also continue to resonate and they may challenge the dominance of formally liberal political institutions. Thus, the notion of Japanese uniqueness remains alive and well in the ideology of *Nihonjin Ron*, favored by some intellectuals and conservative LDP members. Advocates of this view explain the Japanese economic miracle as the triumph of the traditional work ethic centered on the group, not the individual. They explicitly point to non-liberal values and institutions as the explanation for Japan's superiority. That superiority, in turn, has been used as an argument for Japan's seeking a world role other than timidly following the American lead. Because stress is put on the traditional elite culture of Japan, loyally followed by the masses, the simultaneous acceptance of democratic institutions at the mass level sets the scene for continued ambivalence about consistent

---

of dozens of small extreme right-wing groups espousing *kokutai* themes and the repudiation of "alien" democracy. They called themselves, among other names, New Life Japan People's League, Harmony Party, Anti-Bolshevik Corps, Great Japan Patriots' Party, and Chrysanthemum Flag Association.

liberalism. *Nihonjin Ron*, though definitely anti-individualistic and antiu-tilitarian, is not totally inconsistent with political liberalism. Conservatives such as Ishihara Shintaro have long accused their compatriots of lacking the traditional moral sense, a feeling of national purpose and identity. *Nihonjin Ron* ideologues, eschewing the physical and verbal symbols of *kokutai*, find the uniqueness and the superiority of Japanese culture and society in ethnic homogeneity, purity of race, historical continuity, and the mystique of the language—the stuff of fascist and traditional-syncretist nationalists. Although they wish to amend the constitution, they do not call for a militarily aggressive foreign policy.

Until recently, ideologues of nativism have identified all Japanese culture with the traditional culture of the elite; they have rejected as "un-Japanese" the many Marxist intellectuals as well as the numerous liberals. Yet they also rejected Japanese "folk" culture as primitive, condemning it to acceptance by a few extreme right-wing groups. In recent decades, as the Japanese masses have become devotees of Western popular culture, conservative ideologues have begun to fear a new threat to the cultural essence they defend. They manipulated the myth of Showa as a special era in the life of the nation (after the death of the Showa Emperor) to stand for the continuity of all things Japanese despite the lost war and the experience of the occupation. Those who identify with the Meiji and Taisho eras are thus unified with those who favor the "new Japan."

Consensual Decision Making

"What the Japanese mean by 'democracy,' " wrote Nakane Chie, "is a system that should . . . give consideration to the weaker or lower; in practice, any decision should be made on the basis of a consensus which includes those located lower in the hierarchy."[17] Things appear to be more complicated than this syncretist claim suggests. A government survey of almost 7,400 respondents in 1979 disclosed that 67.5 percent of youth and 60.8 percent of adults thought that decisions by majority vote

[17] Nakane Chie, *Japanese Society* (Berkeley: University of California Press, 1970), p. 144. This argument has been appropriated by many conservatives as constituting the quintessential Japanese doctrine, as evidence that the essence remains even under the auspices of Japanese democracy. Hence respected authors such as Nakane Chie, Yamamoto Shichihei (writing about Japanese capitalism as being different from Western capitalism), and Doi Takeo are used to buttress a distinctly syncretist nationalist ideology within a generally liberal institutional setting. However, many other observers insist that the allegedly unique Japanese traits can be convincingly explained on the basis of institutional incentives and disincentives deliberately put in place after 1945, though sometimes justified by older practices. If so, such institutional innovation is quite consistent with what the Meiji restorers practiced in the 1870s and 1880s.

should be used when long deliberation fails to produce a consensus. Majority voting decides elections. It has been used by the LDP to have its way in parliament.

But it is used much more sparingly than in Western democracies. The majority does not take advantage of the minority's boycotts of meetings, although it did in the 1960s. Accommodation among the parties is prized. The norm of the "concurrent majority" was observed whenever the LDP was weakened; it provides that, unless there is a favorable majority in the LDP and the JSP, no draft legislation is put to a vote. When Prime Minister Nakasone sought to avoid this procedure, he was criticized as acting too much like an American president, whereupon he contrived an elaborate committee system outside Parliament to fashion intergroup consensus for the reforms he was advocating. Formation of concurrent majorities is facilitated by the fact that there seem to be few systematic fundamental value differences between the major parties, as distinguished from differences over policy.

In September 1994 the essayist Kato Shuichi declared that democracy and liberalism are weakly rooted in Japan, that they would remain so until the Japanese people faced up to their national guilt over World War II. The Japanese, on the whole, were said to lack interest in politics, a commitment to the public good, a critical spirit, even interest in their own history. Kato regrets that foreign countries and Western ideas no longer concern them much. He thinks that his compatriots believe the sole purpose of the state is to ensure the high living standard of the population.[18]

Kato was really deploring the commitment to harmony, to consensual public life that is still Japan's civil religion. A glance at Table 7-3, however, shows that high rationalization scores seem to go with the general aversion to social conflict. A commitment to consensual decision making may even ensure the continued integration of Japanese society.

The political history of the late 1950s and the early 1960s lends support to this argument. Left-wing workers and students challenged the authorities frontally in the Miike coal strike and the conclusion of the security treaty with the United States when 350,000 supporters of the strikers and almost that many police converged at Miike. Comparable numbers of students and workers snake-danced through the streets of Tokyo, facing an overwhelming police presence that used very little force

---

[18] Interview in *Le Monde*, 27 September 1994. Even though participation in elections runs around 70 percent of those eligible to vote, between 20 percent and 30 percent of voters consistently refuse to identify themselves with any party. The disaffiliated in early years were indifferent to politics; more recently the nonaffiliated were educated people critical of the parties. See Gerald L. Curtis, *The Japanese Way of Politics* (New York: Columbia University Press, 1988), pp. 200–201.

Table 7-3. Legitimacy of Japanese democracy

Percent who believe that	1970	1980	1993
Constitution is generally good	52	55	83
Constitution ought to be amended, especially Article 9	27	28	50
Some constitutionally guaranteed human rights ought to be restricted	59/70	42	—
Democratic reforms were good on balance	74	72	—
Emperor should be more authoritative	8	8	—
Individual rights are more important than public welfare	16	26	32
People should be oriented more toward individualism	24	29	31

SOURCES: Government surveys, 1963, 1971, 1980, 1987; *Asahi Shimbun*, 1970, 1980, 1983; *Yomiuri Shimbun*, 1980, 1991, 1993; *Mainichi Shimbun*, 1970, 1979. Samples varied between 2,000 and 2,500 adults.

against the self-declared revolutionaries. Prime Minister Kishi Nobusuke rammed the treaty through the Diet in the face of this opposition, which was joined by the Socialist and Communist parties.

Evidently, the norm of consensual decision making arose as a result of these challenges to social harmony. Later efforts by student leaders to mount revolutionary challenges failed because of extreme factionalism and because of successful policies of consensus building on the part of the LDP. Prime Ministers Ikeda and Sato inaugurated the practice of continuous secret consultations with the opposition parties ("teahouse politics"). The "money politics" invented by Tanaka Kakuei and practiced until the scandals of the early 1990s failed to arouse much concern because both the LDP and the opposition benefited from the payoffs, although Tanaka himself became a sacrificial offering. Consensual decision making was also institutionalized in the informal conflict-resolution techniques preferred by Japanese business to legal recourse and formal court action. The bureaucracy, too, prefers consensual modes of regulation, guidance, and even coercion to legal action. These procedures stress the existence of trust among the participants, a feeling that could hardly come into being if the main actors were not active in making decisions, irrespective of constitutional rules. It was the unwillingness of revolutionary students to live by this norm that marginalized them into acts of terrorism by the late 1960s as the population at large condemned them. Moreover, the resilience of the authorities made it more difficult for the student leaders to agree on the identity of "the enemy."

There are limits to the prevalence of the norm of consensual decision making. The norm comes into operation only if there is a lack of clearly accepted hierarchy among groups or individuals. The norm is more widely practiced in face-to-face interactions than in large collectivities. It does not prevent rapid and authoritative decisions based on hierarchy when there is no sharp division of opinion. But when there is, policy making is made very cumbersome.

Corporatism without Labor

Workers avoid conflict. Organized labor, until it was empowered by the U.S. occupation, had always existed at the margin of public life, in opposition to the state and its policies of rapid industrialization. Its Marxism made it an ally of the left-wing parties, a fact that contributed to a decade of active industrial strife in Japan. The Ikeda reforms, which combined the encouragement of productivity with an active redistributional policy, brought this phase to an end. The Socialist labor federation was discredited, its place taken by "enterprise unions" loyal to their employers.[19] Enterprise unions provide workers with security of employment and with a more personalistic forum for wage bargaining. The aura of trust and the commitment to consensual decision making at the enterprise level ensures some measure of participation in management.[20]

Wage bargaining is ritualistic. Every spring, the unions' coordinating committee demands wage increases justified by inflation; every fall, the employer associations admonish their workers to respect the challenge of competitiveness and to practice restraint. Government ministries and research institutes publish "data" to support a compromise settlement. The unions accept, but only after pretending to argue and to organize a strike. A few strikes may actually take place, but everyone falls in line after a few large firms have settled at the enterprise level.

---

[19] Only about 33 percent of the work force is unionized, and of the unionized group only 37 percent belongs to the national (socialist) federation Sohyo, which lacks recognition by the state. Between 700 and 800 of the largest firms are members of a powerful trade association, Keidanren. Almost all farmers (6 million families) belong to the National Association of Agricultural Cooperatives. Japan loses about as many days per year in industrial disputes as such strong corporatist countries as Germany and Sweden (i.e. very few). Workers overwhelmingly feel that they have a right to be consulted by management. Koike Kazuo, "Human Resource Development and Labor-Management Relations," in Yamamura Kozo and Yasuba Yasakichi, eds., *The Political Economy of Japan*, vol. 1 (Stanford, Calif.: Stanford University Press, 1987), pp. 292, 320.

[20] The institutions of lifetime guaranteed employment and promotion according to seniority are both inconsistent with an individualistic achievement orientation demanded by formal rationality. However, neither is consistently practiced in Japan, and industrial-commercial personnel practices there are not very different from West European practices. Moreover, it is a mistake to consider the keiretsu firms to be familylike cartels organized along economically nonoptimal lines. There are four different types of keiretsu, none of which corresponds to this tradition-tinged view. See Imai Kenichi and Komiya Ryutaro, eds., *Business Enterprise in Japan* (Cambridge, Mass.: MIT Press, 1994), chaps. 1, 6.

Firms pay a percentage of profits as an annual bonus to *every* employee to give workers a stake in the firm. Managers consider both employees and shareholders as members of the firm; they often mediate, at wage bargaining time, between unions and shareholders. The *Rinri* (Ethics) Movement seeks to institutionalize management–employee trust and harmony by running very popular training schools for workers and supervisors. Once again, Japanese leaders have certainly learned, by drawing on traditional values, to channel and reduce industrial strife.

Industrial governance is designed to avoid unlimited competition. Large firms maintain a network of suppliers in a web of mutual trust and dependence; these suppliers are small and medium-size firms. Much of Japanese industry can be visualized as a huge set of small firms clustered around a single-patron large firm. Industrial governance seeks to limit competition by means of interfirm understandings within each network. Sectoral industrial associations are closely consulted by the bureaucracy in drawing up guidelines for indicative planning. The same industrial associations, by virtue of the interpenetration of key personnel, were almost indistinguishable from the old LDP, a situation that would have prevailed under the unreformed electoral system even if industry had not also regularly bribed politicians.

Industrial governance avoids the unregulated market, but it stops far short of merely following state commands:

> Japan is said to be plan-rational as opposed to a market-rational nation, a mixed capitalist state, a capitalist development state, a technocratic state, a neomercantilist state, a "smart" state, a network state. . . . It practices industrial policy, administrative guidance, "window" guidance, patterned pluralism, canalized pluralism, bureaucracy-led mass-inclusionary pluralism, administered competition, compartmentalized competition, guided free enterprise, managed capitalism, quasi-capitalism, state-directed capitalism.[21]

All this is true. In addition, Japanese business leaders, encouraged by the bureaucracy and unhindered by a tame labor force, have learned to substitute these methods of organizing themselves for their earlier imperialism. They no longer need the Greater East Asia Co-Prosperity Sphere; they have learned to fashion voluntary networks with enterprises in East and Southeast Asia that allow even greater profits while ensuring the security of supply for many goods and commodities.

The concerns of rural folks sometimes challenge the norm of consensual politics. The relentless advance of cities has about eliminated traditional villages and village life. Most farmers hold part-time jobs in cities. Many subsist

---

[21] John W. Dower, "The Useful War," *Daedalus* (Summer 1990): 65.

only because of the generous rice subsidy paid by the government, which had ensured for decades healthy LDP majorities in the countryside. Farmers' representatives participate with several ministries and the LDP central office in the process of setting the price annually. Consensus decision making prevails here because of the equality in status of the participating organizations, although ritual conflict posturing similar to that shown in wage negotiations also is featured. In other situations, however, consensus is conspicuously lacking.

Rural Japan has a long tradition of unrest and rioting. One of the postwar rightist movements, Ishiwara Kanji's National Party, claims a rural base and advocates a return to rural purity in which the allegedly authentic Japanese version of Buddhism (the Lotus Sutra of Nichiren) can best be practiced. In more recent years, rural Japan has been the home of the ever more powerful environmental movement. Sparked by concern over toxic wastes, the movement took off in the 1970s as a grassroot citizens effort to sidestep the established parties and interest groups and their concerns over hobbling economic prowess with environmental regulations. In later years the movement adopted mass civil disobedience to block the expansion of military bases and of Narita airport. Environmental regulations adopted at local levels tend still to be more rigorous than national legislation. The breakdown of the LDP was hastened by the impatience with the established system of unaffiliated citizens groups.

The State: How Strong, How Honest?

In 1988 Japan was hit by its worst political scandal: a number of major political leaders, including two former prime ministers, and many Diet members of all parties, were found to have been systematically "bought" by the Recruit investment firm. One disgraced official hanged himself; two were convicted; but the majority was never tried. This scandal followed many previous ones. The public's approval rating of the cabinet sank to 4 percent. Yet, even though the political careers of Prime Ministers Nakasone and Takeshita were severely damaged, the public cynically accepted the corruption *and* the failure to punish it. How can tolerance for this behavior be reconciled with the evident respect that the Japanese people bestow on their state?

The reasons for the continued legitimacy of the state, in the face of widespread and known corruption among elected officials, are to be found in the consistent centralization of public authority, administrative and legislative, and the containment of occasional conflict within the structure of consensual decision making. Passing legislation is centralized in the House Management Committee, where concurrent interparty majorities are arranged after laws are prepared by the Cabinet legislative bureau. Both are assisted by about 250 advisory and "research" committees that allow for the representation of most interest and professional groups. Conferences of vice ministers (i.e., the highest ranked civil servants in each ministry) work out interministerial compromises to coordinate legislation, as do functional cross-ministerial liaison bodies in such areas as science and defense policy. Local governments, although legally autonomous, get two-thirds of their funds from the central government. Tight personal networks among officials help things along, and the LDP functioned until 1993 as an electoral machine that represented most conservative interests; moreover, it was efficient in delivering, more often than not, the stability sought by private interests to advance their fortunes.

The corruption of the elected officials stands in sharp contrast to the perceived purity of the bureaucracy, a true mandarinate in the midst of an increasingly popular mass culture. A Weberian merit-based civil service was in place by the 1880s, designed deliberately by the Meiji Restorers to supplant familial and parochial ties among administrators. All civil servants must pass examinations administered by the National Personnel Authority. But 65 percent of those who pass the Type A Higher Civil Service examination studied law, economics, or public administration at Tokyo and Kyoto Universities; that number rises to 75 percent for those who study law alone. Only half of those who pass are actually taken on.

Once a person becomes a bureaucrat, his or her career is assured. Higher civil servants spend their entire careers in a single ministry, in which they are rotated from job to job. Close professional friendships are thus formed, especially among those who enter the service at the same time. Higher bureaucrats are expected to retire in their mid-fifties; their "descent from heaven" is rewarded with prestigious positions in major corporations or as members of the LDP delegation to the Diet. Officials with law and economics degrees enjoy higher prestige and reach higher ranks than those with other professional qualifications. Even though rank determines power within a given bureaucratic unit, junior civil servants are given a great deal authority in the initial preparation of decisions; still, the minister, should he or she so choose, can always step in and dictate the outcome.

Socialization and further training stress cross-departmental thinking. The MITI emphasizes such skills, whereas officials of the Ministry of Finance are known for sectoral loyalties to their particular bureau within the ministry. Business and farm leaders have easy access to the bureaucracy, on which they depend for guidance and subsidies and from which they take some of their executives, but bureaucrats are trained not to favor one firm over another. A service class chosen from Japan's "brightest" had been seen until 1996 as incorruptible, very competent, and devoted to the welfare of the nation.

Bureaucratic Coherence and Political Adjustment

As in any other bureaucracy in advanced countries, there is plenty of redundancy and overlap among ministries, units, and parastatal enterprises. In fact, the toleration of redundancy is a technique for minimizing intrabureaucratic conflict, particularly in instances in which the respective units have close ties to competing interest groups.

Overt cleavages also characterize some aspects of administration, in addition to the normal "turf battles" among ministries. Competing private interests seek to colonize specific units within the LDP and the bureaucracy. In addition, there are long-lived conflicts among ministries over basic policy issues, most notably between MITI, the Ministry of Finance, and the Economic Planning Agency.

Unlike the American pattern, however, no single powerful defense ministry acts as a magnet for a myriad of private interests aggregated as "the military-industrial complex." The Self-Defense Force is kept dependent on and marginal to the bureaucratic turf game; its suppliers have no single focal point for seeking influence. And there are also splits between cliques identified with universities of origin, age, and rank groups.

Before the advent of privatization in the 1990s there were almost 100 parastatals of a bewildering variety linked to and subsidized by the central government; there were 3,300 more at the local level. Some strengthened industrial infrastructure by doing research or construction or subsidized private firms to do so. Others sought to aid backward regions of the country, promote foreign trade, or spur scientific research. Because they controlled funds that amounted to 40 percent of the national budget (or 5 percent of GNP) and 9.2 percent of employees, their impact on public life and on the private sector was enormous. Since 1985 the largest have been privatized because of the advent, even in Japan, or more free market thinking, and a voters' revolt against the payment of subsidies to parastatals unable to match revenue with costs.[22]

Taking advantage of this mood, and of a growing popular willingness to accept a Japan that was more active in international affairs, Prime Minister Nakasone skillfully brought about an administrative reorganization in 1986 that both centralized and limited the power of the bureaucracy. He was able to reverse twenty-five years of expanding welfare payments and state services by catering to the demand for smaller gov-

---

[22] Imai and Komiya, *Business Enterprise in Japan*, pp. 315–17.

ernment. His reforms put a cap on budgetary increases and began the liquidation of parastatals, although he allowed defense and foreign aid outlays to rise. The reform was legitimated by a prior "expert study" in which big business participated. The result was a sharp increase in the power of the bureaucracy and of the Prime Minister's Office, of centralized governance.

Learning How to Preserve Legitimacy

The breakup of the LDP and the governmental instability that has plagued Japan since 1993 are matched by other evidence of dissatisfaction over social and economic conditions not seen since 1960. However, Japan is still much more cohesive than Britain, France, Germany, and the United States, all liberal-nationalist industrial giants. Yet there are suggestions that rationalization, as expressed in the institutions of democratic decision making, is being buffeted. The conflict is between two ideological attitudes toward national institutions: a tendency toward more individualistic liberalism as opposed to a desire to retain and even reaffirm a liberalism tinted with reformist syncretism.

Some indicators suggest the persistence of weak liberalism. Most Japanese ignore the presence of ethnic and other minorities because they dislike the implied challenge to the belief in Japan's racial homogeneity. They are uncomfortable with internal dissent because it challenges the myth of middle-class harmony. They stress consensual decision making for the same reason and because they dislike the use of force. The "mistakes" of wartime leaders are attributed to violations of these norms. One reason for the popularity of the police and the eventual acceptance of the Self-Defense Force (note the calculated avoidance of the term "army") is probably the avoidance of coercive measures by both.

These syncretist beliefs may border on self-delusion, but they are buttressed by the cult of *Nihonjin Ron*. One Western critic calls it "the commercialized expression of Japanese nationalism," which "answers to profound needs, since it is echoed repeatedly at every level of discourse." These needs are thought to be a response to the trivialities and banalities of everyday urban life.[23] Others regard the ideology as the effort by Japanese business elites to give themselves "cultural authenticity" in the face of Western charges that Japanese culture amounts to no more than crass economic self-interest with a thin overlay of exotic Orientalism.

The extraordinary ability of Japanese political leaders to sidestep and, in the longer run, to resolve conflict by using liberal institutions argues against the dom-

[23] Peter Dale, *The Myth of Japanese Uniqueness* (New York: St. Martin's Press, 1986), pp. 14, 18.

inance of reformist syncretism. Skillful prime ministers, such as Ikeda and Yoshida, have found ways around conflict by creating channels of co-operation and consultation between the LDP, its parliamentary group, and the bureaucracy. The Office of the Prime Minister and the LDP's Policy Affairs Research Council serve this function. Both broker compromises between factions and functional groups within the LDP and units in the ministries.

But, some observers insist, consensus must be contrived by these means; it does not occur naturally as a result of a Japanese cultural predisposition. Many ingenious means of mediation and consultation are necessary to bring about the much-vaunted consensus. Far from being a free-floating norm, the practice of consensus seeking is a deliberately designed way for overcoming endemic conflict. It is a learned response.

Change comes about most often when dissatisfaction rises to the surface. The system is conservative to the core; it does not anticipate crises or prepare for them; it adjusts to crises by combining the co-optation of the dissatisfied with informal bureaucratic mediation. Conflicts are hardly ever resolved by a formal decision that allows the identification of winners and losers.

These means, however, are used brilliantly and they may well result in the jettisoning of past notions of effective causation and lead to the adoption of new ones. The LDP learned to co-opt its opposition a number of times since 1960. In each case, prior to 1994, the dissatisfied were given symbolic or material benefits that made them better off and into better allies of the LDP. But not everyone outside of the LDP family was always equally well treated. Major crises over toxic wastes and pollution were litigated, but the final settlements were always negotiated by the bureaucracy. Informal mediation by civil servants is far more common in institutionalizing changes in policy than are formal laws and court decisions.

The same ability to learn was demonstrated by the JSP in 1995. Its leader, Prime Minister Murayama Tomiichi, announced the dissolution of the party and the reorganization of its moderate wing into a self-defined liberal group devoted to the same democratic reforms to which the leader who had brought about the split in the LDP, Ozawa Ichiro, had earlier devoted himself: to get rid of local clientelism and of the financial grip of interest groups on the party.

What some might condemn as lack of principle is seen by analysts as flexibility, the capacity to give up a way of thinking when its limitations to overcome dissatisfaction become apparent. Learning, however, is not fully proven unless these enemies of the old party system actually manage to run things on a basis different from the established one. If the new parties continue to behave much as their predecessors, then elites critical of the past will be disappointed once more, and their alienation from the political system will be confirmed.

If we compare today's Japan, with all its institutional and behavioral ambiguities and contradictions with its pre-1945 predecessor, there can be no doubt that a form of liberalism has triumphed, embedded in and aided by a very weak sense of national identity. Attachment to the old civil religion is gone. Materialism has taken over. Individualism is growing, as are crime and disrespect for the hierarchies once considered the essence of Japanese life. Japan looks more and more like other industrial countries that tend toward derationalization.

JAPAN AND THE WORLD

After decades of sailing in a convoy of states led by Washington, Japanese leaders are more and more talking of making a "normal nation" of their country. "Gone is the automatic readiness to unite against communist power and ideology," one observer wrote in 1991. "Gone is America's overweening confidence and unquestioning generosity; gone also is Japan's deep feeling of dependence and humility."[24] Until the end of the Cold War, few Japanese rethought the alliance with the United States, the American-dictated constitution, or the possibility of an independent military stance.

Main Lines of Foreign Policy

Before the interest in "normalcy," the main themes of foreign policy were known as the "Yoshida doctrine," the postwar leadership's instrumental adaptation to the constraints of world politics. The themes were relying on the United States for military protection; following the lead of the United States on core defense and Cold War issues; looking for ways to establish closer ties with China despite the Cold War; abandoning any military role for Japan; adopting a self-effacing posture as the country's policy; accepting the MacArthur constitution, and concentrating on international trade relations by insisting on free trade for everybody while continuing to practice mercantilism. This policy coincided with the view that pacifism symbolized the "true" Japan, held by many on the Left and by some bureaucratic postwar reformers.

For a former great power, this was certainly not a "normal" policy. Articulate nationalism was banned from the Yoshida doctrine, although

[24] Ezra F. Vogel, "Japanese-American Relations after the Cold War," *Daedalus* (Fall 1992): 35.

a nationalist stance was clearly implied by Japan's economic policies. Even then the Yoshida doctrine struck many Japanese as obsolete by the mid-1970s. The terms of the American alliance were being questioned; whom were the American troops in Japan deterring? Would Japan always play second fiddle in alliance matters? Should Japan favor regional ties with Asian countries rather than a global trade-and-investment policy? Those who suggested that Japan was overdependent on export markets in the United States especially stressed the advantages of a Japan-dominated East and Southeast Asian economic zone. The habit of pleasing the United States was increasingly resented, but people differed on whether Japan should multilaterize all of its foreign relations by relying more on the United Nations or by increasingly striking out on its own. And then, unspoken but undeniable, there was always the possibility that Japan might acquire nuclear weapons and abandon pacifism.

Those who after 1975 wanted Japan to be a more normal nation articulated themes consistent with liberal nationalism without at the same time challenging American hegemony. Prime Ministers Ohira Masayoshi, Suzuki Zenko, and Nakasone Yasuhiro adopted an overtly anti-Soviet stance in linking Japanese defense policy to the Western alliance. On economic matters, these leaders realized that protectionist policies would have to yield to more consistent free trading and that Japan would have to take strong and visible positions, especially on monetary and energy questions. Ohira had initiated this reassessment by organizing a group of academic research teams whose judgment he and his successors sought to turn into government policy.

At the base of much of this effort was a persistent fear that Japan, despite its economic miracles, was still insecure. The normalizers argued that the very success of the policies of export-led growth, following intensive technological and industrial innovation, was becoming problematic. Domestic welfare and stability were seen as imperiled unless Japan was able to make decisions more independently in serving its own interests of access to oil, a stable international monetary system, and secure export markets. Security also called for unbroken technological innovation, the need to be "number one" industrially. Many leaders thought of technological power as being fungible, as useful for both wealth and military purposes. Being a normal nation, not merely a follower of the strongest, did not imply any return to the thematic content of prewar nationalism.

However, the advocates of *Nihonjin Ron* called for something suggesting a nostalgia for the old syncretism. Their overall argument in favor of the cultural uniqueness of Japan and their dislike of Western ways also found expression in the advocacy of a much more independent foreign and defense policy, more Japanese and less cosmopolitan than the line urged by the LDP leadership in the 1980s. The Meiji era is seen by the syncretists as having expressed authentic nationalism, whereas the Showa era represents the pathologies of extreme militarism to be shunned by a Japan loyal to its true syncretist culture, the Japan that "can say no."

Japanese Attitudes: How Self-Effacing, How Cosmopolitan?

The following list suggests that, despite these views, the Yoshida doctrine remains extremely popular. Respondents polled between 1989 and 1994 said they favored the following:

Japanese leadership	15%
Aid to LDCs	30
International environmental action	28
Personnel contribution to Gulf War	30
More help in Gulf War	38
Membership of UN Security Council	50

Most Japanese are uncomfortable with a more visible global posture. They lack self-confidence about their global reputation; in 1989 and 1991, respectively, only 35 percent thought Japan was liked or trusted by foreign countries.

The armed forces (SDF) remain totally marginal to national life, even though in 1994 the army numbered 156,000 men, the air force disposed of 9 state-of-the art fighter squadrons, and the navy had 14 submarines and 55 surface vessels. The SDF represents exactly the opposite image from that formerly projected by the imperial army and navy; it minimizes any continuity in institutions, training, and socialization with its predecessors. There is no special military law. Designations of rank are new. The emperor has no link to SDF, and no member of the SDF may visit Yasukuni Shrine. The military mission is deemphasized in favor of disaster relief and other civic actions. Loyalty to the prime minister is stressed.

Opinion toward the military is linked to prevailing attitudes about Japan's role in World War II. The SDF is seen as representing the "good" and "true" Japan, whereas the imperial military is portrayed as disloyal and corrupt. Even though leftist intellectuals generally consider the mere existence of the SDF a violation of the peace constitution, public opinion overwhelmingly supports the military as necessary, perhaps because over half of the Japanese tend to say that they would not fight in case of an invasion. When Japan was asked to contribute troops to the United Nations enforcement action against Iraq, the pacifist sentiments prevailed after an open debate. Few seemed to care that aggression was being punished, that collective security was at stake, and that Kuwait's right to self-determination was being protected. There was not even much concern over a safe oil supply, although some sympathy for the "small Asian country" being pushed around by the West was also expressed. The majority was determined not to compromise Article 9 of the Constitution.

Hence liberal reformers such as Ozawa Ichiro have had a hard time persuading their compatriots that a "normal" Japan should be an active contributor to peacekeeping and other highly visible multilateral security actions. His efforts to amend Article 9 have not been successful.

Between the West and Asia

Supporters of "Japan as a normal nation" profess a sense of national identity that sees their country as a perpetual learner, made up of groups of organizations who continually adjust to perform optimally in a global competitive setting. The future is never assured; one's place in it must be earned. It follows that Japanese culture ought to be less insular than it is, more committed to a permanent dialogue with the West in which Japanese justify their uniqueness while affirming their commitment to a cosmopolitan culture. Self-effacement is part of Japanese uniqueness. The normalizers argue that their version of liberal nationalism will always contain differences from the West's. But they flaunt the difference, as Nakasone did in 1983 at the Summit of the Group of Seven even as he proclaimed Japan's right to be one of the world's hegemons. The continued commitment to the West and to its institutions is seen as fully compatible with the view that the alliance with the United States ought to be scrapped or amended.

These versions of liberal nationalism clash with those of "Asia firsters" who are also much more inclined to stress the syncretism in Japan's sense of identity. They tend to argue that there is a distinct Asian style of capitalist industrial governance, more humane and restrained than the American. Cultural affinities with Asian countries outweigh admiration of the West. The emotional friction caused by American "Japan bashing" over trade and investment issues translates to an endorsement of an "Asia first" policy that seeks the construction of a commercial version of the Greater East Asia Co-prosperity Sphere. This attitude implies the full rejection of an identity of interests with the West, with the West as a role model and as an ally. It is not clear to what extent this stance also implies an indifference to liberal values and institutions.

Asia-first views, although never triumphant in the political establishment, found occasional expression in foreign policy. The recovery of

316

Okinawa and the Kurile Islands was a paramount objective for all postwar governments. Tokyo attached great importance to establishing close relations with South Korea. The creation of a special relationship with, though not recognition of, mainland China was policy since the days of Yoshida Shigeru. Full-scale normalization was sought in 1972; its establishment in 1978 was preceded by many symbolic humiliations imposed by Beijing and swallowed by Tokyo, to the delight of the Japanese Left, but over bitter opposition from the right wing of the LDP. At first there was jubilation in the press as pan-Asian cultural themes were touted, a mood that gave way to disappointment in the 1980s as the Chinese bargainers got the better of Japanese industry in several large investment and trade deals. These experiences made the public feel more ambivalent toward Asia; contempt for the Chinese was commonly expressed; the reluctance to revise history textbooks remained.[25] Japan briefly suspended aid to China after the Tiananmen Square massacre, but was the first country to minimize Chinese violations of human rights.

Despite some real interest in fostering an Asian-Pacific or an East Asian regionalism that caters to Japan's special needs in access to raw materials and is animated by informal networks of off-shore suppliers of exportable manufactures, Japan's foreign policy is still dominated by a cautious globalism. Still, this tendency is moderated by the lack of interest in global human rights programs and the tepid interest in collective security. Moreover, commitment to multilateral processes and institutions is not seen as incompatible with the establishment of special ties. "National security," for the post–Cold War Japanese, means not merely military defense of the home islands, of less importance than before, but also special access to China, close relations with Russia, and the maintenance of a high domestic standard of living. Japan contributes more to multilateral aid programs than any other country, and there is resentment of the lack of appreciation shown by the recipients.

The War Guilt Issue

For the first forty-five years after World War II, the Japanese government made only the most perfunctory gestures toward acknowledging any war guilt. Until the death of the Showa Emperor in 1989 Japanese opinion makers held the "disobedient military" responsible for any acts that might be considered aggressive or involve atrocities. The emperor himself and the rank-and-file military were held blameless, patriotic heroes

---

[25] People answered the question "among the peoples on this list who do you think are superior?" for 1958 and 1973, respectively, as follows: Japanese, 57 percent and 50 percent; Chinese, 9 percent and 21 percent; Germans, 52 percent and 36 percent; Americans, 47 percent and 25 percent (*Nihonjin no kokuminsei*, vol. 3 [Tokyo: Idemitsushoten, 1975]).

bravely defending the realm against Western imperialism. Many, including Nakasone Yasuhiro, denounced the war crimes trials as the victors' revenge; many also were more concerned with protecting the honor of veterans and their survivors than with acknowledging any collective guilt. Japan was painted by its leaders as a victim of nuclear barbarism, not a brutal aggressor. School textbooks made no self-critical reference to wartime events.

Only the disintegration of the LDP changed things. Even though the Diet as late as 1995 would accept war guilt only in a very indirect and circumspect way, Prime Minister Murayama admitted full and unqualified responsibility for Japan's aggression. Textbooks were finally revised to reflect the admission, as had long been demanded by the Socialist Teachers' Union. The change in policy was forced partly by the demands of the countries courted by Japan for her East Asian special zone, but partly it reflects a genuine change of opinion.[26]

LEARNING LIBERAL NATIONALISM

Many observers see a policy cycle in Japan: long periods of rigidity alternating with bursts of self-examination, reform, and innovation. Linked to this cycle is the paradox that outsiders see Japan as a successfully rationalized, secure, and effective society whereas Japanese often see themselves as perpetually poised on the edge of national failure, if not disaster. Collective self-analysis that can lead to true learning occurs when such fears are haunting people.

The most striking crisis of innovation occurred after the defeat of 1945. Members of the policy elite, mostly from the imperial bureaucracy, deliberately jettisoned the core policy of achieving security and internal harmony through empire building. They substituted the policy of security and internal harmony derived from prosperity based on economic innovation and reliance on the United States. They quite deliberately mapped new policies and refurbished older ones designed to achieve these objectives: provide lifetime employment for most workers and salaried employees, limit interfirm competition without stifling it, foster state-guided policies of industrial innovation and export promotion. None were entirely new because all contained adaptations carried over

[26] In 1993 Asahi Shimbun reported that 76 percent of respondents to a poll supported admission that Japan had waged aggressive war and that 50 percent were willing to pay reparations to the victims. Reparations were paid to Korean "comfort women," whose very existence had been denied before 1994. Peace museums illustrating Japan's atrocities are being opened. Nobel Laureate Oe Kenzaburo campaigned strongly in favor of these measures.

from the imperial period. Yet the entire package represents learning because of its derivation from a discredited paradigm. Older means were reshaped to serve a brand-new purpose. The lessons were derived from the appreciation that the old paradigm produced too many unintended and unwanted consequences. The total abandonment of the old national myth and the substitution of an official policy of pacifism as national policy were complete innovations, not changes based on incremental steps of adaptation.

As a result of this foresight it was possible in 1960 to plan and execute a scheme to double the income of each Japanese. The encouragement of science and export-relevant technology was stressed as well. Even though fewer funds were then devoted to R&D than in other industrial countries, Japan moved from an economy in which unskilled labor-intensive and medium capital-intensive manufacturing in a few sectors had prevailed as late as 1959 to a one by 1985 in which knowledge-intensive and medium capital-intensive manufacturing dominated all industries.

Rigidities persisted, however, after and within this shift. Success was confined to sectors characterized by broad consensus: economic growth with low inflation, competitiveness in exports, education, self-sufficiency in rice production, access to cheap oil. It took another crisis in the mid-1970s to make social welfare entitlements part of the consensus, an adaptation of an instrumental kind implying no shift to new knowledge about the causes of social harmony. The increase in R&D funding and the even higher respect for science and technology that came at the same time reflects another adaptation to what was perceived as faltering competitiveness, not a new mode of causal inference about the happiness of society.

Moreover, Japan's global economic successes owe a good deal to circumstances far removed from the government's control. The most that can be said is that the bureaucracy took full advantage of what external conditions allowed. Without generous reconstruction aid from the United States nothing like the rapid recovery from the war would have occurred. The initial spur to the economy came from the Korean War–triggered procurement orders. Japanese exports could not have prospered without the global trend toward free trade actively pursued by the United States. The stability of the yen owed a good deal to the monetary discipline of the Bretton Woods regime. And Japanese protectionism, practiced despite the free trade commitment of her best customers, was tolerated by them for a long time. Japan did not learn to give large amounts of foreign aid, contribute to international monetary stability, or gradually relax its discrimination against foreign investors and traders; it was shamed and coerced into these steps, though there had always been reformist voices in the bureaucracy and the LDP whose claims did represent true learning. Some of them were key actors in the 1994 crisis of the party system when they sought to break with the LDP old guard. But all Japanese leaders learned to abandon the mercantilist paradigm for one of moderate international competition. They also learned how to make democracy work despite its being imposed on Japan. They learned to take the imposed institutions and to alter them to suit their collectivist and consensus-oriented values. But, they also became more tolerant of conflict, debate and uncertainty. In 1989, 7,406 people were polled on these issues. These are the percentages of respondents saying "more importance" or "great importance" should be attached to the issue:

Respect law and order	92
Improve living conditions, quality of life	90
Protect the poor and the weak	87
Preserve traditional morals	87
Make more people voice their opinions	87
Defend freedom of speech	83
Maintain economic growth	83
Have a strong defense	38

When asked about Japan's future social goals, 2,186 respondents between the age of 44 and 46 expressed these views:

Stick to pacifist ideology	64%
Enrich people's lives	61%
Enrich social welfare	59%

These were the three top choices. None of the others received scores above 23 percent.

Japan's liberalism is not exactly like Europe's or North America's. Traces of reformist-syncretist views and institutions are easily discerned. Collectivism still trumps individualism in some spheres. Probably, if it were not for the fascinating melange of syncretist and liberal institutions that prevailed in the 1920s and since 1945, Japan would not have modernized and recovered so quickly and so relatively free of social turmoil. Possibly, that mixture is the glue that makes today's Japan appear still more rationalized than the largest countries of Europe and North America.

However, syncretism is in retreat. In every major sphere Japan's public and collective life is becoming more liberal, not more syncretist. Integralism is completely discredited. The syncretist features that seem attractive to some find most of their appeal among the oldest generation of leaders. Traditional institutions seem to lack attractiveness to young people. But the fact remains that liberalism, too, seems shallowly rooted in people's affections. Japan has shed its past so much that the fanatic collective national identity once professed by almost all seems ludicrous to today's young adults. Even if not consistently liberal by Western standards, and even if the prevailing liberalism is not fervently espoused by most, the public culture of today's Japan contains no trace of the militantly hostile stance toward the outside world that so etched Imperial Japan.

But there is little evidence of Japan's outgrowing nation-statehood in favor of a new identity. Unlike France and Germany and unlike the United States, the unresolved conflict among liberal and syncretist nationalists does not contain the ideological seeds of shifting one's identity to a global, regional, or subnational focus of attachment. Japan's espousal of multilateralism remains cautious and muted. Her endorsement of regionalism does not go beyond the qualified free trade rhetoric of the Asian-Pacific Economic Conference. The enmeshment in East and Southeast Asian trade and financial ties remains instrumental. Moderate derationalization has not led elites to conclude that no sweeping intergroup bargains are possible in the future and that new transnational institutions and loyalties are therefore required to survive. The nation-state remains intact. Our theory of learning suggests that far more troublesome crises have to be experienced by the leaders of Japan before such a reassessment will occur.

CHAPTER EIGHT

Liberal Nationalism and Collective Learning

As Robert Schuman, former foreign minister of France and one of the fathers of the movement for the unification of Europe, said: "Political borders are the result of a respectable historic and ethnic evolution, of a long effort at national unification. One shouldn't think of erasing them. In other times one eliminated them by violent conquest or fruitful marriages. Today, it is good enough to de-emphasize them."[1] Schuman's words remind us that nationalism, for many decades, was a positive force, a force that gave coherence and meaning to people. He also reminds us that in order to have a peaceful world it may not be necessary to abolish the nation-state, just to "de-emphasize" it.

This chapter is devoted to comparing and summarizing five different experiences of creating national borders—and of de-emphasizing them, too. I am taking stock, seeking answers from five narratives to the questions raised in Chapters 1 and 2. That done, I recapitulate the core concepts used in this study: progress, modernization, social mobilization, nationalist sentiment, ideology and myth, rationalization, and collective learning. After that we can see whether the putative associations and relationships among these concepts claimed in the first chapters can actually be mapped and projected.

I greatly appreciate the research assistance of Karen Adelberger, and I gratefully acknowledge the financial support of the Center for German and European Studies at the University of California at Berkeley.
[1] Robert Schuman, *Pour l'Europe* (Paris: Nagel, 1963), p. 23. My translation.

THE QUESTIONS RESTATED

This inquiry into the history of five old nation-states is justified by my social construction of historical reality. I entertain the hypothesis that reason, in the form of science, increasingly informs collective decisions. When actors choose on the basis of scientific reasoning, the hypothesis continues, they usher in more and more progress. This happens more consistently when the political context involves popular participation or the institutions of the nation-state. When disappointment with the performance of the nation-state sets in—actors try to yoke even more scientific reasoning to the solutions they seek to fashion. Eventually, political cognition based on reason comes to the conclusion that the nation-state may be unable to fuel the train of progress. At that point, reason leads actors to entertain transnational political formulas to solve their problems.

My reality thus leads me to ask the same three core questions of all the historical cases studied to be able to judge the doings and ruminations of actors and their organizations. Are they behaving as my hypothesis postulates? The questions are:

1. Are the historical paths trod by polities determined by the initial ideological choices the nation-building elites adopt? Do the five profiles that describe the origin of the nation-building process determine the eventual beliefs and institutions of the nation-state?
2. Who learns what about diffusely reciprocal exchange relations? Is rationalization prevented by the persistence of clashing substantive rationalities in the same polity? Are practitioners of liberal nationalism more likely to learn the rules of diffuse reciprocity than believers in other nationalist ideologies?
3. Who learns to outgrow the nation-state as the terminal human community? Are liberal nationalists likely to outgrow it sooner than integralists and syncretists?

CHANGE RECAPITULATED

Progress is my term for the improvement of every person's lot with respect to health, wealth, and peace. A country that has benefited from progress is one in which the citizenry lives free from the danger of war and civil war and enjoys a higher living standard and a better health (including a cleaner and safer environment) than in the past. People in the industrialized world have been free of war with one another since 1945. Only Britain (in Ireland) and Spain (in the Basque country) have suffered

323

from civil wars, in which, fortunately, relatively few fatalities have occurred.

As for wealth and health, Hugh Heclo sums matters up as follows:

> Politically, the welfare state was an amalgam of extraordinarily diverse ideas and interests: of crusading liberalism, with its confidence in the possibilities of social betterment, human progress, and secular individualism; of traditional conservatism, with its stress on paternalistic steps to safeguard institutions and social order against radical change; to undertake collective responsibilities. . . . Viewing it through the eyes of those who had endured the turmoil of the interwar and war years we can see how well balanced such a mixture of ideas might be. It tended to achieve for the postwar democracies the kind of mutual check and balance among principles that had served so well in the creation of representative government two centuries earlier.[2]

Welfare standards have risen sharply since 1945, although they declined somewhat after 1980 as opinion in the West turned against governmental regulation and Keynesian economics, to embrace free markets and monetarism instead (Table 8-1). As we know, the confrontation between free marketeers and regulators continues. In short, there has been a great deal of progress.

Progress is associated with *modernization*. As measured by the indicators listed in Chapter 2, modernization is the ability to apply tested knowledge to the solution of problems in all branches of production; it therefore includes education as well as manufacturing, urbanization, and commercial agriculture (any movement away from local isolation and subsistence agriculture). *Social mobilization* occurs when the people who are modernized become available to play new social roles: factory workers, soldiers, civil servants, engineers, elected representatives of some constituency. People who are socially mobilized may choose to *assimilate* to the dominant cosmopolitan culture; or they may deliberately *differentiate* themselves from it and form their own culture, which may or may not contain elements of the traditional culture from which they recently emerged.

Their choice determines whether a *nation-state* comes into being. Mobilized-differentiated intellectuals often form *nationalist sentiments* to define their own collective identity against some group they dislike and wish to displace in the process of modernization. "Self" becomes a group of the like-minded, the "nation," juxtaposed to the "other" outside the charmed circle. When social mobilization continues, it results

---

[2] Hugh Heclo, "Toward a New Welfare State?," in Peter Flora and Arnold Hiedenheimer, eds., *The Development of Welfare States in Europe and America* (New Brunswick, N.J.: Transaction, 1981), pp. 392–93.

Table 8-1. Social insurance spending, military spending, enrollment ratios in higher education, and GDP in twenty-five countries, 1966–93

	Per capita GDP ($U.S.)[a]		Social insurance spending (% of GNP)		Military spending (% of GNP)		Enrollment ratios for total population 20–24 in higher education	
	1966	1993	1966	1986	1966	1993	1965 or nearest year	1989 or nearest year
Australia	2,129	15,963	9.0	9.2	3.8	2.6	16	32
Austria	1,411	22,787	21.0	25.4	1.5	1.0	9	31
Belgium	1,873	21,037	18.5	26.4	3.3	1.8	15	34
Canada	2,957	19,001	10.1	16.2	3.6	2.0	21	66
Denmark	2,329	26,204	13.9	26.3	3.1	2.0	13	32
Finland	1,948	16,540	13.1	22.8	1.8	2.2	11	43
France	2,186	21,706	18.3	28.6	5.9	3.4	14	37
Germany[b]	1,726	23,537	19.6	23.4	4.7	2.2	9	34
Greece	774	7,071	12.0	19.5	4.2	5.5	10	28
Iceland	3,249	23,369	8.7	7.2	0.0	0.0	6	25
Ireland	1,032	13,392	11.1	23.2	1.5	1.3	12	26
Italy	1,380	17,371	17.5	11.2	3.8	2.1	12	29
Japan	1,073	33,802	6.2	12.2	1.0	1.0	12	31
Luxembourg	2,405	32,477	17.5	23.4	1.6	0.8	3	3
Mexico	521	3,968	2.9	2.7	0.8	0.5	4	15
Netherlands	1,768	20,211	18.3	28.6	4.1	2.4	16	32
New Zealand	2,178	12,630	11.8	17.9	2.2	1.5	14	41
Norway	2,036	23,995	12.6	29.8	4.0	3.1	8	36
Portugal	530	8,688	5.8	10.4	6.0	3.0	5	18
Spain	835	12,227	4.3	18.1	3.3	1.8	6	32
Sweden	3,079	21,254	17.5	31.3	4.4	2.8	12	31
Switzerland	2,493	33,453	9.5	14.7	2.8	1.7	6	26
Turkey	444	2,928	2.0	3.6	5.2	5.8	4	12.7
United Kingdom	1,962	16,279	14.4	20.4	6.5	3.6	10	24
United States	3,923	24,302	7.9	12.5	9.1	4.7	40	63

SOURCE: Updated version of Harold L. Wilensky's t. 4 in the appendix to his *Welfare State and Equality* (Berkeley: University of California Press, 1975), pp. 122–24. Per capita GDP data: OECD, *National Accounts 1960–1993*, vol. I, *Main Aggregates* (Paris: OECD, 1995), pp. 132–33, t. 21. Social insurance, spending: ILO, *The Cost of Social Security, 1964–66* (Geneva: ILO, 1972) and *The Cost of Social Security, 1984–1986* (1992). Military spending: U.S. Arms Control and Disarmament Agency, *World Military Expenditures, 1971* (Washington, D.C.: U.S. Army Control and Disarmament Agency, 1972), and *World Military Expenditures and Arms Transfers 1993–1994* (1995). Data for Australia and New Zealand are from the Stockholm International Peace Research Institute, *SIPRI Yearbook of World Armaments and Disarmaments, 1969–70* (Uppsala: SIPRI, 1970), pp. 274–76. Higher education data: UNESCO, *Statistical Yearbook 1971* (Louvain: UNESCO, 1972), t. 2.7 and *Statistical Yearbook 1991* (Paris: UNESCO, 1991), t. 3.2.

[a]Per capita GDP at current prices and current exchange rates.

[b]Figures for 1966 are West Germany only. Social security (1986) and school enrollment (1989) figures are for West Germany. Per capita GNP (1993) and military spending (1993) are for united Germany.

in the creation of a large mass of dissatisfied people, also differentiated from tradition, to whom the intellectuals appeal for the creation of a *nation-state* that challenges the right of the traditional rulers to continue to define the political community. They do so by formulating *nationalist ideologies*, programs and doctrines proclaiming the character of the nation-state to be created. A nationalist ideology that gains general acceptance in the state's population is called a *national myth.*

How do countries that are modernizing and are peopled by socially mobilized masses led by intellectuals of diverse beliefs survive the tensions and conflicts associated with change? How can unity emerge from cacophony and suffering? Our main purpose is to show how *rationalization* takes place and how nationalism can serve as a rationalizing formula. Conversely, we are concerned with determining when nationalism ceases to serve as an effective rationalizer, when the nation-state decays or disintegrates. Rationalization is the coming together into a single coherent set of all contradictory institutions and beliefs impinging on the modernizing society from its premodern past and its current aspirations. Whether to accept, modify, or reject religion is the major task of the rationalizer.

There are many ways in which the changes that may add up to rationalization may occur. I am concerned mostly with collective *learning*, the application of formal reason to the solution of collective social problems, the search for consensual knowledge about causality to be used in the making of public policy. But there are more common ways of achieving rationalization. Sometimes leaders rely simply on their ideology, unaided by any formal knowledge about causality, to rule and to introduce change. More often they *adapt*, rather than learn. Adaptation involves the deliberate search for new means to achieve unvarying ends if the first set of means proved inadequate. Learning involves the search for new means *as well as* the substitution of new ends for old ones as a result of an altered understanding of causality.

Rationalization that relies on ideology or adaptation is not likely to work for long. As Max Weber might have put it, rationalization based on substantive or technical rationality is temporary at best. Theoretical rationality might do better, but only formal rationality—learning, in my universe—is likely to provide lasting social integration because it allows for constant self-examination and self-reform.

But, as Weber also taught us, formal rationality leads to the loss of affect, the death of emotional ties among people, to the Iron Cage. And that is why even a formally rationalized society may disintegrate; if it does, its leaders search for a way to rerationalize, perhaps as something other than a nation-state. Rationalization and rerationalization are rooted in instrumental collective behavior, not in commitment to principle, to all-enveloping faith, or in devotion to a charismatic leader, institution, or idea. Instrumental behavior has a closer affinity to liberalism than to any of the other ideologies we explored in our case studies. Will liberalism thus remain the privileged formula of governance?

PROGRESS, RATIONALIZATION, LEARNING: SOME FINDINGS

Do Structural Features at the Origin of Nation-States Determine the Content of Rationalization?

Social mobilization may be well advanced at the time agitation for the creation of a nation-state sets in; or the agitation may begin with a small mass base during the early stages of the mobilization process. Will rationalization be smooth, or will it elude the active counterelite challenging the ancien régime? Will rapid (late) or slow (early) social mobilization favor a rationalization formula that features liberalism, syncretism, or integralism?

Political and economic institutions supporting the modernization process may already be in place when nation-state formation begins; or their creation may be one of the demands made by the nationalist counterelite. If such institutions are in place, relatively smooth adaptation or even learning rationalization will be simpler than if the opposite is the case. Open decision-making institutions (elected parliaments, extensive civil rights, relatively free markets) allow more adaptive behavior than syncretist institutions that bear the weight of hallowed sacred doctrines or integralist institutions that respond only to the will of a charismatic leader or party.

The mobilized-differentiated elites and their mass followers may respond in different ways to the established culture: they may wish to join it, or they may prefer to destroy it and substitute their own. Rationalization is much harder where the desire to create a new culture prevails.

In short, structural considerations suggest that rationalization will be smooth, though slow, and show an elective affinity for liberal nationalism (or reformist syncretism) if (1) social mobilization proceeds slowly and is not far advanced at the onset of the nationalist movement; (2) relatively open decision-making institutions already exist; and (3) the mobilized-differentiated (the actively dissatisfied) have no wish to supplant the existing culture. What do our five cases reveal (Table 8-2)?

First of all, we note that, even though the starting conditions in the five cases were very different, all eventually achieved rationalization under liberal-nationalist auspices, albeit after jumping over very different historical hurdles. Incomplete and slow social mobilization was helpful

Table 8-2. Structural conditions of rationalization

Country	Early rationalization	Slow Social Mobilization	Open Institutions	No challenge to culture
Britain	Yes	Yes	Yes	Yes
France	No	Yes	Some	Yes
Germany	No	No	No	Yes
Japan	Yes	No	No	Yes
United States	No	No	Yes	Yes

in Britain and France, not elsewhere. The prior existence of open institutions facilitated adaptation only in Britain and America. An uncontested culture was present in all cases, in those who achieved rationalization easily as well as in more troublesome cases. The hypothesis that prior structural conditions predict successful rationalization is clearly wrong. Type A, B, or C may tell us something about patterned events at the point when the nationalist counterelite mounts an active challenge against the traditional forces, but it certainly predicts nothing about later developments.

Is Liberal Nationalism as It Emerged in Type A the Most Efficient Rationalizer?

Even though today almost all Western countries have liberal institutions and are animated by the ideas of liberal nationalism—insofar as any nationalism still commands the attention of the public—it was not always so. Before we conclude that today's progress is indeed associated with liberalism, in its free market as well as in its social democratic costume, we had better have another look at the historical record.

Among industrialized countries, the following achieved nation-statehood by following the pattern of Type A: Britain, France, Spain, Japan, Denmark, Sweden, Netherlands, Luxembourg, New Zealand. In all of them, the old regime was challenged by mobilized educated middle classes who resented their exclusion from governance by the nobility and disagreed with the insufficiently "modern" policies pursued by traditional monarchs. In all of them, the challengers did not wish to supplant the traditional culture: they wanted to participate in it on terms of equality. Social mobilization had not yet engulfed most of the masses and proceeded slowly when the challenge to tradition arose, except in Japan and New Zealand.

But liberal nationalism did not take hold immediately in all of them. In France, rationalization did not finally occur until 170 years after the first nationalist revolution; the first spurt of liberal nationalism lasted barely a decade and was frequently interrupted thereafter until the rise of the Fifth Republic. In Japan, rationalization was accomplished rapidly under the auspices of reformist and traditional syncretism, not liberalism. And in Spain rationalization was achieved under integralist auspices, and liberal nationalism took over only after the death of Francisco Franco, 150 years after the first liberal revolution.

Nor did liberal nationalism perform consistently well in rerationalizing or healing Type A nation-states severely buffeted by crises. France, Spain, and Japan were victims of derationalization not repaired by liberalism. Liberalism failed to prevent the Great Depression or to avoid decisions by liberal statesmen that led to two world wars. Progress, until after 1945, was spotty. Liberal nationalism did little to ensure it.[3] The residues of syncretist and integralist ideas and institutions in many of the countries reviewed made the practice of learning very difficult until the most recent times.

Is Liberal Nationalism Unlikely to Rationalize Type C States?

The record is a mixed one. Liberal nationalism is positively associated with rationalization, and rerationalization after crises were experienced in the United States, Belgium, Australia, Canada, Switzerland, and interwar Czechoslovakia. In all these cases the nation-state was constructed by elites who rebelled against their former rulers in such a way as to secede to form a new state, although they did not challenge the culture of the former elite. (This characterization does not fully fit Switzerland in the nineteenth century.) In some cases social mobilization was far advanced at the time of secession; in others it was not. In all these cases the new state was constructed by combining several units that originally had been autonomous, or belonged to another state.

However, in the cases of Germany, Italy, Austria, and Poland the secessionist pattern did not result in a liberal nation-state. The fact that today all these countries are successfully rationalized under liberal auspices was the result of many intervening crises, of several branching points; only defeat in war or expulsion of foreign imperial rulers made it possible for the contemporary elite to take the liberal road.[4]

These case histories cast more doubt on the determining force of the

---

[3] See Peter B. Evans, Harold K. Jacobson, and Robert D. Putnam, eds., *Double-Edged Diplomacy* (Berkeley: University of California Press, 1993), for a fully illustrated discussion of discontinuities in policymaking.

[4] There were no Type B cases in our studies. However, the history of Europe suggests that liberalism is the predominantly successful rationalizer for this type, as shown by the cases of Norway and Ireland. Finland's liberal rationalization was in some doubt in the 1920s; Hungary's is in doubt still.

patterns that dominate at the origin of the nation-state. Opportunities and costs encountered at branching points in later history, usually in the form of severe crises of derationalization, are of greater—if unpredictable—causal significance. Yet the pre-1945 histories of Germany, Italy, Austria, and Poland suggest that, if the early institutions lacked liberal content, the preferred road to lead one out of a crisis turned out to be integralist.[5]

Is Syncretist Nationalism a Better Rationalizer in Type C States?

Many traditional themes and institutions remained in nineteenth-century Germany, before and after unification. No national myth emerged until the 1890s, and even then it contained contradictory ideas, some liberal and some syncretist. Exactly the same is true of Austria, Poland, and Italy before the advent of fascism. In each the Catholic Church and the army represented traditional-syncretist notions of nationhood.

An interesting issue about collective action is posed here. Modernization and social mobilization (in all cases except Germany) remained incomplete; the power of traditional institutions and elites was considerable. How can a nationalist movement based on mass participation gain influence under these premodern conditions? Obviously, social mobilization, though incomplete, must be advanced enough to provide the prophet of nationalism with an audience. How else can a nation-state be created by an act of secession and fusion that requires some mass participation and often results in war?

Premodern networks of partially mobilized people are the answer. There are usually guilds and artisanal professional associations, religious brotherhoods, and churches—orthodox as well as heretical. America had the Sons of Liberty and Committees of Correspondence as nationalist networks.[6] Few of these are likely to meet the core conception of liberalism; most of them are still embedded in traditional institutions and ideas that are much more akin to those of syncretist nationalism. However, although such networks explain secession, they are not likely to lead to the simple and rapid rationalization of the newly independent polity that follows.

---

[5] The fact that fascist integration was terminated by war in France, Germany, and Italy, and weakened in Spain by the allied victory, fortunately deprives us of adequate case material for judging the long-run rationalizing power of fascism.

[6] For a powerful work in support of this argument, see Sidney Tarrow, *Power in Movement* (Cambridge: Cambridge University Press, 1994).

No Rationalization Formula Works Forever

All countries in our case studies experienced crises after they were successfully rationalized. Britain's came around 1900 and again after 1930; France unraveled after 1934 and again in 1958; America experienced derationalization after 1970; Japan's crises came in the late 1920s, Germany's after 1918. In each case a formula for rerationalization was found, an integralist one in three cases.

In most cases the rerationalization before the Great Depression relied on adaptation or ideological reorientation; collective learning was confined to a few instances of economic and social welfare legislation. During the Great Depression and especially after 1945, collective learning was overwhelmingly important in Germany, Japan, and France, as well as in almost all West European continental countries; it was less systematically practiced in Britain and the Commonwealth or in America, although there were many instances of it.

Ideology-based change is not likely to favor the practice of diffuse reciprocity in social exchange. Behavior deduced from ideological tenets rarely encourages compromise with opponents or the deferring of benefits. Adaptation is less hostile to diffuse reciprocity, but those who adapt do not necessarily favor accommodation by compromise and deferred gratification as a matter of principle. Actors who learn to review and change their basic goals, however, must almost by definition welcome compromise if they expect to persuade their opponents to share a new vision of causality. Another pattern is conceivable only in the rare instance of outright conversion to a new dispensation.

Therefore we can say that the integration and reintegration of a nation-state can be made to work for long periods if leaders rely entirely on technical and substantive rationality; but in no case did the formula work indefinitely to stave off crises. Formal rationality takes over in the form of analytic problem solving based on consensual technical knowledge when the survival of the nation-state seems in doubt *and* when the means for finding better causal links become available to elites. This did not occur often until the Great Depression. Put differently, forms of nationalism that spurned formal collective learning did very well in giving satisfaction to the citizenry in many countries, until a crisis more threatening than any previous one engulfs the country. Only when the costs incurred by having followed one road become too high are countries tempted to follow another, a newer and less familiar one. One such road leads to the deemphasis of the nation-state evoked by Robert Schuman.

Liberalism And Collective Learning: Some Ambiguities

We now know that in some of the industrial world liberal nationalism acquired an elective affinity with successful rationalization and rerationalization only after serious crises were experienced. We have yet to show that successful rationalization also comes about as a result of collective learning. Does collective learning, then, have an elective affinity for liberal nationalism?

The stories we now summarize add up to an ambiguous lesson. I look at economic policy making, measures to ensure social harmony, and lessons learned about peaceful conflict management. Collective learning is a sometime thing; epistemic communities come and go; politicians and bureaucrats, especially in democracies, cannot be depended on to make use of consensual knowledge. The link between liberalism and learning is far from sturdy.

Why Liberal Nationalism Facilitated, but did not Cause, Economic Policy Learning

Before the Great Depression Western governments did not make much economic policy. They were particularly unconcerned about unemployment; and they did consider it their business to moderate the business cycle. The gold standard provided for a minimum of international coordination to facilitate international trade and financial flows. Central banks mounted the appropriate interventions to aid domestic interests, *not* to maintain the international economic system by means of well-internalized rules. We recall from our case studies that unemployment insurance was rudimentary, if it existed at all, prior to the 1930s. The notion that unemployment was directly related to undermining political legitimacy was not something that was generally understood or appreciated before then.[7]

The theoretical explanation about the link between economic performance, unemployment, and political legitimacy, of course, was provided

[7] I appreciate the research assistance of Jacqueline Reich for this part of the chapter. I am grateful also to Barry Eichengreen for his help. See Jacob Viner, *Studies in the Theory of International Trade* (New York: Harper's, 1937); Joseph Schumpeter, *Economic Doctrine and Method* (London: Oxford University Press, 1954); Robert Lekachman, *The Age of Keynes*, (New York: McGraw Hill, 1966). The entire panoply of fiscal and monetary tools was not brought to bear by governments until well into the twentieth century because the modern macroeconomic discourse is of very recent origin. See also Arthur I. Bloomfield, *Monetary Policy under the International Gold Standard* (New York: Federal Reserve Bank of New York, 1959); John S. Odell, *U.S. International Monetary Policy* (Princeton: Princeton University Press, 1982). Richard Cooper explains the lack of consensual knowledge among economists since the decline of Keynesianism in "International Economic Cooperation: Is It Desirable?," *Bulletin of the American Academy of Arts and Sciences* (November 1985).

by John Maynard Keynes in a series of essays written in the late 1920s and early 1930s. Until then, few questioned the orthodox prescription that balanced budgets and tight money were the antidote to depression. There was little understanding during the 1920s that prosperity was blocked by the interaction between the debts incurred by European countries to American banks, the failure of Germany to pay reparations, the overvaluing of the pound and the undervaluing of the French franc, and the restored automaticity of the gold standard. At the World Economic Conference of 1933 some suggested that a new international monetary mechanism be created to transcend competing national measures to combat the depression, but the United States rejected the idea in favor of seeking to isolate its economy from Europe's.

Bretton Woods represents a major lesson learned. There the United States and Britain decided to make the world safe for the national practice of embedded liberalism, the use of governmental power to steer industrial economies toward prosperity and full employment. This program required the coordination of foreign exchange policies that had been lacking in the interwar years, and it was provided by the fixed, but flexible, exchange rate regime put in place and supported by the international lending to be undertaken by the International Monetary Fund. By merging the postwar plans of Britain and of the United States, both inspired by Keynesian thinking and drawn up by Keynesian epistemic communities, the new regime was to neutralize the effect of exchange rate fluctuation on domestic policies to maintain full employment.

The scheme, however, was not based on solid Keynesian consensual knowledge. True, Australia, Canada, and Sweden adopted Keynesianism as official government policy. But neither France, the United States, or Britain consistently practiced such policies during the ensuing decades. Germany went Keynesian only during the 1970s, and Japan never followed that path. The reasons for the failure of Keynesianism to become consensual vary from case to case. Political opportunism and factionalized policymaking were evident in all instances, and neither is consistent with systematic learning.

In any event, it did not seem to matter because the West prospered as never before until the mid-1970s; a full-fledged welfare state was installed everywhere, and political legitimacy flourished as well. Nor did the unilateral scuttling of the Bretton Woods system by the United States upset matters greatly. Through consistent deficit financing and heavy foreign borrowing the United States managed to finance the Vietnam War while greatly expanding the domestic welfare state. When the burden of these commitments got in the way of also acting as the banker of last resort for the Bretton Woods system, the United States simply abandoned fixed exchange rates and compelled its allies to follow in adopting the system of managed-floating rates instead. The jettisoning of the old system can hardly be portrayed as an instance of consensual economic coordination, but the rapid substitution of the successful system of floating did represent an act of collective learning, albeit not one consistent with the previous canon.

The massive globalization of national economies during the 1970s went hand in hand with rapid technological innovation and with the reappearance of unemployment. Instead of looking to Keynesianism, whose policy instruments failed to correct the stagflation of the 1970s, a new canon arose that worships unfettered markets, a minimum of government regulation, sharply reduced public entitlements, and monetarist fiscal and monetary policies. This canon, formalized by its own epistemic community, took hold in Britain, made many converts in the United States, and by the 1980s made itself felt on the European continent and in Japan, although not with the determination and consistency seen in Thatcherite Britain and Reaganite America.

Has a new economic policy consensus emerged, based on a new agreed theory? Has the derationalization of economic life of the 1970s been followed by rerationalization based on a new body of consensual knowledge? The continuing controversy about the causes of slow growth and persistent unemployment says "no." The derationalization we observed in all our cases during the 1990s confirms the doubt. Free markets and monetarism have not swept away the welfare state.

Like Janus, the economic face of liberal nationalism remains double-sided. One side is devoted to the attainment of economic efficiency and to individual achievement; it worships free markets and decries group entitlements. The other side embraces social equity and redistribution and therefore looks to the state for active help; it prefers communitarian democracy to individualism. Put differently, one side opts for Whig nationalism, the other for the Jacobin variety.

The quarrel between the two liberalisms is far from settled in any Western country. Privatization of state firms, deregulation, and the reduction of real wages and social entitlements are still opposed by the many remaining acolytes of Keynes. Unfettered competition, especially in international trade, is unacceptable to advocates of managed trade. The uneven performance of post–Bretton Woods intergovernmental economic coordination, some say, demands institutional reform. The drop in real wages and the decay of the nuclear family in today's capitalist economies are seen by hard-core social democrats as a challenge for designing a leaner welfare state. Observers disagree on whether the admitted globalization of corporate affairs is undermining the liberal nation-state and pushing it toward the supranational pooling of sovereignty or whether the liberal nation-state remains the core decision maker, able to choose whether to be Whig or Jacobin.[8]

For both Whig and Jacobin liberals, however, redistribution of wealth remains the core task of the nation-state, although they differ about the appropriate means: individual or corporate initiative versus state guidance and subsidies. Potentially, at least, devotees of both equity and efficiency are willing to seek and use consensual knowledge in their separate quests for a more perfect liberal nation-state.

Liberal Nationalism and Learning to Practice Domestic Harmony

In Britain, the United States, and France the liberal nation-state has a good record of extending the circle of groups and classes who gradually came to participate in public life. By the turn to the twentieth century inclusion of the working and peasant classes was far advanced in these countries and the sweep of civil rights was being extended. By the 1930s the practice of democratic corporatism was taking hold on the Continent, although in Britain and America a less organized form of pluralism extended the influence of trade unions and farmers' and business associations. Yet, these changes were basically adaptations, not formally learned adjustments.

Nevertheless, liberalism is not the only formula for successfully extending political participation: Germany and Japan achieved much the same results under reformist-syncretist auspices before 1914. What they failed to achieve is the practice of diffuse reciprocity among social groups, a mutual deferring and compromising based on the existence of trust. Germany and Japan did not learn to practice diffuse reciprocity until after 1945, under crisis-imposed liberal auspices; the industrial democracies in our sample internalized that lesson thirty years earlier without suffering the trauma of military defeat. It does appear as if there is an elective affinity between liberal ideology and the capacity to improve domestic harmony when it comes to ensuring peaceful political change, political participation, willingness to serve one's nation in the military. But does that same elective affinity exist in the realm of interethnic relations and religious tolerance? Can successful change initiated by adaptation or ideology be institutionalized as collective learning?

There has been agreement on peaceful political succession in all our cases since 1945. In Britain, America, and Japan the issue had never

---

[8] I am indebted to manuscripts by and discussions with Jeffrey A. Frankel and Richard N. Cooper for some of these points. The argument that the liberal nation-state remains in charge of its destiny is made by Michael Mann, "Nation-States in Europe and Other Continents," *Daedalus* (Summer 1993): 115–39.

been in doubt, though not in France and Germany. But no formal learning was required to bring about this result. Matters are far more complicated when we turn to the place of ethnic minorities in the polity and to issues of religious toleration and state–church relations.

Liberal nation-states have not learned to cope with multiculturalism. They sought to deal with the fact of ethnic diversity by practicing active melting pot policies to encourage rapid assimilation into the majority culture, although Japan never made strong efforts to assimilate any foreigners. These efforts were generally successful before 1945 as long as the groups to be assimilated were Europeans. Poles and Czechs joined the mainstream German population; Irish and Jewish immigrants melted reasonably well into Britain's. France assimilated eastern European immigrants and successfully forced the majority culture on native ethnic minorities, though not totally eliminating resentment. American's success at assimilating Europeans while segregating Asians, Blacks, and Native Americans is legendary. Since 1945, however, none of these countries successfully met the challenges of native and immigrant ethnic groups who were of non-European origin. Successful assimilation, or recognized-equal, but separate, communal status, would have constituted learning because it would have implied rethinking the causes of similarity and difference; but neither full assimilation nor recognized separation has occurred. New controversies about official languages have arisen as well.

It is not clear whether the remarkable trend toward the acceptance of religious diversity is a learned or an adaptive response. To the extent that secular modes of thinking have supplanted faith as a basis of collective social choice learning has taken place. This has occurred in all Western countries and in Japan. That being the case the toleration of religious diversity in the context of private devotions is hardly surprising. The separation of church and state, however, may be a mere adaptive or ideological response to accommodate the demands of skeptics and secularists. In any event, controversy about the relationship between religion and the state ceased to shape political discourse early in the century. But some of the old controversy came back in the form of fundamentalism in the United States during the 1980s. *The elective affinity between liberal nationalism and religious toleration (or indifference) is based on ideology, not on consensual knowledge about causality. The traditional-nationalist challenge to that toleration is equally ideological.*

If little has been learned about multiculturalism and church–state relations, much has been learned about military conscription, warfighting, and peaceful change. Conscription has been abandoned in all countries in which it was perceived by the ruling elites to run counter to mass public opinion and to be unnecessary for defense: in the United States, France, Britain, Japan. The future of conscription in Germany, as well as the willingness of German conscripts to fight, remains in doubt. The learned consensus on warfighting, of course, means that none of the liberal nation-states in question is willing to risk military operations that are likely to involve heavy casualties.

The rapid healing of domestic wounds after 1945 in France, Germany, and Japan is truly remarkable. Fascists were rapidly readmitted to normal life with the exception of the small number of war criminals. It was as if everyone was determined to put the integralist interlude behind them, to banish the bad years from consciousness, to start the life of the nation all over again. In other words, the public had learned to shape new practices to hold the nation together in freedom; it had learned to practice diffuse reciprocity as a result of the trauma of fascism and defeat. In their trauma-induced commitment to peaceful change procedures as the only acceptable ones the three mass publics conferred legitimacy on their new liberal institutions.

Liberal Nationalism, Conflict Management, Global Involvement

Liberal countries have learned not to fight one another. Liberal democracies have learned to master ethnic conflicts because primordial loyalties do not define their people's identities. Liberal democracies have learned to treasure multilateral processes of negotiation and cooperation because instrumental rationality trumps emotive and symbolic behavior. All of these claims are commonly made. Are they true? A careful answer requires another look at two concepts: identity and rationalization.

How do we define "us" as juxtaposed to the "other"? This study is linked to the claim that people behave instrumentally, that they *choose* an identity when circumstances allow a choice. The purpose of the choice is to improve one's position in state and society, to better realize whatever values and interests motivate one's actions. Instrumental behavior implies willingness to compromise, to avoid dogmatic claims.

Others, however, insist that behavior relating to the integration of states is determined by ethnic ties and loyalties (subsuming racial, religious, and linguistic ones). These observers insist that monoethnic states alone are fated to become liberal because multiethnic entities are more likely to fight civil wars. In any event, the argument goes, societies united by a primordial ethnic identity may be rationalized along syncretist or integral lines as well as liberal ones, whereas instrumentally defined identities have an elective affinity for liberalism alone.

Much depends on what we mean by rationalization here. Is it any formula that holds the society together, or a particular one? The advocate of instrumental behavior (and of liberalism) holds that a particular kind of rationalization must prevail to avoid integration under authoritarian auspices. Rationalization must include the idea of fairness as a commonly accepted norm for dispute settlement and decision making. Behavior and institutions must tend toward formal rationality in the sense that there must be proportionality between substantive (value-defined) choices and the selection of efficient means. The proper mix of substantive and procedural rationality will ensure fairness and reciprocity because it precludes the marriage of extreme means to fanatic ends. Ethnonationalism guarantees no such thing.

Thus, we ask: does the history of nationalism in industrialized countries conform to the instrumentalist's notion of rationalization? Does liberal nationalism imply learning to avoid war and collaborate peacefully in monoethnic as well as in multiethnic settings?

Learning to Manage Ethnic Conflict. There have been only two lethal ethnic conflicts since 1945 in industrial countries: the Ulster civil war and the Basque revolt. There were a few others, less lethal, in east-central Europe in the aftermath of World War I. However, we also witnessed a large number of conflicts among indigenous minorities and majorities that involved relatively little violence: in Belgium, France, Spain, Britain, Canada, the United States, Czechoslovakia, New Zealand, and even Italy. We already know that ethnic conflict between nonwhite immigrants and the majority populations is not being managed to everyone's satisfaction.

With the exception of the Northern Irish, Basque terrorists, and most of Japan, the liberal countries have displayed admirable skill in learning to defuse conflict between ethnic minorities and official majorities. They practice precisely the kind of compromise an instrumental rationality suggests as appropriate, the policies that primordialists consider impossible. These compromises, except in the peacefully resolved case of Slovakia, have avoided the changing of political boundaries by the deft use of nonconfrontational conflict management techniques.

It remains true, however, that ethnic conflicts outside Western and Central Europe arouse far less interest. The Yugoslav tragedy illustrates that learning to manage ethnic conflict at home is not diffused to the south and east. Citizens of liberal democracies are unwilling to suffer military casualties to prevent ethnic massacres, impose peace among warring groups, protect the human rights of the persecuted if such events do not occur at home.

Fighting interstate wars. No doubt these successes in Europe and North America owe something to the fact that ethnic conflict in Western countries is not an everyday event. But liberal democracies did equally well in disposing of their colonial empires with a minimum of violence, at least after 1962. The ideology of anticolonialism played a role. Adaptation was practiced in the sense that fatigue and weakness conditioned the acquiescence in the independence of most of the former colonies.

Yet surely a lesson was learned, earlier by Britain and America than by France, *that the objectives of embedded liberalism are incompatible with fighting against national self-determination in Asia and Africa.*

But Immanuel Kant's dictum about the avoidance of war by "republican" states was not inspired by colonial and postcolonial conflicts. Kant's reasoning projected into international politics the instrumentalist logic used to explain the liberal-nationalist identity: fighting wars interferes with trade and imposes heavy transaction costs on democratic deliberations. Furthermore, republics whose constitutions enshrine the norms associated with Kant's ethics should lack a motive for attacking other republics.

Statistically, Kant is proven correct: there have been almost no wars in this century pitting one liberal-nationalist state against another, none since 1945. But that record is not satisfactorily explained by the dominance of the instrumentalist identity and the rationality of proportionality. It is hard to find a motive or an interest that might have inspired aggression in Western Europe, North American, or Australia. Liberal nation-states in these regions had no claims against one another serious enough to evoke violence. None threatened another's existence. None experienced a security dilemma against another. Moreover, nuclear deterrence and a hegemonic America were responsible for defending the West against the Soviet Union. So why fight one another?[9] Thus, we cannot conclude that the avoidance of war between democracies is a lesson learned by liberal nation-states. We can only find that there have been no compelling reasons for ruling elites to wage such wars since 1945. The record of the United States, Britain, and France shows that no such inhibition governs the use of force against nondemocracies.

But did not ordinary patriotic French citizens hate Germans, and did not Germans reciprocate the feeling? The same has been said of the feelings Britons entertained for the French during much of the nineteenth century, and Germans toward Britons in the twentieth. Possibly, without ethnic hatred anchored in mass opinion, neither of the murderous world wars of this century could have been fought. No doubt, enthusiasm for fighting was whipped up by government propaganda, including a great deal of historical falsification. But the propagandists must have had a receptive audience to inspire the kind of self-sacrifice conscripts and volunteers exhibited in the first years of both world wars, among liberal as well as integralist nationalists.

It is therefore remarkable that nothing like this kind of ethnic hatred,

[9] Edward Mansfield and Jack Snyder argue that countries that find themselves in the transition from authoritarian to democratic governance are especially likely to resort to war to gain their way. They illustrate this tendency and explain it on the basis of insecurity of the new rulers. "Democratization and War," *Foreign Affairs* (May–June 1995): 79–97.

neither for each other nor for third parties, has been discernible since 1945. Wars are fought reluctantly, if at all, by the countries in our sample. Most are unwilling to risk incurring even modest casualties. Ethnic prejudice may subsist, but it no longer finds the kind of expression in warfare that we witness in other parts of the world. Somebody learned something.

Military strategy as learning. Nuclear weapons not only revolutionized warfare, but also they made people rethink the very basics of how to wage war and peace. In the past, military planners thought in terms of compelling the enemy to do one's will, or of defending against him; they did not think of using force to *deter* the enemy from striking in the first place. Nuclear weapons created the culture of deterrence, especially the American-invented variant called Mutual Assured Destruction. The technology made military strategists learn how to protect the home state without calling the enemy's right to exist into question. Strategists came to the conclusion that the security of the home state required that the enemy state be assured about *its* security, too.

These considerations, when tied to the intrinsic horror of nuclear destructiveness and the dangers of radiation, led to the series of ever more comprehensive nuclear arms control agreements. They were inaugurated with the ban on atmospheric nuclear testing and came to include the massive builddown of nuclear arsenals, the cessation of all testing, and the controls on vertical and horizontal nuclear proliferation. Equally important, arms control led to the creation of special communications networks among enemies, to the toleration of satellite overflights, the sharing of information, and the mutual inspection of arms builddowns. This system was extended to the elimination of biological and chemical weapons in the 1990s.

True, the initial learning took place in the United States, thus confirming the proposition that liberalism favors learning, largely because of its instrumentalist bias. But the American epistemic community soon went international, including Soviet members by no means raised in the liberal ambience of discussion, debate, or consideration of opposing evidence. No doubt, liberal institutions did favor the early learning of the strategic and arms control lessons. But the diffusion of the lesson to integralist settings suggests that liberals have no monopoly on learning.

Liberalism Favors Multilateral Cooperation — Sometimes

The entire array of multilateral organizations, especially those that make up the United Nations system, are the result of initiatives of Western liberal nation-states. The West invented the very idea of a world order based on intergovernmental organizations that act as fora for continual multilateral negotiations and are the creators of new norms of conduct. Moreover, the tendency to give nongovernmental organizations increasing scope and influence in this world also is the result of Western initiatives. Does that mean that liberal nationalism has a special affinity for multilaterally organized cooperation among states? On balance, the answer is positive.

Western democracies take more interest in the creation of new international norms of conduct than do other regimes. Unlike others, they do not propose norms they do not intend to implement. But they also are careful of what they ratify; Western governments avoid ratifying international agreements for symbolic purposes alone. Once the agreements are ratified, Western governments tend to live by the norms to which they have committed themselves—unlike many others.

Western governments have disproportionately supported the United Nations system financially and by earmarking military forces for peacekeeping and enforcement purposes, though they are also the most disenchanted after the failures of such efforts. They also have committed themselves very heavily to an array of regional intergovernmental organizations in Europe and North America: the Organization for Economic Cooperation and Development, the Council of Europe with its supranational machinery for protecting human rights, the Organization for Security and Cooperation in Europe, the North American Free Trade Association. That said, it also is true that Western governments are not enthusiastic participants in activities of the United Nations system that seem to them largely symbolic and not likely to lead to an improvement of the human condition.

It seems unlikely that the march toward European economic and political integration, launched in 1952 by six founder nations and leading by 1995 to the European Union of fifteen members, could have been undertaken without a special affinity between liberal-national and supranational institutions. Lessons learned earlier about postwar rerationalization were clearly projected into the arena of regional European international relations by the integrating elites. Some observers argue that the process of European regional unification is driven by governments that redefine their interests before pooling them.[10] It is their very liberalism, at the national level, that gives these elites the ability to think regionally and to act multilaterally, the argument runs. I, however, argue that the undisputed pooling of sovereignty is due to the erosion of the national state in Europe, to the weakening of national identities, to the transnational activities of many interest groups and political parties, and

---

[10] Andrew Moravcsik, "Preferences and Power in the European Community," *Journal of Common Market Studies* (December 1993): 473–524.

to the growth of epistemic communities of national bureaucrats devoted to regional solutions to common problems. In this explanation, too, the liberal character of the participants' identities and institutions makes possible the supranational integration process. In short, weakened liberal nationalism does favor supranational integration and cooperation in Europe. But it does so not merely because liberals possess institutions that favor the creation of new norms by discussion but also because the perceived interests of political elites dictated the integrationist course.

But serious ambiguities remain about the special ability of liberal nationalists to learn multilateral cooperative lessons.[11] Possibly, liberalism has reached the limits of its ability to serve human progress by means of multilateral cooperation. All along, a world order based on this creed stressed national sovereignty, national self-determination, free markets, welfare democracy, and the protection of basic human rights. But all along, there have been tensions among these aspirations. Is the protection of human rights by international organizations consistent with respect for sovereignty or the attainment of national self-determination? Usually it is not. Is the attainment of free markets always consistent with the continuation of welfare democracy? Not very often. Are both, when actively sought by the United Nations system, consistent with national sovereignty? Many developing countries say "no."

So far, these tensions were kept mostly within bounds because the liberal world order was being sought and protected by the Western alliance: normative and security interests usually coincided, so that the liberal norms were able to free-ride on the security objectives.

Since the end of the cold war this is no longer the case. Moreover, derationalization and conflict are sharply rising within the very states— our cases—that advocated a liberal world order. This gives rise to the problem of what to do in civil wars and under what conditions intervention may be justified. It begs the question of whether the creation of peace is more important than supporting democracy or protecting human right or whether the reverse is true. The weakening of the liberal state entails uncertainty over the fate of refugees, humanitarian intervention, and the prevention of genocide. Maybe the lessons learned on these counts are not sweeping enough after all?

A second force, economic globalization, has seriously weakened the liberal state. Much of economic life now escapes its sovereign sway. Reduced control creates an angry backlash among citizens who have been harmed by the growth of unregulated global markets, further contrib-

---

[11] This section draws heavily on Stanley Hoffmann, "The Crisis of Liberal Internationalism," *Foreign Policy* (Spring 1995): 159–77. However, I have interpreted his argument to suit my own in several particulars.

uting to derationalization. Multinational firms and currency speculators are accountable to nobody, and nobody has regulated them.

A cacophony of norms now rules, not a liberal consensus. Every one of the traditional liberal world order norms is being challenged somewhere, domestically and internationally, even as new norms are built up within the fields of human rights and trade relations, only to clash with the norms of sovereignty and welfare democracy. Unless a consensus on priorities among norms develops first, continued learning among liberal elites is not garanteed.[12]

LIMITS OF COLLECTIVE LEARNING

Massive Change, Sparse Learning

There are good reasons why liberal governmental institutions often inhibit collective learning, although they also permit it to take place from time to time when urgent crises allow a disregard of familiar practices. We know that there was little collective political learning before World War II. We also know that the Great Depression, the war, and postwar reconstruction were the great crises that triggered learning. There was little consensual knowledge before the 1930s about defense, international cooperation, or macroeconomic steering to achieve mass social welfare. The rise of scientific rationality in general in the early part of the twentieth century surely facilitated the learning that eventually occurred.

Who learned what? We know that, most broadly, political elites learned to practice diffuse reciprocity in their mutual relations, domestic and international. That practice was most pronounced with respect to the rise of *mutual* defense postures, multilateral cooperation, the growth of democratic corporatism, and the mounting of macroeconomic policies to enhance mass social welfare. The picture is as shown on Table 8-3, though we must recall that Britain engaged in learning about social welfare and Japan about military defense as early as the 1880s.

Evidently, liberal nationalism is no panacea when it comes to collective learning. The United States and Britain did learn first to use analytical means to improve social welfare. But Nazi Germany ventured into mac-

---

[12] Hoffmann's solution calls for rethinking the foundations of liberal nationalism along lines of *voluntary* multiculturalism, not the ethnonationalism of communitarian thought. He wants to institutionalize the multilateral pooling of sovereignty. The ill effects of economic globalization are to be overcome by a collective rethinking of international collective goods, a rethinking that would subordinate the freeing of all markets to collective welfare considerations. Absolute devotion to sovereignty, national self-determination, and free markets would have to go in this revised liberal world order vision.

Table 8-3. Differential learning since 1945

Issue	Most ←				→ Least
Multilateral cooperation	Germany	France	United States	Britain	Japan
Mutual security	United States	Britain	France	Germany	Japan
Democratic Corporatism	Germany	Japan	France	Britain	United States
Welfare state	Japan	Germany	France	Britain	United States

roeconomic steering at the same time as the oldest democracies, and integralist Japan soon followed. The most impressive episodes of learning occurred when France, Germany, and Japan rerationalized after 1945; but only in France could elites draw on a residue of liberal values and institutions. Why, then, was learning so sporadic?

Why Adaptation Is Easier than Learning

Some conditions that lead to learning stem from the political environment in which decision makers are placed. Other conditions refer to the microworld of bureaucracy. The predictors of learning are the *desirability* of finding new cause-and-effect chains, the *possibility* of finding them, and the *urgency* for finding them. Learning occurs when desirability is high, the possibility reasonable, and the urgency heightened by a crisis.

Desirability refers to the incentives motivating the bureaucratic units to engage in soul searching. Actors' career goals and political opportunities to prosper are heavily identified with pleasing a certain constituency, with helping that constituency to solve its problems. Issues that offer decision makers incentives are more likely to be dealt with than issues that do not present the same opportunities. From the vantage point of desirability, it makes more sense to reexamine one's ends and values when fighting epidemics than mounting campaigns in favor of human rights.

The lack of predictable incentives motivating bureaucrats to rethink their causal schemata is a serious hurdle facing epistemic communities in their efforts to penetrate administrative agencies. Epistemic communities—networks of experts who possess the consensual knowledge necessary to solve some public policy problem—must gain access to decision makers in order to prevail, preferably so as to acquire a monopoly over the knowledge available for policymaking. Bureaucratic inertia with respect to innovation prevents effective access. New knowledge will not be used if bureaucrats lack the incentives of better career, increased funds,

344

expanding mandate, higher pay, and faster promotion. Hence, epistemic communities will lack the receptive audience in government that they seek.

The existence of political incentives is not enough to trigger learning. The *possibility* of redefining ends along new causal chains also must exist. This possibility, of course, is a function of the state of scientific knowledge, the degree of consensus it enjoys, and the availability of epistemic communities for spreading the word. The possibility of learning refers to the availability of new means that entitle actors to consider new ends not previously accessible to them.

The availability of consensual knowledge is not the only possible hurdle over which the learning decision maker must jump. Unless the prevailing *bargaining style* among agencies and governments allows the introduction of consensual knowledge, the mere availability of applicable specialized lore will not result in learning. Diverse bargaining styles can be visualized in the following way.

There are four possibilities on how to use knowledge in bargaining. (1) An *eclectic* style makes no effort to link issues on the agenda with any kind of knowledge-based logic; (2) an *analytical* style is based on the systematic use of knowledge; (3) a *pragmatic* style seeks to insert consensual knowledge into objectives that do not transcend short-run calculations; and (4) a *skeptic* style is characterized by inattention to consensual knowledge, but a concern with long-run objectives.[13] We must know, then, whether bargaining styles pitting negotiators against each other are similar or different.

We must also know at what level our negotiations take place and be mindful that most bargaining of interest to us can take place, more or less simultaneously, at three levels. (1) Intragovernmental negotiations are important because they (a) determine the outcomes the international negotiator ought to seek and (b) ratify the accord he or she brings home. (2) Intracoalitional negotiations seek to unify a single bloc or alliance of governments behind a preferred position (or range of positions) before the full international talks begin. Both types are essentially encounters among the like-minded, a feature that ought to caution us about the generalizability of studies of national-level decision making. (3) Finally, the international negotiations themselves must be included, and we must remind ourselves that these are negotiations among antagonists, parties that cannot be expected to share many meanings or that dispose, between them, of a large "win set."[14]

---

[13] For a complete discussion of bargaining styles, see Ernst B. Haas, *When Knowledge Is Power* (Berkeley: University of California Press, 1990), pp. 73–80.

[14] The logic of this discussion is derived from Robert D. Putnam, "Diplomacy and Domestic Politics: The Logic of Two-Level Games," *International Organization* 42, 3 (Summer

Therefore, arriving at an agreement at the international level is more difficult than at the other two levels, especially if we recall that the size of the win-set at levels 1 and 2 determines the range of possible outcomes at level 3. The possibility of agreement at level 2 is also constrained (at least in the case of pluralistic and/or democratic polities) by the number of actors and the complexity of their demands at level 1: the larger the number and the more intricate their nested demands, the smaller the win set. Moreover, bargaining styles at level 1 will tend toward dissimilarity if there are very numerous participating constituencies. Styles will tend to be quite similar at level 2 because the knowledge that the coalition will eventually have to face an opposing coalition is a powerful incentive to hold the members together. Dissimilarity has an elective affinity for adaptive behavior; therefore, bargaining at level 3, which probably pits opposing styles against each other, is not likely to lead to learning.

The *urgency* of the problem is the chief cause for a high rate of learning. Is there a crises that calls out for immediate action, such as famine, the imminent bankruptcy of a large country and its creditors, or an AIDS epidemic? If the requisite knowledge exists (or can rapidly be found) and if bureaucratic incentives are aligned with crisis management, we would expect rapid learning to occur, *provided* the administrators or negotiators agree on how to conceptualize the causal dimensions of the crisis.

Crisis management can be used as an indicator for successful learning if the decision makers agree on the nesting. A crisis is a sudden concatenation of circumstances that threatens the major values of the bulk of the actors, such as a major war, famine, depression. A crisis presents the actors with an unfamiliar set of problems in the sense that the causes of the disturbance are seen as complex and not amenable to single-shot solutions. It is not that they never experienced war, famine, or depression previously. A crisis consists not in the recurrence of these events, but in the actors' recognition that the recurrence is due to the fact that previous institutional routines have been insufficient to avert it.

If the available consensual knowledge is used to sort out the causes of the crisis, the decision makers are likely to arrive at a program of action in short order. However, if they have to bargain over the manner of

---

1988): 427–60. A win set for any one constituency is "the set of all possible agreements that would 'win'—that is, gain the necessary majority among the constituents—when simply voted up or down" (ibid., p. 437). Putnam uses the notion of a set as meaning the *number* of possibly acceptable agreements, without worrying about the content of the agreements in terms of the complexity or type of linked issues in the set. Putnam is not responsible for my connecting his logic with my concern with bargaining styles.

nesting most appropriate for finding a solution to the crisis, learning is impeded.[15]

The simplest way to reach agreement is to consider the set as fully decomposable; but doing so risks not finding a good solution because the conceptualization downplays the existence of links among the components of the crisis. Conversely, arriving at a fully nondecomposable set of causes makes the task so complex that adequate knowledge for a conclusion may not exist; in that case an overly tightly nested conception may condemn the decision makers to inability to act. Agreeing to a nearly nondecomposable set is optimal for learning.

Learning, then, is impeded by a variety of obstacles. Some are endemic in modern bureaucracies. Others have to do with the difficulty of creating, and making accessible, sufficient consensual knowledge. A crisis is needed to overcome both forms of inertia, but the solution to the crisis has to be conceptualized in the proper manner to favor learning.

In addition, there are institutional constraints, such as voting rules, standard operating procedures, and court decisions. The effectiveness of epistemic communities as consensus builders may be blocked by any of these. The prevailing norms of society may be at odds with the needs seen by an epistemic community, particularly norms associated with free market thinking and with feudalist-patriarchal institutions.

It seems clear that the shock of war and of disappointment with economic development are major occasions for learning to think anew about the adequacy of international institutions in the second half of the twentieth century. Threats to the environment and to the global commons can also be powerful stimuli. The most consistent and the most impressive sequences of attempted problem solving, which resulted in the elaboration of more complex problem sets, all hinged on the demands for programs, services, and rules that conform to Western political principles and responded to secular knowledge purveyed by epistemic communities. The logical and epistemological properties featured in modern Western thought were important facilitators of learning because they helped to focus research and program making around the substantive strategic variables that determine degrees of decomposability.

Between Adaptation and Learning

All institutional actors are habit-driven, but not to the same degree and not at a constant rate through time. To be able to learn demands that

---

[15] The source of the vocabulary of decomposability is, of course, Herbert Simon's work. For a discussion of these distinctions, see his *Reason in Human Affairs* (Stanford: Stanford University Press, 1983).

the bonds of habit be light. Adaptation, however, is quite possible to all but the most taboo-ridden. Few modern public entities are so encrusted with habit and routine as to be unable to shift from ineffective to more efficacious means, or to add new purposes to old ones, although neither the new nor the old need be attained with speed and efficiency. Although most habit-driven bureaucracies can adapt, only a few seem to be able to learn.

How rapidly and how readily political leaders are willing to reexamine and revaluate themselves is a wholly empirical question. No formalized script can capture the process. As argued, we can only claim that epistemic communities, as triggers for learning, are likely to be listened to when political decision makers find it congruent with their career interests to listen; and this is more likely to happen when knowledge promises better solutions to old problems in a setting of crisis.

The discussion of habit, and how to cope with it, suggests that perhaps the contrast between learning and adaptation is not as stark as we have painted it. Habits are a drag on innovation, but not an absolute one. Routines confine, but they can be altered. We could think of the effects of many acts of adaptation in dealing with a single issue as becoming cumulative. A given bureaucracy or polity, we think, adapts many of its routines as small crises and minor inconsistencies in implementation come to its attention and as it comes under pressure from restricted groups of constituents for reform. The piecemeal reforms of social security, of the tax code, and of foreign aid measures in the United States come to mind. After decades of adaptations, however, the ensemble begins to resemble a major change. At this point, perhaps triggered by a major new crisis, the entire program is scrutinized by the legislature in the light of causal thinking not current at the time of program initiation. The new problem set that emerges from the reanalysis may be more nearly nondecomposable or more decomposable; it will be nested differently from the way it was before the accumulated adaptations. Cascading adaptations, in short, may add up to collective learning after all, if only by inadvertence.[16]

For these reasons, then, the learning game should not be seen as heroic epistemic communities facing off against silent, undifferentiated, malign habit. Rather we should see the game as a slow historical movement in which *some* epistemic communities successfully shake up *some* aspects of habitual behavior. Organizations, because they adapt and sometimes even learn, permit change to occur, even if they do not ac-

---

[16] I am indebted to Jennifer McCoy for this line of thought. Habit-driven actors and institutions are discussed by James H. Rosenau, "Before Cooperation: Hegemons, Regimes and Habit-Driven Actors," *International Organization* 40 (Autumn 1986): 864–65.

tively favor it. Habit is neither totally banished nor an inevitable block to new ways.

TRIUMPH OR TWILIGHT OF LIBERAL NATIONALISM?

Nationalism on the whole has been a powerful rationalizing agent; without it, it is unlikely that progress would have come to countries that severed their ties to tradition under violent and disruptive conditions. Liberal nationalism, the ideology that informed modernization in most of the West, shaped western civilization more than any other faith after the decline of Christianity. It vanquished its syncretist, racist, and Marxist rivals.

But now it seems to be in trouble in countries where it remains the national myth. Moreover, the intensity of that myth has weakened under the blows of globalism, regionalism, and localism. What once seemed instrumentally desirable to most people—assimilation into the nation-state—is far less rational today because the state no longer can deliver the goods unaided it once offered in abundance all by itself.

Domestically, the state seems unable to perform all the welfare services the poor expect, and the gap between rich and poor increases. Many want more regulation of industry and commerce; many want less. As the cultural diversity of the population increases (except in Japan), some demand more autonomy and special entitlements for the unassimilated minorities; others want fewer rights for fewer minorities. The procedures and the redistributive ethic of liberal nationalism no longer satisfy everyone.

Internationally, only the United States seem strong enough to arrange for its own defense unaided by alliances. But again, discord over responsibility for others is rife. Cosmopolitan internationalists and accommodationists argue for a stronger United Nations, more collective security, more international peacekeeping, more assistance to developing countries, and more concern for global sustainable development. Those distrustful of other cultures argue against all these choices, preferring to huddle in the no longer very comforting shell of their nation-state to wholesale involvement with the fate of others. Again, *the old link between liberal nationalism and cosmopolitan internationalism is now weaker.*

Before we conclude that liberal nationalism is fading away—disputed in the industrial world as a national myth and seen as inadequate to garantee progress—we ought to take a further look at what is being discredited. Derationalization there surely is; but is it clearly associated with the demise of liberal nationalism as the rationalizer of choice?

The nation-state, as the core western political institution, has not been discredited finally and decisively. It is competing with novel political institutions; sovereignty is "shared," "pooled," even "layered." "Multi-level governance" is being practiced and conceptualized theoretically in Europe. The resistance to having the nation-state shed power and tasks is still considerable, especially in America and Japan.

Neither has liberal nationalism been forgotten as the myth informing the citizens' links with the nation-state. Even in countries suffering from large-scale public dissatisfaction the procedural character of liberalism continues almost unchallenged. The isolationists and xenophobes in Europe and America have not opted for integralist political institutions and practices. However, the religious fundamentalist revival in America and Japan displays strong signs of restorative syncretism—one protestant and the other Buddhist and Shinto. In the Western Hemisphere, Australasia and Japan, however, neither the nation-state nor liberal nationalism have gone the way of feudalism, fascism, and Marxism. The glow of liberalism has dimmed, although no substitute ideology to rerationalize the country has been found.

But liberalism may well have passed its peak as a potential rationalizer *outside* the industrialized world. It is quite possible that the conquest of the world by liberal ideas and institutions, supposedly triggered by the defeat of Communism, will turn out to be an illusion, a flash in the pan of history during the final decade of the twentieth century. In Western and central Europe, though liberalism has no strong competitor, the present nation-states show signs of obsolescence. The situation in eastern Europe is quite the opposite; here national self-determination has gotten its strong second wind as nation-states are still being born or reborn, while the fate of liberalism as their future national myth remains very clouded.

Liberal triumphalism holds that, despite these signs, the future east and west, north and south, is liberal. All other ideologies having demonstrated their bankruptcy, liberalism is declared the winner by default.[17] This claim points to liberalism as the hegemonic political and economic idea, to democratic constitutionalism married to free markets as the victorious institutions. There is, of course, evidence to support this claim. But the evidence is strong only if we stress ideas and institutions apart from the material aspirations of citizens. The precariousness of liberalism in countries with declining living standards and failing markets makes it doubtful that a rationalized polity can be built by liberal nationalists. Critics of liberal triumphalism point to the likelihood of conflict between the West—liberal civilization—against various nonliberal

---

[17] Francis Fukuyama, "The End of History," *The National Interest* (Summer 1989): 3–18, makes the triumphalist case.

civilizations elsewhere. These non-Western civilizations (in which some include Japan) are thought not to be interested in the political or economic aspects of liberalism, though very envious of the material progress of the West.[18]

These are concerns that apply to the former Second and Third Worlds, not directly to the themes of this book except insofar as they seek to predict the global entanglements of our case study countries. Triumphalists see peace, harmony, and universal progress. Some of their critics see a revival of Western imperialism as the still-liberal West flexes its economic and military muscles; others foresee a Fortress West, as the still-liberal countries defend themselves against the onslaught of envious non-Western civilizations.

Less apocalyptic speculations about the health of the West open up a different perspective altogether. What if the rise of the West was unusual historically because if featured the rare instance of a charismatic idea linked to a charismatic elite determined to make it real? Ken Jowitt interprets the history of the West prior to 1944 as the triumph of a uniquely rational-creative civilization that began with Catholic Christianity and culminated in liberal nationalism. But that history, he thinks, is finished: it spawned elites that run "those flabby, prosperous, self-satisfied, inward looking, weak-willed states whose grandest project was nothing more than the creation of the Common Market."[19] These critics regard as the stigmata of decline the very features that, I argue, furnish evidence of the capacity to learn, to gear rationality to continued progress. Charismatic and instrumental behavior are, after all, incompatible. One constructs one's social reality in terms of one or the other, not both.

My reading of the fate of liberal nationalism in the West and in Japan is close to the formulation suggested by Charles Maier. He sees the current derationalization of the West as a recurrence, a trough in a moral cycle of disillusionment and recovery observable since the 1870s. Peaks are associated with belief in cosmopolitan internationalism, troughs with xenophobic isolationism and intergralist ideologies, with "territorial populism." Human intervention, he believes, is capable of making nations rise from the trough or of preventing their descent into it. Such intervention must call on the essence of liberal nationalism, its capacity to fashion compromise by peaceful and deliberately rational procedures.

[18] For doubts about the triumphalist case, see Donald J. Puchala, "The History of the Future of International Relations," *Ethics and International Affairs* 8 (1994): 177–202; Samuel Huntington, "The Clash of Civilizations," *Foreign Affairs* (Summer 1993): 22–49.

[19] Quoted from Fukuyama, "End of History," p. 5, by Ken Jowitt, "No More Normans in Europe," unpublished manuscript, October 1995, kindly made available to me by the author. The case that American yuppie elites have betrayed their own virtuous past is made by Christopher Lasch, "The Revolt of the Elites: Have They Cancelled Their Allegiance to America?," *Harper's*, November 1994, pp. 39–49.

Maier wants to weaken nationalism further by deemphasizing the territorial nation-state as the font of benefits. "It is time for confederalism," he writes, "cantonization and overlapping citizenship . . . participants that are not drawn directly from the contested territory."[20] He sees regional organizations and new subnational entities as appropriate antidotes to tired nationalism and to claims for revived primordial nationhood.

In my judgment, compromise in the current era calls for this and more. It demands the acceptance of a degree of multiculturalism shorn of the features of cultural separatism. It demands the reassertion of individualism tempered at the margin with concessions to communalism. And compromise must find a formula for tempering the embrace of free markets and small government with the maintenance of adequate service for those whom free markets punish relentlessly.

If human behavior were really based on emotional drive alone this hope would be forlorn; primordial primitivism would win out. Belief in instrumental behavior, rationally informed behavior, justifies our confidence that these new lessons may be learned. They will rerationalize and rejuvenate liberalism, even if it is no longer practiced exclusively within the boundaries of the familiar nation-states, but beyond and across them. Liberalism allows for open political space, for alternative solutions, because it features rational discourse and compromise, not decisions based on faith and force. The present travail, therefore, ought to be seen as an opportunity to fill open political space with new institutions and practices that will assimilate, or reassimilate, those who are currently differentiated, dissatisfied, and thus potential constituents for nonliberal ideas. The present offers the same opportunities as did the nation-state in its infancy to those who are able to migrate into new spaces, to prosper even if the revived liberalism is no longer embedded in the nation-state.

[20] Charles S. Maier, "Democracy and Its Discontents," *Foreign Affairs* (July/August 1994): 63–64.

Index

355

Cornell Studies in Political Economy

Edited by Peter J. Katzenstein